Graphic Standards Field Guide to Residential Construction

Graphic Standards Field Guide to Residential Construction

DENNIS HALL, NINA GIGLIO

WILEY
John Wiley & Sons, Inc.

This book is printed on acid-free paper. 

Published by John Wiley & Sons, Inc., Hoboken, New Jersey

Published simultaneously in Canada

For general information about our other products and services, please contact our Customer Care Department within the United States at (800) 762–2974, outside the United States at (317) 572–3993 or fax (317) 572–4002.

Wiley also publishes its books in a variety of electronic formats. Some content that appears in print may not be available in electronic books. For more information about Wiley products, visit Web site at www.wiley.com.

Library of Congress Cataloging-in-Publication Data:

Hall, Dennis J., 1954-

Graphic Standards Field Guide to Residential Construction / Dennis J. Hall, Nina M. Giglio.

p. cm. — (Graphic Standards Field Guide series ; 18)

Includes bibliographical references and index.

ISBN 978-0-470-63504-9 (pbk. : acid-free paper); 978-047-0-90626-2 (ebk.); 978-047-0-90627-9 (ebk.); 978-047-0-90628-6 (ebk.); 978-047-0-95129-3 (ebk.); 978-047-0-95148-4 (ebk.)

1. Building--Details—Drawings—Handbooks, manuals, etc. 2. Building—Details—Drawings—Standards. 3. Dwellings—Designs and plans—Handbooks, manuals, etc. I. Giglio, Nina M. II. Title.

TH2031.H33 2011

690'.8370218—dc22

2010048283

Printed in the United States of America

10 9 8 7 6 5 4 3 2 1

Contents

Introduction

Welcome to Wiley's Graphic Standard Field Guide!

We know that when you're on a jobsite or in a meeting, questions come up. Even the most seasoned professionals may wish they could look up just that one piece of information that is just outside their instant recall or just beyond their current experience. There is a real need to make immediate on-site decisions—to access information on the spot, no matter where you are.

Graphic Standards Field Guide to Residential Construction is designed to be a quick and portable reference for busy professionals like you. It focuses on just the information you need away from the design desk, no matter where you are.

Who This Book Is For

As a companion to the recently completed *Architectural Graphic Standards for Residential Construction, 2nd ed.* this handy guide provides quick reference to professional, homeowners and the do-it-yourself handyman. This book is intended to assist the person in the field when they are looking at a situation and are in need of a ready recommendation or solution. This book also provides numerous references to organizations and resources should additional information be required.

How This Book Is Organized

The content of this book is organized according to CSI's MasterFormat. Each chapter covers a specific division, and includes topics appropriate to residential construction. Use the chapter opening pages to find a specific topic within a division, or refer to the index to find exactly what you need.

Information on specific topics is presented in lists and tables, making it easy to find and reference quickly. Architectural details and drawings demonstrate standards and help you evaluate what you may encounter on-site.

Each topic contains the following sections:

Description: A brief overview of the topic, to provide some context.

Assessing Existing Conditions: Key things to look for when you're in the field that will help guide your decisions.

Acceptable Practices: Keys to what constitutes good-quality work and references to industry standards.

Practices to Avoid: A quick list of what to look out for.

References: Look to this section for where to find more information about the topic within this book or in other sources.

How to Use This Book

The Field Guides are meant to go anywhere you go. Take them to jobsites that are under construction and to meetings, so that you have solutions right at your finger tips, or keep one in the glove compartment just in case—the book is a handy reference to have on hand whenever you are away from the design desk and out of the office.

Use the Field Guide to:

- Help a client evaluate a prospective property
- Find information on unexpected on-site conditions
- Remind yourself of possibilities and alternatives
- Create a checklist to make sure you asked all the right questions during a site visit
- Expand your expertise on practices that are common in residential construction

About The Authors

Dennis J. Hall and Nina M. Giglio, have guided the production of this work, drawing upon their experience with the Graphic Standards series, including *Architectural Graphic Standards*, 11th ed., and *Architectural Graphic Standards for Residential Construction*, 2nd ed. The Graphic Standards Field Guide to Residential Construction is a compilation of topics, researched and developed by the staff of HALL | Building Information Group, LLC. As with many endeavors, collaboration and input from many people with expertise as well as the once-burned experiences make this guide more direct and appropriate for residential construction applications that arise.

Topic Authors

Julie I. Carlsen CDT, LEED AP
Sandy M. Carter CSI, CCS, CCCA, SCIP
Nina M. Giglio Assoc. AIA, CSI, CCS, SCIP
Dennis J. Hall FAIA FCSI, CCS, CCCA, SCIP, LEED AP
Leslie H. Schlesinger CSI, CDT, SCIP Affiliate
Herb Sprott AIA
Michael E. Wilson RA CSI, CDT

About Graphic Standards

First published in 1932, *Architectural Graphic Standards (AGS)* is a comprehensive source of architectural and building design data and construction details.

Now in its eleventh edition, *AGS* has sold more than one million copies and has become one of the most influential and indispensable tools of the trade for architects, builders, draftsmen, engineers and students, interior designers, real estate professionals and many others. The entire family of *Graphic Standards* resources are ready to help you in your work. In recent years the franchise has expanded to *include Interior Graphic Standards, Planning and Urban Design Standards,* and the most recent publication, *Landscape Architectural Graphic Standards*. Each of these major references follows in the tradition *of Architectural Graphic Standards* and is the first source of comprehensive design data for any design or construction project. Explore what these products have to offer, and see how quickly they become an essential part of your practice.

Visit www.graphicstandards.com for more information.

PART I

GENERAL REQUIREMENTS

Chapter 1

Construction Information

Weights of Materials

Thermal Conductivity

Weights of Materials

Description

Table 1.1 provides weights of some common materials used in residential construction. Many times when in the field, changes are required, and the variation in weight of the material may need to be taken into consideration. Because of the infinite possibilities, the table provides only a sampling of common materials, and should be used only for rules of thumb. Once the actual product is selected, a final evaluation related to weight and the relationship to the structure and supporting elements should occur.

Table 1.1 Weight of Common Building Materials

Brick and Block Masonry		
4-in. brick		40 PSF
4-in. concrete block, stone or gravel		34 PSF
4-in. concrete block, lightweight		22 PSF
4-in. concrete brick, stone or gravel		46 PSF
4-in. concrete brick, lightweight		33 PSF
6-in. concrete block, stone or gravel		50 PSF
6-in. concrete block, lightweight		31 PSF
8-in. concrete block, stone or gravel		55 PSF
8-in. concrete block, lightweight		35 PSF
12-in. concrete block, stone or gravel		85 PSF
12-in. concrete block, lightweight		55 PSF
CONCRETE		
Plain	Cinder	108 PCF
	Expanded slag aggregate	100 PCF
	Expanded clay	90 PCF
	Slag	132 PCF
	Stone and cast stone	144 PCF
Reinforced	Cinder	111 PCF
	Slag	138 PCF
	Stone	150 PCF

(Continued)

Table 1.1 (*Continued*)

FINISH MATERIALS	
Fiberboard, ½-in.	0.75 PSF
Gypsum board, ½-in.	2 PSF
Marble and setting bed	25–30 PSF
Plaster, ½-in.	4.5 PSF
Plaster on wood lath	8 PSF
Plaster suspended on lath	10 PSF
Plywood, ½-in.	1.5 PSF
Tile, glazed wall ⅜-in.	3 PSF
Tile, ceramic mosaic, ¼-in.	2.5 PSF
Vinyl tile, ⅛-in.	1.33 PSF
Hardwood flooring, 25/32-in.	4 PSF
Wood block flooring, 3-in. on mastic	15 PSF
GLASS	
Polished float, ¼-in.	3.28 PSF
Polished float, ½-in.	6.56 PSF
Insulated unit ⅝-in. overall thickness	3.25 PSF
Glass block	18 PSF
INSULATION	
Blanket per 1-in. thickness	0.1–0.4 PSF
Corkboard per 1-in. thickness	0.58 PSF
Foamed board insulation—1-in. thickness	2.6 oz per SF
Board insulation	0.75 PSF
METALS	
Aluminum, cast	165 PCF
Brass, cast, rolled	534 PCF
Bronze, statuary	509 PCF
Copper, cast or rolled	556 PCF
Gold, cast, solid	1205 PCF
Iron, cast gray, pig	450 PCF
Iron, wrought	480 PCF
Lead	710 PCF
Nickel	565 PCF
Silver, cast, solid	656 PCF
Stainless steel, rolled	492–510 PCF

(*Continued*)

Table 1.1 (*Continued*)

Steel, rolled, cold drawn	490 PCF
Zinc, rolled, cast or sheet	449 PCF
MORTAR AND PLASTER	
Mortar, masonry	116 PCF
Plaster, gypsum, sand	104–120 PCF
PARTITIONS	
2 x 4 wood stud, gypsum board, two sides	8 PSF
4-in. metal stud, gypsum board, two sides	6 PSF
4-in. concrete block, lightweight, gypsum board	26 PSF
6-in. concrete block, lightweight, gypsum board	35 PSF
2-in. solid plaster	20 PSF
4-in. solid plaster	32 PSF
ROOFING MATERIALS	
Built up	6.5 PSF
Concrete roof tile	9.5 PSF
Copper	1.5–2.5 PSF
Corrugated iron	2 PSF
Deck, steel without roofing or insulation	2.2–3.6 PSF
Fiberglass panels (2½-in. corrugated)	5–8 oz per SF
Galvanized iron	1.2–1.7 PSF
Lead, ⅛-in.	6.8 PSF
Plastic sandwich panel, 2½-in. thick	2.6 PSF
Shingles, asphalt	1.7–2.8 PSF
Shingles, wood	2–3 PSF
Slate, 3/16-in. to ¼-in.	7–9.5 PSF
Slate, ⅜-in. to ½-in.	14–18 PSF
Stainless steel	2.5 PSF
Tile, cement flat	13 PSF
Tile, cement ribbed	16 PSF
Tile, clay shingle type	8–16 PSF
Tile, clay flat with setting bed	15–20 PSF
Wood sheathing per inch	3 PSF
SOIL, SAND, AND GRAVEL	
Ashes or cinder	40–50 PCF
Clay, damp and plastic	110 PCF
Clay, dry	63 PCF

(*Continued*)

Table 1.1 *(Continued)*

SOIL, SAND, AND GRAVEL	
Clay and gravel, dry	100 PCF
Earth, dry and loose	76 PCF
Earth, dry and packed	95 PCF
Earth, moist and loose	78 PCF
Earth, moist and packed	96 PCF
Earth, mud, packed	115 PCF
Sand or gravel, dry and loose	90–105 PCF
Sand or gravel, dry and packed	100–120 PCF
Sand or gravel, dry and wet	118–120 PCF
Silt, moist, loose	78 PCF
Silt, moist, packed	98 PCF
STONE (ASHLAR)	
Granite, limestone, crystalline	165 PCF
Limestone, oolitic	136 PCF
Marble	173 PCF
Sandstone, bluestone	144 PCF
Slate	172 PCF
STONE VENEER	
2-in. granite, ½-in. parging	30 PSF
4-in. granite, ½-in. parging	59 PSF
6-in. limestone facing, ½-in. parging	55 PSF
4-in. sandstone or bluestone, ½-in. parging	49 PSF
1-in. marble	13 PSF
1-in. slate	14 PSF
SUSPENDED CEILINGS	
Mineral fiber tile ¾-in., 12″ x 12″	1.2–1.57 PSF
Mineral fiberboard ⅝-in., 24″ x 24″	1.4 PSF
Acoustic plaster on gypsum lath base	10–11 PSF
WOOD	
Ash, commercial white	40.5 PCF
Birch, red oak, sweet and yellow	44 PCF
Cedar, northern white	22.2 PCF
Cedar, western red	24.2 PCF

(Continued)

Table 1.1 *(Continued)*

Cypress, southern	33.5 PCF
Douglas fir (coast region)	32.7 PCF
Fir, commercial white, Idaho white pine	27 PCF
Hemlock	28–29 PCF
Maple, hard (blacks and sugar)	44.6 PCF
Oak, white and red	47.3 PCF
Pine, northern white sugar	25 PCF
Pine, southern yellow	37.3 PCF
Pine, ponderosa, spruce: eastern and sitka	28.6 PCF
Poplar, yellow	29.4 PCF
Redwood	26 PCF
Walnut, black	38 PCF

Thermal Conductivity

Description

Table 1.2 provides conductivity values for some common building materials. Because changes often are required in the field, and variation in conductivity may play into decision making, it is important to have comparative values available. The values indicated are for dry materials in common use and are intended only as for use in preliminary calculations. Once the actual product is selected, additional evaluation and verification may be required.

Unless shown otherwise, descriptions of materials are for 75°C mean temperature.

Table 1.2 Thermal Conductivity Values of Common Building Materials

Material and Description	Density (pcf)	Conductivity/ in. Thickness (k)	Conductance for Thickness Listed (c)
BUILDING BOARDS, PANELS, FLOORING, ETC.			
Gypsum or veneer plaster base	50	1.11	—
Plywood	34	0.81	—
Sheathing, fiberboard	18	0.38	—
	22	0.41	—
	25	0.44	—
Wood fiberboard, laminate, or homogeneous	30	0.50	—
Hardboard	50	0.73	—
Particleboard	40	0.76	—
Wood subfloor	—	0.80	—
BUILDING PAPER			
Vapor—permeable 15-lb felt	—	—	16.70
Vapor—seal, two layers of mopped 15-lb felt	—	—	8.35

(Continued)

Table 1.2 *(Continued)*

Material and Description	Density (pcf)	Conductivity/ in. Thickness (k)	Conductance for Thickness Listed (c)
FINISH FLOORING MATERIALS			
Carpet and fibrous pad	—	—	0.48
Carpet and rubber pad	—	—	0.81
Hardwood	45	1.10	—
Tile—asphalt, linoleum, vinyl, rubber	—	—	20.00
INSULATING MATERIALS			
Blanket and batt[a]			
Mineral wool, fibrous form processed from rock, slag, or glass:			
Approximately 3–3½ in.	0.3–2.0	—	0.09
Approximately 5½–6½ in.	0.3–2.0	—	0.05
Approximately 6–7 in.	0.3–2.0	—	0.05
Approximately 8½—9 in.	0.3–2.0	—	0.03
Approximately 12 in.	0.3–2.0	—	0.03
Boards			
Cellular glass	8.5	0.35	—
Glass fiber	4.9	0.25	—
Expanded rubber (rigid)	4.5	0.22	—
Expanded polyurethane (R-11 blown)	1.5	0.16	—
Expanded polyurethane (extruded)			
Cut cell surface	1.8	0.25	—
Smooth skin surface	1.8–3.5	0.20	—
Expanded polyurethane (molded beads)	1.0	0.20	—
Mineral fiber with resin binder	15	0.29	—
Mineral fiberboard (wet felted)			
Core or roof insulation	16–17	0.34	—
Acoustic tile	18	0.35	—
Acoustic tile	21	0.37	—
Mineral fiberboard (wet molded)			
Acoustic tile[b]	23	0.42	—

(Continued)

Table 1.2 (*Continued*)

Material and Description	Density (pcf)	Conductivity/ in. Thickness (k)	Conductance for Thickness Listed (c)
Wood or cane fiberboard			
Acoustic tile[b] ½ in.	—	—	0.84
Acoustic tile[b] ¾ in.	—	—	0.56
Interior finish (plank, tile)	15	0.35	—
Cement fiber slabs (shredded with Portland cement boards)	25.0–27.0	0.50	—
Loose fill			
Mineral fiber (glass, slag, rock) 5 in.	0.6–2.0	—	0.09
6½–8¾ in.	0.6–2.0	—	0.05
10¼–13¾ in.	0.6–2.0	—	0.03
Vermiculite (exfoliated)	4.0–6.0	0.44	—
	7.0–8.2	0.47	—
Perlite (expanded)	2.0–4.1	0.29	—
	4.1–7.4	0.33	—
	7.4–11.0	0.38	—
Wood fiber, softwoods	2.0–35.0	0.30	—
MASONRY—CONCRETE			
Cement mortar	116	5.0	—
Gypsum fiber concrete: 87.5 percent gypsum, 12.5 percent wood chips	51	1.67	—
Lightweight aggregates including	120	5.26	—
Expanded shale, clay, or slate	100	3.57	—
Expanded slags, cinder, pumice	80	2.50	—
Perlite, vermiculite	60	1.69	—
Cellular concrete	40	1.16	—
	30	0.90	—
	20	0.70	—
Sand and gravel or stone aggregate (oven dried)	140	9.1	—

(*Continued*)

Table 1.2 (*Continued*)

Material and Description		Density (pcf)	Conductivity/ in. Thickness (k)	Conductance for Thickness Listed (c)
Sand and gravel or stone aggregate (not dried)		140	12.5	—
Stucco		116	5.0	—
MASONRY UNITS				
Brick, common		120	5.0	—
Brick, face		130	9.1	—
Concrete blocks, 3 oval core:				
Sand and gravel aggregate	4 in.	—	—	1.41
	8 in.	—	—	0.90
	12 in.	—	—	0.78
Cinder aggregate	3 in.	—	—	1.16
	4 in.	—	—	0.90
	8 in.	—	—	0.58
	12 in.	—	—	0.53
Lightweight aggregate (expanded shale, clay, slate, or slag; pumice)	3 in.	—	—	0.78
	4 in.	—	—	0.67
	8 in.	—	—	0.50
	12 in.	—	—	0.44
Concrete blocks, rectangular core: sand and gravel aggregate 2 core, 8 in., 36 lb		—	—	0.96
Lightweight aggregate (expanded shale, clay, slate, or slag; pumice:[c]				
3 core, 6 in. 19 lb		—	—	0.60
2 core, 8 in. 24 lb		—	—	0.46
3 core, 12 in. 38 lb		—	—	0.40
Granite, marble		150–175	20.0	—
Stone, lime, or sand		—	12.5	—
METALS				
Aluminum		171	1428	—
Brass, red		524–542	1000	—

(*Continued*)

Table 1.2 *(Continued)*

Material and Description	Density (pcf)	Conductivity/ in. Thickness (k)	Conductance for Thickness Listed (c)
Brass, yellow	524–542	833	—
Copper, cast rolled	550–555	2500	—
Iron, gray cast	438–445	333	—
Iron, pure	474–493	434	—
Lead	704	243	—
Steel, cold drawn	490	312	—
Steel, stainless, type 304	—	181	—
Zinc, cast	—	770	—
PLASTERING MATERIALS			
Cement plaster, sand aggregate	116	5.0	—
Sand aggregate ½ in.	—	—	10.0
Sand aggregate ¾ in.	—	—	6.67
Gypsum plaster:			
Lightweight aggregate ½ in.	45	—	3.12
Lightweight aggregate ⅝ in.	45	—	2.56
Lightweight aggregate, on metal lath ¾ in.	—	—	2.12
Perlite aggregate	45	1.49	—
Sand aggregate	105	5.55	—
Sand aggregate ½ in.	105	—	11.1
Sand aggregate ⅝ in.	105	—	9.1
Sand aggregate, on metal lath ¾ in.	—	—	7.69
Vermiculite aggregate	45	1.69	—
ROOFING			
1-ply membrane 0.048 in.	83	—	2.0
Asphalt roll roofing	70	—	6.67
Asphalt shingles	70	—	2.27
Built-up roofing ¾ in.	70	—	3.03
Slate ½ in.	—	—	20.0
SIDING MATERIALS (ON FLAT SURFACE)			
Shingles			
Wood, 16 in., 7½ in. exposure	—	—	1.15

(Continued)

Table 1.2 *(Continued)*

Material and Description		Density (pcf)	Conductivity/ in. Thickness (k)	Conductance for Thickness Listed (c)
Wood, double, 16 in. 12 in. exposure		—	—	0.84
Wood, plus insulation backer board, 5/16 in.		—	—	0.71
Siding:				
Aluminum (hollow backed over sheathing)		—	—	1.64
Vinyl (hollow backed over sheathing)	0.04 in.	—	—	1.00
Cedar shakes	1/2 in.	—	—	1.06
	1/3 in.	—	—	0.59
Wood, drop. 1 by 8 in.		—	—	1.26
Wood, bevel, 1/2 by 8 in., lapped		—	—	1.23
Wood, bevel, 3/4 by 10 in., lapped		—	—	0.95
Architectural glass		—	—	10.0
WOOD				
Maple, oak, and similar hardwoods		45	1.09	—
Fir, pine, and similar softwoods		32	0.8	—
Fir, pine, and similar softwoods				
	25/32 in.	32	—	1.02
	1 1/2 in.	32	—	0.53
	2 1/2 in.	32	—	0.32
	3 1/2 in.	32	—	0.23
Door, 1 3/4 in. thick solid wood core				0.32
1 3/8 in. hollow core				0.45
STEEL DOORS (nominal thickness 1-3/4 in.)				
Mineral fiber core		—	—	0.59
Solid urethane foam core (with thermal break)		—	—	0.18
Solid polystyrene core (with thermal break)		—	—	0.47

(Continued)

Notes:
[a]Includes paper backing and facing if any. In cases where insulation forms a boundary (highly reflective or otherwise) of an air space, refer to appropriate table for the insulating value of the air space. Some manufacturers of blanket insulation mark their products with an R-value, but they can ensure only the quality of the material as shipped.
[b]Average values only are given because variations depend on density of the board and on the type, size, and depth of perforations.
[c]Weight of masonry units measuring approximately 7-5/8-in. high by 15-5/8-in. long is given to describe blocks tested. Values are for 1-sq. ft. area.

Resources

- American Institute of Architects, *Architectural Graphics Standards*, 11th ed. Hoboken, NJ: John Wiley and Sons, 2007.
- American Institute of Architects, *Graphic Standards for Residential Construction*, 2nd ed. Hoboken, NJ: John Wiley and Sons, 2010.

Chapter 2

Common Building Code Requirements

Loads and Allowable Deflection

Fire Resistance Ratings for Exterior Walls

Minimum Fixture Clearances

Loads and Allowable Deflection

Description

Various environmental factors are considered during the design stage, but it is also imperative to evaluate and consider conditions when renovating or remodeling a space or residence. It seems obvious that the column in the middle of the room cannot be removed or omitted without other resolution.

The tables in this chapter are based on information from the 2009 International Residential Code (IRC). Because conditions vary, these tables should be used only for reference.

Other Live-Load Considerations

- Elevated garage floors shall be capable of supporting a 2,000-pound load applied over a 20-square-inch area.
- Attics without storage are those where the maximum clear height between joist and rafter is less than 42 inches, or where there are not two or more adjacent trusses with the same web configuration

Table 2.1 Minimum Uniformly Distributed Live Loads

Use	Live Load
Attics without storage	10 PSF
Attics with limited storage	20 PSF
Habitable attics and attics served with fixed stairs	30 PSF
Balconies (exterior) and decks	40 PSF
Fire escapes	40 PSF
Guardrails and handrails	200 PSF
Guardrails in-fill components	50 PSF
Passenger vehicle garages	50 PSF
Rooms other than sleeping room	40 PSF
Sleeping rooms	30 PSF
Stairs	40 PSF

capable of containing a rectangle 42 inches high by 2 feet wide, or greater, located within the plane of the truss. For attics without storage, this live load need not be assumed to act concurrently with any other live-load requirements.

- Individual stair treads shall be designed for the uniformly distributed live load or a 300-pound concentrated load acting over an area of 4 square inches, whichever produces greater stresses.
- A single concentrated load applied in any direction at any point along the top.
- Guard in-fill components (all those except the handrail), balusters, and panel fillers shall be designed to withstand a horizontal applied normal load of 50 pounds on an area equal to 1 square foot. This load need not be assumed to act concurrently with any other live load requirements.
- For attics with limited storage and constructed with trusses, this live load need be applied only to those portions of the bottom chord where there are two or more adjacent trusses with the same web configuration capable of containing a rectangle 42 inches high or greater by 2 feet wide or greater, located within the plane of the truss. The rectangle shall fit between the top of the bottom chord and the bottom of any other truss member, provided that each of the following criteria is met.

  1. The attic area is accessible by a pull-down stairway or framed opening.
  2. The truss has a bottom chord pitch less than 2:12.
  3. Required insulation depth is less than the bottom chord member depth.

  The bottom chords of trusses meeting the indicated criteria for limited storage shall be designed for the greater of the actual imposed dead load or 10 psf, uniformly distributed over the entire span.
- Glazing used in handrail assemblies and guards shall be designed with a safety factor of 4. The safety factor shall be applied to each of the concentrated loads applied to the top of the rail, and to the load on the in-fill components. These loads shall be determined independent of one another, and loads are assumed not to occur with any other live load.

For cantilever members, L shall be taken as twice the length of the cantilever.

For aluminum structural members or panels used in roofs or walls of sunroom additions or patio covers, not supporting edge of glass or sandwich panels, the total load deflection shall not exceed L/60.

Table 2.2 Minimum Roof Live Loads in Pounds-Force per Square Foot of Horizontal Projection

Roof Slope	Tributary Loaded Area in Square Feet for Any Structural Member		
	0 to 200	201 to 600	Over 600
Flat or rise less than 4 in. per ft. (1:3)	20	16	12
Rise 4 inches per ft. (1:3) to less than 12 in. per foot (1:1)	16	14	12
Rise 12 in. per ft. (1:1) and greater	12	12	12

Table 2.3 Allowable Deflection of Structural Members

Structural Member	Allowable Deflection
Rafters having slopes greater than 3:12 with no finished ceiling attached to rafters	L/180
Interior walls and partitions	H/180
Floors and plastered ceilings	L/360
All other structural members	L/240
Exterior walls with plaster or stucco finish	H/360
Exterior walls—wind loads with brittle finishes	H/240
Exterior wall—wind loads with flexible finishes	L/120
Lintels supporting masonry veneer walls	L/600

Note: L = span length, H = span height.
The wind load shall be permitted to be taken as 0.7 times the component and cladding loads for the purpose of the determining deflection limits herein.
Deflection for exterior walls with interior gypsum board finish shall be limited to an allowable deflection of H/180.

For continuous aluminum structural members supporting edge of glass, the total load deflection shall not excess L/175 for each glass lite or L/60 for the entire length of the member, whichever is more stringent. For sandwich panels used in roofs or walls of sunroom additions or patio covers, the total load deflection shall not exceed L/120.

Fire Resistance Ratings for Exterior Walls

Description

Life safety is critical in all facilities, but in spaces where sleeping occurs it becomes even more critical. When evaluating existing conditions, the following tables based on information from the International Residential Code are helpful rules of thumb. Once actual conditions have been evaluated, it is important to consult local code requirements that are applicable to specific conditions.

Table 2.4 Exterior Walls

Exterior Wall Element		Minimum Fire-Resistance Rating	Minimum Fire Separation Distance
Walls	(Fire-resistance rated)	1 hour—tested in accordance with ASTM E119 or UL 263 with exposure from both sides	< 5 ft.
Walls	Not-fire-resistance rated)	0 hours	≥ 5 ft.
Projections	(Fire-resistance rated)	1 hour on the underside	≥ 2 ft. to 5 ft.
Projections	Not-fire-resistance rated)	0 hours	5 ft.
Openings in walls	Not allowed	Not applicable	< 3 ft.
Openings in walls	25% maximum of wall area	0 hours	3 ft.
Openings in walls	Unlimited	0 hours	5 ft.
Penetrations		Refer to local jurisdiction	< 5 ft.
Penetrations	All	None required	5 ft.

Table 2.5 Dwelling/Garage Separation

Separation	Material
From the residence and attics	Not less than ½-inch gypsum board or equivalent applied to the garage side
From all habitable rooms above the garage	Not less than ⅝-inch Type X gypsum board or equivalent
Structure(s) supporting floor/ceiling assemblies used for separation required by this section	Not less than ½-inch gypsum board or equivalent
Garages located less than 3 ft. from a dwelling unit on the same lot	Not less than ½-inch gypsum board or equivalent applied to the interior side of exterior walls that are within this area

Minimum Fixture Clearances

Description

Plumbing- and electrical-code-required clearances are important when installing residential fixtures. The International Residential Code (IRC) outlines the codes by location and type, and should be used when determining the minimum fixture clearances.

A plumbing fixture is described as a device that delivers and drains water to and from a system that has particular use. The most common are water closets, toilets, urinals, sinks/faucets, bathtubs/showers, bidets, drinking fountains, hose bibs, and terminal valves from dishwashers, and refrigerators/freezers with icemakers.

A lighting fixture is described as a device used to create artificial light or illumination. The most common fixed lighting are recessed, which includes can lights and cove lights, and surface-mounted, which includes chandeliers, pendant lights, and track lights.

Assessing Existing Conditions

To ensure the proper installation of plumbing fixtures, assess the following conditions:

- Each fixture shall have a means of connection to water supply line, and fixture drain that is within regulation distance from other fixtures, walls, or vanity.
- Check clearance behind plumbing fixtures for plugs, connectors, and pipes and tubing.

To ensure the proper installation of lighting fixtures, assess the following conditions:

- Some lighting fixtures can only be installed as recessed due to their mounting location in regards to other fixtures or surroundings.
- Lighting fixture controls shall be located at regulation heights in accordance with the current IRC.

Acceptable Practices

By plumbing code, each fixture requires a minimum distance from a wall or another fixture. When planning, consider the plumbing fixtures and the spaces in which they will function. Measuring to the centerline of all fixtures while keeping the desirable fixture clearances in mind can come in handy as the planning progresses. The following are minimum clearances, according to the IRC:

- A water closet, lavatory, or bidet shall not be set closer than 15 inches from its center to any sidewall, partition, or vanity. *IRC P2705.1*
- A minimum of 30 inches, center-to-center, is required between adjacent fixtures. *IRC P2705.1*
- Allow for 21 inches clearance in front of the water closet, lavatory, or bidet to any wall, fixture, or door. *IRC P2705.1*
- Shower compartments shall have at least 900 square inches of interior cross-sectional area, and not less than 30 inches in minimum dimension measured from the finished interior dimension of the shower. *IRC P2708.1*
- Allow a minimum of 22 inches of clear and unobstructed space to access the shower compartment. *IRC P2708.1.1*

Lighting fixture clearances are also regulated by codes, according to the IRC. The following are current residential regulations:

- Surface-mounted incandescent or LED light fixtures with enclosed light source can be installed on the wall above the door or on the ceiling, provided that there is a 12-inch minimum clearance between the fixture and the nearest storage. *IRC E4003.12*
- Surface-mounted and recessed fluorescent light fixtures can be installed on the wall above the door or on the ceiling, provided that there is a 6-inch minimum clearance between the fixture and the nearest storage. *IRC E4003.12*
- Recessed incandescent or LED light fixtures with enclosed light source can be installed on the wall above the door or on the ceiling, provided that there is a 6-inch minimum clearance between the fixture and the nearest storage. *IRC E4003.12*
- Recessed light fixtures shall be either marked as "Type IC," or shall have at least ½-inch clearance from combustible materials. *IRC E4004.8*
- Recessed light fixtures shall be either marked as "Type IC" or have at least 3-inch clearance from insulation. *IRC E4004.9*

Appliances also have minimum clearances from unprotected combustible materials. Most can be found on a fixed label or in the manufacturer's written installation instructions. However, the following are required by the current IRC:

- Not less than 1 inch of air space shall be provided between the appliance and combustible construction. *IRC M1306*
- Freestanding or built-in ranges shall have a vertical clearance above the cooking top of not less than 30 inches to unprotected combustible materials unless otherwise indicated on the appliance label or installation instructions. *IRC M1901*

Practices to Avoid

Since electrical and/or lighting fixtures carry electrical charges and could be dangerous, building codes have been mandated to ensure the safety of facility users. Common construction practices to avoid, unless approved by authorities having jurisdiction, include:

- Light fixtures located within 8 feet, measured vertically, above the bathtub rim or shower threshold, and within 3 feet, measured horizontally, of the bathtub rim or shower threshold, must be approved for use in damp locations. *IRC E4003.11*
- Pendant, cord-connected and chain-, cable-, or cord-suspended light fixtures are not allowed to be within 3 feet horizontally and 8 feet vertically of a bathtub rim or shower threshold. *IRC E4003.11*
- Ceiling fans are not allowed to be within 3 feet horizontally and 8 feet vertically of a bathtub rim or shower threshold. *IRC E4003.11*
- Track lighting is not allowed to be within 3 feet horizontally and 8 feet vertically of a bathtub rim or shower threshold. *IRC E4003.11*

When installing kitchen appliances and fixtures, avoid these construction practices:

- No two primary work centers including primary sink, refrigerator, or cooktop/range shall be separated by a full-height, full-depth tall cabinet.
- No entry door, appliance door, or cabinet door should interfere with another door.
- Countertop receptacle outlets should be placed every 24 inches on center along the counter surface. Mounting height should not exceed 20 inches above the countertop surface. *IRC E3901.4*

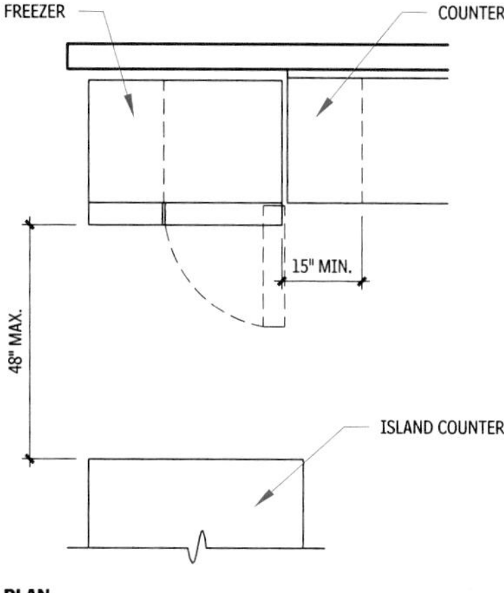

Figure 2.1 Refrigerator work area

Source: AIA, *Architectural Graphic Standards,* 11th ed. Copyright 2007, John Wiley & Sons, Inc.

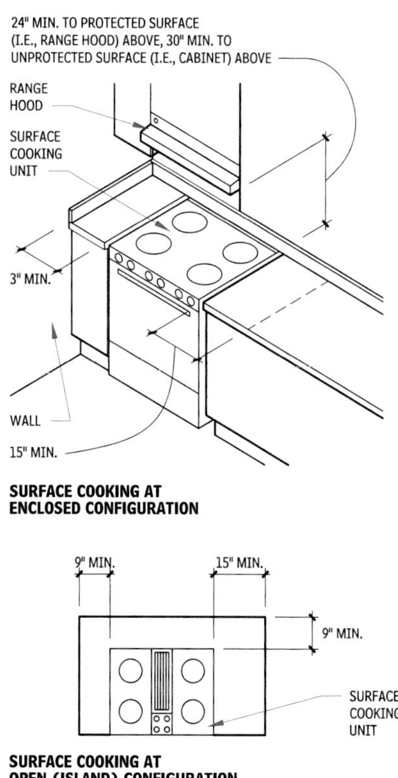

Figure 2.2 Surface cooking work area

Source: AIA, *Architectural Graphic Standards,* 11th ed. Copyright 2007, John Wiley & Sons, Inc.

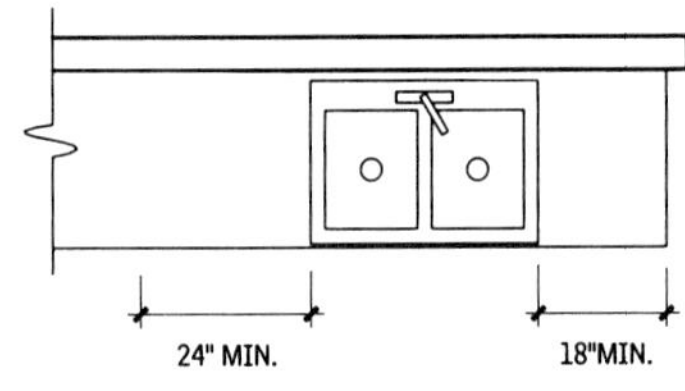

LINEAR COUNTER FRONTAGE

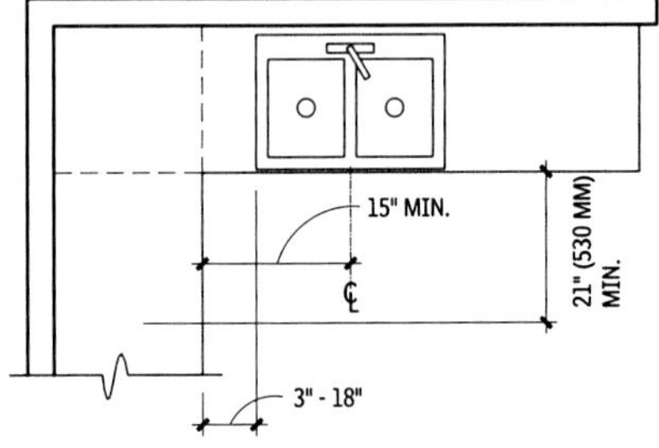

SINK ADJACENT TO CORNER

Figure 2.3 Sink work area

Source: AIA, *Architectural Graphic Standards,* 11th ed. Copyright 2007, John Wiley & Sons, Inc.

Resources

WITHIN THIS BOOK

- Chapter 31 Plumbing
- Chapter 33 Electrical

REFERENCE STANDARDS

- ASTM E 119—Standard Test Methods for Fire Tests of Building Construction and Materials.
- ANSI/UL 263—Fire Resistance Ratings, Underwriters Laboratories, Inc.

OTHER RESOURCES

- American Institute of Architects, *Architectural Graphics Standards,* 11th ed. Hoboken, NJ: John Wiley and Sons, 2007.
- American Institute of Architects, *Architectural Graphic Standards for Residential Construction*, 2nd ed. Hoboken, NJ: John Wiley and Sons, 2010.
- 2009 International Residential Code for One and Two-Family Dwellings. Washington, DC: International Code Council, Inc, 2009.

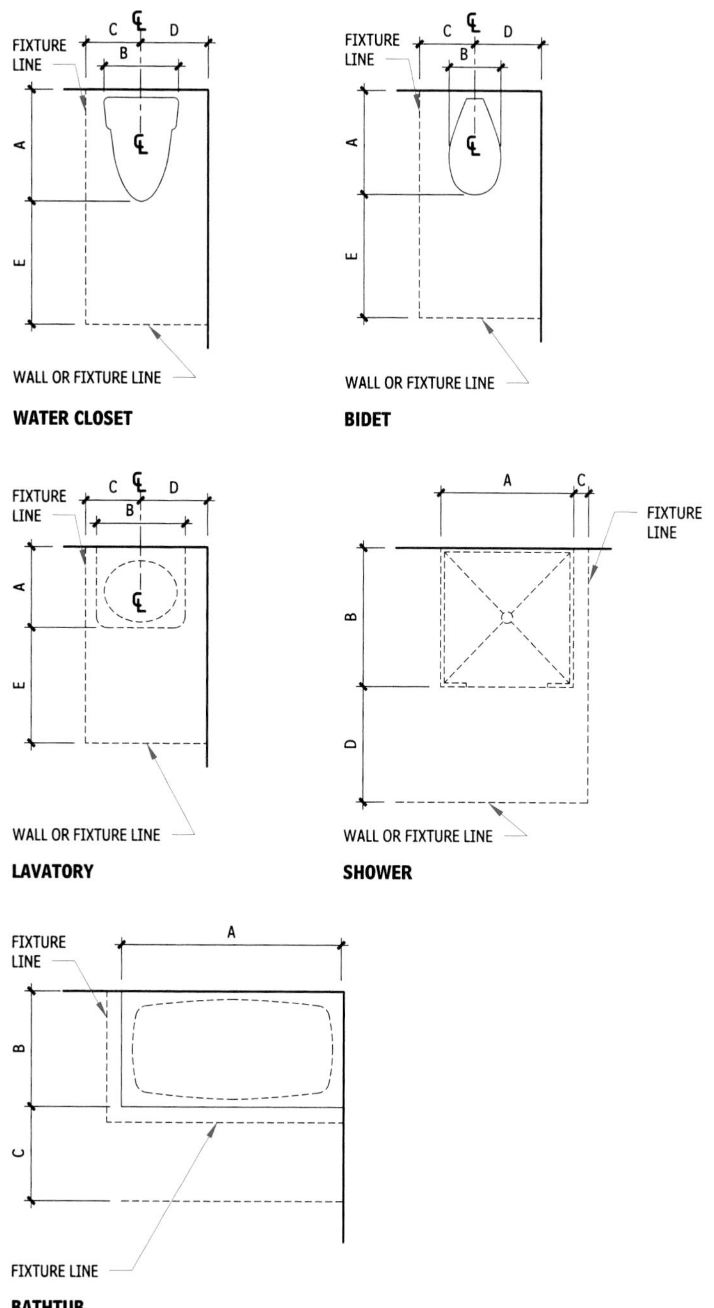

Figure 2.4 Typical bathroom fixture design parameters

Source: AIA, *Architectural Graphic Standards for Residential Construction*, 2nd ed. Copyright 2010, John Wiley & Sons, Inc.

Table 2.6 Fixture Sizes and Clearances (in.). Values in Table 2.6 refer to Figure 2.4.

	A		B		C		D		E	
Fixture	Minimum	Liberal	Minimum	Liberal	Minimum	Liberal	Minimum	Liberal	Minimum	Liberal
Water closet	27	31	19	21	15*	18	15*	22	21*	36
Bidet	25	27	14	14	15*	18	15*	22	21*	36
Lavatory	16	21	18	30	2	6	14*	22	21*	30
Shower (interior dimension)	30*	36	30*	36	2	8	24*	34	N/A	N/A
Bathtub	60 standard	72	30 standard	48	21	34	**		**	

Note: * IRC Minimum

Chapter 3

Accessibility Guidelines

Basic Accessible Clearances

Accessible Routes

Basic Accessible Clearances

Description

There are many standards and rules of thumb that are appropriate for use in residential design and construction. The most commonly used are *ANSI A117.1, Accessibility Guidelines for Buildings*, and the Department of Justice's *ADA Standards*. These guidelines are not requirements in single-family homes, but in conditions where accessibility or adaptability may be desirable, the guidelines should provide rules of thumb.

Assessing Existing Conditions

- Identify areas required to be accessible.
- Consider insulating lavatory pipes under sinks when installing wall-mounted or pedestal-mounted units.
- Check door swing, direction, and clearance, doors shall not swing into required clear floor space.

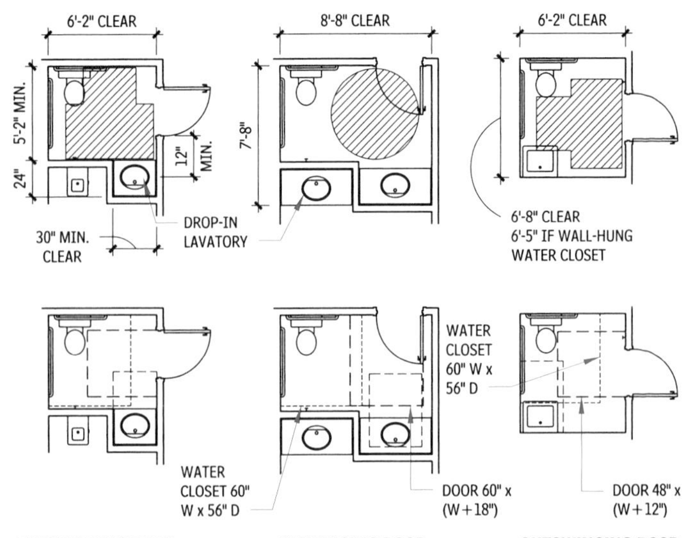

Figure 3.1 Bathroom layout

Source: AIA, *Architectural Graphic Standards*, 11th ed. Copyright 2007, John Wiley & Sons, Inc.

Acceptable Practices

Wall- and post-mounted cantilevered lavatories and sinks shall have a clear knee space between the bottom of the apron and the floor or ground at least 27 inches high, 30 inches wide, and a toe clearance at least 9 inches deep. Free-standing or built-in units not having a clear space under them shall have a clear floor space at least 30 inches by 48 inches that allows a person in a wheelchair to make a parallel approach to the unit.

For a hinged door, the clear width is measured between the face of the door and the doorstop with the door open at a 90° angle. For a sliding or folding door, the clear width is measured between the edge of the door and the jamb with the door fully open. Hardware must be accessible with the door in fully open position. Openings and doors without doorways more than 24 inches in depth must have a clear width of 36 inches minimum. Doors in dwelling units covered by Fair Housing Act Guidelines are required to have a "nominal" 32-inch clear opening width, an accessible threshold, and maneuvering clearances on both sides of the door.

If the clear floor space only allows forward approach to an object, the maximum high forward reach allowed shall be 48 inches. The minimum low forward reach is 15 inches. If the clear floor space allows parallel approach by a person in a wheelchair, the maximum high-side reach allowed shall be 54 inches and the low-side reach shall be no less than 9 inches above the floor.

Practices to Avoid

- Avoid installing grab bars onto walls without proper blocking and mounting plates.
- Avoid installing floor covering that will interfere with mounting heights.
- Avoid locating light switches, receptacle outlets, thermostats, and other wall-mounted controls at heights outside of wheelchair reach ranges.
- Avoid installing ceiling fans without wall switches and/or remote control.

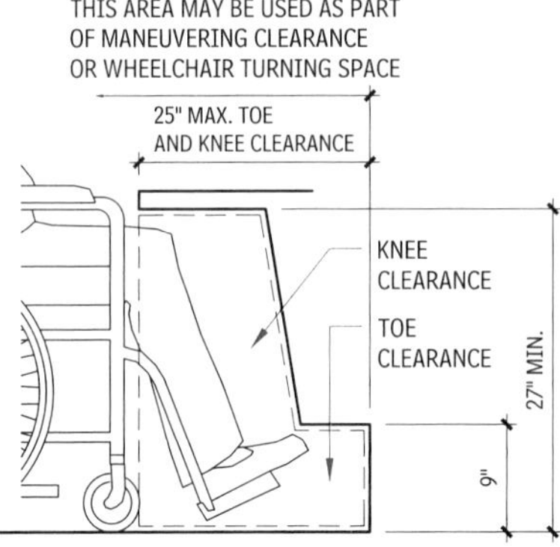

THIS AREA MAY BE USED AS PART
OF MANEUVERING CLEARANCE
OR WHEELCHAIR TURNING SPACE
25" MAX. TOE
AND KNEE CLEARANCE
KNEE
CLEARANCE
TOE
CLEARANCE
27" MIN.
9"

MAX. CLEARANCE

THIS AREA MAY BE USED AS PART
OF MANEUVERING CLEARANCE
OR WHEELCHAIR TURNING SPACE
17" MIN. TOE
AND KNEE CLEARANCE
11" MIN.
6" MIN.
8" MIN.
KNEE
CLEARANCE
TOE
CLEARANCE
27" MIN.
9"

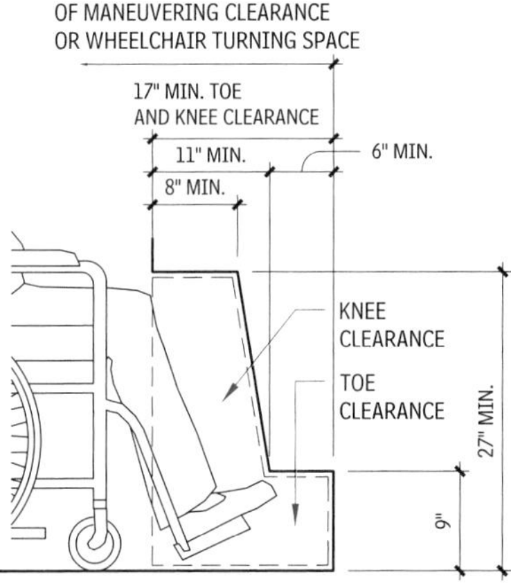

MIN. CLEARANCE

THIS AREA MAY BE USED AS PART
OF MANEUVERING CLEARANCE
OR WHEELCHAIR TURNING SPACE
6" MAX.
TOE CLEARANCE
9"

TOE CLEARANCE ONLY

Figure 3.2 Knee and toe clearances

Source: AIA, *Architectural Graphic Standards,* 11th ed. Copyright 2007, John Wiley & Sons, Inc.

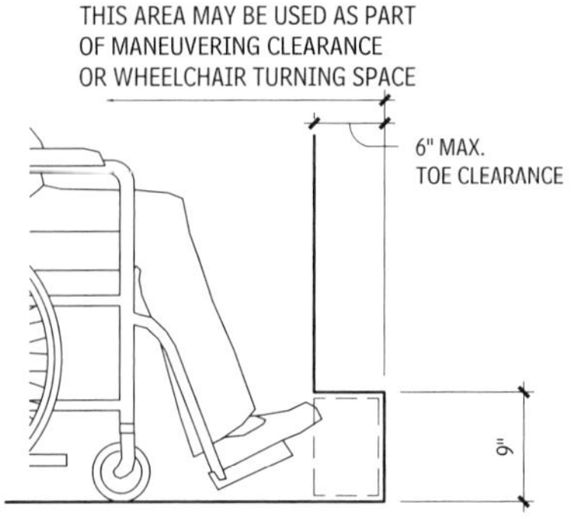

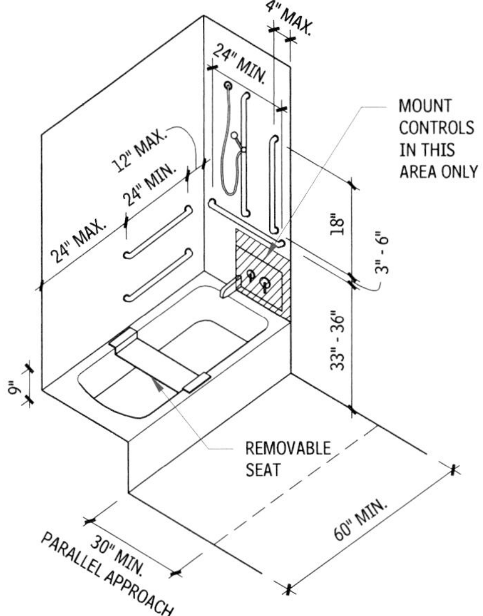

Figure 3.3 Shower and tub grab bar locations
Source: AIA, *Architectural Graphic Standards,* 11th ed. Copyright 2007, John Wiley & Sons, Inc.

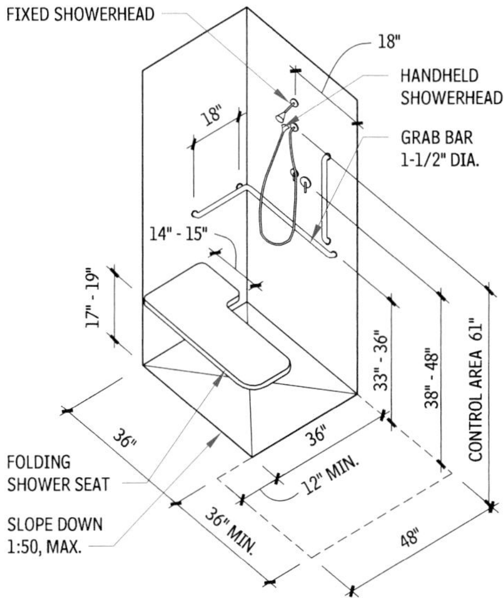

Figure 3.4 Shower grab bar locations
Source: AIA, *Architectural Graphic Standards,* 11th ed. Copyright 2007, John Wiley & Sons, Inc.

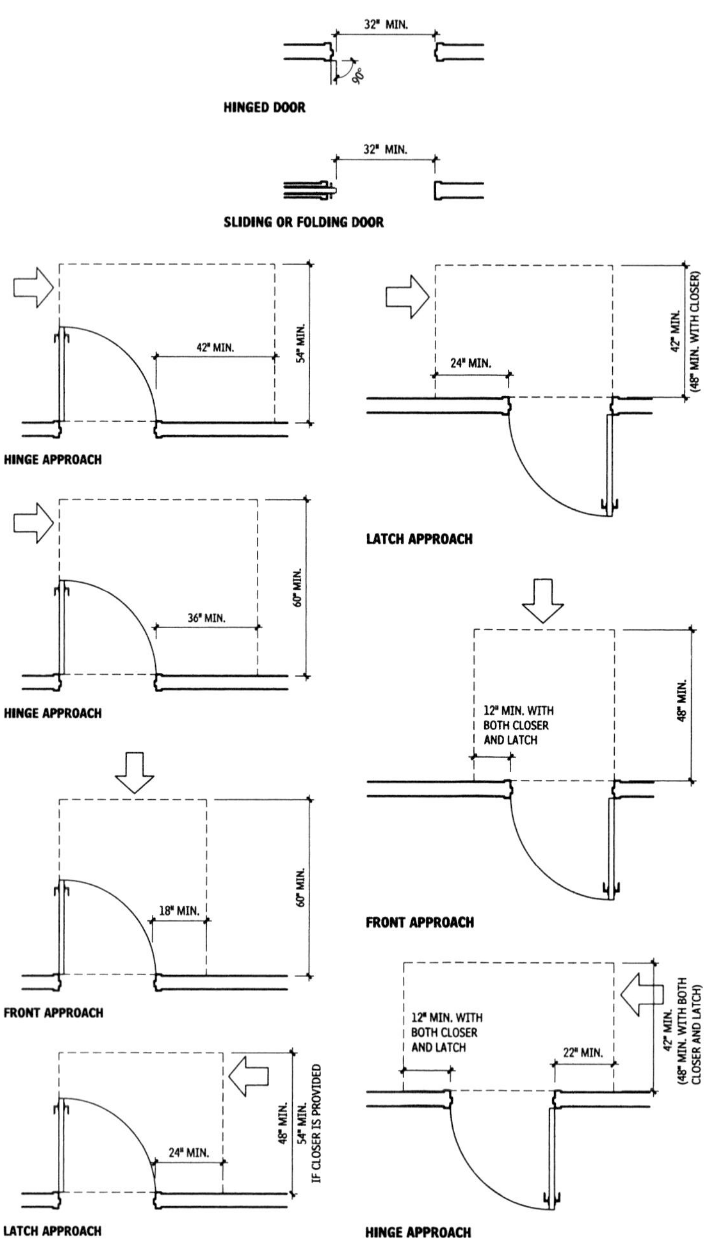

Figure 3.5 Accessible clearance at doorways

Source: AIA, *Architectural Graphic Standards,* 11th ed. Copyright 2007, John Wiley & Sons, Inc.

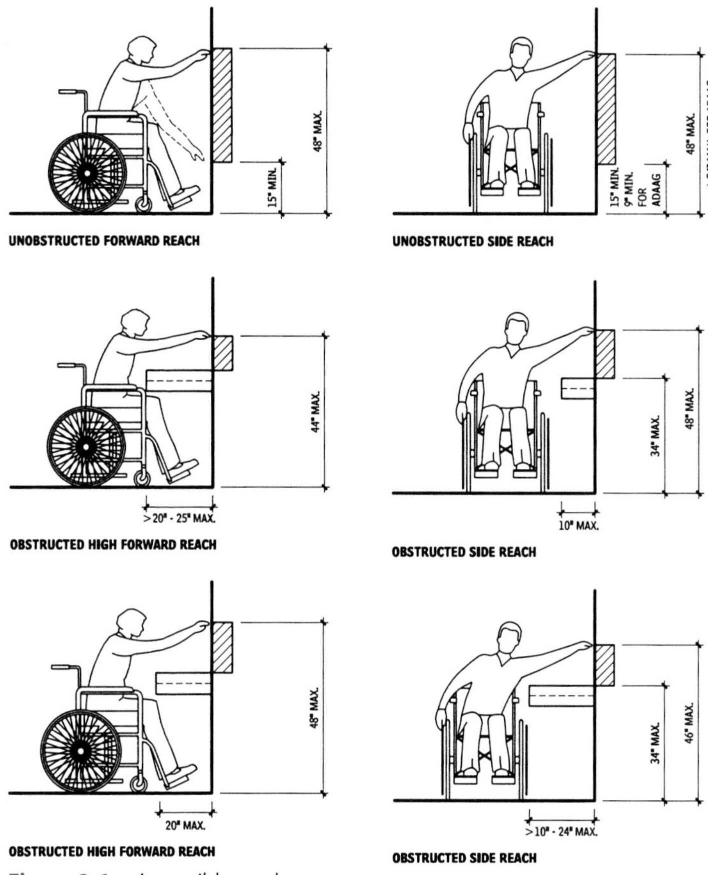

Figure 3.6 Accessible reach ranges

Source: AIA, *Architectural Graphic Standards,* 11th ed. Copyright 2007, John Wiley & Sons, Inc.

Accessible Routes

Description

Similar to the basic clearances, accessible routes allow for travel between one area and another and should be considered in residential construction.

Assessing Existing Conditions

Accessible routes are permitted to include the following elements:

- Walking surfaces with a slope of less than 1:20
- Curb ramps
- Ramps
- Elevators
- Platform (wheelchair) lifts

Each component has specific technical criteria that must be applied for use as part of an accessible route. Consult the applicable code or regulation.

Acceptable Practices

The minimum clear width of an accessible route shall be 36 inches except at doors. If an accessible route has less than 60 inches clear width, then passing spaces at least 60 inches by 60 inches shall be located at reasonable intervals not to exceed 200 feet. A T-intersection of two corridors or walks is an acceptable passing place.

If a person in a wheelchair must make a turn around an obstruction, the minimum clear width of the accessible route shall be as shown in Figure 3.8.

If an accessible route has changes in level greater than 1/2 inch, then a curb ramp, ramp, elevator, or platform lift shall be provided.

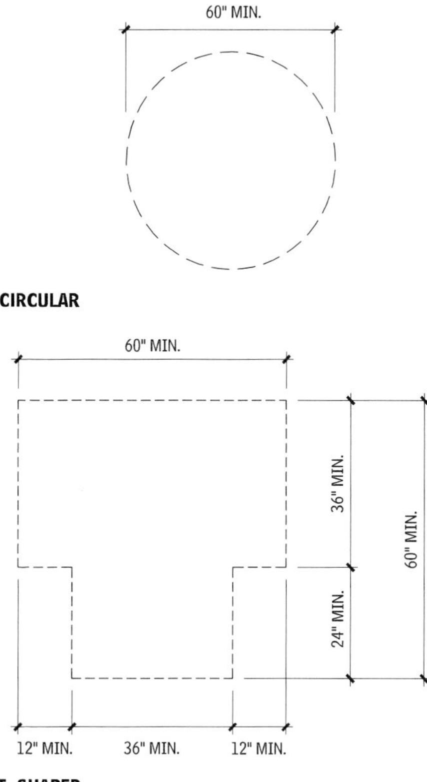

Figure 3.7 Accessible route and maneuvering clearances
Source: AIA, *Architectural Graphic Standards,* 11th ed. Copyright 2007, John Wiley & Sons, Inc.

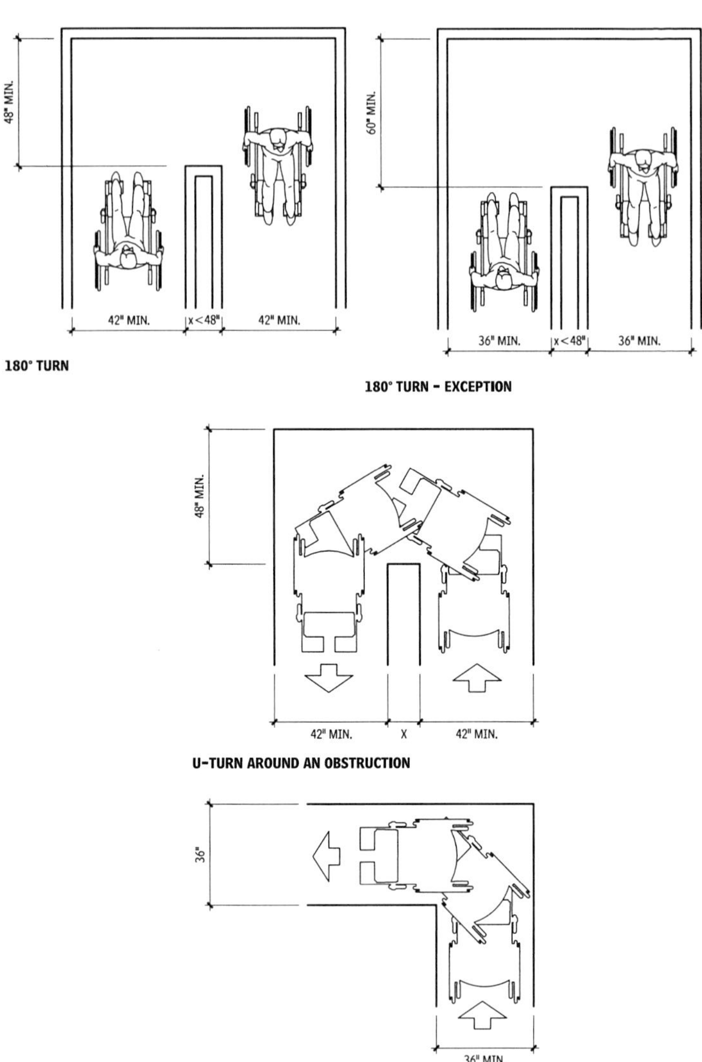

Figure 3.8 Accessible route clear width at turns

Source: AIA, *Architectural Graphic Standards,* 11th ed. Copyright 2007, John Wiley & Sons, Inc.

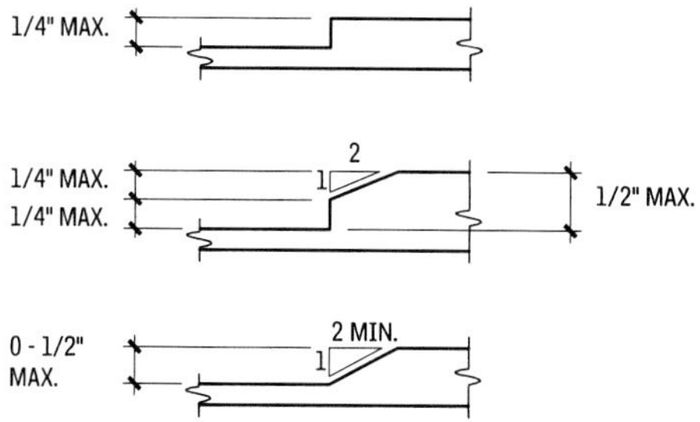

Figure 3.9 Accessible route changes in level
Source: AIA, *Architectural Graphic Standards,* 11th ed. Copyright 2007, John Wiley & Sons, Inc.

Practices to Avoid

- Avoid making the accessible route a "second-class" means of circulation.
- Avoid using surfaces that are not firm, stable, and slip resistant.

Resources

- 2009 International Residential Code for One and Two-Family Dwellings. Washington, DC: International Code Council, Inc., 2009.
- American Institute of Architects, *Architectural Graphics Standards,* 11th ed. Hoboken, NJ: John Wiley and Sons, 2007.
- American Institute of Architects, *Graphic Standards for Residential Construction,* 2nd ed. Hoboken, NJ: John Wiley and Sons, 2010.
- Department of Housing and Urban Development, *Fair Housing Accessibility Guidelines.* Washington, DC: Department of Housing and Urban Development, 1991.
- ICC/ANSI A117.1, Accessible and Usable Buildings and Facilities. Washington, DC: International Code Council, Inc., 2003.

Chapter 4

Sustainability Rating Systems

LEED™ for Homes

NAHB Green Home Building Guidelines

ENERGY STAR

LEED™ for Homes

Description

LEED (**L**eadership in **E**nergy and **E**nvironmental **D**esign) for Homes is a rating system that promotes the design and construction of high-performance sustainable homes. Both single-family and low-rise multifamily residential developments can utilize this program to use resources more efficiently, provide healthier living environments, improve air and water quality, and often pursue a LEED rating for the facility. These ratings, Certified, Silver, Gold, and Platinum, are achieved by earning predetermined amounts of points, as shown in Table 4.1, for performing credits in eight categories.

The strength of the LEED for Homes program is its third-party verification through LEED for Homes Providers and Green Raters. These are local and regional organizations chosen by USGBC to provide certification services to LEED for Home projects in their local or regional markets.

Acceptable Practices

The following LEED for Homes rating system's eight categories are subdivided into prerequisites/credits: (maximum points available):

1. *Innovation and design process (ID):* Special design methods, unique regional credits, measures not currently addressed in the rating system, and exemplary performance levels
2. *Location and linkages (LL):* The placement of homes in socially and environmentally responsible ways in relation to the larger community

Table 4.1 LEED for Homes Certification

Levels	Number of LEED for Homes Points Required
Certified	75–59
Silver	60–74
Gold	75–89
Platinum	90–136
Total Available Points	136

3. *Sustainable sites (SS):* The use of the entire property so as to minimize the project's impact on the site
4. *Water efficiency (WE):* Water-efficient practices, both indoor and outdoor
5. *Energy and atmosphere (EA):* Energy efficiency, particularly in the building envelope and heating and cooling design
6. *Materials and resources (MR):* Efficient utilization of materials, selection of environmentally preferable materials, and minimization of waste during construction
7. *Indoor environmental quality (EQ):* Improvement of indoor air quality by reducing the creating of and exposure to pollutants
8. *Awareness and education (AE):* The education of homeowners, tenants, and/or building manager about the operation and maintenance of the green features of a LEED home

Assessing Existing Conditions

In order to ensure that LEED for Homes credits are not being violated, verify the following:

- Review the projects LEED for Homes checklist to see which prerequisites and credits are being targeted to achieve the level of certification desired.
- Review shop drawings and product data and become familiar with products to be installed on the project site; verify that the products submitted are the products being used on the project site.
- Confirm that a third-party inspector has been on project site per project requirements.
- Review with contractor how implementation of a waste management plan is to be handled to comply with the project's required waste diversion rate to meet project goals.
- Confirm that interior ductwork and vents have been sealed to prevent contamination during construction activities.

Acceptable Practices

The following standards are guidelines for verifying that appropriate products are being administered to ensure achievement of LEED for Homes goals. VOC levels are within levels stated in Tables 4.2 and 4.3.

Table 4.2 Standards for Environmentally Preferable Paints and Coatings

Component	Applicable Standard (VOC Content)
Architectural paints, coatings, and primers applied to interior walls and ceilings	Flats: 50 g/L Nonflats: 150 g/L
Anticorrosive and antirust paints applied to interior ferrous metal substrates	250 g/L
Clear wood finishes	Varnish: 350 g/L Lacquer: 550 g/L
Floor coatings	100 g/L
Sealers	Waterproofing: 250 g/L Sanding: 275 g/L All others: 200 g/L
Shellacs	Clear: 730 g/L Pigmented: 550 g/L
Stains	250 g/L

Adapted from Table 25 Standards for Environmentally Preferable Paints and Coatings of the LEED for Homes Rating System

Table 4.3 Standards for Low-Emissions Adhesives and Sealants

Architectural Applications	Applicable Standard (VOC Content)
Indoor carpet adhesives	50 g/L less Water
Carpet pad adhesives	50 g/L less Water
Wood flooring adhesives	100 g/L less Water
VCT and asphalt adhesives	50 g/L less Water
Gypsum board and panel adhesives	50 g/L less Water
Cove base adhesives	50 g/L less Water
Multipurpose construction adhesives	70 g/L less Water
Specialty Applications	
Contact adhesive	80 g/L less Water
Special-purpose contact adhesive	250 g/L less Water
Sealants	
Architectural	250 g/L less Water

Adapted from Table 26 Standards for Low-Emissions Adhesives and Sealants of the LEED for Homes Rating System

Practices to Avoid

The LEED for Homes rating system requires integrated project planning, project delivery, and closeout. The following are practices to avoid, to ensure that the project is finished in a timely manner and to LEED requirements.

- Construction waste and recycling going into one dumpster. Contractors should provide a separate dumpster for recycling, and may be required to have different containers for different types of recycling like glass and wood.
- Smoking inside or around the openings of the facility.
- Skipping or not allowing enough time for the indoor air quality preoccupancy flush. This process takes time and needs to be incorporated into the overall construction schedule.
- Leaving dirty air filters in when construction is complete.

NAHB Green Home Building Guidelines

Description

The National Association of Home Builders (NAHB) and the International Code Council (ICC) partnered to form a standard definition of "green building." The National Green Building Standard (ICC 700–2008) for all residential construction, including single-family homes, apartments, condos, land developments, remodeling, and renovation, was the outcome of the partnership.

Key features of the standard include the following:

- Construction of smaller homes to conserve resources
- Energy performance a minimum of 15 percent better than the 2006 International Energy Conservation Code
- Use of low VOC materials
- Homeowner education on proper maintenance and operation

As with most of the rating systems, the Green Building Standard requires that a minimum number of features be incorporated in the following areas:

- Energy, water, and resource efficiency
- Lot and site development
- Indoor environmental quality
- Homeowner education

There are four performance levels that can be achieved: Bronze, Silver, Gold, and Emerald. These exemplify the highest achievement in residential green construction. Similar to other systems, verification by a third party is required.

Acceptable Practices

Common practices utilize the following:

- Environmental considerations should be incorporated into the project as early as possible.
- The house should be looked at as a whole as the builder determines which of the green home guidelines to put into the house.

- Verify there is a green building program coordinator or other third party. The guidelines and point system can be used independently even if a formal green building program does not exist.

Table 4.4 Points Required for the Three Levels of Green Building

	Bronze	Silver	Gold	Emerald
Lot design, preparation, and development	39	66	93	119
Resource efficiency	45	79	113	146
Energy efficiency	30	60	100	120
Water efficiency	14	26	41	60
Indoor environmental quality	36	65	100	140
Operation, maintenance, and homeowner education	8	10	11	12
Additional points from sections of your choice	50	100	100	100

ENERGY STAR

Description

ENERGY STAR is a joint program of the U.S. Environmental Protection Agency and the U.S. Department of Energy, focusing on protecting the environment through energy-efficient products and practices. Products that meet the standard should be clearly labeled with the ENERGY STAR logo. These can include but are not limited to appliance, heating and cool equipment, water heaters, building envelope product, home electronics, and lighting products.

ENERGY STAR–qualified homes have energy-efficient features that contribute to improved home quality, lower energy demand, and reduce air pollution. These homes are at least 15 percent more energy efficient than homes built to the 2004 International Residential Code (IRC), and include additional energy-saving features that typically make them 20 to 30 percent more efficient than standard homes.

The ENERGY STAR label can be applied to any home that is three stories or less, single family, and multifamily, and of various construction types.

Assessing Existing Conditions

In order to ensure that ENERGY STAR products are meeting requirements, verify the following:

- The home energy rater is using correct climate zone, location product is being used, and product has current regionally developed requirements. Hot climates require more efficient-cooling equipment, whereas mixed and cold climates require more efficient heating equipment.
- The National Performance Path Requirements, or National Builder Option Package, can be utilized by the home energy rater. Individual requirements vary and should be reviewed by the energy rater prior to qualifying products for ENERGY STAR label.

Figure 4.1 ENERGY STAR label

Acceptable Practices

To qualify for the ENERGY STAR label, a variety of energy-efficient features must be addressed:

- *Effective insulation:* Properly installed insulation in the floors, walls, and attic spaces create more uniform temperatures throughout the house, thus reducing energy consumption and increasing comfort.
- *High-performance windows:* Protective coatings and improved frame construction assist in keeping the heat in during the winter and out during the summer. The coating also assists in minimizing ultraviolet damage caused by direct sunlight.
- *Tight construction and ducts:* Seal holes and cracks in the exterior envelope of the home and also the heating and cooling ductwork reduces drafts, moisture, dust, pollen, and noise. A tightly sealed home improves comfort and indoor air quality while reducing utility and maintenance costs.
- *Efficient heating and cooling equipment:* In addition to using less energy to operate, efficient heating and cooling systems improve the overall comfort of the home by reducing humidity and noise.
- *Efficient products:* The use of ENERGY STAR–qualified products, including lighting fixtures and appliances, reduces the energy and resource consumption of the home.
- *Third-party verification:* Home energy raters will conduct on-site testing and inspections to verify the energy-efficient measures. A home energy rater may utilize either the National Performance Path Requirements or the National Builder Option Package.

Resources

- American Institute of Architects, *Architectural Graphics Standards*, 11th ed. Hoboken, NJ: John Wiley and Sons, 2007.
- American Institute of Architects, *Architectural Graphic Standards for Residential Construction*, 2nd ed. Hoboken, NJ: John Wiley & Sons, 2010.
- National Green Building Standard, NAHB/ICC, Washington, DC, 2008.
- LEED for Homes Reference Guide v2009. Washington, DC: USGBC, 2009.

Part II

Concrete

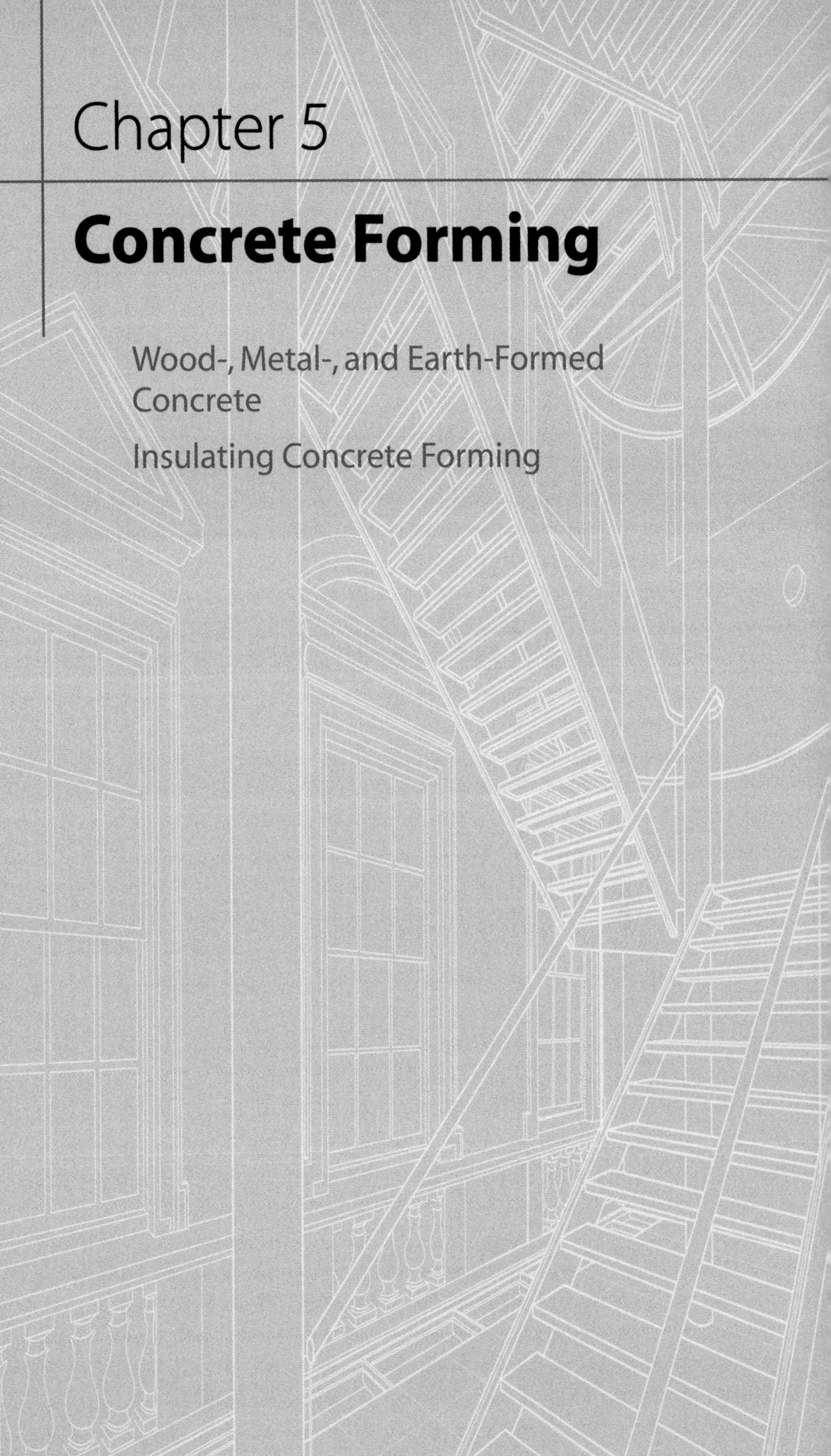

Chapter 5

Concrete Forming

Wood-, Metal-, and Earth-Formed Concrete

Insulating Concrete Forming

Wood-, Metal-, and Earth-Formed Concrete

Description

When placing concrete to form vertical walls, because concrete starts out as a liquid, forms must be built to contain the concrete while it cures. Common materials used to fabricate forms for concrete are wood, metal, and earth.

Wood forms are generally fabricated on site from dimension lumber and plywood. Formwork must be fabricated in such a way as to resist the pressure of the concrete in its liquid form. Concrete in its liquid form exerts pressure on formwork. As the formwork gets higher, so does the amount of pressure the concrete is exerting at the base of the wall. As shown in Figure 5.1, formwork is fabricated using plywood

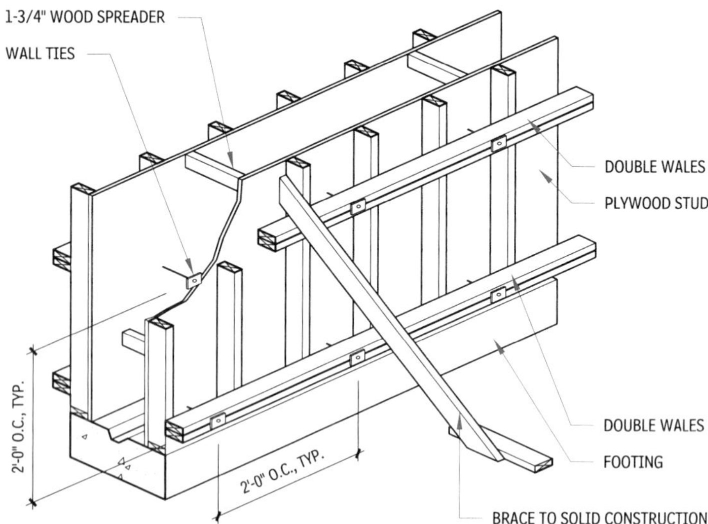

Figure 5.1 Typical site-built wall formwork
Source: AIA, *Architectural Graphic Standards for Residential Construction*, 2nd ed. Copyright 2010, John Wiley & Sons, Inc.

sheathing as the surface against which the concrete hardens. Dimension lumber is placed alongside the sheathing and helps to keep the sheathing flat, plumb, and resistant to the force exerted by the concrete. In addition, metal ties are used to help with the pressure exerted by the concrete.

Metal formwork is generally made in a shop or factory, can be a modular size, and is generally reused. It is a framework that is fabricated of steel plate, angles, tubes, or miscellaneous shapes for the supporting framework and can use plywood or metal plate as a sheathing material to retain the concrete.

Formwork, because it is retaining concrete in a liquid state, must be fabricated in such a way as to prevent leaking of water from the concrete. The loss of water from the concrete will cause the concrete to lose strength; therefore, joints in the formwork must be made in such a way that eliminates leaks.

Earth-formed concrete can be accomplished in different ways. If what needs to be formed is a spread footing or perimeter footing, then a trench or hole can be dug in the shape needed for the footing and concrete can be placed along with the required reinforcing in the hole or trench. Perimeter stem walls or basement walls can be earth formed, but only on one side of the wall. The other side of the form must be fabricated from wood or steel. Earth-formed concrete stem or basement walls are not very common anymore because it is difficult to apply any kind of waterproofing or dampproofing on the outside of the wall.

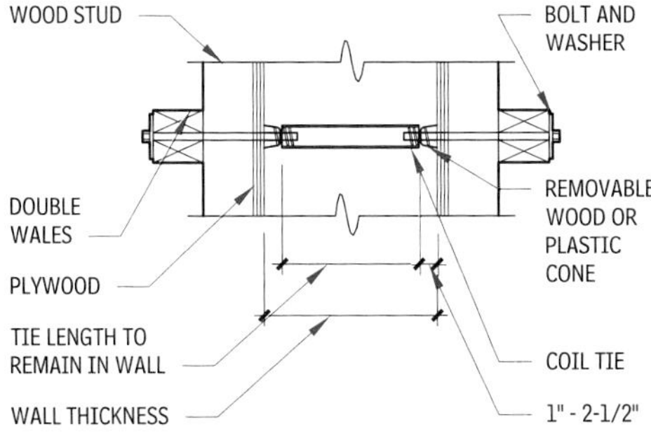

Figure 5.2 Site-built wall forms
Source: AIA, *Architectural Graphic Standards*, 11th ed. Copyright 2007, John Wiley & Sons, Inc.

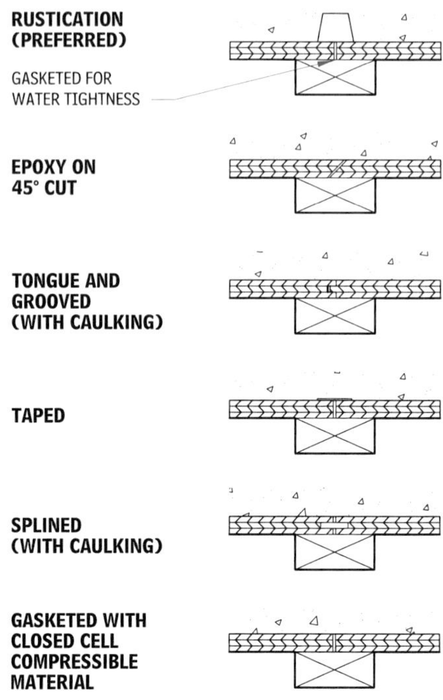

Figure 5.3 Form sheathing joint details

Source: AIA, *Architectural Graphic Standards,* 11th ed. Copyright 2007, John Wiley & Sons, Inc.

Assessing Existing Conditions

Verify the following conditions:

- Formwork is adequately braced and attached at bottom and top of wall.

Acceptable Practices

- Concrete starts to cure within two hours of beginning of the pour.
- Provide a keyed concrete joint between perimeter footing and stem or basement wall.

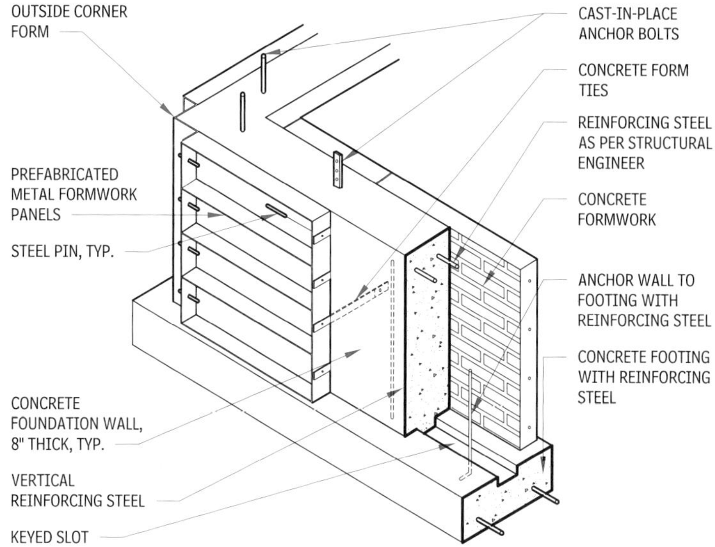

Figure 5.4 Typical concrete foundation wall
Source: AIA, *Architectural Graphic Standards for Residential Construction*, 2nd ed. Copyright 2010, John Wiley & Sons, Inc.

Practices to Avoid

- If waterproof membrane or dampproofing needs to be placed on blind side of foundation wall, then earth-formed concrete placement cannot be used.

Insulating Concrete Forming

Description

Insulating concrete forms (ICFs) are rigid plastic foam blocks, used to hold poured concrete in place during curing, that remain in place afterward as permanent thermal insulation. Together, the concrete, steel reinforcement bar, and foam insulation become a solid structural wall, floor, or roof structure that is resistant to strong winds, seismic forces, fire, insects, and rot.

ICFs are made from two panels of expanded polystyrene (EPS) or extruded polystyrene (XPS) held together by plastic ties or integral foam cores. ICFs are available in a variety of shapes, but the strength of an ICF structure depends on the configuration, thickness, and reinforcement of the concrete. Refer to the IRC and ASTM E2634 before using forms that do not result in a uniform monolithic concrete core. Openings in ICFs are easily cut to required rough dimensions before the concrete is poured. Buck systems or block-outs made from wood, metal, or plastic can be used to speed up construction and provide anchor points for windows and doors.

There are many benefits to using ICFs over traditional framing. High sound absorption is one, but better thermal resistance is usually at the top of everyone's list. ICFs should be chosen by their insulating value, which typically ranges from R-17 to R-26, depending on the thickness and type of foam used. ICF walls form a solid air barrier with minimal leaks, enabling HVAC systems to be sized smaller and energy savings to be seen from day one.

The cost to construct an ICF structure in relation to traditional methods varies by how the ICFs are used. Formwork can be a major cost for any concrete work, but ICFs are easily constructed by dry-stacking interlocking modular units. Where used for long spans of foundation wall or shapes designed to the modulus of available forms, ICFs are almost 40 percent less due to simplified construction and the elimination of field errors. Complicated structures are often more expensive because they can be difficult to form, but some savings can occur at openings where framing is simplified, less materials are need, and less waste is produced.

ICFs can be finished with a variety of products, including siding or direct applied stucco. Weather-resistant barriers are no longer required over ICFs above grade; however, some local conditions and materials may benefit from additional protection. Waterproofing should always be installed over ICFs used below grade.

Assessing Existing Conditions

In order to ensure the proper installation of ICFs, verify the following conditions:

- Footings are properly installed. Footing should be smooth, square, and level to ensure straight, plumb, and level walls.
- Formwork is properly attached to footings using either glue, metal tracks, or wood cleats.
- Bottom course is level.
- Corner joints are staggered and secured with fiber-reinforced tape.
- Horizontal and vertical reinforcements are provided per code and manufacturers' requirements.
- All openings are blocked out, including vents, outlets, fixtures, and utility lines.
- Each wall is braced every 5 feet on center along either side of wall.
- Openings are braced separately from walls.
- Concrete is placed in multiple lifts at a maximum of 4 feet each.
- Waterproofing membrane is installed at below-grade installations.
- Wall finishes are attached using recessed fastening strips, located every 6 inches on center on the ends of form ties.
- Per code, ICFs are covered by a 15-minute thermal barrier (½-inch gypsum board).

Acceptable Practices

Although ICF walls are often covered and unseen, they are a structural part of a home that provides an important thermal barrier to exterior conditions. ICF construction is becoming more familiar in many markets but remains somewhat uncharted. It is important to access local conditions and review manufacturer installation recommendations before using any ICF system.

Common construction practices for ICFs include the following:

- Shim or shave the bottom course to level it.
- Anchor bolting a ledger board prior to concrete to allow joist hangers to be used to frame floors.

- Use buck systems to block out openings.
- Install nails into bucks so they will become embedded in the concrete.
- Cut channels into IFCs to install utilities.

Practices to Avoid

The best ICF system can become one of the worst structures if not properly installed using recommended tools and methods. Common construction practices to avoid include the following:

- Unlevel or improperly prepared foundations for the IFCs.
- Use of a buck with a material that may be detrimental to a wall. Wood is inexpensive but can decay, expand, absorb moisture and create a thermal bridge, metal is strong but expensive and should be insulated, and plastic is good for uncommon shapes but needs lots of support.
- Pouring concrete without adequate blocking and support. Lack of support could result in a blowout.
- Using sealants or membrane products that are incompatible with the ICF foam material.
- Forgetting to cut an opening in the bottom of the buck for concrete pouring.
- Failing to plan ahead. Do not make plan or opening modifications once installation is complete.

Resources

WITHIN THIS BOOK

- Chapter 6 Concrete Reinforcing
- Chapter 7 Cast-In-Place Concrete

REFERENCE STANDARDS

- ASTM E2634—Standard Specification for Flat Wall Insulating Concrete Form (ICF) Systems

OTHER RESOURCES

- 2009 International Residential Code for One and Two-Family Dwellings. Washington, DC: International Code Council, Inc., 2009.
- 2009 International Building Code. Washington, DC: International Code Council, Inc., 2009.

- American Institute of Architects, *Architectural Graphics Standards*, 11th ed. Hoboken, NJ: John Wiley and Sons, 2007.
- American Institute of Architects, *Architectural Graphic Standards for Residential Construction*, 2nd ed. Hoboken, NJ: John Wiley and Sons, 2010.
- American Concrete Institute, www.concrete.org.
- Insulating Concrete Form Association, www.forms.org.

Chapter 6

Concrete Reinforcing

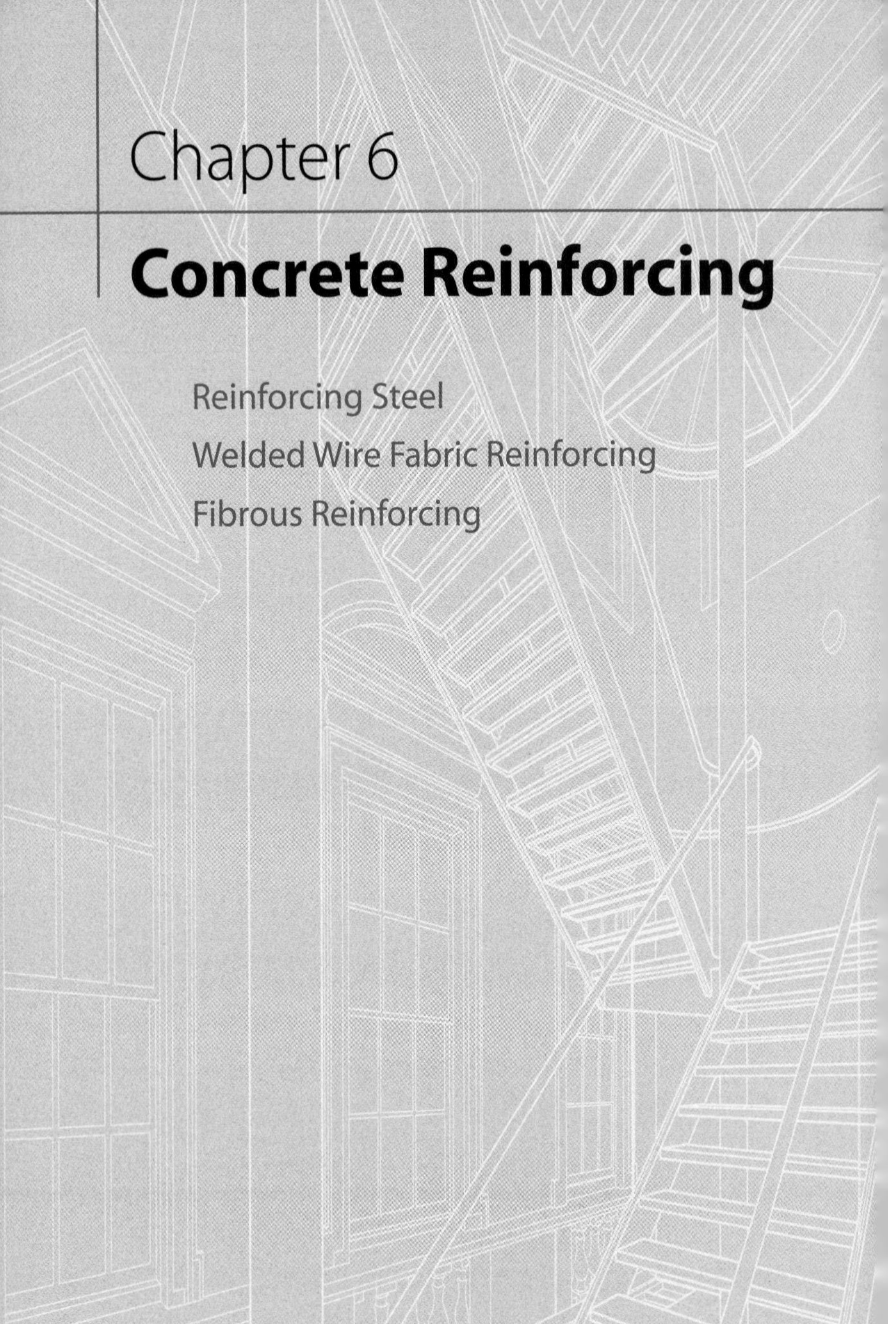

Reinforcing Steel

Welded Wire Fabric Reinforcing

Fibrous Reinforcing

Reinforcing Steel

Description

Reinforcing steel is commonly used in concrete to increase the tensile strength of the concrete. Reinforcing steel, often called rebar, is formed from carbon steel and is typically fabricated with ridges on the bar for better mechanical anchoring in the concrete. Rebar can also be fabricated smooth, without ridges, which is typically used for expansion, or cold joints in concrete. Rebar comes in three grades of steel—40, 60, and 75. The grade designation indicates the minimum yield strength of the rebar in ksi units ("ksi" stands for kilo-pounds per square inch; a "kilo-pound" equals 1,000 pounds) so grade 40 rebar has a maximum yield strength of 40,000 psi, or 40 ksi. In residential construction, grade 40 rebar is commonly used for foundation walls and footings. In seismic zones, generally grade 60 rebar is required.

Bars are marked showing where the bar was manufactured, what size the bar is and what type of steel it is. In residential construction, generally billet (Type "S") steel is used.

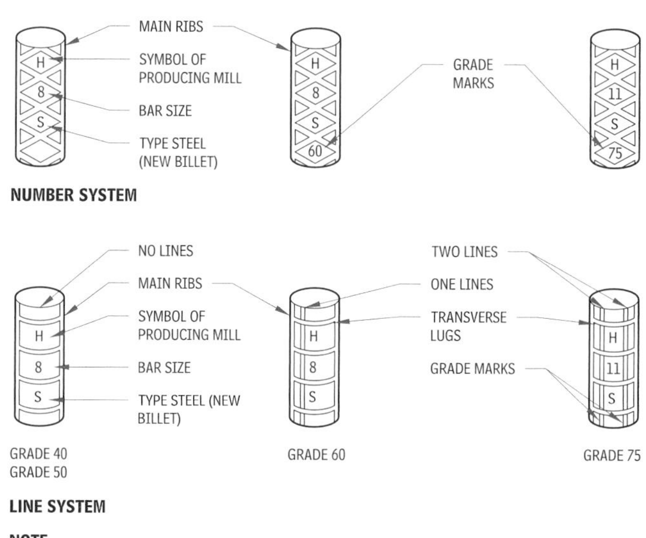

Figure 6.1 Reinforcing bar grade mark identification

Source: AIA, *Architectural Graphic Standards for Residential Construction*. Copyright 2003, John Wiley & Sons, Inc.

Assessing Existing Conditions

Prior to the placement of concrete, verify that reinforcing is correctly located as follows:

- *Slabs on grade:* If required, locate in the upper third of the slab.
- *Footings:* If required by code, minimum 3 inches clear from the bottom of the footing.
- Stem walls: Locate reinforcing in center of wall. Do not vary from the center of the wall by more than 10 percent of the wall thickness. Reinforcing must be covered by a minimum 1¼ inches of concrete

Acceptable Practices

- Adequately support reinforcing bars to prevent displacement while placing concrete.
- Placing one continuous rebar (#4) at the top and bottom of thickened slab edges.

Practices to Avoid

- Be sure to provide enough concrete cover over reinforcing. Otherwise, this will cause premature corroding of the reinforcing steel, weakening the concrete in tensile strength.

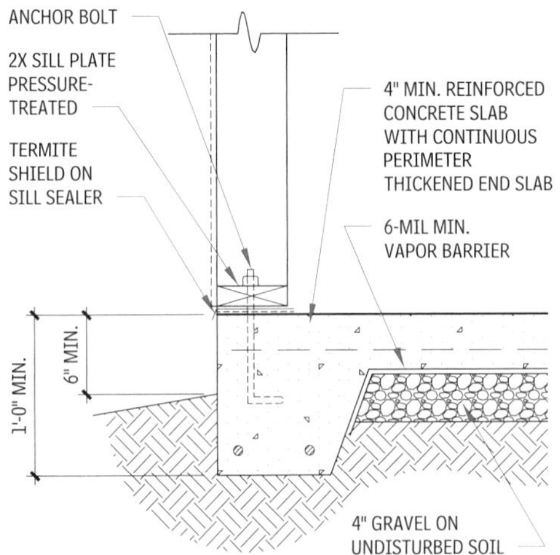

Figure 6.2 Slab edge section
Source: AIA, *Architectural Graphic Standards for Residential Construction*. Copyright 2003, John Wiley & Sons, Inc.

Welded Wire Fabric Reinforcing

Description

Welded wire fabric reinforcing is commonly used in concrete slab-on-grade construction to increase the tensile strength of the concrete. Welded wire fabric reinforcing is formed from carbon steel and is typically fabricated with ridges on the wire for better mechanical anchoring in the concrete (denoted as "D"). Welded wire fabric can also be fabricated smooth or plain, without ridges (denoted as "W"). Welded wire fabric is fabricated in sheets 5 to 10 feet wide by 10 to 20 feet long. It is also fabricated in rolls up to 200 feet in length (see Figure 6.3).

Figure 6.3 Welded wire fabric

Assessing Existing Conditions

Before placing the concrete, verify that reinforcing is correctly located as follows:

- Slabs on grade: If required, locate in the upper third of the slab.

Acceptable Practices

- Adequately support welded wire fabric to prevent displacement while placing concrete.
- Use spacing suggested in Table 6.1.

Practices to Avoid

- Avoid walking on wire reinforcement while placing concrete.

Table 6.1 Recommended Support Spacing

Suggested Support Spacing		
Welded Wire Reinforcement Range	Welded Wire Spacing (inches)	Suggested Support Spacing (feet)
W or D9 or larger*	12 and greater	4–6
W or D5 to W or D8	12 and greater	3–4
W or D9 and larger	Less than 12	3–4
W or D4 to W or D8	Less than 12	2–3
Less than W or D4	Less than 12	2–3 (or less) **

* Spacings of supports for WWR with wires larger than W or D9 can possibly be increased over the spacings shown, depending on the construction loads applied.

** Consider using additional rows of supports when large deflections or deformations occur.

Fibrous Reinforcing

Description

Fibrous reinforcing is added to a concrete mix to control shrinkage, cracking, and flexural strength, and to improve toughness and hardness of concrete. Small-diameter synthetic fibers (nylon, glass, steel, or polypropylene) are added to concrete and are primarily used in nonstructural concrete applications.

There are three types of fiber reinforcement, according to ASTM C1116:

- Type I: Includes steel fiber reinforcement and contains stainless-steel, alloy-steel, or carbon-steel fibers. Type I fiber is not common in residential construction.
- Type II: Includes glass-fiber reinforcement using alkali-resistant glass fibers.
- Type III: Includes synthetic-fiber reinforcement using polypropylene or polyethylene, nylon, carbon, or other deterioration-resistant synthetic fibers.

Acceptable Practices

- Fibrous concrete reinforcing is used in lieu of placing welded wire fabric or reinforcing steel in slabs on grade.
- Fibrous concrete reinforcing is used when hard, dense concrete is desired and when shrinkage cracks would deter from the appearance of the finished concrete.

Practices to Avoid

- Do not use glass fibers that are not alkali resistant. Because of the texture of fibrous reinforced concrete, aesthetics may play into where this type of reinforcing is used.

Resources

WITHIN THIS BOOK

- Chapter 5 Concrete Forming
- Chapter 7 Cast-In-Place Concrete

REFERENCE STANDARDS

- ASTM A185/A185M—Standard Specification for Steel Welded Wire Reinforcement, Plain, for Concrete.
- ASTM A615/A615M—Standard Specification for Deformed and Plain Carbon-Steel Bars for Concrete Reinforcement.
- ASTM C1116—Standard for Fiber-Reinforced Concrete.

OTHER RESOURCES

- 2009 International Residential Code for One and Two-Family Dwellings. Washington, DC: International Code Council, Inc., 2009.
- 2009 International Building Code. Washington, DC: International Code Council, Inc., 2009.
- American Institute of Architects, *Architectural Graphics Standards,* 11th ed. Hoboken, NJ: John Wiley & Sons, 2007.
- American Institute of Architects, *Architectural Graphic Standards for Residential Construction,* 2nd ed. Hoboken, NJ: John Wiley & Sons, 2010.
- American Concrete Institute, www.concrete.org.

Cast-in-Place Concrete

Placing Cast-in-Place Concrete

Finishing Cast-in-Place Concrete

Curing Cast-in-Place Concrete

Placing Cast-in-Place Concrete

Description

When the concrete has been mixed, the act of taking the concrete from the mixer and pouring the concrete within the confines of the formwork is called *placing concrete*. Concrete can be placed either vertically or horizontally. Concrete is placed vertically in situations such as foundations or retaining walls. Concrete is placed horizontally in situations such as concrete slabs on grade, either for basement floors, driveways, the main floor of a home, or exterior patio surfaces. After the concrete is placed, formwork must stay in place for a minimum of 12 hours when the ambient temperature is at least 50°F or greater in accordance with the American Concrete Institute (ACI) publication SP-4. In most circumstances, 24 hours is common practice. After placing horizontal concrete, the concrete must be consolidated and screeded to the proper height.

Assessing Existing Conditions

Prior to the placing of concrete, the following must be verified:

- Verify that all utility work under slabs on grade is complete and pipe work penetrating slab on grade is complete, or blocked out, and ready for the concrete work.
- Verify that penetrations in foundation walls are secure and ready for placement of vertical concrete.
- Under slabs on grade in occupied basements, a vapor retarder should be placed over a minimum 4-inch-thick gravel base. It is up to the design professional to determine what an appropriate vapor retarder is. A minimum 6-mil-thick polyethylene sheet is typical for underslab vapor retarders. Joints in the vapor retarder should be lapped a minimum of 6 inches and sealed.
- Verify that formwork is adequately shored and supported.
- Verify that rain is not in the forecast for the length of day required to finish the work.

Acceptable Practices

Below are practices commonly used in residential construction:

- Concrete foundation or retaining walls are generally poured in two pours. The first pour is the spread footing at the base of the wall; the footing must cure for a minimum of seven days. The second pour is the vertical foundation or retaining wall.

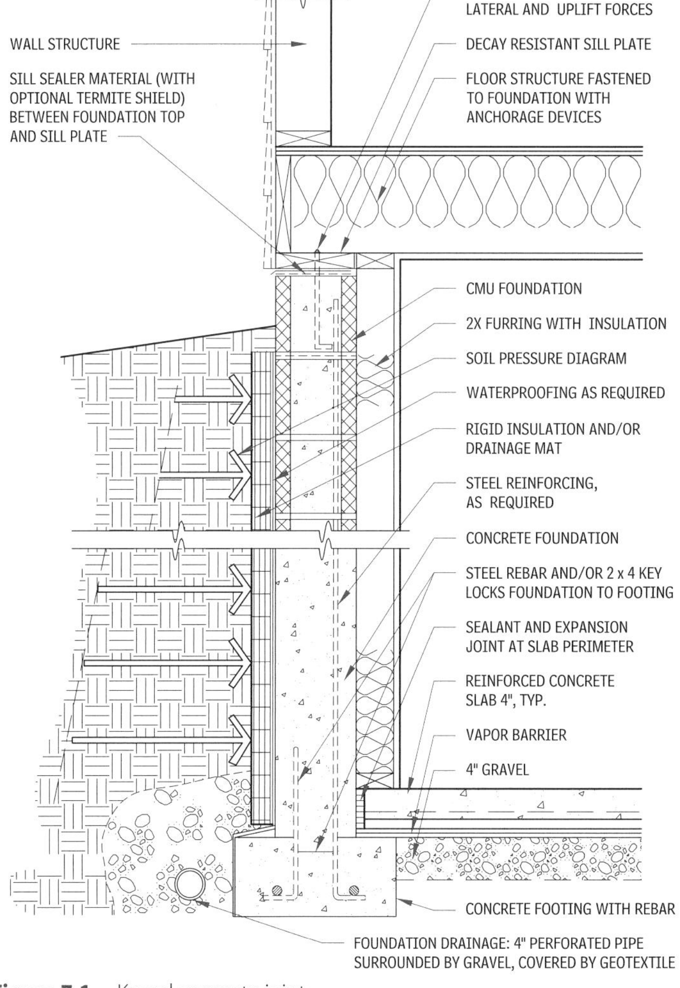

Figure 7.1 Keyed concrete joint

Source: AIA, *Architectural Graphic Standards for Residential Construction.* Copyright 2003, John Wiley & Sons, Inc.

- The joint between the footing and the wall is a *keyed* joint, which helps prevent movement of the wall after backfilling against the wall.
- When placing concrete for foundation or retaining walls, care must be taken to not allow concrete to segregate. Concrete should be placed in maximum 36-inch-high lifts and should be adequately machine vibrated to eliminate air pockets and rock pockets.
- When placing concrete horizontally, start concrete placement in the corner of the pour. Concrete is placed where it is to be used, not placed and then moved to where it will be used. Moving concrete after it has been placed promotes segregation of materials.
- Concrete should be screeded as soon as possible after concrete is placed—low spots should be filled and the surface made level.
- If the concrete area is too large for one day's work or placement of concrete has to stop longer than the setting time of concrete, then a construction joint should be formed using a form board. The concrete is then poured to form a straight edge. A construction joint is placed where two successive placements of concrete meet.
- After forms are stripped, exterior basement walls should be adequately braced with a minimum 2 × 8 lumber at 25 feet on center prior to backfilling.

Practices to Avoid

- Early removal of formwork.
- Premature backfilling of below-grade walls.

Finishing Cast-in-Place Concrete

Description

Finishing of concrete between vertical surfaces and horizontal surfaces are two completely different processes. For vertical concrete surfaces in residential construction, there are two common ways of finishing concrete to be left exposed.

The first is to leave the somewhat-smooth board form surface from the formwork exposed. The tie holes can be filled with grout; any fins or irregularities in the concrete should be removed using a carborundum brick. Rub all exposed concrete surfaces to be left exposed with carborundum brick.

Other common finishing techniques for foundation walls include parging a coat of Portland cement plaster directly onto concrete surface and adhering a layer of stone cladding, brick, or stone veneer to the face of the concrete foundation wall. Refer to Chapter 10, "Stone Assemblies" and Chapter 20, "Exterior Wall Covering," for additional information.

Finishing of horizontal surfaces such as a slab-on-grade consists of screeding the concrete as it is placed and then using a darby to further consolidate the concrete, which helps bring the water to the surface of the slab. Next, the finisher uses an edger tool to round the exposed edges and then cuts in the control joints. The final steps are to float and trowel the surface. Floating the surface helps to flatten the concrete surface to obtain the required level surface of the slab. Troweling with a steel trowel helps to give the concrete surface it final smooth finish. For interior slabs, this allows the installation of floor finishes. On exterior slabs, the surface is then given a broom finish, or the top layer of cement can be removed with water, leaving an exposed aggregate finish.

Stamped concrete is also a finish option for concrete slabs. The stamping process must be done while the concrete is still in its plastic state. Stamping of concrete requires the use of special molds that are pressed into the concrete, forming patterns such as cobblestone, slate, brick, or stone, to name a few. In addition, color can be added to the concrete to make the impressions more closer resemble the material being imitated. Color can be applied as an integral color, which is added when the concrete is being mixed; as a dry shake powder, which is a powder added to the top of the slab as the concrete is being finished; as an acid stain, which is done after the stamping; or by low-pressure sprayed color hardeners.

Assessing Existing Conditions

Prior to the finishing of concrete the following must be verified:

- Verify that concrete has been screeded to the appropriate height. The finishing process should begin on the concrete as soon as possible after screeding.
- For vertical concrete, formwork should be removed.

Acceptable Practices

The following are common trade practices used in residential construction. There are two different types of joints in concrete slabs:

- *Isolation joints or expansion joints* are used to relieve stresses due to vertical movement of slab-on-grade applications that adjoin fixed building elements. Examples would be isolating floor slabs from columns or building foundations, and isolating driveway slabs from garage slabs or cast-in-place concrete stairs.
- *Control or contraction joints* are placed to control random cracking of slabs. The rule of thumb for joints is a minimum 1/4-inch-deep joint with a joint spacing of two times the slab thickness in feet (i.e., 4-inch thick slab, maximum spacing 8 feet on center). In larger slabs, control joints are generally placed in two directions perpendicular to each other. Generally, joints should be placed in a square pattern. Where slabs are long and narrow, such as sidewalks, control joints should be placed at a distance equal to the narrow width of the sidewalk.

Exposed edges of slabs should be rounded with a trowel called an edger. This prevents the exposed edges of the slab from spalling off due to use or abuse.

Concrete slab-on-grade surface finishes:

- *Exposed concrete, carpet, resilient flooring, ceramic tile, or quarry tile*: Provide a trowel finish. Should be maximum of 3/16-inch gap under an unleveled 10-foot straightedge.

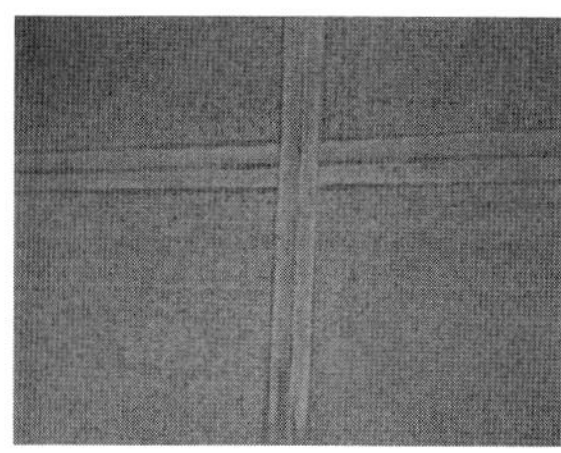

Figure 7.2 Broom finish

- *Exterior surfaces or inclined surfaces*: Medium or course broom finish. Medium broom surfaces are standard; course broom finishes are used on steep slopes for traction or heavy use.

Practices to Avoid

- Exposed aggregate finishes on inclined surfaces that are subject to continual wetting or surface water tend to be slippery
- Smooth troweled finishes on exterior slabs

Figure 7.3 Exposed aggregate concrete

Curing Cast-in-Place Concrete

Description

Curing of concrete is the most important part of the entire concrete process. Hydration and hardening of concrete during the first three days is critical. Fast drying and shrinkage because of wind or high temperatures during placement may lead to shrinkage cracking and curling of slab edges. Properly curing concrete leads to increased strength and lower permeability and can help to avoid unwanted cracking.

There are several different ways to cure concrete:

- Moisture curing of concrete involves keeping the concrete surface continuously wet for not less than seven days.
- Membrane curing of concrete surfaces is when a chemical compound is sprayed over exposed concrete surfaces, which retards the evaporation of water from the concrete slab.
- Sheet curing requires the use of a moisture-retaining cover to prevent evaporation of water from concrete surfaces. Joints in sheets must be sealed using either a waterproof tape or adhesive. All tears in the sheet must be repaired.

Assessing Existing Conditions

Before curing the concrete, the following must be verified:

- Verify that finish work is complete; immediately begin curing techniques to protect concrete work from cold temperatures.
- In hot weather, protect concrete work from rapid evaporation of slab moisture.

Acceptable Practices

Below are common practices in residential construction:

- Cold weather moisture retaining materials: Insulated blankets or tarps
- Straw covered with 4-mil polyethylene plastic sheets
- Enclosures or insulated forms

Below are some hot weather moisture retaining materials:

- Liquid membrane-forming curing compounds
- Minimum 4-mil polyethylene sheets
- Waterproof paper
- Burlap or cotton mats and rugs used with a soaker hose or sprinkler to keep materials wet
- Ponding water
- 6 inches of straw sprinkled with water regularly

The ideal concrete temperature is between 50 and 85°F. Concrete surface should be kept moist for a minimum of 7 days. Membrane forming curing compounds can be used where a slab is to be left exposed. If the curing compound is certified by the manufacturer to not interfere with bonding of floor covering then the curing compound can be used under floor coverings.

Practices to Avoid

- Avoid freezing of concrete. Temperature of concrete should remain above 25°F.
- In cold weather, moisture curing should be avoided.
- If concrete slab is to be left exposed and appearance is a concern, using polyethylene sheets as moisture retaining materials should be avoided, because wrinkles touching uncured concrete surface can leave dark streaks on concrete surface.
- Ponding water on slabs on grade increases the time it takes for moisture to exit the slab. If construction schedules are critical or tight, another method of slab curing should be used, as most floor coverings require a relatively low-slab moisture content prior to the installation of the floor coverings.
- Avoid hot, dry winds on the surface of curing concrete; immediately cover with moisture-retaining materials or construct wind breaks around concrete pour.

Resources

WITHIN THIS BOOK

- Chapter 5 Concrete Forming
- Chapter 6 Concrete Reinforcing
- Chapter 10 Stone Assemblies
- Chapter 20 Exterior Wall Covering

REFERENCE STANDARDS

- ACI 117—Specifications for Tolerances for Concrete Construction and Materials
- ACI 308R—Guide to Curing Concrete
- ACI 308.1—Standard Specification for Curing Concrete

OTHER RESOURCES

- 2009 International Residential Code for One and Two-Family Dwellings. Washington, DC: International Code Council, Inc., 2009.
- 2009 International Building Code. Washington, DC: International Code Council, Inc., 2009.
- American Institute of Architects, *Architectural Graphics Standards,* 11th ed. Hoboken, NJ: John Wiley & Sons, 2007.
- American Institute of Architects, *Architectural Graphic Standards for Residential Construction,* 2nd ed. Hoboken, NJ: John Wiley & Sons, 2010.
- American Concrete Institute, www.concrete.org.

Part III

Masonry

Chapter 8

Common Work Results for Masonry

Mortar and Grout

Bonding Patterns

Masonry Anchorage and Reinforcing

Mortar and Grout

Description

Mortar is a paste used to bind blocks together while filling the spaces between them. It is used most commonly in the masonry trade to bind stone, brick, or concrete blocks. Mortar is a combination of sand, a binder such as lime or concrete, and water. It creates a tight seal between bricks to prevent the entry of air and moisture into the structure. It bonds with any joint reinforcements, anchor bolts, or metal ties, and compensates for size variations in the bricks to create an aesthetically pleasing and structurally sound building.

Grout is a type of mortar used to fill joints, cracks, and cavities in tiles, masonry, and brickwork. Used in semi-liquid form, it may be pumped, spread, or poured into cavities and allowed to harden, creating a tight, water-resistant seal.

Assessing Existing Conditions

- Replace set mortar that can easily be scraped out with a sharp knife.
- Consistency of material must meet slump test measurements. Mortar or grout that is too fluid or stiff to work with, can also damage properties like bond and compressive strength.

Acceptable Practices

The big difference between mortar and grout is in their plasticity or fluidity in the initial stage.

Mortar is relatively stiff, with a slump of 5 to 8 inches. Mortar must be relatively stiff in order to be handled on a trowel, to be spread on the masonry unit and to evenly support the masonry units placed on it. Although mortar has a low water/cement ratio, this ratio is further decreased after the mortar is spread on the bed and the masonry units are placed on it. Any excess water in the mortar is absorbed both

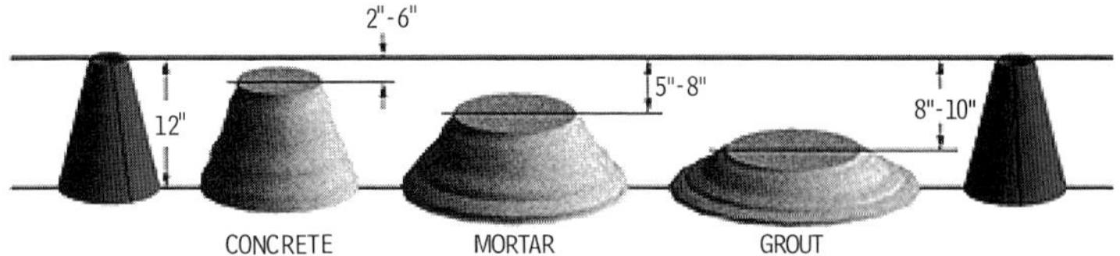

Figure 8.1 Slump tests of concrete, mortar, and grout

down into the masonry unit on which the mortar is spread and up into the masonry unit that is placed on the mortar bed. This absorption helps create bond between the mortar and the masonry unit.

Three main types of mortar:

- Portland cement mortar (OPC) is a mixture of portland cement, sand, and water. It sets quickly, requires less skill to use, and increases construction speed.
- Polymer cement mortar (PCM) is created by replacing the cement binders of traditional mortar with polymers. PCM reduces shrinkage cracking and is primarily used for repairing concrete construction.
- Lime mortar sets almost instantly upon contact with water. It is used as a binder in the mortar mixture instead of concrete or polymers. Lime mortar is breathable when set, and allows moisture to move freely and evaporate from the surface.

Mortar is specified as one of four types according to compressive strength:

- Type M has a high compressive strength (at least 2500 psi) and is recommended primarily for walls bearing heavy loads, but also, due to its durability, for masonry below grade or in contact with the earth.
- Type S is sometimes specified for masonry at or below grade, and it also has a high compressive strength (1800 psi). Type S yields maximum flexural strength to fight wind, soil pressure, or earthquakes.
- Type N is a medium compressive-strength (750 psi) mortar, recommended for most exterior, above-grade walls exposed to severe weather, including chimneys.
- Type O has a low compressive strength (about 350 psi), and is recommended for interior and limited exterior use in non-load-bearing walls.

Grout has plasticity far greater than normal concrete. Grout is placed in the cells of hollow masonry units and in relatively narrow grout spaces in brick walls in heights of anywhere from just a few inches to as high as 25 feet, as in the case of high lift grouting. Accordingly, it must completely fill the cells, the grout space, and the joints between masonry units in order to provide a solid, homogeneous grouted masonry wall.

If the grout is stiff, it will not flow into the cells or grout space, but will hang up and leave voids within the wall. Grout must have fluidity with a slump of 8 to 10 inches. This fluidity allows the grout to flow through the grout space, around the reinforcing bars, and completely surround and bond to the steel and masonry unit. The excess water, which is a placement vehicle for the grout and helps it flow throughout the wall, is absorbed by the masonry units, whether brick or block, and thus the final water/cement ratio of the grout is reduced to a point where the strength of the hardened grout is in accordance with the specification or code requirements.

The three main types of grout are epoxy, portland cement-based, and furan resin.

- The epoxy type is strong and water resistant. It is available in 100 percent epoxy resin and modified epoxy emulsion form. Although epoxy grout is generally more expensive, it's effective when water and stain resistance is desired.
- Portland cement-based grout is available in sanded, unsanded, pre-mixed, or powdered form. Portland cement-based grout is weaker than the epoxy type.
- Furan resin grout utilizes alcohol instead of water. It is rarely used in residential construction.

Practices to Avoid

- Avoid pouring any mortar or grout residue down a drain, as doing so could lead to serious pipe damage.
- Avoid using mortar that does not adhere to surface or support the weight of the unit being adhered.

Masonry Bonding Patterns

Description

There are various types of bonding patterns that can be used when laying masonry. The most common bond pattern is the running bond for both exposed and concealed masonry. Combinations of various bond patterns produce more aesthetically interesting construction and may be combined with various types, textures, and colors of masonry.

Joint types also allow for variations in overall appearance. Figure 8.3 shows the more common types of joints.

Acceptable Practices

If a parge coat of plaster is being placed over the masonry surface or a backup masonry wall is used behind brick veneer, then generally a flush joint (plain cut joint) is appropriate.

Vertical control joints in masonry construction:

- At or near corners
- At wall intersections
- At changes in wall height
- Where wall backing systems change

Horizontal joints in brick veneer:

- In multistory construction below shelf angles

Practices to Avoid

When exposed to weather conditions, extruded, beaded, struck, and raked joint types should be avoided because they allow water to sit on the joint, which may lead to spalling of the brick surface in freezing conditions:

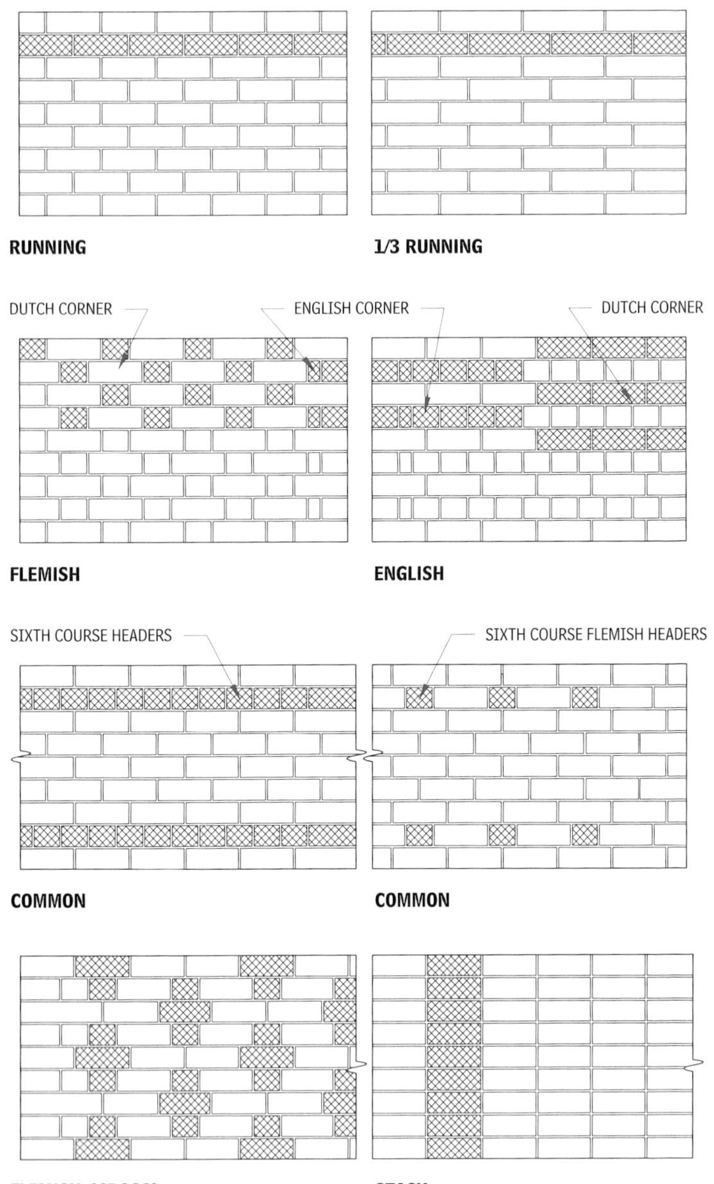

Figure 8.2 Common bond patterns

Source: AIA, *Architectural Graphic Standards,* 11th ed. Copyright 2007, John Wiley & Sons, Inc.

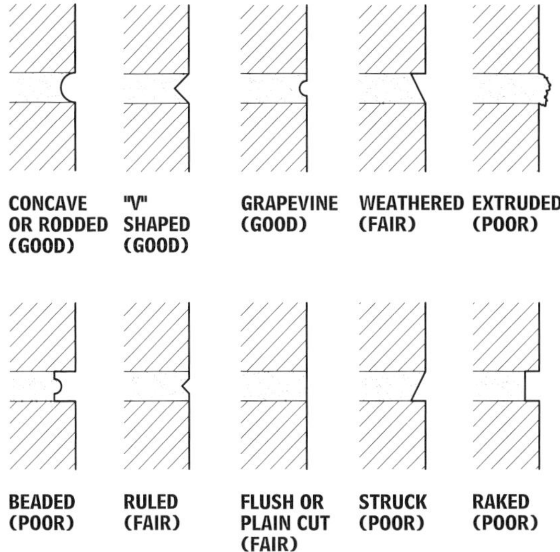

Figure 8.3 Common joint types
Source: AIA, *Architectural Graphic Standards*, 11th ed. Copyright 2007, John Wiley & Sons, Inc.

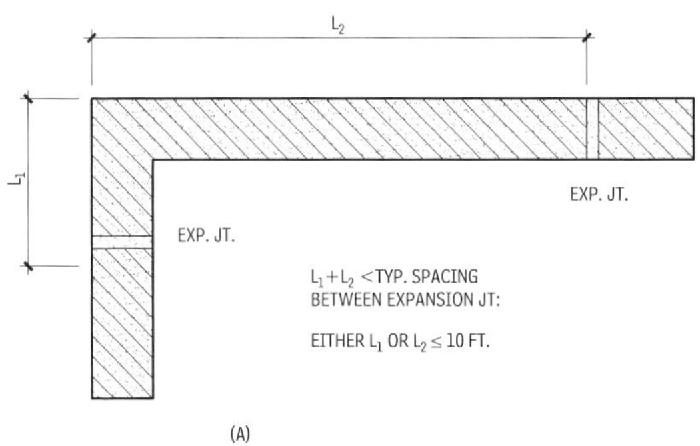

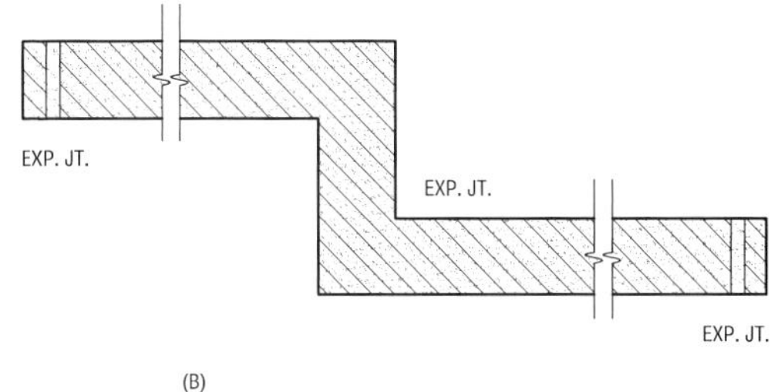

Figure 8.4 Vertical expansion joints at corners
Source: Brick Industry Association

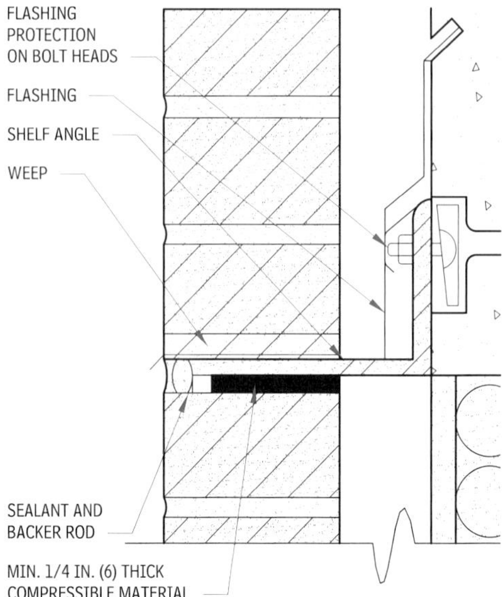

Figure 8.5 Expansion joint at shelf angle
Source: Brick Industry Association

Masonry Anchorage and Reinforcing

Description

Reinforcing and anchorage are used in single-wythe, multi-wythe, and veneer masonry for stability, strength, and to help control thermal movement of materials.

Single-wythe reinforcing is accomplished through the use of steel reinforcing bars. Reinforcing is placed in the open cells of the CMU. The open cells are then filled with grout. In essence, when the grout is cured, this creates a beam within the masonry that gives the wall strength. In CMU construction, horizontal beams are created using either wire reinforcing in the mortar joints or special units called bond

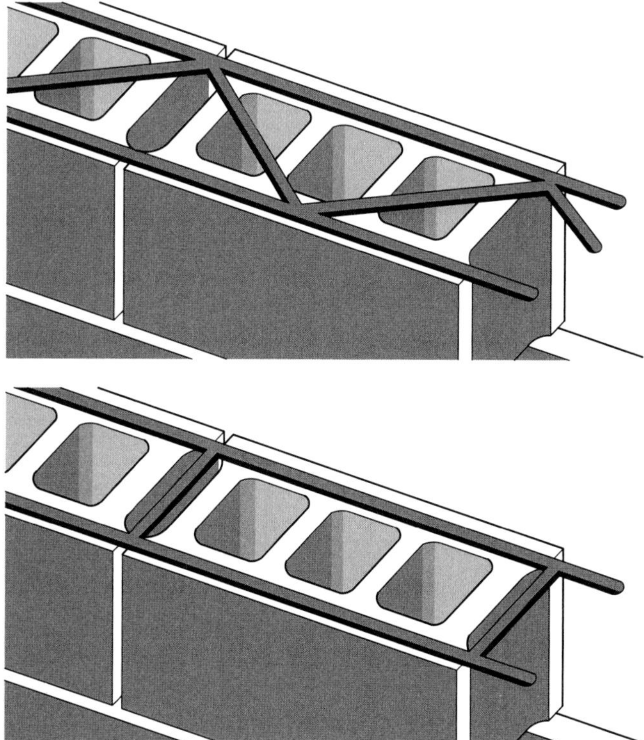

Figure 8.6 Single-wythe joint reinforcement

beams. The bond beam provides an area to place reinforcing bars; the bond beam is then filled with grout.

Multi-wythe reinforcing and anchorage are accomplished by using either steel reinforcing bars or wire reinforcing, or both. Wire reinforcing is also known as either truss or ladder type wire reinforcing and is fabricated of a minimum of 9-gage wire. Wire-type reinforcing can be either nonadjustable or adjustable. Adjustable reinforcing allows variation between mortar joints in multiple-wythe walls of up to 1¼ inch.

Veneer masonry can be anchored to either masonry or concrete structural backup walls or to a framed wall covered with sheathing. If the backup is a concrete wall, the anchors can be surface attached or cast into the concrete. If the wall is framed, then the anchors must be attached at a stud over the sheathing and weather barrier.

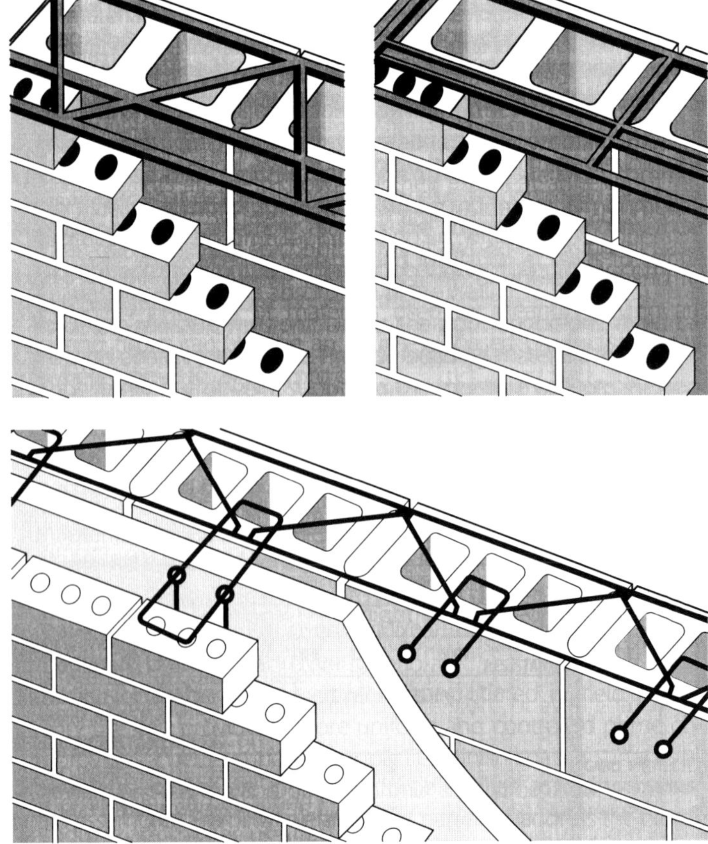

Figure 8.7 Multi-wythe joint reinforcement

Table 8.1 Recommended Minimum Tie Diameters and Gauges

Tie System		Minimum Specified Dimension	
		Diameter (in.)	Gauge
Standard Ties	**Unit**		
	Rectangular and "Z"	3/16	—
	Corrugated	—	22
	Joint reinforcement		
	Ladder and truss	—	9
	Tab	—	9
Adjustable Ties	**Unit**		
	Rectangular and "Z"	3/16	—
	Dovetail/channel slot		
	Wire	3/16	—
	Corrugated	—	16
	Connector slot	—	22
	Slotted plate		
	Wire	3/16	—
	Slotted plate	—	14
	Backer plate	—	14
	Joint reinforcement		
	Standard section	—	9
	Tabs	3/16	—

Source: AIA, *Architectural Graphic Standards for Residential Construction*. Copyright 2003 by John Wiley & Sons, Inc.

Masonry anchorage for veneer masonry is generally a galvanized or stainless-steel tie spaced between 16 and 24 inches on center in each direction, vertically and horizontally. In some situations, joint reinforcing is added to veneer masonry in the form of a 9-gage wire that runs continuously in the masonry veneer joint.

Assessing Existing Conditions

- Veneer anchors are required to have a corrosion-resistant coating like galvanizing, or be fabricated from stainless steel.

Acceptable Practices

- Veneer anchor spacing: One anchor for each 2.67 square feet of wall area for all seismic zones except zone D, which is 1 anchor for each 2 square feet of wall area.
- Anchors around wall openings must be placed within 12 inches of wall opening in any direction.
- Structurally reinforce single-wythe or multi-wythe walls in seismic zones C, D, and E.
- Structural reinforcing of walls in seismic zones A and B is not required unless required by the structural design.

Practices to Avoid

- On framed walls, veneer anchors cannot be attached just to sheathing.

Resources

WITHIN THIS BOOK

- Chapter 9 Unit Masonry
- Chapter 10 Stone Assemblies

OTHER RESOURCES

- 2009 International Residential Code for One and Two-Family Dwellings. Washington, DC: International Code Council, Inc. 2009.
- 2009 International Building Code. Washington, DC: International Code Council, Inc., 2009.
- American Institute of Architects, *Architectural Graphics Standards*, 11th ed. Hoboken, NJ: John Wiley and Sons, 2007.
- American Institute of Architects, *Architectural Graphic Standards for Residential Construction*, 2nd ed. Hoboken, NJ: John Wiley & Sons, 2010.
- The Brick Industry Association, *Technical Notes on Brick Construction*. Reston, VA: BIA (undated).
- The Brick Industry Association, www.gobrick.com.
- National Concrete Masonry Association, TEK Manual for Concrete Masonry Design and Construction (Collection of TEK Bulletins). Herndon, VA: NCMA (undated).

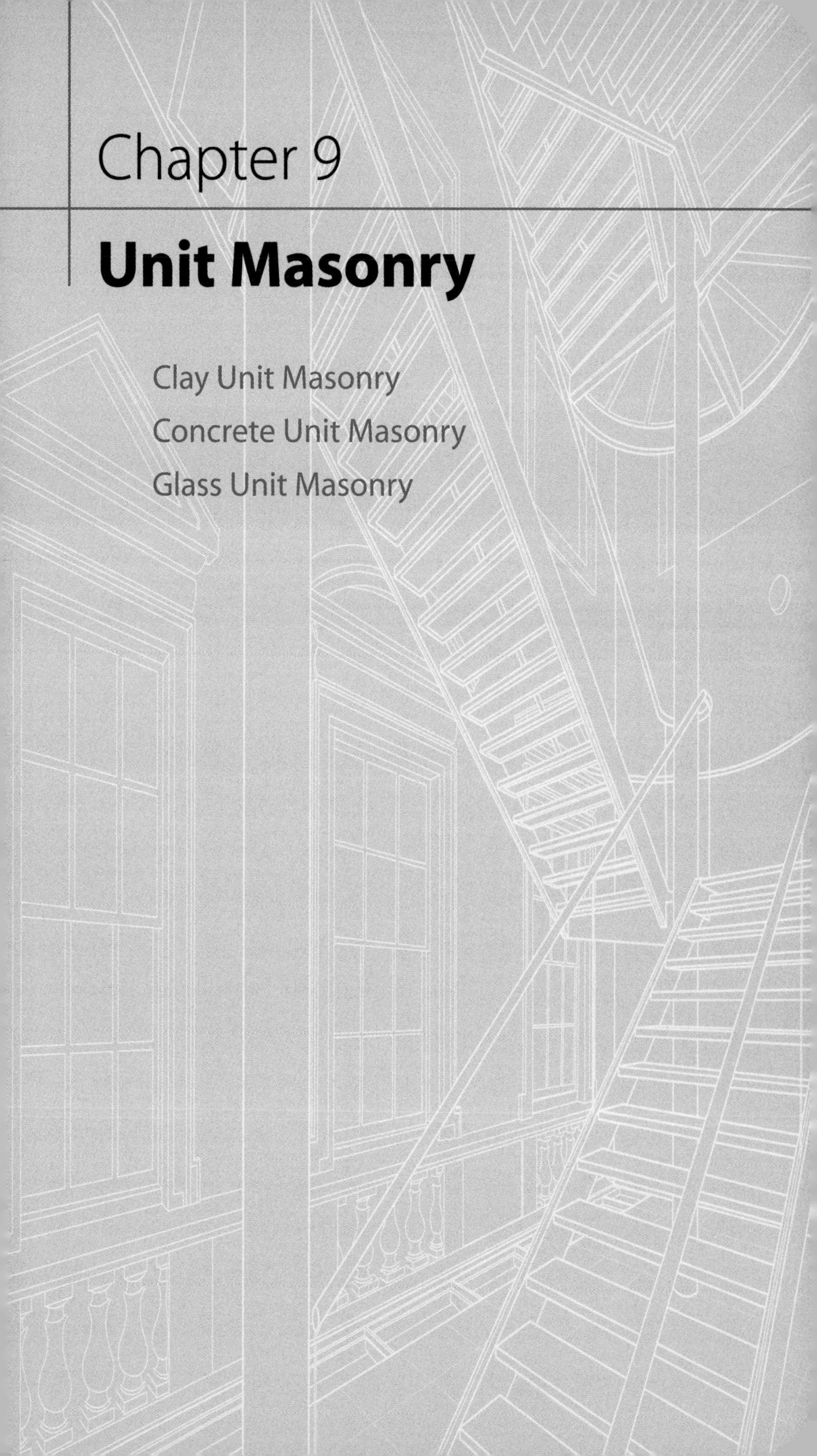

Chapter 9

Unit Masonry

Clay Unit Masonry

Description

Clay masonry units in the form of brick are one of the world's oldest building materials: Brick offers a homeowner many advantages over other exterior materials: it is available in a wide variety of colors and textures, it is pest-and weather-resistant, fireproof, energy efficient, low maintenance, and typically increases a home's resale value. Brick homes built hundreds of years ago are still standing and look as distinguished today as when first built. Genuine clay brick is also environmentally friendly; all of these attributes make it an excellent choice for long-term value.

The typical clay masonry unit wall assembly for residential construction is brick veneer on a wood stud wall.

Brick is available in a variety of shapes and sizes. For convenience and convention, different names are used to indicate the size of brick.

Modular brick: 3⅝ in. × 2½ in. × 7⅝ in.

Standard brick: 3⅝ in. × 2¼ in. × 8 in.

Jumbo brick: 3⅝ in. × 2¾ in. × 8 in.

King brick: 3⅝ in. × 2¾ in. × 9–5/8 in.

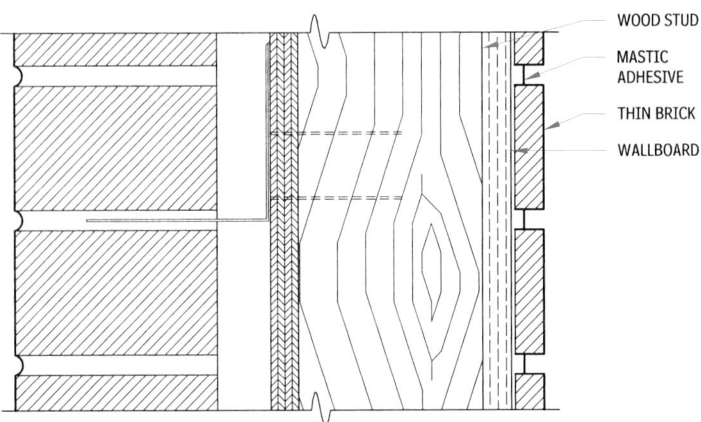

Figure 9.1 Typical brick veneer/wood stud wall section
Source: Brick Industry Association

Roman brick: 3⅝ in. × 1⅝ in. × 11⅝ in.
Norman brick: 3⅝ in. × 2¼ in. × 11⅝ in.
Jumbo Norman brick: 3⅝ in. × 2¾ in. × 11⅝ in.
Economy brick: 3⅝ in. × 3⅝ in. × 8 in.
Utility brick: 3⅝ in. × 3⅝ in. × 11⅝ in.

Bricks are classified by ASTM C216 in grades according to their resistance to damage by freezing when saturated:

- Grade SW (severe weathering) is for brick intended for use where a high and uniform resistance to damage caused by cyclic freezing is required and where the brick may be frozen when saturated with water.
- Grade MW (moderate weathering) is for brick intended for use where a moderate and somewhat nonuniform resistance to freezing is allowable or where brick is unlikely to be saturated with water when exposed to temperatures below freezing.

ASTM C216 further classifies face brick into three types :

- **Type FBS** allows a normal range of size variations.
- **Type FBX** requires a high degree of mechanical perfection and minimum permissible variations in size. More severe restrictions on allowable percentages of chippage and dimensional tolerances are required for Type FBX than for Type FBS.
- **Type FBA** is manufactured and selected for nonuniformity in size and texture, such as in hand-molded or tumbled brick. It is used for special architectural effects.

Hollow brick is a term used in ASTM C652, *Standard Specification for Hollow Brick (Hollow Masonry Units Made from Clay or Shale),* to describe clay masonry units manufactured with cores or cells that reduce the net cross-sectional area to less than 75 percent but not less than 40 percent of the gross cross-sectional area.

Following are the types and classes that are included in ASTM C652 for hollow brick:

- **Type HBS** allows a normal range of size variations.
- **Type HBX** requires a high degree of mechanical perfection and minimum variation in size.
- **Type HBA** applies to units selected to produce a distinctive appearance resulting from nonuniformity in the size and texture of individual units.
- **Type HBB** permits greater variation in size than Type HBS and is not controlled for color and texture. These units are generally for applications where masonry is not exposed.

- **Class H40V** permits reduction of net cross-sectional area up to 40 percent—the brick is at least 60 percent solid.
- **Class H60V** permits reduction of net cross-sectional area up to 60 percent—the brick is at least 40 percent solid.

Thin-fired clay masonry units are often referred to as thin brick and can be used as interior or exterior wall coverings. Thin brick units are much like facing brick except they are approximately ½ to 1 inch thick and weigh considerably less. Face sizes are normally the same as face brick; therefore, when installed (adhered or fastened veneer applications), thin brick gives the appearance of a conventional clay masonry unit or brick masonry wall.

ASTM C 1088, *Standard Specification for Thin Veneer Brick Units Made from Clay or Shale,* covers two grades for exposure conditions to weather, which are defined as exterior and interior. The three types of thin veneer brick are based on appearance:

- **Type TBS** (Standard): General masonry use
- **Type TBX** (Select): Produced with higher degree of precision
- **Type TBA** (Architectural): Selected to produce characteristic architectural effects resulting from nonuniformity in size and texture

The typical thin-fired clay masonry unit wall assembly for residential construction is thin brick veneer on a wood stud wall, as illustrated in Figure 9.2.

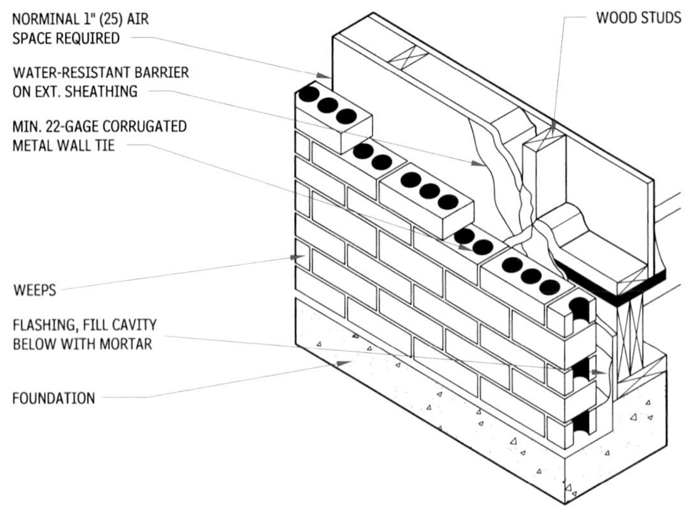

Figure 9.2 Typical adhered thin brick veneer / wood stud wall section
Source: Brick Industry Association

A thick bed procedure may be used on interior or exterior installations when the substrate material is masonry, concrete, steel stud, or wood stud framing. Figure 9.3 illustrates the thick bed setting over concrete masonry. The wire lath shown may be eliminated if the masonry wall is heavily scarified or sand-blasted. For applications over steel or wood studs, procedures are similar; however, sheathing and building felt must be installed over the studs before the lath and mortar bed are placed.

Assessing Existing Conditions

- Determine which masonry walls are load bearing and which are not.
- Check that exposed masonry has no cracking, spalling, bowing bulging vertically, sweeping (bulges horizontally), leaning, or mortar deterioration.
  - Bulging brick walls: Likely to be a bond course failure and potentially dangerous; may cause building collapse.
  - Cracks and bulges may be due to frost and earth loading.
- Efflorescence has the appearance of white powder on the surface of clay masonry and is caused by water in the wall dissolving mineral salts in the brick or mortar. When this leaches to the surface, the

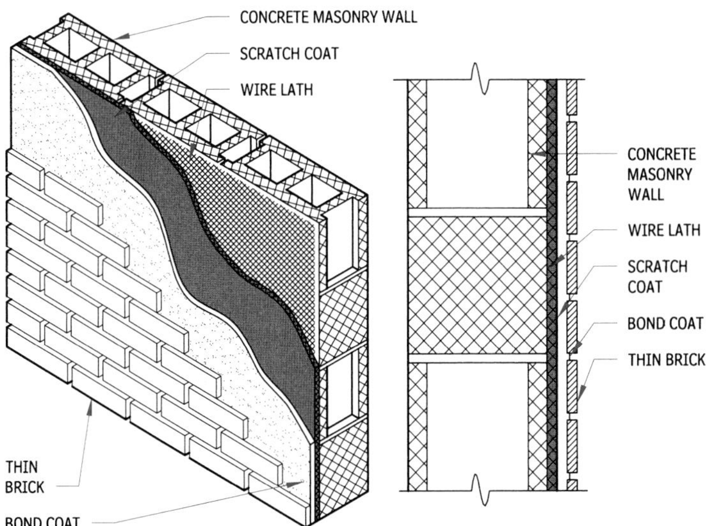

Figure 9.3 Typical thick set thin brick veneer/concrete masonry wall section
Source: Brick Industry Association

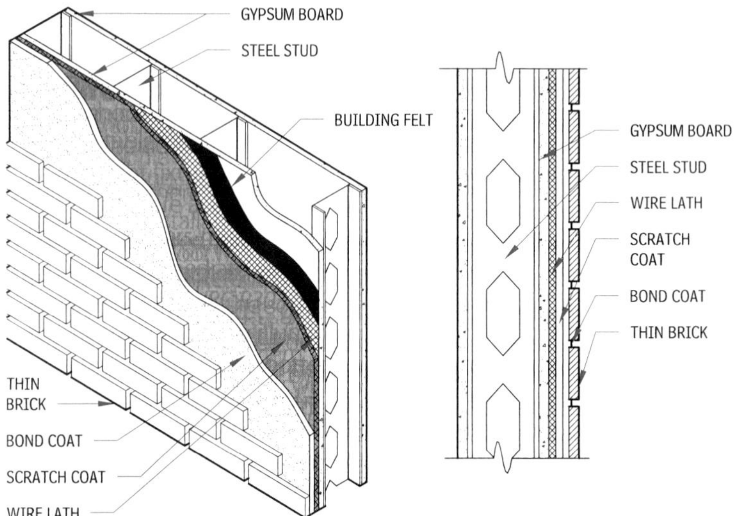

Figure 9.4 Typical thick set thin brick veneer/steel stud wall section
Source: Brick Industry Association

water evaporates, leaving a whitish mineral-salt residue. The principal objection to this condition is an unsightly appearance, though it typically is not harmful to brick.

- Most efflorescence is water soluble, so it can usually be removed by washing with plain water when the weather and the wall are warm and dry. This helps keep the cleaning water from causing additional efflorescence. The only long-term cure for this condition is to stop water from entering the wall by ensuring that any flashing or caulking is correctly installed and defect free.

Acceptable Practices

- Continuous flashing must be installed under the first course of brick under sills and heads of windows and doors in a brick veneer wall and the flashing should extend to the exterior face of the masonry wall. A self-adhered bitumen flashing is preferred over asphalt-impregnated felt.
- Weepholes should be installed at 24 inches on center when using open-head joint-type weepholes; when using cotton sash cords as a wicking material, space them at 16 inches on center.
- For one-and two-family wood-frame construction, the corrugated sheet metal anchor spacing must be one anchor for each 2.67 square feet of wall with a maximum spacing of 32 inches horizontally and

18 inches vertically on center with a minimum embedment depth of 1-1/2 inches into the bed joints for the veneer (with 5/8 inch mortar cover to the outside face). Also place anchors within 12 inches of openings.

- It is essential to maintain a 1-inch minimum air space between the back of the brick veneer and the sheathing to ensure proper drainage.
- It is recommended to only use Grade SW brick in most climates.
- For most brick veneer, Type N mortar is suitable; however, Type S may be required. Head joints and bed joints should be full with tooled vee or concave joints.
- The exterior face of the poured concrete or concrete block foundation, which the brick veneer sits on, should be in the same plane as the finished brick's wall plane.
- The finished grade must be below the weepholes (preferably 2 to 3 inches below the flashing line). If brick goes below the flashing, fill the space between the brick and the foundation with grout or mortar.
- Make sure the flashing is placed behind the building paper or house wrap (not in front of the building paper, or water will run between and appear at the wooden sill plate).
- Use flashing end dams at the edges of openings and prefabricated flashing for inside and outside corners.

Practices to Avoid

- Do not build masonry walls that do not allow water to escape.
- All brick veneer walls are drainage walls and their design should be based on the premise that water is going to enter the wall system. Therefore, to ensure that wall's successful performance, its design must incorporate a means of water egress.
- For a cavity wall to function properly, water that collects on flashing must be able to drain through weepholes to the exterior of the building. If weepholes do not function properly, water collecting in the cavity can infiltrate to the building's interior.

Concrete Unit Masonry

Description

Concrete masonry units (CMUs) are made from cast concrete with fly ash, clinker, sand, or fine gravel aggregate. It is primarily used for foundations, basement perimeter walls, or structural walls. Because CMU is so versatile, the finish appearance can vary due to size, color, or surface.

Assessing Existing Conditions

In order to ensure the proper installation of concrete unit masonry in an opening, verify the following conditions:

- Verify the weight classification, and local availability (especially medium weight) of the CMUs.
- Control joints should be spaced no more than 25 feet apart, with the length-to-height ratio of masonry panels not greater than 1.5 to 1.
- Fire-resistance ratings must meet requirements.
- Verify if waterproofing is necessary for building application.
- Reinforcing bars must be properly lapped before surrounding by grout.

Acceptable Practices

Although CMUs can come in several sizes, the most common is 8 inches by 8 inches by 16 inches. Actual sizes are typically the nominal size minus the thickness of a 3/8-inch mortar joint. Although there are three weight classifications for CMUs, lightweight units that weigh less than 105 lb/cu are predominantly used in residential construction because of their lower shipping cost, lower labor cost, higher fire-resistance ratings, and higher thermal resistance.

Single-wythe construction is most common for residential applications. Hollow-core concrete masonry units (CMUs) are installed utilizing grout-filled cells with embedded reinforcing steel, for vertical construction.

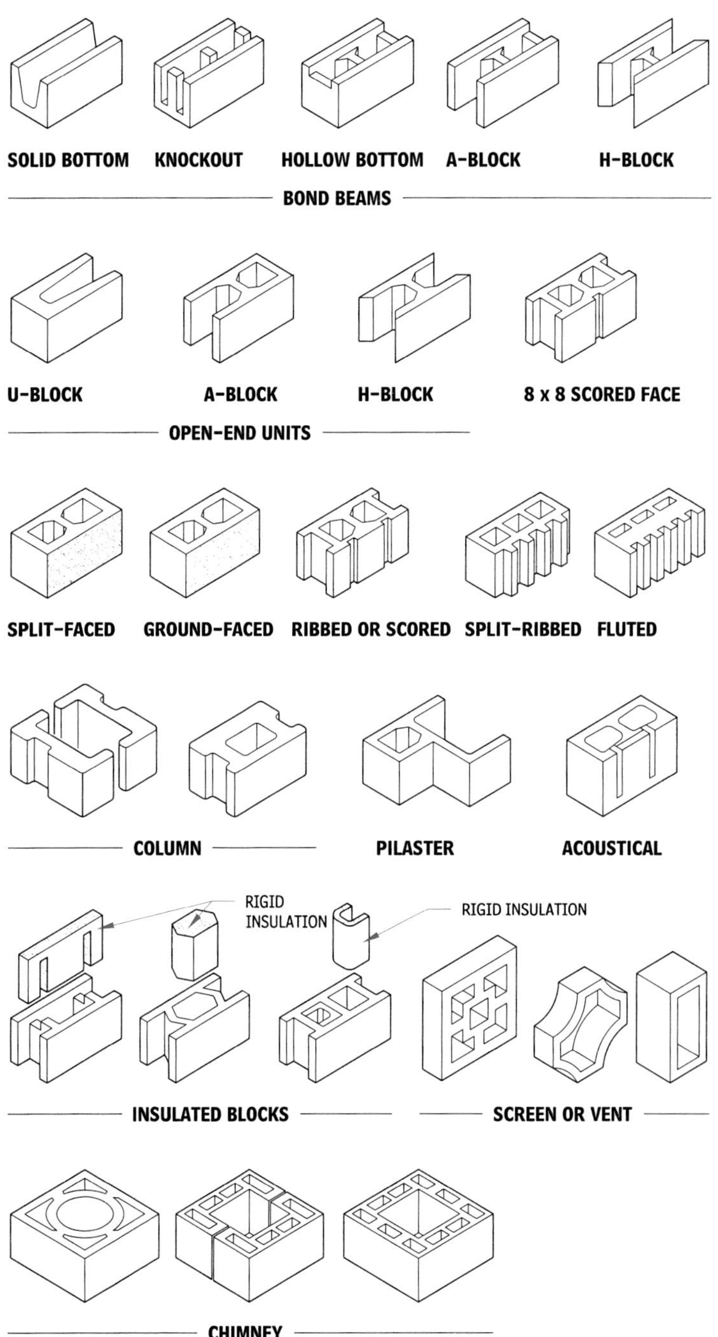

Figure 9.5 Common concrete masonry unit shapes

Source: AIA, *Architectural Graphic Standards for Residential Construction,* 2nd ed. Copyright 2010, John Wiley and Sons, Inc.

According to the International Residential Code, reinforced hollow-unit masonry shall conform to all the following requirements:

- Reinforced hollow-unit masonry shall be built to preserve the unobstructed vertical continuity of the cells to be filled. Walls and cross webs forming cells to be filled shall be full-bedded in mortar to prevent leakage of grout. Head and end joints shall be solidly filled with mortar for a distance in from the face of the wall or unit not less than the thickness of the longitudinal face shall. Bond shall be provided by lapping units in successive vertical courses.
- Vertical reinforcement shall be held in position at top and bottom and at intervals not exceeding 200 times the diameter of the reinforcement.
- Cells containing reinforcement shall be filled solidly with grout. Grout shall be poured in lifts of 8-foot maximum height. When a total grout pout exceeds 8 feet in height, the grout shall be placed in lifts not exceeding 5 feet, and special inspection during grouting shall be required.
- Horizontal steel shall be fully embedded by grout in an uninterrupted pour.

Practices to Avoid

- Avoid installing cinder blocks (made with clinker as opposed to sand or gravel in CMUs) where structural performance is critical.
- Avoid using defective units, including units that contain chips or cracks that will be exposed in the completed product.
- Avoid cutting CMU if possible. If cutting is required, use a motor-driven saw and then install with cut surfaces concealed.

Glass Unit Masonry

Description

Glass masonry units come in a variety of shapes, sizes, and finishes, and are commonly used in residential construction as windows and interior partitions where a partially transparent effect is desired. Common benefits of using glass unit masonry panels include added security and privacy and noise reduction.

Exterior openings that use glass unit masonry most commonly use single wythe construction, making weatherproofing of joints critical to avoid leakage. Mortar should be type S or N with joints that are between 1/4 and 3/8 inch thick. Glass unit masonry will not absorb the water from mortar and will require longer installation times. Edges of the units in contact with mortar should be treated with a polyvinyl butyral coating or latex paint to improve mortar bonding. Plastic spacers are often used to prevent squeezing of mortar and keep joints uniform in width.

Expansion joints are also critical in glass unit masonry panel construction since glass masonry units have a higher thermal expansion rate than most surrounding materials. Glass unit masonry panels should be mortared at the sill support and expansion joints should be located at the head and jamb to allow for movement and settling. Reinforcement should not extend across any expansion joint.

Assessing Existing Conditions

In order to ensure the proper installation of glass unit masonry in an opening, verify the following conditions:

- Glass masonry units meet minimum code requirements as follows:
  - Minimum average glass face thickness of hollow units: 3/16 inch.
  - Minimum thickness of standard units: 3-7/8 inches.
  - Minimum thickness of thin hollow units: 3–1/8 inches.
  - Minimum thickness of thin solid units: 3 inches.
- Structural members supporting glass unit masonry are designed and sized for a maximum deflection of L/600.

- Isolated exterior standard-unit panels subjected to design wind pressures of 20 psf are no larger than 144 square feet nor 25 feet in width or 20 feet in height.
- Isolated exterior thin-unit panels subjected to design wind pressures of 20 psf are no larger than 85 square feet nor 15 feet in width or 10 feet in height.
- Isolated interior standard-unit panels are no larger than 250 square feet nor 25 feet in width or 20 feet in height.
- Isolated interior thin-unit panels are no larger than 150 square feet nor 25 feet in width or 20 feet in height.
- Horizontal reinforcement is spaced a maximum of 16 inches on center.
- Edge drips are installed to prevent moisture run-down on the surface.
- Curved wall panels have expansion joints at each change in direction.
- Sill area is covered by 1/8-inch minimum thick, asphaltic-emulsion coating before mortar bedding.

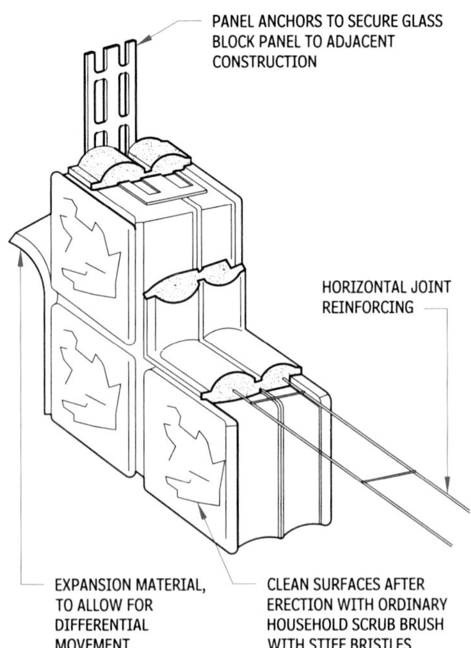

Figure 9.6 Glass block
Source: AIA, *Architectural Graphic Standards for Residential Construction,* 2nd ed. Copyright 2010, John Wiley and Sons, Inc.

Acceptable Practices

There are many options to consider in the construction of glass unit masonry panels. As with other types of glazed openings, glass unit masonry panels can be supported and framed to form large areas. Properties of the glass masonry units can be selected for view, fire protection, thermal properties, and even noise.

Common construction practices include the following:

- Vertical and horizontal stiffeners can break large areas into required sizes.
- Panels can be held in place by bent plate channels, perimeter recesses, or panel anchors.
- Coatings and inserts can be used to help control heat gain, glare, and brightness.
- Solid glass block units can be used for impact resistance and some bullet-proof requirements.
- Glass unit masonry panels can be fire rated up to 45 minutes according to UL 9, Fire Tests of Window Assemblies or NFPA 257, Fire Test of Window and Glass Block Assemblies.
- Coated units require periodic cleaning to remove alkali and metal ions that will harm the coating.
- Edge coating can affect the perceived color of the block.

Practices to Avoid

Since glass unit masonry panels can carry as much weight as concrete or brick masonry units yet are used as windows within framed openings, they must be constructed carefully with structural, thermal, and moisture in mind. Common construction practices to avoid include the following:

- Reusing glass masonry units.
- Cutting glass masonry units.
- Imposing loads on glass unit masonry panels.
- Expansion joints less than 3/8-inch thickness at heads and jambs.
- Mortarless installations at fire-rated assemblies.

Resources

WITHIN THIS BOOK

- Chapter 8 Common Work Results for Masonry
- Chapter 10 Stone Assemblies

REFERENCE STANDARDS

- ASTM C216—Standard Specification for Facing Brick (Solid Units Made from Clay or Shale).
- ASTM C652—Standard Specification for Hollow Brick (Hollow Masonry Units Made from Clay or Shale).
- ASTM C1088—Standard Specification for Thin Veneer Brick Units Made from Clay or Shale.

OTHER RESOURCES

- 2009 International Residential Code for One and Two-Family Dwellings. Washington, DC: International Code Council, Inc., 2009.
- 2009 International Building Code. Washington, DC: International Code Council, Inc., 2009.
- American Institute of Architects, *Architectural Graphics Standards,* 11th ed. Hoboken, NJ: John Wiley and Sons, 2007.
- American Institute of Architects, *Architectural Graphic Standards for Residential Construction*, 2nd ed. Hoboken, NJ: John Wiley and Sons, 2010.
- The Brick Industry Association. Technical Notes on Brick Construction, Reston, VA: BIA (undated).
- The Brick Industry Association: www.gobrick.com.
- National Concrete Masonry Association, TEK Manual for Concrete Masonry Design and Construction (Collection of TEK Bulletins). Herndon, VA: NCMA (undated).

Chapter 10

Stone Assemblies

Stone

Description

Stone assemblies include both natural and cut stone that can be used in many construction applications. The major factors affecting the suitability and use of stone for construction fall under two broad, but overlapping categories: physical and structural properties, and aesthetic qualities. The three factors of building stone that most influence their selection by design professionals for aesthetic reasons are pattern, texture, and color. Consideration also should be given to cost, availability, weathering characteristics, physical properties, and size limitations.

Pattern, texture, and color all are affected by how the stone is fabricated and finished. Granites tend to hold their color and pattern, whereas limestone color and pattern changes with exposure. Textures may range from rough and flamed finishes to honed or polished surfaces. The harder the stone, the better it takes and holds a polish.

Assessing Existing Conditions

- Review the physical properties of the stones to confirm it is suitable for its intended purpose.

Acceptable Practices

Stone is obtained by quarrying and has two general shapes. The first is rubble, which is irregular in shape and size. Examples are natural collected stone and quarry rubble, which is stone left over after cutting and removal of stone slabs. The second type of shape is the cut stone, which can be either dimension stone or cleft-face. Although dimension is typically larger blocks cut to specific size, cleft-face stone is generally smaller squares or rectangles without specific sizes.

All stone types have different properties, but the most important is durability, which can be determined by hardness or porosity. Thermal expansion can cause some fine-grained stones to permanently increase in volume, allowing the stone to become more porous and vulnerable to atmospheric acids and freezing, which can damage the stone. The following are stone types and their properties:

- **Granite:** Colors vary from red, pink, brown, buff, gray, and cream to dark green and black. Granite is classified as fine, medium, or coarse grained. It is very hard, strong, and durable, and is noted for its weathering and abrasion resistance.
- **Limestone:** The most pure form of limestone, crystalline limestone, which is highest in strength and lowest in absorption of the various types of limestone, has a fairly uniform white or light gray stone of smooth texture. Because limestone can vary in density, three different classifications have be established: I (low density), II (medium density), and III (high density). Although it is quite soft when first taken from the ground, limestone weathers hard upon exposure. Its durability is greatest in drier climates.
- **Marble:** Marble is a form of noncrystalline limestone that can have a wide range of colors, depending on its crystalline structure. When used in dry climates or in areas protected from precipitation, the stone is durable; however, some varieties deteriorate by weathering or exposure to industrial fumes, and are suitable only for interior work. Although there are four classifications for marbles (A, B, C, and D), exterior applications should use only group A because it has the highest-quality materials.
- **Slate:** Slate is fine and compact, and commonly dark colored such as black, blue, and gray or red and purple (if iron oxide is present) or green (if chlorite is present). Slate provides an extremely durable material that is weather resistant.
- **Sandstone:** Formed of sand or quartz, sandstone's properties such as hardness, durability, and color depend on the type of cementing agent. If cemented with silica and hardened under pressure, the stone is light in color, strong, and durable. If the cementing agent is largely iron oxide, the stone is red or brown, and is softer and more easily cut.

Much of the stone that is produced for building construction has a sawn finish, but stone may also be further dressed with hand or machine tools for hammered finishes, polished finishes, and honed or rubbed finishes. Polished surfaces require repeated rubbing with increasingly finer abrasives, and only granite, marble, and some very dense limestones will take and hold a high polish. Granite can be fabricated with a flame cut or thermal finish, to produce a fractured surface texture. It is most often selectively applied to portions of a surface to contrast with polished finish areas.

Stone assemblies included stone walls and stone claddings. Stone cladding uses a structural framing behind the stone and is covered later in this chapter. Stone walls use stones with high compressive strength as the structure of the wall. Some of the most common construction methods for erecting stone walls include:

- *Dry-laid walls:* Drystone walls are capable of moving and settling, as well as letting water penetrate through them. They will outlast with a mortared wall.
- *Rubble-filled, mortared walls:* Although a rubble-filled wall looks similar to a dry-laid wall on the exterior, the interior is composed of broken, damaged, or poor-quality stones held together by mortar. In this application, the appearance should not show mortar.
- *Slip-form stone walls:* Forms are placed on both sides of the wall and stones are then placed on the inside of the forms and the forms are filled up with concrete behind the stones. Rebar can be placed within the wall for added strength.

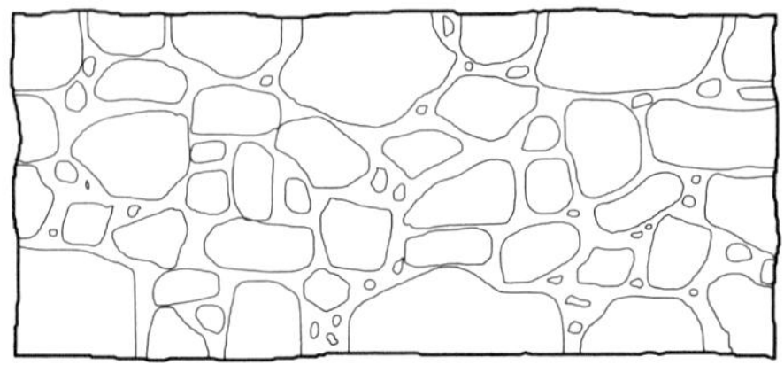

Figure 10.1 Uncoursed rubble stone masonry patterns—elevations
Source: AIA, *Architectural Graphic Standards for Residential Construction*, 2nd ed. Copyright 2010, John Wiley and Sons, Inc.

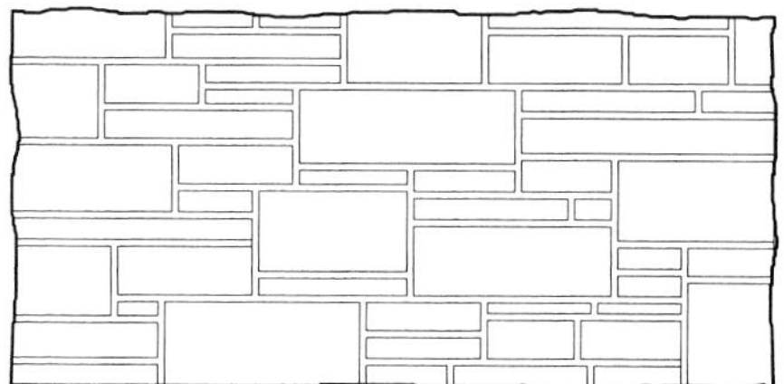

RANDOM BROKEN COURSED ASHLAR

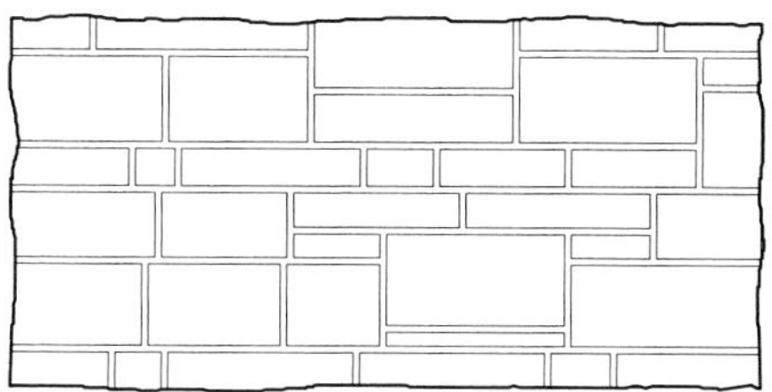

RANDOM COURSED ASHLAR

COURSED ASHLAR-RUNNING BOND

Figure 10.2 Coursed cut stone masonry patterns—elevations
Source: AIA, *Architectural Graphic Standards for Residential Construction*, 2nd ed. Copyright 2010, John Wiley and Sons, Inc.

Practices to Avoid

- Avoid using soft or porous stone in colder environments; it can absorb and retain water causing flaking, cracking, and damage in heavy frost.

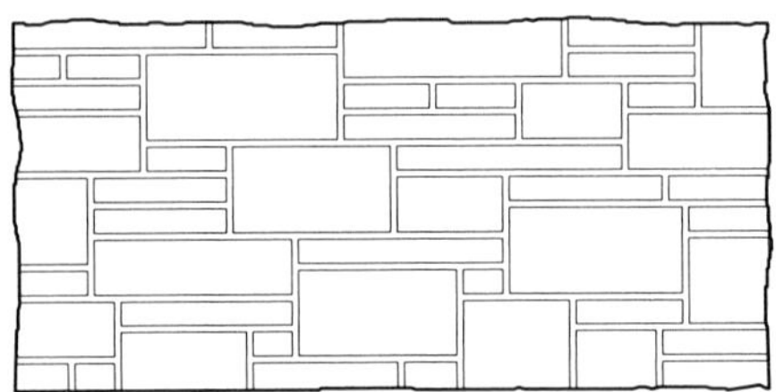

THREE-HEIGHT PATTERN (15% AT 2-1/4 IN.; 40% AT 5 IN.; 45% AT 7-3/4 IN.)

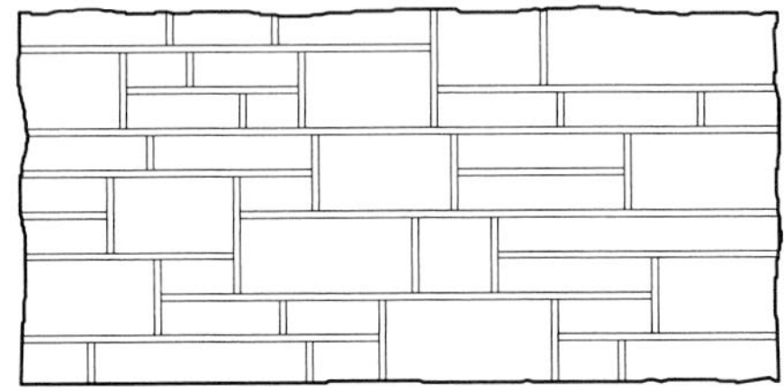

TWO-HEIGHT PATTERN (40% AT 2-1/4 IN.; 60% AT 5 IN.)

Figure 10.3 Cut stone masonry height patterns

Source: AIA, *Architectural Graphic Standards for Residential Construction*, 2nd ed. Copyright 2010, John Wiley and Sons, Inc.

Stone Cladding

Description

Stone cladding may be anchored or adhered to solid concrete or masonry, or over structural framing to form an exterior weather-resistant siding. Stone cladding is typically constructed from granite, limestone, or quartz-based stones.

Granite is impervious to water making it resistant to abuse and weathering with little maintenance. Its strength, however, makes it expensive since it is difficult to shape or finish. Limestone is easily worked and available but is limited in color. Quartz-based stones vary widely in workability and strength.

Adhered stone cladding uses a solid backing of mortar to form a water barrier and hold stones in place. Mortar backings, which should be filled as the stone is laid, are required by code to be between 1 and 2 inches thick to ensure a solid backing and still support the stone adequately. The size of adhered stone is also limited by code. The IRC limits their weight to 15 pounds/square feet, thickness to 1-5/8 inches and faces to 36 inches or 720 square inches in area. Stones less than 1 inch thick and 81 square inches in area may also be set using a tile-setting method.

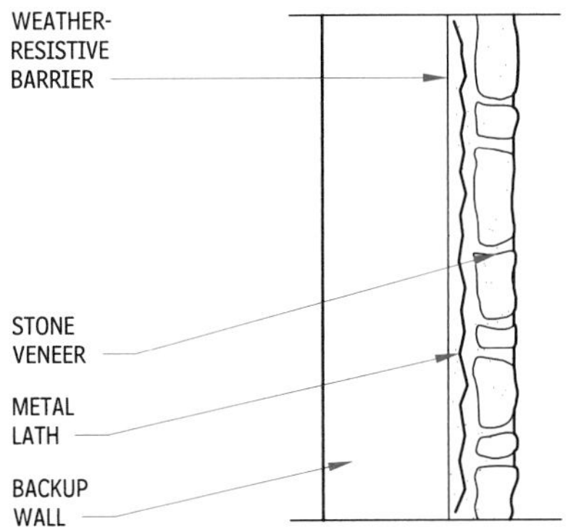

Figure 10.4 Typical adhered stone-cladding wall section
Source: AIA, *Architectural Graphic Standards for Residential Construction*, 2nd ed. Copyright 2010, John Wiley and Sons, Inc.

Anchored stone cladding is constructed with an air space behind it and held in place by anchors. The air space not only allows the cladding to move independently from the structure, but also allows for air circulation behind the cladding. A water-resistant barrier, asphalt felt or another approved barrier, is required over studs or sheathing. The type and placement of anchors used for stone cladding are governed by IRC table R703.4. It also requires anchors to be noncorrosive to prevent rusting, which could stain and damage the adjacent mortar and stone. Corrugated, galvanized metal strips are most common, since they are easily bent or cut to fit the irregular mortar joints caused by stone irregularities. Mortar spots should be used to eliminate excessive play in the anchors and increase their resistance to compression forces.

Mortar used installation of stone cladding includes portland cement-lime, masonry cement, and mortar cement. Portland cement-lime mortar is most common since it can be mixed to achieve a workable mortar with high compressive strength and increased bond strength. Masonry cements are proprietary mixes. Although they simplify job mixing, they are not required to comply with performance tests for flexural bond strength.

Mortar joints in stone cladding are wide to allow for the unevenness of stone. Often they are tooled to avoid varying depths at the middle of the joints making them susceptible to spalling. *Spalling,* or deterioration of the mortar at the stone edges, is caused when setting mortar

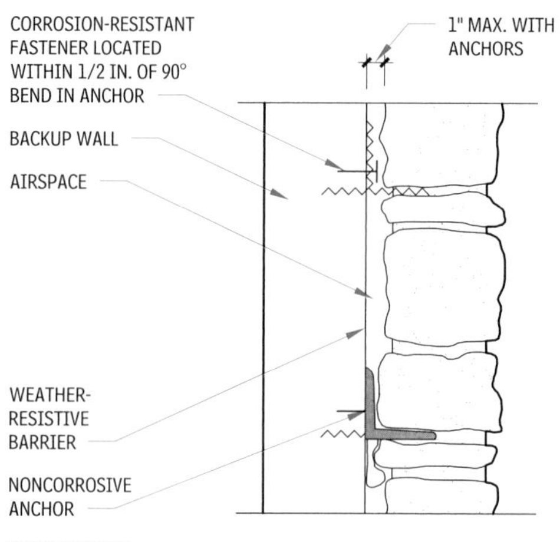

Figure 10.5 Typical anchored stone-cladding wall section

Source: AIA, *Architectural Graphic Standards for Residential Construction*, 2nd ed. Copyright 2010, John Wiley and Sons, Inc.

hardens on the surface before the center and results in less shrinkage at the face joint. Raking of mortar joints allows the setting mortar to harden before the face of the joint is filled by pointing.

Assessing Existing Conditions

- Movement joints are provided where stone veneer is supported by wood or cold-formed steel adjoins veneer supported by a foundation.
- Stone veneer above openings is supported by corrosion-resistant lintels with bearing not less than 4 inches.
- Anchored stone veneer is attached in accordance with IRC Table R703.4, typically one corrosion-resistant veneer anchor for every 2.67 square feet of veneer, with anchors spaced not more than 32 inches on center horizontally and 18 inches on center vertically, using approved corrosion-resistant fasteners.
- Metal ties are embedded 1-1/2 inches minimum in mortar or grout and 5/8 inches minimum cover to the outer face.
- Metal ties are spaced not more than 24 inches apart.
- Additional metal ties spaced 3 feet along the edge within 12 inches are provided at wall openings greater than 16 inches.
- Air space is between 1 inch wide, minimum.
- A water-resistant barrier is installed where the air space is filled with mortar or grout.
- Flashing is located beneath the first course of stone units above ground above the foundation wall and at other points of support, including structural floors, shelf angles, and lintels.
- Flashing is corrosion resistant, applied shingle fashion, extends to the surface of exterior wall finish at all window and door openings, built in gutters, wall and roof intersections, projecting wood trim, exterior attachments or penetrations, and under copings and sills (IRC R703.8).
- Weepholes are provided a maximum of 33 inches on center immediately above the flashing. Weepholes should always be placed at every course of flashing to expedite the exit of any moisture and reduce the growth of mildew and staining from dissolved substances within the wall.
- Sealant joints are located directly adjacent to control joints in masonry backup.
- Building expansion joints continue through stone cladding.
- Control joints for adhered cladding are not more than 18 feet apart, areas do not exceed 144 square feet, and the length-to-width ratio is less than 2.5 to 1.

Acceptable Practices

- Use of stainless-steel anchors to eliminate the possibility of rusting in areas where an industrial or marine environment causes increased corrosion.
- Use of 1-inch minimum air spaces to ensure they will remain free of mortar droppings.
- Use of a wire mesh and approved water-resistive barrier or water-resistive barrier-backed reinforcement.
- Use of a raised bead in the center of the joint to minimize widely varying joints.
- Use of mortar containing the maximum amount of lime permissible by the lowest acceptable compressive strength. The lime in hairline cracks will react with the air and water and seals the cracks and prevents further water penetration.
- Use of masonry cements only for small projects where simplified mixing and good workability may result in better workmanship.
- Use of latex additives in adhered setting mortars to increase bond strength and flexibility of hardened mortar and retard evaporation during setting.
- Use of Type O pointing mortar where it is not likely to be frozen when saturated, and Type N otherwise.

Practices to Avoid

- Avoid using geologists' classifications or common names, which are often misunderstood, to describe stone cladding.
- Use of marble as a stone cladding, which is subject to fading and susceptible to weather, is not recommended.
- Use of adhered limestone, typically over 1 inch thick, without anchors. Model code limits the weight of adhered veneers to 15 lb/sq. ft. or about 1 inch thick.
- Use of recessed joints which may be susceptible to freeze-thaw damage in harsh weather.

Manufactured Stone Masonry

Description

Manufactured stone masonry is typically a lightweight, non-load-bearing, concrete-based product that is manufactured to simulate the appearance of natural stone. The units are adhered to exterior and interior walls by mortar bonding in a veneer installation. The veneer substrates include wood framing with rigid sheathing, metal framing with gypsum board sheathing, concrete or brick masonry, concrete, and stucco.

Assessing Existing Conditions

- Ensure structural and surface integrity of substrate before stone installation. The substrate must be free of dirt, waterproofing, paint, form oil, or any other substance that may inhibit mortar bonding.
- If a mortar-bondable substrate surface cannot be achieved, fasten corrosion-resistant mesh lath material to act as a base for adhering mortar, using corrosion resistant hardware to secure.
- A water-resistive barrier behind manufactured stone is required by IRC R730.2 to restrict the transmission of moisture to the surface behind.
- Water-resistive barrier must be continuous and integrated with all flashing accessories, doors, windows, wall penetrations, and wall transitions to form a continuous water drainage plane.
- Lath and lath attachments must be corrosion resistant, typically galvanized, and installed horizontally with overlapping seams.
- Flashing materials are installed.

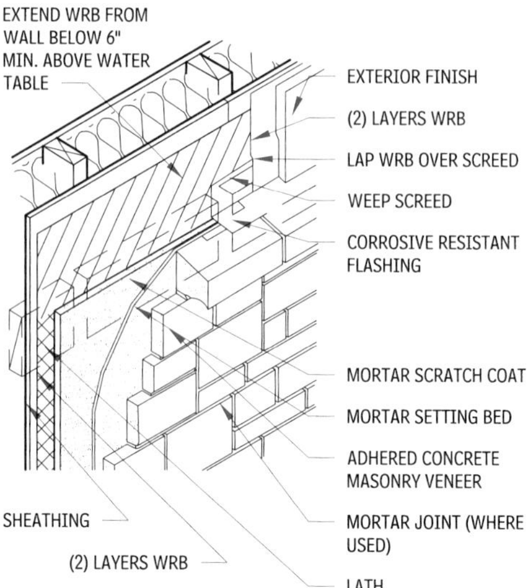

Figure 10.6 Adhered masonry wall assembly
Source: AIA, *Architectural Graphic Standards for Residential Construction*, 2nd ed. Copyright 2010, John Wiley and Sons, Inc.

Acceptable Practices

Successful manufactured stone masonry installations include the following:

- Sealing manufactured stone masonry facing a fireplace installation will assist in the removal of smoke stains.
- For best results, stones must be trimmed so that mortar joints do not exceed 3/4-inch width. For fire-rated walls, joints cannot exceed 1/2-inch width.
- Grouted stone installations are best started at the top of wall and stacked stones installations are best when started at the bottom.
- For final cleaning of mortar joint, ensure that mortar is completely set to avoid smearing mortar on stone masonry.

Practices to Avoid

- Avoid the use of ferrous metals, which can cause two major problems: Stone may fall off wall if lath fasteners rust; rust will leach through mortar and cause stains on manufactured stone masonry.

- Wet mortar that is smeared on manufactured stone leaves a thin film that dulls the stone. Clean with a sponge and clean water right away, and keep washing with clean water until film is completely gone.
- Avoid installations below a water line or in areas with cascading water (swimming pool, water fountain, direct contact with sprinklers, etc.) or water directly sprayed onto stone surface.
- Do not subject manufactured stone masonry to contact with chlorine, de-icing materials, salt, acid, or other harsh chemicals.
- Where rainfall could splash mud on stone masonry, put down hay or straw to prevent mud splashing.

Resources

WITHIN THIS BOOK

- Chapter 8 Common Work Results for Masonry
- Chapter 9 Unit Masonry

REFERENCE STANDARDS

ASTM C15.11, Adhered Manufactured Stone Masonry Veneer
ASTM C 119, Standard Terminology Relating to Dimension Stone
ASTM C 270 - Standard Specification for Mortar for Unit Masonry
ASTM C 1242, Guide for the Selection, Design, and Installation of Exterior Dimension Stone Anchors and Anchoring Systems

OTHER RESOURCES

- 2009 International Residential Code for One and Two-Family Dwellings. Washington, DC: International Code Council, Inc., 2009.
- 2009 International Building Code. Washington, DC: International Code Council, Inc., 2009.
- American Institute of Architects, *Architectural Graphics Standards,* 11th ed. Hoboken, NJ: John Wiley and Sons, 2007.
- American Institute of Architects, *Architectural Graphic Standards for Residential Construction,* 2nd ed. Hoboken, NJ: John Wiley and Sons, 2010.
- The Brick Industry Association, Technical Notes on Brick Construction. Reston, VA: BIA (undated).
- The Brick Industry Association, www.gobrick.com.
- Building Stone Institute, www.buildingstoneinstitute.org.
- National Concrete Masonry Association, TEK Manual for Concrete Masonry Design and Construction (Collection of TEK Bulletins.) Herndon, VA: Val NCMA (undated).

Part IV

Metals

Chapter 11

Common Work Results for Metals

Ferrous Metals

Nonferrous Metals

Galvanic Action

Metal Gauges, Thickness and Weights

Metal Finishes

Ferrous Metals

Description

All metal that contains iron are ferrous metals. All cast irons have high compressive strengths, but tensile and yield strengths vary widely, depending on basic type. Cast iron is relatively corrosion-resistant but cannot be hammered or beaten into shapes. The characteristics of cast iron vary widely among the six basic types:

- **Gray:** Gray irons are brittle due to high carbon and silicon content.
- **Malleable:** Malleable iron is a low-carbon white iron that is cast, reheated, and slowly cooled, or annealed, to improve its workability.
- **Ductile:** Ductile iron contains magnesium, which alters the surface tension, making the iron casting more ductile. It is less brittle, stiffer, stronger, and more shock-resistant than gray iron.
- **White:** White iron is extremely hard and brittle.
- **Compacted graphite:** Compacted graphite iron properties are very difficult to control during production. They are between those of gray and ductile iron.
- **High-alloy iron:** High-alloy irons are gray, ductile, or white irons with an alloy content of 3 percent to more than 30 percent.

Assessing Existing Conditions

An alloy is a mixture of two or more metals. When a pure metal material does not contain necessary properties, combining metals can help achieve these desirable characteristics. Elements typically used to modify steel include the following:

- **Aluminum:** For surface hardening
- **Chromium:** For corrosion resistance
- **Copper:** For atmospheric corrosion resistance
- **Manganese:** In small amounts, for additional hardening; in larger amounts, for better wear resistance
- **Molybdenum:** Combined with other metals, such as chromium and nickel, to increase corrosion resistance and raise tensile strength without reducing ductility

- **Nickel:** To increase tensile strength without reducing ductility; in high concentrations, nickel improves corrosion resistance
- **Silicon:** To strengthen low-alloy steels and improve oxidation resistance. (Larger amounts produce hard, brittle castings that are resistant to corrosive chemicals.)
- **Sulfur:** For free machining
- **Titanium:** To prevent intergranular corrosion of stainless steels
- **Tungsten, vanadium, and cobalt:** For hardness and corrosion resistance

Acceptable Practices

Gray irons are excellent for damping purposes (i.e., absorbing vibrations). Other applications include decorative shapes, such as fences and posts, gratings, and stair components, as well as utility uses such as manhole covers and fire hydrants.

Malleable iron has been used for decades in applications that require durability and high ductility.

White iron castings are used primarily in industrial machinery parts that experience high wear and require abrasion resistance.

High-alloy iron is used as follows:

- Wrought iron is ideal for railings, grilles, fences, screens, and various types of decorative metal.
- Carbon steel uses include structural shapes, such as welded fabrications or castings, metal framing and joists, fasteners, wall grilles, and ceiling suspension grids.
- Stainless steel is used in construction for flashing, coping, fascia, wall panels, floor plates, gratings, handrails, hardware, fasteners, and anchors. Decorative shapes and statuary can be cast in stainless steel.

Practices to Avoid

- Iron that contains no trace of carbon is soft, ductile, and easily worked, but it rusts in a relatively short period of time and is susceptible to corrosion by most acids.
- Low-alloy steels are seldom used in exterior architectural applications that involve water runoff, because adjacent materials could become stained with rust.

Nonferrous Metals

Description

Nonferrous metals do not contain any iron, are not magnetic, and are usually more resistant to corrosion than ferrous metals. Nonferrous metals and their alloys can be categorized into major groups, described as follows.

Aluminum

Aluminum has good forming and casting characteristics and offers good corrosion resistance. When exposed to air, aluminum does not oxidize progressively because a hard, thin oxide coating forms on the surface and seals the metal from its environment.

Aluminum and its alloys, numbering in the hundreds, are widely available in common commercial forms. Aluminum alloy sheets can be formed, drawn, stamped, or spun. Many wrought or cast aluminum alloys can be welded, brazed, or soldered, and aluminum surfaces readily accept a wide variety of finishes, both mechanical and chemical.

Brass, Copper, and Bronze

Good thermal and electrical conductivity, corrosion resistance, and easy forming and joining make copper and its alloys useful in construction. However, copper and many of its alloys have relatively low strength-to-weight ratios, and their strength is even further reduced at elevated temperatures. These metals are offered in rod, plate, strip, sheet, and tube shapes; forgings; castings; and electrical wire.

These metals can be grouped according to composition in several general categories: copper, high-copper alloys, and many types of brass and bronze. Monel metal is a copper-nickel alloy that offers excellent corrosion resistance and is often used for corrosion-resistant fasteners.

Brass is copper with zinc as its principal alloying element. It is important to know that some brass alloys may be called "bronzes," even though they have little or no tin in them. When a metal is identified as bronze, the alloy may not contain zinc or nickel; if it does, it is probably brass. Muntz metal, also called *malleable brass,* is a bronze alloy resembling

Table 11.1 Copper-Based Alloy Characteristics

Name		Architectural Bronze	Commercial Bronze	Muntz Metal
Composition				
	Copper (Cu)	56.5%	90.0%	60.0%
	Zinc (Zn)	41.25%	10.0%	40.0%
	Lead (Pb)	2.25%		
Color		Bronze	Bronze	Light yellow
Cold workability		Very poor	Excellent	Fair
Machinability		Good	Poor	Good
Weldability		Poor	Gas, carbon arc, metal arc	Gas, carbon arc, metal arc, spot and seam welding for thin sheets
Hot workability (and soldering and polishing)		Very good	Very good	Very good
Other properties		Excellent forging and free-machining	Very ductile	High strength; low ductility

extruded architectural bronze in color. It is available in sheets and strips, and is used in flat surfaces in architectural compositions in connection with extruded architectural bronze.

Lead

An extremely dense metal, lead is corrosion-resistant and easily worked. Alloys are added to it to improve properties such as hardness and strength. Typical applications of lead include roof and wall accessories. It can be combined with tin alloy to plate iron or steel, which is commonly called *terneplate.*

Zinc

Although it is corrosion-resistant in water and air, zinc is brittle and low in strength. Its major use is in galvanizing (dipping hot iron or steel in molten zinc), although zinc is also used to create sand-cast or die-cast components.

Tin

The key properties of tin are its low melting point (450°F), relative softness, good formability, and readiness to form alloys. The principal uses for tin are as a constituent of solder, a coating for steel (tinplate, terneplate), and an alloy with other metals that can be cast, rolled, extruded, or atomized. Tin is most popular as an alloy for copper, antimony, lead, bismuth, silver, and zinc. Pewter alloys contain 1 to 8 percent antimony and 0.5 to 3 percent copper. Alloy metal in tin solders ranges from 40 percent lead to no lead and 3.5 percent silver.

Nickel

Whitish in color, nickel is used for plating other metals or as a base for chromium plating. Nickel polishes well and does not tarnish. It is also widely applied as an additive in iron and steel alloys, as well as other metal alloys. Nickel-iron castings are more ductile and more resistant to corrosion than conventional cast iron. Adding nickel makes steel more resistant to impact.

Chromium

A hard, steel-gray metal, chromium is commonly used to plate other metals, including iron, steel, brass, and bronze. Plated cast shapes can be brightly polished and do not tarnish. Chromium does not rust, which makes chromium alloys excellent for exterior uses.

Magnesium

The lightest of all metals used in construction, pure magnesium is not strong enough for general structural functions.

Acceptable Practices

- Architectural brasses and bronzes are used for doors, windows, door and window frames, railings, trim and grilles, and finish hardware.
- Zinc is commonly used for roofing, flashing, nails, plumbing hardware, galvanizing structural components, and decorative shapes.

Practices to Avoid

- Alloys that darken to a brown or black finish when used in exterior applications may also cause staining of surrounding surfaces if not properly isolated.
- Use of uncoated copper surfaces in outdoor weather conditions if the blue-green patina is undesirable.
- Use of lead in areas where there is a potential for human contact or where water sources are nearby. Lead vapors and dust are toxic if they are ingested.

Galvanic Action

Description

Corrosion, which is caused by galvanic action, occurs between dissimilar metals or between metals and other materials when sufficient moisture is present to carry an electrical current. The galvanic series shown in Table 11.2 is a useful indicator of corrosion susceptibility caused by galvanic action. The metals listed are arranged in order from the least noble (most reactive to corrosion) to the most noble (least reactive to corrosion). The farther apart two metals are on the list, the

Table 11.2 The Galvanic Series

Anode (least noble) +	Magnesium, magnesium alloys
	Zinc
	Aluminum 1100
	Cadmium
	Aluminum 2024-T4
	Steel or iron, cast iron
	Chromium iron (active)
Electric current flows from positive (+) to negative (−)	Ni-Resist
	Type 304, 316 stainless (active)
	Hastelloy "C"
	Lead, tin
	Nickel (active)
	Hastelloy "B"
	Brasses, copper, bronzes, copper-nickel alloys, monel
	Silver solder
	Nickel (passive)
	Chromium iron (passive)
	Type 304, 316 stainless (passive)
	Silver
	Titanium
Cathode (most noble) −	Graphite, gold, platinum

greater the deterioration of the less noble metal will be if the two come in contact under adverse conditions.

Metal deterioration also occurs when metal comes in contact with chemically active materials, particularly when moisture is present. For example, aluminum corrodes when in direct contact with concrete or mortar, and steel corrodes when in contact with certain treated woods.

Pitting and concentration cell corrosion are other types of metal deterioration. Pitting takes place when particles or bubbles of gas are deposited on a metal surface. Oxygen deficiency under these deposits sets up anodic areas, which cause pitting. Concentration cell corrosion is similar to galvanic corrosion; the difference is in the electrolytes. Concentration cell corrosion can be produced by differences in ion concentration, oxygen concentration, or foreign matter adhering to the surface.

Assessing Existing Conditions

When assessing galvanic corrosion, be aware that:

- Nails, screws, bolts, and other attachments must be coated with or separated by a nonabsorbent nonconductive material.

Acceptable Practices

- Coat metal surfaces that must be in contact with dissimilar metals.

Practices to Avoid

- Do not put dissimilar metals in contact with each other where water or high humidity may be present.
- Do not use coated surfaces that are dented and scratched. Imperfections in the coating may cause metal substrate to corrode more quickly.

Metal Gauges, Thickness and Weights

Description

Sheet metals are often described in gauges and in decimal-inch thickness. The decimal-inch thicknesses of different metals of the same gauge vary, and it may be important to consider when in the field. Table 11.3 provides a convenient guide in comparing metal gauges, thickness and weights.

Table 11.3 Weights of Sheet Metals

Gauge	Steel		Galvanized Steel		Stainless			Aluminum	
	Decimal Thickness	Lb/sq ft	Decimal Thickness	Lb/sq ft	Decimal Thickness	Lb/sq ft		Decimal Thickness	Lb/sq ft
						Chrome Alloy	Chrome Nickel		
32	0.0100		0.0130	0.563	0.0100	0.418	0.427	0.008	0.115
31	0.0110		0.0140	0.594	0.0109	0.450	0.459	0.009	0.130
30	0.0120	0.500	0.0157	0.656	0.0125	0.515	0.525	0.010	0.144
29	0.0135	0.563	0.0172	0.719	0.0140	0.579	0.591	0.011	0.158
28	0.0149	0.625	0.0187	0.781	0.0156	0.643	0.656	0.012	0.173
27	0.0164	0.688	0.0202	0.844	0.0171	0.708	0.721	0.014	0.202
26	0.0179	0.750	0.0217	0.906	0.0187	0.772	0.787	0.016	0.230
25	0.0209	0.875	0.0247	1.031	0.0218	0.901	0.918	0.018	0.259
24	0.0239	1.000	0.0276	1.156	0.0250	1.030	1.050	0.020	0.286
23	0.0269	1.125	0.0306	1.281	0.0281	1.158	1.181	0.022	0.331
22	0.0299	1.250	0.0336	1.406	0.0312	1.287	1.312	0.025	0.360
21	0.0329	1.375	0.0366	1.531	0.0343	1.416	1.443	0.028	0.403
20	0.0359	1.500	0.0396	1.656	0.0375	1.545	1.575	0.032	0.461
19	0.0418	1.750	0.0456	1.906	0.0437	1.802	1.837	0.036	0.518
18	0.0478	2.000	0.0516	2.156	0.0500	2.060	2.100	0.040	0.576
17	0.0538	2.250	0.0575	2.406	0.0562	2.317	2.362	0.045	0.648
16	0.0598	2.500	0.0635	2.656	0.0625	2.575	2.625	0.050	0.734
15	0.0673	2.812	0.0710	2.969	0.0703	2.896	2.953	0.056	0.821

(continued)

Gauge	Steel		Galvanized Steel		Stainless			Aluminum	
	Decimal Thick-ness	Lb/ sq ft	Decimal Thick-ness	Lb/ sq ft	Decimal Thick-ness	Lb/sq ft Chrome Alloy	Lb/sq ft Chrome Nickel	Deci-mal Thick-ness	Lb/ sq ft
14	0.0747	3.125	0.0785	3.281	0.0781	3.218	3.281	0.063	0.992
13	0.0897	3.750	0.0934	3.906	0.0937	3.862	3.937	0.071	1.040
12	0.1046	4.375	0.1084	4.531	0.1093	4.506	4.593	0.080	1.170
11	0.1196	5.000	0.1233	5.156	0.1250	5.150	5.250	0.090	1.310
10	0.1345	5.625	0.1382	5.781	0.1406	5.793	5.906	0.100	1.470
9	0.1494	6.250	0.1532	6.406	0.1562	6.437	6.562	0.112	1.640
8	0.1644	6.875	0.1681	7.031	0.1718	7.081	7.218	0.125	1.760
7	0.1793	7.500			0.1875	7.590	7.752	0.140	1.980

Metal Finishes

Description

The finishes commonly used on architectural metals fall into three categories:

- **Mechanical finishes:** The result of physically changing the surface of the metal through mechanical means. The forming process itself or a subsequent procedure is performed either before or after the metal is fabricated into an end-use product.
- **Chemical finishes:** Finishes are achieved by means of chemicals, which may or may not have a physical effect on the surface of the metal.
- **Coatings:** Applied as finishes, either to the metal stock or the fabricated product. These coatings either change the metal itself, through a process of chemical or electrochemical conversion, or they are simply applied to the metal surface.

Assessing Existing Conditions

Application environments, service requirements, and aesthetics together determine which metal finish or coating is best to specify. Finishes are usually selected for both appearance and function; chromium plating on metal bathroom water faucets and handles, or baked enamel on sheet metal lighting fixtures, for example, must be attractive as well as functionally protective.

For structural and exterior metal building products, such as metal framing, steel siding, and exterior lighting, function and operating environments are the more important criteria. From a design standpoint, it is important to recognize how finishes and coatings resist wear and corrosion. To choose the right coating or finish, design professionals must understand which material or process is best suited for a specific application.

Acceptable Practices

Table 11.4 Comparative Applicability of Various Finishes for Architectural Applications

Type of Finish or Treatment	Metal			
	Aluminum	Copper Alloys	Stainless Steel	Carbon Steel and Iron
MECHANICAL FINISHES				
As-fabricated	Common to all of the metals (produced by hot rolling, extruding, or casting)			
Bright rolled	Commonly used (produced by cold rolling)			Not used
Directional grit textured	Commonly used (produced by polishing, buffing, hand-rubbing, brushing, or cold rolling)			Rarely used
Non-directional matte textured	Commonly used (produced by sandblasting or shot blasting)			Rarely used
Bright polished	Commonly used (produced by polishing and buffing)			Not used
Patterned	Available in light sheet gauges of all metals			
CHEMICAL FINISHES				
Nonetch cleaning	Commonly used on all of the metals			
Etched matte finish	Etched finishes widely used	Seldom used	Not used	Not used
Bright finish	Limited uses	Rarely used	Not used	Not used
Conversion coatings	Widely used as pretreatment for painting	Widely used to provide added color variation	Not used	Widely used as pretreatment for painting
COATINGS				
Organic	Widely used	Opaque types rarely used; transparent types common	Sometimes used	Most important type of finish
Anodic	Widely used	Not used	Not used	Not used
Metallic	Rarely used	Limited use	Limited use	Widely used
Laminated	Substantial uses	Limited use	Not used	Substantial uses

Mechanical Finishes

Mechanical finishes fall into the following categories:

- **As-fabricated finishes:** The texture and surface appearance given to a metal by the fabrication process.
- **Polished or buffed finishes:** Produced by successive polishing and buffing operations. Polishing and buffing improve edge and surface finishes and render many types of cast parts more durable, efficient, and safe.
- **Patterned finishes:** Produced by passing an as-fabricated sheet between design rollers to imprint a pattern.
- **Directional textured finishes:** Produced by making tiny parallel scratches on the metal surface. Metal treated this way has a smooth, satin sheen.
- **Nondirectional textured finishes:** Produced by blasting metal, under controlled conditions, with small metal shot, silica sand, glass beads, and aluminum oxide.

Chemical Finishes

Chemical finishes are produced in four ways.

- **Chemical cleaning** cleanses the metal surface without affecting it in any other way.
- **Etched finishes:** Produce a matte, frosted surface with varying degrees of roughness by treating the metal with an acid (sulfuric and nitric acid) or alkali solution.
- **Bright finish:** The process, not used widely, involves chemical or electrolytic brightening of a metal surface, typically aluminum.
- **Conversion coating:** Usually categorized as a chemical finish, but since a layer or coating is produced by a chemical reaction, it could be considered a coating. Conversion coatings typically prepare the surface of a metal for painting or for receiving another type of finish, but they are also used to produce a patina or statuary finish.

Coatings

Organic coatings on metal can provide protection and may also be decorative. When protection is the sole purpose, primers or undercoats, pigmented topcoats in hidden areas, and clear finishes are used. Organic coatings used for decorative and protective applications include pigmented coatings, clear finishes used for gloss, and transparent or translucent clear finishes with dyes added.

Anodic coatings are widely used to protect aluminum and many of its alloys from corrosion. When the metal is anodized in one of a variety of acids, a protective oxide is formed on the surface. Depending on the acid, the oxide may range from thin and nonporous to thick and porous. Anodic processes produce porous aluminum-oxide coatings, sealing is usually desirable. Three types of anodizing are used for aluminum: chromic, sulfuric, and hardcoat. The coating is immersed in hot water, the oxide is hydrated, and the pores swell shut. Chromic- and sulfuric-anodized coatings almost always are sealed, but hardcoats are not.

- **Chromic anodizing:** This type of anodizing, which results in a relatively soft coating, is the least used of the three types.
- **Sulfuric anodizing:** This is the most widely used method. It produces a harder coating than chromic anodizing, but it can be scratched. It offers a pleasing appearance and can be dyed in several colors. Corrosion resistance is good.
- **Hardcoat anodizing:** This method produces a relatively thick, extremely hard coating that can be dyed in a range of colors. Hardcoats are porous, making them suitable as a base for paints and adhesives.

Metallic plating is achieved by electroplating. In electro-deposition, an electrical current is carried across an electrolyte, and an organic resin is deposited on an electrode (the metal object being painted). Materials widely used to plate complex metal components include bronze, brass, chromium, cadmium, chromates, copper, lead, lead-tin, nickel, phosphates, silver, tin-nickel, and tin-zinc.

Lamination involves bonding preformed plastic films to metals with adhesives. Laminated coatings provide finishes for products such as interior paneling, partitions, and exterior metalwork. The following are types of plastic film that are widely used:

- **Polyvinyl chloride (PVC):** Films provide excellent stain and abrasion resistance. Available in a variety of types, these laminates may come with graining or embossing to simulate wood grain, leather, or fabric.
- **Polyvinyl fluoride (PVF):** Films have a smooth, medium-gloss surface, they are very strong, tough, and weather-resistant, making them particularly suited to exterior applications such as siding

materials. Their color range is limited, but they resist staining and chemical damage well.

- **Acrylic:** Films are low-cost products that stand up well to weather and are widely used for exterior metalwork. They resist UV radiation and yellowing and retain their flexibility with aging.

Practices to Avoid

- In high-traffic, areas coated finishes are more susceptible to wear and damage than chemical finishes.

Resources

WITHIN THIS BOOK

- Chapter 12 Cold-Formed Metal Framing
- Chapter 13 Metal Fabrications

OTHER RESOURCES

- American Institute of Architects, *Architectural Graphics Standards*, 11th ed. Hoboken, NJ: John Wiley and Sons, 2007.
- American Institute of Architects, *Architectural Graphic Standards for Residential Construction*, 2nd ed. Hoboken, NJ: John Wiley and Sons, 2010.
- National Association of Architectural Metal Manufacturers, www.naamm.org.

Chapter 12

Cold-Formed Metal Framing

Framing Details

Bracing

Fasteners and Connectors

Framing Details

Description

Cold-formed metal framing consists of the elements of the structural frame, which include the structural members, bracing and blocking, and a connection method and/or hardware. Components are manufactured by brake or cold roll forming and punching galvanized coil and sheet stock, which make it very strong and versatile. The strength and load-carrying capacity of a member can be increased simply by increasing the thickness, or gauge, of the metal. The dimensions of the member, or the spacing, do not necessarily have to be increased.

Assessing Existing Conditions

In order to ensure cold-formed metal framing is installed properly, verify the following:

- There is little limitation on the length of steel framing members; joists or studs may be fabricated in lengths up to 40 feet.
- Dimensions have been accurately measured so that extra cost and time can be avoided.
- Assemblies shall have structural members that are cut and assembled in accordance with tolerances prescribed in the International Residential Code (IRC).

Acceptable Practices

The building elements that are most often framed with cold-formed steel are floors, roofs, and walls, although other building elements and both structural and decorative assemblies may be steel framed. Although cold-formed steel is used for several products in building construction, framing products are different in that they are typically used for wall studs, floor joists, rafters, and truss members.

Cold-formed framing members consist of two basic types of components that are C-shaped in section:

1. Quarter-inch flanges folded inward to stiffen studs, joist, and rafters so they will more readily stand vertically
2. No flanges or (commonly called tracks), which have unpunched solid webs

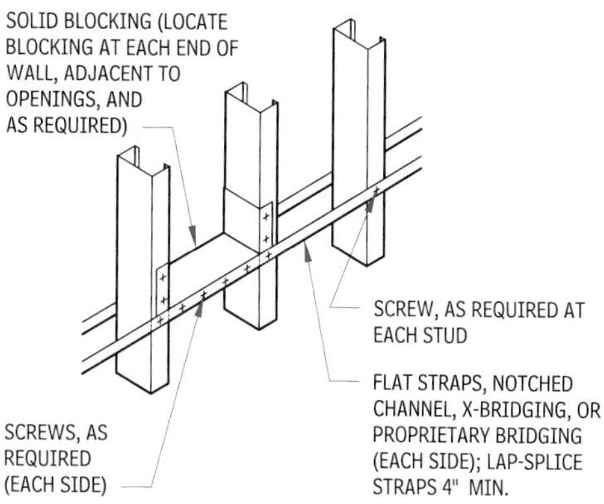

Figure 12.1 Wall bridging
Source: AIA, *Architectural Graphic Standards,* 11th ed. Copyright 2007, John Wiley & Sons, Inc.

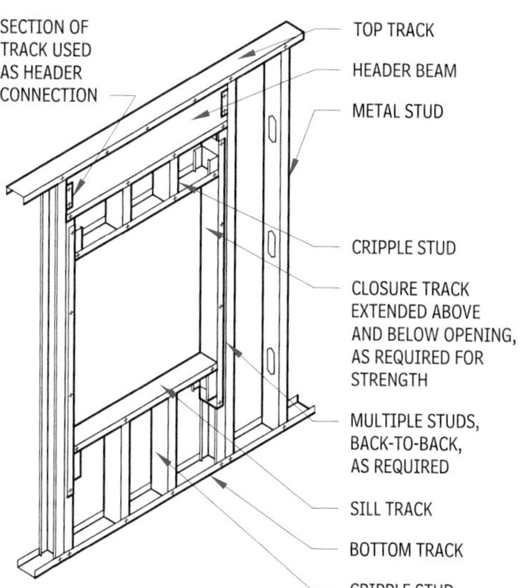

Figure 12.2 Window opening
Source: AIA, *Architectural Graphic Standards,* 11th ed. Copyright 2007, John Wiley & Sons, Inc.

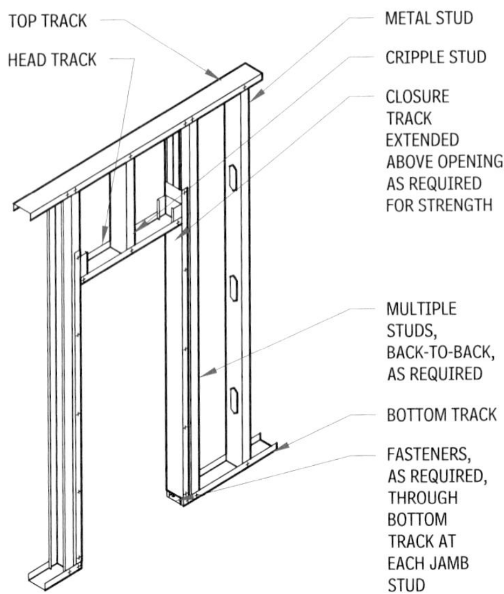

Figure 12.3 Door opening
Source: AIA, *Architectural Graphic Standards*, 11th ed. Copyright 2007, John Wiley & Sons, Inc.

Framing members are typically spaced at 16 or 24 inches on center, with spacing variations lower and higher depending on the loads and coverings. Wall members are typically vertical lipped channel or stud members, which fit into unlipped channel or track sections at the top and bottom. Similar configurations are used for both floor joist and rafter assemblies, but in a horizontal application for floors, and a horizontal or sloped application for roof framing.

Practices to Avoid

Common construction practices to avoid include the following:

- Avoid cutting whenever possible, as edges become sharp and dangerous.
- Avoid using hot-rolled steel members because their relatively thin walls are susceptible to buckling.

Bracing

Description

Bracing is the use of structural elements that are installed to provide restraint or support (or both) to other framing members so that the complete assembly forms a stable structure.

Assessing Existing Conditions

In order to ensure structural bracing is installed properly, verify the following:

- The bracing will resist forces and tension that will be applied during construction.

Acceptable Practices

Buildings must be properly braced to resist racking under wind and seismic loads. Diagonal-strap bracing is sloped to resist forces in tension and is fastened by screws or welds to studs and plates. This can be accomplished because diagonal bracing helps transfer some portion of any concentrated load or localized overload to an adjacent joint or stud.

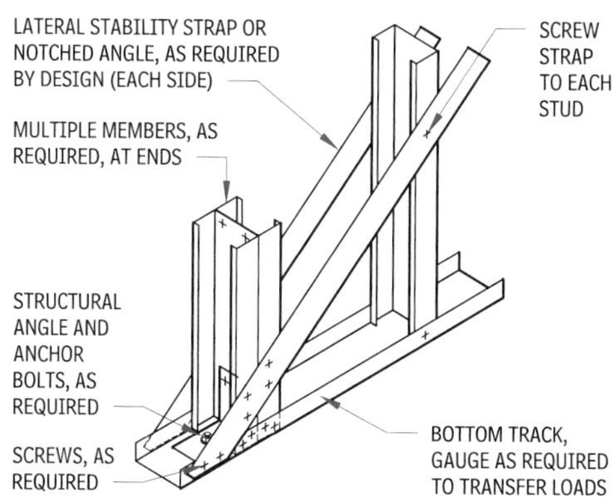

Figure 12.4 Diagonal bracing
Source: AIA, *Architectural Graphic Standards*, 11th ed. Copyright 2007, John Wiley & Sons, Inc.

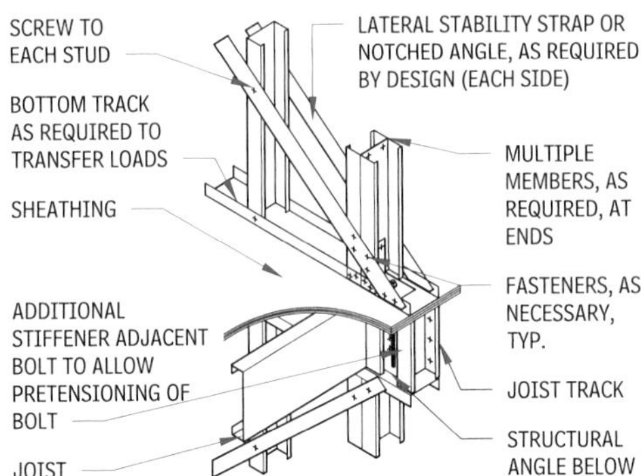

Figure 12.5 Horizontal bracing
Source: AIA, *Architectural Graphic Standards*, 11th ed. Copyright 2007, John Wiley & Sons, Inc.

Horizontal bridging does not transfer any load capacities to other members because it has no potential vertical component of force. It is primarily used to increase lateral stability through a bridging system. A horizontal bridging member is mounted between a pair of studs to prevent relative motion between the two studs.

Practices to Avoid

Common construction practices to avoid include the following:

- Avoid installing sheathing or finishes to steel bracing that is not properly spaced, as minor axis bending under wind, seismic, and axial loads can cause stud rotation and damage to finishing products.

Fasteners and Connectors

Description

Connectors are used in cold-formed steel construction to attach members such as studs and joists to each other or to the primary structure for the purpose of load transfer and support.

Acceptable Practices

There are two main connection types, fixed and movement-allowing (slip). Fixed connections of framing members don't allow movement of the connected parts. They can be found in axial-load-bearing walls, curtain walls, trusses, roofs, and floors. Movement-allowing connections are designed to allow deflection of the primary structure in the vertical direction due to live load, or in the horizontal direction due to wind or seismic loads, or both vertical and horizontal directions.

Fixed Connectors

Welding is a process that joins metals by melting the members together and adding a filler material to form a pool of molten material that cools to become a joint. Weldability refers to the capacity of steel to be welded into satisfactory, crack-free, sound joints. When welding cold formed steel members follow the current standards by AISI S100, section E:

- The various possible welds in cold-formed steel sections where the thickness of the thinnest element in the connection is 3/16-inch or less are as follows:
  - Groove welds in butt joints
  - Arc spot welds
  - Arc seam welds
  - Fillet welds
  - Flare groove welds
- Welded connections in which thickness of the thinnest connected arc is greater than 3/16-inch shall be in accordance with ANSI/AISC-360.

Movement-Allowing Connectors

Embedded anchors are structural anchor or devices like bolts, straps, or plates intended for fastening cold-formed steel structural framing to masonry or concrete that is installed prior to hardening of the grout or concrete. Embedded anchors are manufactured in several configurations and geometrical shapes depending on their intended purpose and/or location.

Practices to Avoid

Common construction practices to avoid include the following:

- Avoid using fastening methods such as clinching, power-actuated fasteners (PAF), mechanical anchors, adhesive anchors, and structural glue unless recommended by the manufacturer's instructions.

Resources

WITHIN THIS BOOK

- Chapter 11 Common Work Results for Metals
- Chapter 13 Metal Fabrications

REFERENCE STANDARDS

- ANSI/AISC-360—Specification for Structural Steel Buildings
- AISI S100—North American Specification for the Design of Cold-Formed Steel Structural Members

OTHER RESOURCES

- American Institute of Architects, *Architectural Graphics Standards*, 11th ed. Hoboken, NJ: John Wiley and Sons, 2007.
- American Institute of Architects, *Architectural Graphic Standards for Residential Construction*, 2nd ed. Hoboken, NJ: John Wiley and Sons, 2010.
- American Iron and Steel Institute, www.steel.org.
- Steel Framing Alliance, www.steelframing.org.
- Steel Stud Manufacturers Association (SSMA), www.ssma.com.

Chapter 13

Metal Fabrications

Metal Railings

Description

Railings are guards that protect occupants from falling at edges of openings and open-sided floors and stairs, act as visual separators, and offer protection and support for people with disabilities.

Metal railings, although primarily functional, can also be ornamental. They can be made of steel, aluminum, wrought iron, or stainless steel in pipe or tube materials. Railings are effective in many different design configurations, both horizontal and vertical.

Metal railings are attached by brackets, flanges, fittings, and anchors that can be cast or formed metal, typically finished to match supported railings. Components of metal railings may be welded or nonwelded to achieve desired configuration, depending on materials used. Changes in direction may be formed by bending or by inserting elbow fittings, depending on materials used and configuration desired.

Railings may be factory fabricated or fabricated in the field. Field-fabricated railings may be less expensive, but it is important to comply with code requirements.

Assessing Existing Conditions

In order to ensure the proper installation of metal railings, verify the following conditions:

- No rust should exist on railings or attachments.
- Metal railings should be securely attached to the structure and set accurately in location, alignment, and elevation.
- Manufactured metal railings should have been tested for compliance with structural performance requirements.
- Confirm local building code restrictions for railings that are used as ornamental and not functional railings, as they may have different code restrictions.
- Wrought iron for exterior applications rusts easily and should not be used in direct connection with concrete. Also check for rust through at the weld joints between railings and at mechanical fasteners.

Acceptable Practices

Common construction practices for metal railings include the following:

- Structural performance and spacing of vertical and horizontal members is critical and must comply with requirements of local building codes and occupancy requirements. For residential stairs, handrails are required on only one side of stair, without top and bottom extensions.
- Set posts plumb within a tolerance of 1/16 inch in 3 feet.
- Align rails so variations from level for horizontal members and variations from parallel with rake of steps and ramps for sloping members do not exceed 1/4 inch in 12 feet.
- For corrosion protection, coat concealed surfaces of aluminum that will be in contact with grout, concrete, masonry, wood, or dissimilar metals with a heavy coat of bituminous paint.
- Embed metal railing posts in concrete by inserting into preset metal pipe sleeves or formed/core-drilled holes and grouting annular space.
- For welded connections, cope components at connections to provide close fit, or use fittings designed for this purpose. Weld all around at connections, including at fittings.
- Bend members in jigs to produce uniform curvature for each configuration required; maintain cross-section of member throughout entire bend without buckling, twisting, cracking, or otherwise deforming exposed surfaces of components.
- Close exposed ends of hollow metal railing members with prefabricated end fittings.
- Secure wall brackets and railing end flanges to building construction by mechanical fastening as follows:
    - For concrete and solid masonry anchorage, use drilled-in expansion shields and hanger or lag bolts.
    - For hollow masonry anchorage, use toggle bolts.
    - For wood stud partitions, use hanger or lag bolts set into studs or wood backing between studs and coordinate with carpentry work to locate backing members.
- The finish used on metal railing is dependent on the material:
    - Aluminum railing finish is generally determined by concerns about appearance, corrosion, and abrasion resistance.
    - Steel railings used on the exterior should be galvanized or primed with a zinc-rich primer and finish painted, preferably with a high-performance coating. On interiors, steel railings can generally be

primed with a good-quality, rust-resistant primer and finished with enamel paint. For interior spaces subject to high humidity, steel railings should be finished as they would be for exterior applications.
  - Stainless-steel Type 304 typically provides a sufficient corrosion resistance, except in marine environments where Type 316L is more suitable. Finishes available range from a directional brushed (no. 4) finish to highly polished mirror finish.

- Code requirements for railings are as follows (see Figure 13.1):

  - Railing must be at least 36 inches in height, when the offset is more than 30 inches.
  - Bottom rail is less than 4 inches above the finished surface.
  - Rail spacing should not allow a 4-inch-diameter ball to pass between the rails.
  - Railing must be able to withstand a 200-pound force anywhere and in any direction along the top of the rail.
  - Deck railing balusters must resist 50 pounds in a 1-square-foot area.
  - Rail posts should be spaced no greater than 6 feet apart.

Figure 13.1 Railing with dimensions

Practices to Avoid

Common construction practices to avoid include:

- Contact between dissimilar metals including screws. Refer to "Galvanic Action" in Chapter 11.
- Railings that are loose. These are even more dangerous than railings that are missing because they provide a false sense of security. Test use every railing and pull on it with progressive and considerable force to ensure that it is secure.
- Railings that are freestanding at one or both ends. They are also much more difficult to build. Pay particular attention to these.
- Welding, cutting, or abrading surfaces of metal-railing components that have been coated or finished after fabrication and that are intended for field connection by mechanical or other means without further cutting or fitting.

Metal Lintels and Shelf Angles

Description

Lintels are structural members used to support carry a load over an opening in a wall. Openings in walls generally include doors and windows. Although lintels can be precast concrete, reinforced masonry, or heavy timber, most lintels used in residential construction are steel angles and are used to support masonry veneers. Lintels are commonly loose steel angles with simple spans bearing on the masonry veneer, but in longer spans can be attached to masonry, concrete, or wood or metal framing.

Shelf angles are similar to lintels. They are structural angles used to support masonry veneers above nonloading construction, above exterior wood construction, and where the veneer cannot be self-supporting. Shelf angles are typically supported by fasteners to structural members. Often, these conditions include chimneys, masonry veneer above roofs, and three-story masonry veneer walls.

The proper sizing of steel angles used for lintels and shelf angles can be calculated by an engineer based on span and load or selected from a span table in the IRC (see Table 13.1). Flashing and weepholes must be installed at all lintels and shelf angles in exterior locations to provide for cavity drainage of the wall.

Assessing Existing Conditions

When reviewing the installation of lintels and shelf angles, verify the following conditions:

- Check to see if the steel angle has a shop-applied rust-inhibited paint, is made of corrosion-resistant steel, or is treated with coatings to provide corrosion resistance.
- Steel angle should be appropriately sized for the span and condition.
- The long leg of a shelf angle should be placed in the vertical position.
- The span should not exceed 18 ft. 3 in.
- Minimum veneer of each side of opening is 18 in.

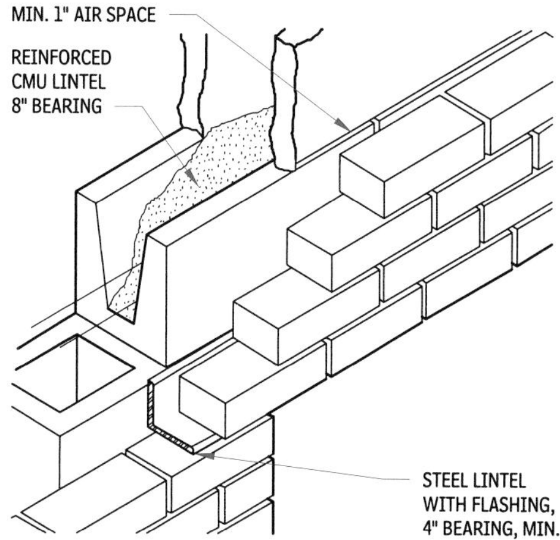

Figure 13.2 Lintel detail
Source: AIA, *Architectural Graphic Standards for Residential Construction*, 2nd ed. Copyright 2010, John Wiley & Sons, Inc.

- Minimum bearing is 4 in.
- Flashing is installed to the exterior of masonry.
- Weephole spacing does not exceed 33 in.

Acceptable Practices

Lintels and shelf angles provide structural support of masonry veneer at wall openings and other locations. They also create a horizontal obstruction in the drainage cavity or air space of masonry veneer walls, which requires flashing and weepholes to direct moisture outboard of the wall.

Consider the weight of a triangular section of wall above the opening. The height of the triangle should be equal to the width of the opening.

Practices to Avoid

- Deflection in the lintel or shelf and cracking of masonry can occur in long span conditions when the steel angle is not supported for at least seven days until the mortar cures.

Table 13.1 Steel Angle Lintel Sizing Chart—Allowable Loads

Horizontal Leg	Angle Size	Weight per Foot	Span (Center to Center of Required Bearing)									
			3′	4′	5′	6′	7′	8′	9′	10′	11′	12′
3 1/2	3 × 3 1/2 × 1/4	5.4 lb	956	517	262	149	91	59				
	× 5/16	6.6 lb	1,166	637	323	184	113	73				
	3 1/2 × 3 1/2 × 1/4	5.8 lb	1,281	718	406	232	144	94	65			
	× 5/16	7.2 lb	1,589	891	507	290	179	118	80			
	4 × 3 1/2 × 1/4	6.2 lb	1,622	910	580	338	210	139	95	68		
	× 5/16	7.7 lb	2,110	1,184	734	421	262	173	119	85	62	
	× 3/8	9.1 lb	2,434	1,365	855	490	305	201	138	98	71	
	× 7/16	10.6 lb	2,760	1,548	978	561	349	230	158	113	82	60
	5 × 3 1/2 × 1/4	7.0 lb	2,600	1,460	932	636	398	264	184	132	97	73
	× 5/16	8.7 lb	3,087	1,733	1,106	765	486	323	224	161	119	89
	× 7/16	12.0 lb	4,224	2,371	1,513	1,047	655	435	302	217	160	120
	6 × 3 1/2 × 1/4	7.9 lb	3,577	2,009	1,283	888	650	439	306	221	164	124
	× 5/16	9.8 lb	4,390	2,465	1,574	1,090	798	538	375	271	201	151
	× 3/8	11.7 lb	5,200	2,922	1,865	1,291	945	636	443	320	237	179

Note: Allowable loads to the left of the heavy line are governed by moment, and to the right by deflection. Fy = 36,000 psi. Maximum deflection is 1/600. Consult structural engineer for long spans. Allowable uniform loads are indicated in pounds per linear foot.

- Avoid insufficient bearing of masonry veneer on steel angles by ensuring the bottom leg of steel angles are deep enough to support the veneer masonry including any corbelling of the masonry.
- Flashing and weepholes must be installed above the lintel when the opening exceeds 33 inches wide and when a single piece lintel such as stone or precast concrete is used.

Resources

WITHIN THIS BOOK

- Chapter 2 Common Building Code Requirements
- Chapter 3 Accessibility Guidelines
- Chapter 11 Common Work Results for Metals
- Chapter 12 Cold-Formed Metal Framing

OTHER RESOURCES

- 2009 International Residential Code for One and Two-Family Dwellings. Washington, DC: International Code Council, Inc., 2009.
- American Institute of Architects, *Architectural Graphics Standards*, 11th ed. Hoboken, NJ: John Wiley & Sons, 2007.
- American Institute of Architects, *Architectural Graphic Standards for Residential Construction*, 2nd ed. Hoboken, NJ: John Wiley & Sons, 2010.
- ICC/ANSI A117.1—Accessible and Usable Buildings and Facilities. Washington, DC: International Code Council, Inc., 2003.

Part V

Wood, Plastics, and Composites

Chapter 14

Common Work Results for Wood, Plastics, and Composites

Wood Treatment

Fastening/Connectors

Wood Treatment

Description

Preservative Treatment

Where wood may be subject to deterioration by moisture or insect attack, pressure-preservative-treated material must be used. Wood should always be preservative treated when used with roofing and flashing, on the damp side of vapor barriers and waterproofing, and items such as sills, sleepers, furring, blocking, and stripping if in contact with masonry or concrete or located below grade. Most building codes require the use of preservative wood treatment or naturally resistant wood species for these areas as well as floor joists and crawl space support members within 12 to 18 inches of exposed soil.

Fire-Retardant Wood Treatment

Fire-Retardant-Treated (FRT) Wood Standards and Classifications

Interior fire retardants meet Class I ratings, which are required by code for vertical exits and special areas. Class II ratings are required for horizontal exits, but this rating is rarely reached with untreated wood. FRT lumber and plywood are recognized substitutes for noncombustible materials, for insurance purposes. Many codes allow FRT wood products for a variety of applications.

Both the flame spread index and smoke developed index give numerical scales for a material's fire classification. The flame spread index is the primary test for fire performance, according to ASTM E84. In the International Building Codes, flame spread ratings are classified as 0–25 (Class I or A), 26–75 (Class II or B), and 76–200 (Class III or C).

A smoke-developed index of 450 or less is permitted for FRT wood used for interior wall and ceiling finishes. The UL FR-S listing applies only to treated products with a UL-723 (ASTM E84) flame and smoke classification not exceeding 25 in a 30-minute test. The classification applies to the species tested and does not pertain to the structures in which the materials are installed.

Fire retardants come in interior and exterior types. Interior fire retardants are used on wood trusses and studs; exterior retardants protect exterior lumber, siding, roof shakes and shingles, and scaffold planking.

The latter type offers durable, nonleachable, long-term fire protection in outdoor or moist (relative humidity of 95 percent or greater) conditions.

Class C or Class B FRT shingles and shakes may be considered non-combustible materials. For wood exposed to the weather, use exterior-type retardants that retain their protective properties under the standard rain test.

Interior Type A wood is appropriate for interior and weather-protected applications with less than 95 percent relative humidity. In rare instances, when relative humidity is less than 75 percent, Type B can be specified. Interior Type A is used when a wood with low hygroscopicity (the rate at which the chemical draws moisture from the air) is required.

Assessing Existing Conditions

To ensure the proper installation of preservative- and/or fire-retardant-treated wood, consider the following:

- Preservative-treated wood can be identified by an identification mark such as shown in Figure 14.1:
  - A: Trademark of inspection agency certified by the American Lumber Standard Committee (ALSC). Contact the Southern Pine Council (SPC) or the ALSC for a list of certified inspection agencies.
  - B: Applicable American Wood Preservers' Association (AWPA) standard.
  - C: Year of treatment.
  - D: Preservative used for treatment.
  - E: Retention level.
  - F: Dry or KDAT (kiln-dried after treatment), if applicable.
  - G: Proper exposure conditions.
  - H: Treating company and location.
- FRT wood fasteners must be hot-dipped, zinc-coated, galvanized stainless steel, silicon bronze, or copper; other materials deteriorate upon contact with FRT chemicals.
- FRT wood can be identified by an identification mark such as shown in Figure 14.2.*
- FRT wood has increased weight and decreased strength. Consult a structural engineer and the wood treater for the actual design values for structural applications.

*Wood shakes and shingles are further classified as Class B or C. Rather than stamp each piece, each bundle is tagged with an identification mark.

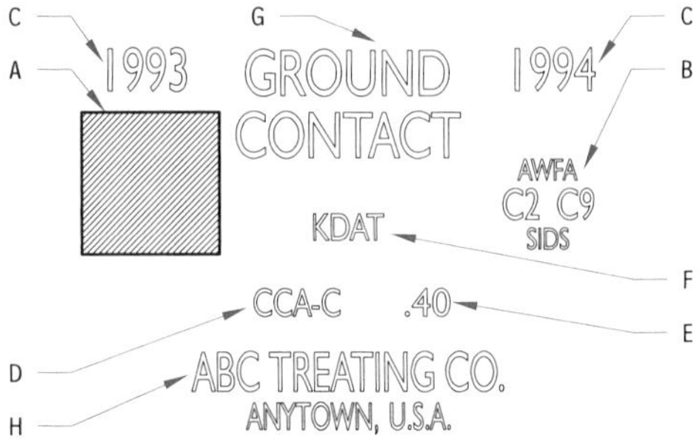

Figure 14.1 Typical quality mark for treated lumber
Source: AIA, *Architectural Graphic Standards for Residential Construction,* 2nd ed. Copyright 2010, John Wiley & Sons, Inc.

Acceptable Practices

- Fire-retardant-treated wood is permitted in lieu of noncombustible materials for certain applications such as non–load-bearing partitions and exterior walls, roof assemblies, and exterior architectural trim.
- Fire-retardant-treated lumber and plywood can be lightly sanded for cosmetic cleaning after treatment. Painting and staining are possible, but not always successful—particularly transparent finishes. Consult finish manufacturer's installation instructions and test finishes for compatibility before applying them.

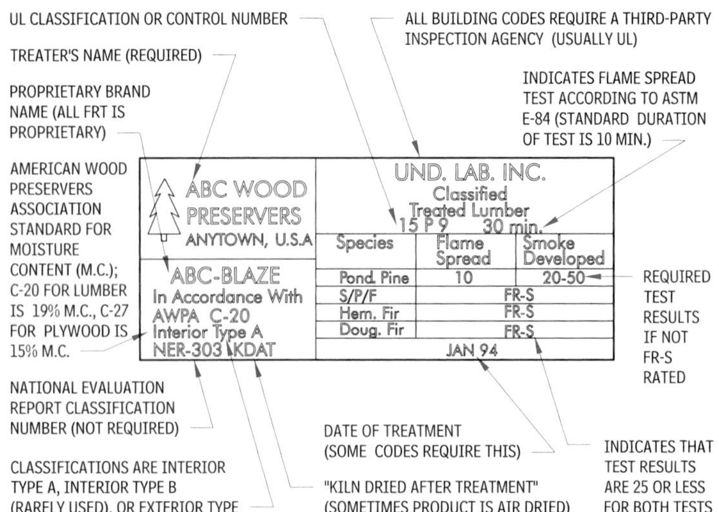

Figure 14.2 Typical fire-retardant treated wood identification mark
Source: AIA, *Architectural Graphic Standards for Residential Construction,* 2nd ed. Copyright 2010, John Wiley & Sons, Inc.

- Treated lumber may be end-cut, but ripping and extensive surfacing will normally void the UL label. To the extent possible, materials should be precut before treatment; otherwise, a wood treater should be consulted. Treated plywood can be cut in either direction without the loss of fire protection.
- Increased corrosion of steel and even galvanized fasteners is a concern with preservative treatments, especially those containing ammonia and higher concentrations of copper (which will generally replace those containing arsenic). For this reason, hot-dip galvanized steel or stainless-steel fasteners should be used with pressure-preservative-treated lumber.
- Use of preservative-treated wood for applications subject to decay and insect attack is a positive measure for the environment because it eliminates the need to routinely replace such items. Use of preservative-treated wood also decreases the consumption of naturally decay-resistant species, some of which have become far less abundant than they once were because of overuse.
- Finishing preservative-treated wood can be a challenge. Painting wood treated with oil-borne preservatives is not recommended and requires extensive care and an aluminum-based paint. When clean, odorless, and paintable wood is required, a waterborne preservative is recommended. Guidelines for precautions in these cases are outlined in an EPA-approved consumer information sheet for each preservative treatment.

Practices to Avoid

- Dual treatment with both preservative and fire-retardant treatments is not feasible because the preservative treatment affects the performance of the fire retardant.
- Never burn treated wood in open fires or in stoves, fireplaces, or residential boilers. Dispose of treated wood by ordinary trash collection or burial.
- Avoid frequent inhalation of sawdust from treated wood. Whenever possible, perform sawing and machining of treated wood outdoors.
- Avoid frequent or prolonged skin contact with penta- or creosote-treated wood.
- After handling treated wood products, wash skin thoroughly before eating or drinking.

Fastening/Connectors

Description

There are several types of wood fasteners or connectors. Some of the most common include:

- *Adhesives:* Composed of a base component, dispersion medium, and various additives that impart specific properties.
- *Nails:* Nails are measured, or sized, according to length. This is expressed by the letter "d" (called penny).
- *Shields and anchors:* Shields and anchors are both stronger fasteners than screws and nails.
- *Screws and bolts:* Screws are stronger than nails and can be removed with less damage to the material.

Assessing Existing Conditions

Nails are made of many types of metal, for diverse uses. When selecting nails, follow the recommendations of the manufacturer of the material to be fastened, as well as applicable building codes. General guidelines include:

- Select nails so as to avoid galvanic action between the nail and the nailed material.
- Select the nail head size according to the strength and area of the material to be held.
- In wood framing, use the correct size and number of nails to withstand stress. Procedures for calculating nailed connections can be found in the National Design Specifications for Wood Construction.
- Base your nail selection on the type(s) of wood or other materials to be assembled, joined, or connected.
- Be aware that nails with serrated or helically threaded shanks have increased holding power, but such nails are difficult to remove without destroying the surrounding material.
- Where nails are exposed to moisture or weather—for example, in exterior stucco lath—use nonferrous (aluminum) or zinc-coated nails.
- Choose nails for automatic nailing equipment specifically for the equipment used. See ANSI's *Safety Requirements for Power-Actuated Fastening Systems* and OSHA regulations.

Acceptable Practices

Many jurisdictions are enacting clean air statutes that, among other things, target organic solvents as air pollutants. Organic solvents also can have adverse affects on the workers who apply them, as well as on future building occupants. One drawback to most water-based adhesives, however, is that they tend only to resist water, whereas the solvent-based adhesives are waterproof.

Construction adhesives used for building have been formulated to tolerate many of the often-adverse conditions that exist at most job sites, such as extreme temperatures and temperature fluctuations. They are excellent for filling gaps and thus work on both smooth and rough surfaces. The degree of adhesion depends on the surface conditions of the materials: ice, dirt, grease, or other contaminants will all have a negative effect.

Performance depends on careful consideration of the physical and chemical compatibility of glue and wood, processing requirements, mechanical properties, and durability under design conditions.

Adhesives should be applied to one surface and as recommended in Figure 14.3.

Hollow Wall Anchors

Also called molly bolts or molly screws, hollow wall anchors provide a cheap, fast method for attaching heavy items. The user threads a screw, or thread-ended hook, through the hollow wall anchor, then pushes it through the gypsum board into the hollow space in the wall. The anchor is placed into the hole before driving the screw or attaching the hook.

Screw and Bolt Lengths

The bolt's clamping force causes protrusions on the washer to flatten partially, closing the gap between the washer and the bolt head. Measurement of the gap indicates whether the bolt has been tightened adequately.

High-tension, stainless steel helical inserts are held in place by spring-like pressure, and they are used to salvage damaged threads. They also eliminate thread failure due to stress.

Turnbuckles

A turnbuckle is a coupling device consisting of two eyelets or other connection points connected in screw threads. The joint in between

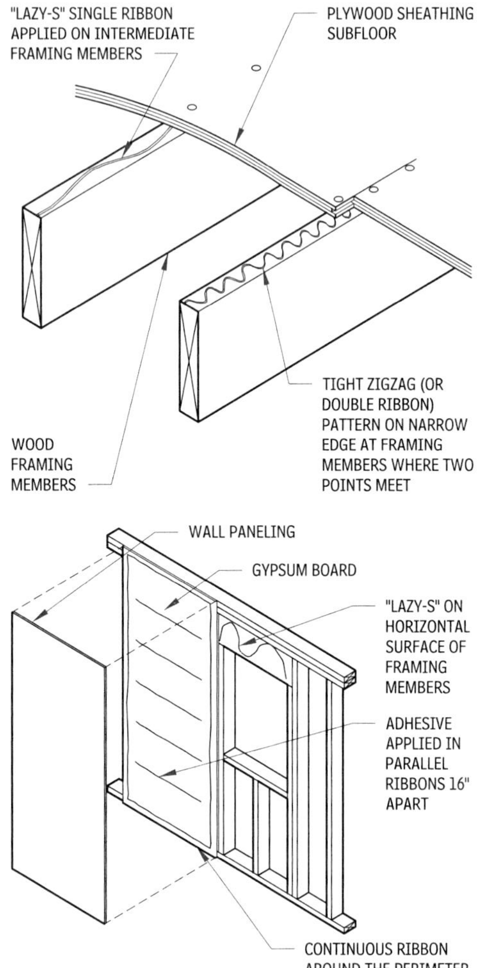

Figure 14.3 Recommended adhesive bead patterns
Source: AIA, *Architectural Graphic Standards for Residential Construction,* 2nd ed. Copyright 2010, John Wiley & Sons, Inc.

can be turned to shorten or lengthen the device with mechanical advantage provided by the screw threads.

Toggle Bolts

Toggle bolts are light-duty anchors used with machine screws. The user drives the machine screw through the hole at the center of the spring-loaded toggle bolts, which then folds for installation through a predrilled hole. Once through the hole, the wings reopen on the other side of surface.

Table 14.1 Common Nail Sizes

Length	Penny (d)	Gauge	Diameter of Head	Nails/lb
1	2	15	11/64 in.	847
1 1/4	3	14	13/64 in.	543
1 1/2	4	12 1/2	1/4 in.	296
1 3/4	5	12 1/2	1/4 in.	254
2	6	11 1/2	17/64 in.	167
2 1/4	7	11 1/2	17/64 in.	150
2 1/2	8	10 1/4	9/32 in.	101
2 3/4	9	10 1/4	9/32 in.	92.1
3	10	9	5/16 in.	66
3 1/4	12	9	5/16 in.	66.1
3 1/2	16	8	11/32 in.	47.4
4	20	6	13/32 in.	29.7
4 1/2	30	5	7/16 in.	22.7
5	40	4	15/32 in.	17.3
5 1/2	50	3	1/2 in.	13.5
6	60	2	17/32 in.	10.7

Table 14.2 Wood Screws

Wood Screw Sizes	Decimal Equivalent	Length
0	0.060	1/4 –3/8 in.
1	0.073	1/4–1/2 in.
2	0.086	1/4–3/4 in.
3	0.099	1/4–1 in.
4	0.112	1/4–1 1/2 in.
5	0.125	3/8–1 1/2 in.
6	0.138	3/8–2 1/2 in.
7	0.151	3/8–2 1/2 in.
8	0.164	3/8–3 in.
9	0.177	1/2–3 in.
10	0.190	1/2–3 1/2 in.
11	0.203	5/8–3 1/2 in.
12	0.216	5/8–4 in.
14	0.242	3/4–5 in.
16	0.268	1–5 in.
18	0.294	1 1/4–5 in.
20	0.320	1 1/2–5 in.
24	0.372	3–5 in.

Practices to Avoid

- Avoid applying adhesives on surfaces with ice, dirt, grease, or other contaminants that may cause materials not to adhere properly.
- Avoid applying adhesives made of organic solvents without properly ventilating area during and after application.

Resources

WITHIN THIS BOOK

- Chapter 15 Rough Carpentry
- Chapter 16 Finish Carpentry

REFERENCE STANDARDS

- ASTM D2898—Standard Practice for Accelerated Weathering of Fire-Retardant-Treated Wood for Fire Testing
- ASTM D3201—Standard Test Method for Hygroscopic Properties of Fire-Retardant Wood and Wood-Based Products
- ASTM E84—Standard Test Method for Surface Burning Characteristics of Building Materials
- ASTM E108—Standard Test Methods for Fire Tests of Roof Coverings *ULI Building Materials Directory* (current edition).

OTHER RESOURCES

- 2009 International Residential Code for One and Two-Family Dwellings. Washington, DC: International Code Council, Inc., 2009.
- American Institute of Architects, *Architectural Graphics Standards*, 11th ed. Hoboken, NJ: John Wiley and Sons, 2007.
- American Institute of Architects, *Architectural Graphic Standards for Residential Construction*, 2nd ed. Hoboken, NJ: John Wiley and Sons, 2010.
- American Forest and Paper Association, www.afandpa.org.
- American Wood Protection Association, www.awpa.com.

Chapter 15

Rough Carpentry

- Wood Framing
- Blocking
- Treated Wood Foundations
- Decking
- Sheathing
- Shop-Fabricated Structural Wood

Wood Framing

Description

Wood framing is the industry standard for home construction in the United States. In general, because of wood's physical properties, it can be used in load-bearing construction. Wood framing includes dimension lumber that is used for the framing of bearing and non-bearing walls, floors, ceilings, and roofs.

Dressed lumber is a term used to indicate that the lumber has been surfaced by a planing machine to a specific finished size. Most lumber used in residential construction is planed on four sides, which is indicated as "S4S" or "surfaced four sides," Industry standard has set specific sizes for dressed lumber. Lumber size is generally referred to in its nominal dimension, which is different from its actual size. Lumber that has a nominal dimension of 1 inch has an actual dimension of 3/4 inch. Lumber that has a nominal dimension of between 2 and 6 inches has an actual dimension of 1/2 inch less than the nominal dimension; therefore, a stud with a nominal dimension of 2 × 4 has an actual dimension of 1-1/2 by 3-1/2 inches. Lumber that is between 7 and 12 inches has an actual dimension of ¾ inches less than the nominal dimension. So a piece of lumber with a nominal dimension of 8 × 8 has an actual dimension of 7-1/4 × 7-1/4 inches and a piece of lumber that has a nominal dimension of 2 × 12 has an actual dimension of 1-1/2 × 11-1/4 inches.

Dressed lumber, when used as framing lumber for residential construction, should be seasoned. Seasoned framing lumber is air dried until there is a consistent moisture content of 19 percent. Lumber inherently has a lot of moisture in it. When seasoned, the lumber loses the moisture and shrinks, which makes the lumber more stable and strong.

In certain construction circumstances, and as required by code, lumber should be treated with either a wood preservative or fire-retardant treatment; refer to Chapter 14 for information regarding wood treatments.

Two common framing methods are used in residential construction: platform framing and balloon framing.

Platform framing is a system of framing for a building of wood construction several stories high, in which the studs are only one story

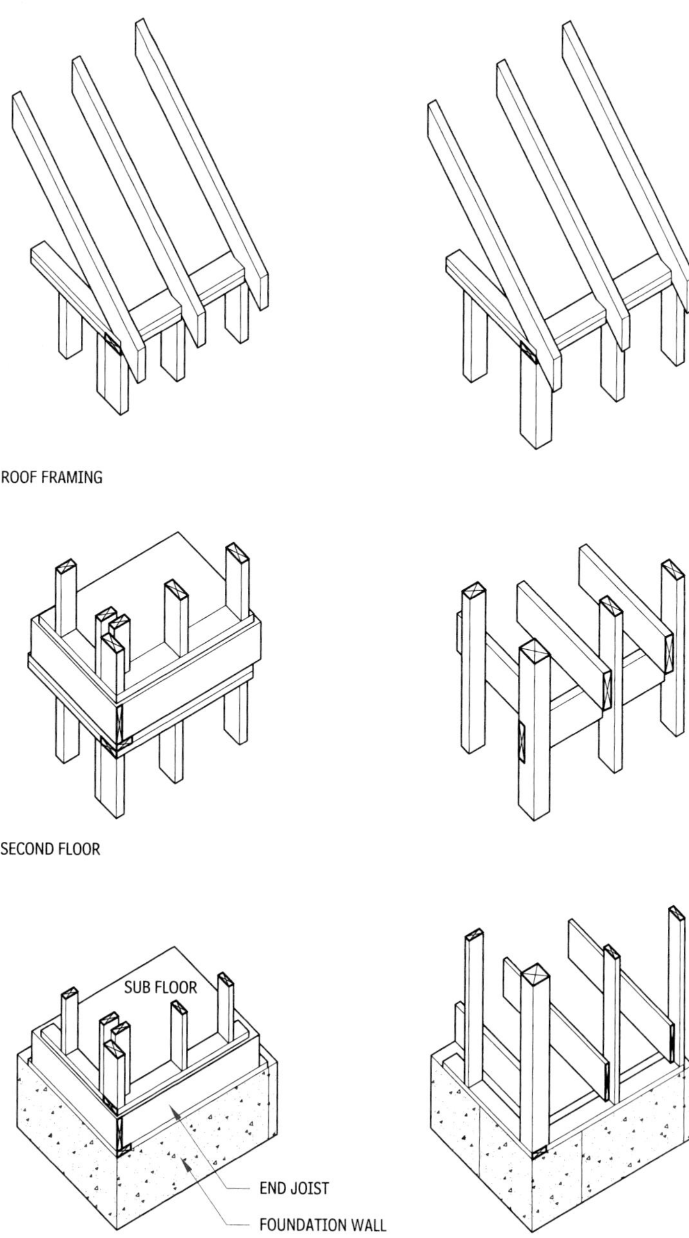

Figure 15.1 Platform framing versus balloon framing isometric
Source: Sears Brands LLC

high; the floor joists for each story rest on the top plates of the story below; the bearing walls and partitions rest on the subfloor of each story. Platform framing is also called western framing.

Balloon framing is where the exterior load-bearing wall studs are continuous from the first floor to the roof, in a multistory structure. Each floor is attached to the exterior stud with a ledger, which has been let into each stud.

Assessing Existing Conditions

When a jobsite observation calls for inspection of framing, verify the following:

- Tops of foundation walls, if concrete or concrete masonry units (CMU), should have a pressure-treated plate continuous on top of the wall. The plate should be attached to the wall with anchor bolts.
- At exterior perimeter foundation walls, floor joists should have a continuous rim joist attached to the ends of each floor joist.
- When floor spans call for an intermediate support beam and the floor joists are resting on top of that beam, then solid blocking should be place between each floor joist.
- On load-bearing walls, there are generally two top plates. The first is attached to the top of each stud, then the wall is erected and the second top plate is installed with the joints between the two plates staggered at least 24 inches.
- Typical stud spacing is 16 inches on center, maximum 24 inches on center.
- Typical ceiling joist spacing is 24 inches on center, maximum.

Acceptable Practices

- Lumber, when delivered to the job site, should be protected from the elements by keeping lumber from being stored directly on the ground. Lumber should be stored a minimum of 6 inches clear above ground. Lumber should be covered with a plastic film.
- Posts or columns in basements or crawl spaces should be supported on concrete piers or pedestals projecting at least 1 inch above concrete floors or 6 inches above exposed earth.

- Posts or columns should be protected from moisture with an impervious moisture barrier between the pier and post to prevent moisture from wicking up from the pier into the wooden post.
- Sheathing edges should rest on a framing member. If sheathing does not, then blocking should be provided between framing members at a maximum spacing of 24 inches on center.
- Solid blocking or bridging should be provided between floor joists to maintain proper alignment of upper edges of joists.
- When a floor joist frames into a girder, it is preferable to frame joists into the side of the girder to minimize overall shrinkage of girders and joists.
- Joist end-bearing should be a minimum of 1½ inches on wood or metal and 3 inches on masonry.
- When framing of floor and roof opening, the header across the opening should be doubled if the span exceeds 4 feet. Headers more than 6 feet long should be supported at the ends by joist hangers, unless bearing on a partition or beam.
- Bearing partitions should be located over girders or walls that support the floor system, unless the floor framing has been designed to support the added load. Bearing partitions may offset the supporting members by no more than the joist depth.
- When non-bearing partitions run parallel to floor joists, the joist under the partition is doubled to support the increased load.
- Cantilevered floor joists should be tied back into the main floor framing a minimum distance of twice the cantilever distance from end of cantilever to supporting wall.
- Exterior wall openings should have solid or composite headers supported by double studs when the span is over 3 feet. If the span is under 3 feet, framing anchors can replace double studs. For spans over 6 feet, triple studs should be used at each end of the header.
- Notching of floor joists is only allowed as shown in Figure 15.3.
- Where building exterior is to be stuccoed or if lap siding is applied directly to studs, exterior walls must be braced at the corners with one of the following methods:
  - 1 × 4 wood bracing at 45 degrees and fastened into each stud, plate, and header.
  - Galvanized metal straps are nailed to studs, plates, and headers per manufacturers recommendations.
  - One structural panel is applied to each wall surface with long direction of panel vertical.

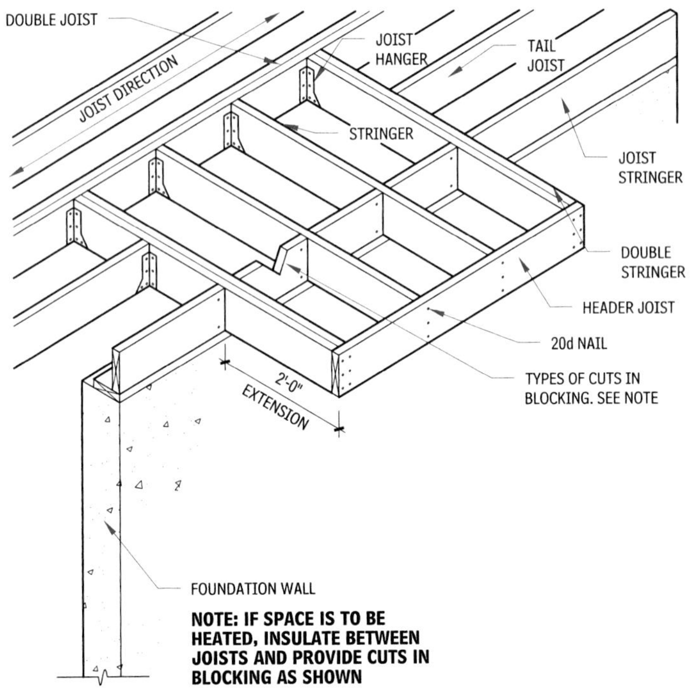

PERPENDICULAR TO JOISTS

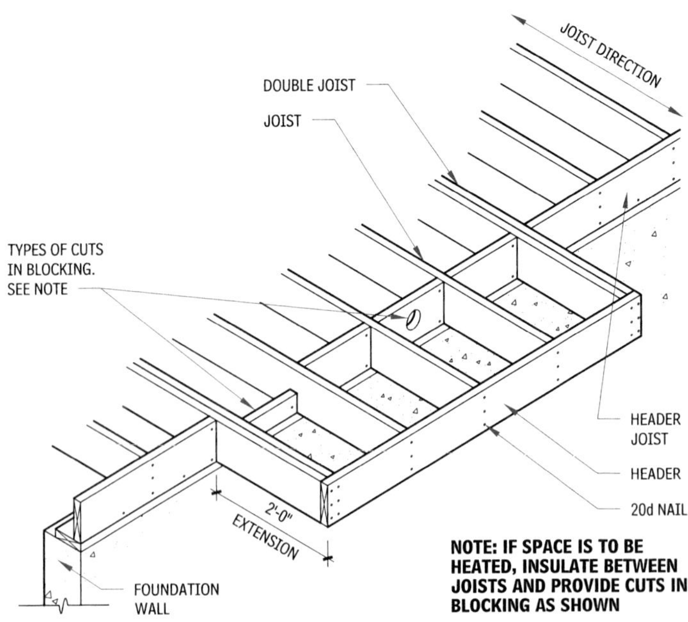

PARALLEL TO JOISTS

Figure 15.2 Cantilevered floor framing detail

Source: AIA, *Architectural Graphic Standards,* 11th ed. Copyright 2007, John Wiley & Sons, Inc.

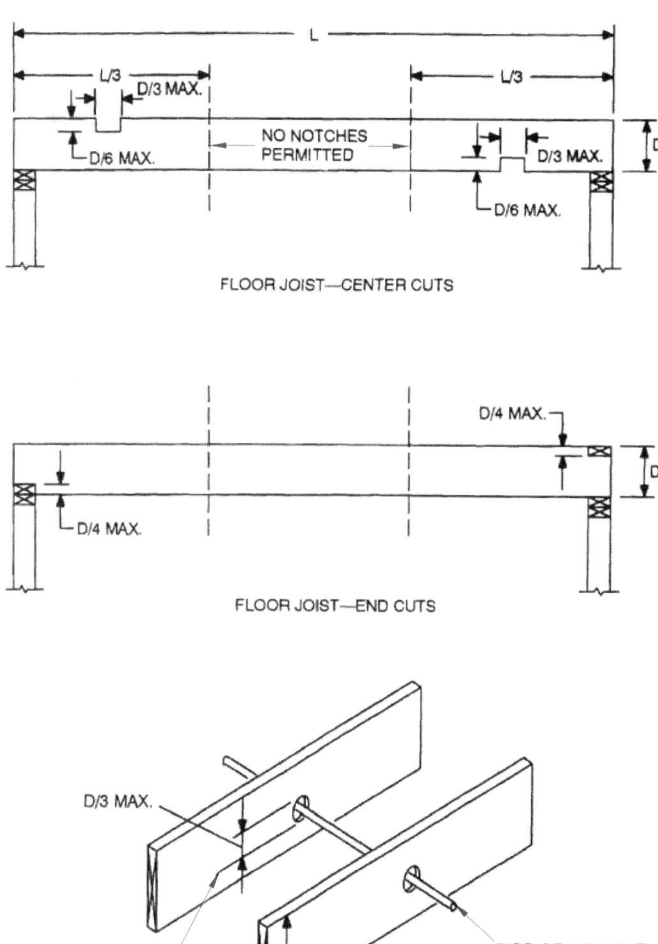

Figure 15.3 Permitted notching of beam locations

Practices to Avoid

- Do not splice structural members between supports.
- Avoid untreated lumber in contact with ground, concrete, or concrete masonry unit.
- Floor joists shall not be notched in center third of span.

Blocking

Description

Support blocking is used extensively in many areas of construction, most commonly as in-wall wood blocking. Blocking is the support material placed within or upon gypsum board or plaster walls to provide support and attachment sites required to distribute the weight load of cabinetry, woodwork, shelving, and other items that are attached to a wall surface. Items that are subject to pulling, as in a hooks or bathroom towel bars, require mechanical attachment to in-wall blocking to prevent detachment from the wall over time and use.

Traditionally 2 × 4 or 2 × 6 boards are cut to size and nailed between wood studs for in-wall blocking. If support blocking is not installed between studs prior to gypsum board installation, external blocking may be surface mounted on the wall by mechanical fastening the blocking through the gypsum board to anchor it into wall studs. Another type of blocking is called *let-in* blocking when wood studs are notched to receive the wood blocking. When light-gauge metal stud wall assemblies are used, metal blocking for support of heavy wall-hung items is installed in appropriate gauge of metal for minimum load resistance.

Once gypsum board, or any other material, covers the wall, it may be difficult to find 2 × 4 studs for attachment and the position of nails and screws must be adjusted to stud location. Properly installed support blocking at a uniform and predetermined height is easier to find and use for attaching wall hardware than studs alone.

Pressure-preservative-treated wood blocking is used in roofing construction to support fasteners for roof specialties such as copings, roof edge fascia, gravel stops, to raise roof edge slightly if needed to ensure proper water draining, and to separate materials from roofing membrane to prevent tearing. Wood nailing strips (nailers) used on roof decks must be securely and firmly attached to the deck or through to its supporting members.

Assessing Existing Conditions

- A site visit prior to gypsum board installation is recommended in order to properly assess the installation of support blocking.
- A thorough review of woodwork/carpentry locations is recommended to know where support blocking is required.
- Confirm support blocking is installed to support fixtures, equipment, casework, heavy trim, furnishings, and similar work requiring attachment to framing.
- Confirm blocking is installed at a uniform and predetermined height so that attachment sites can be found easily.
- Fire-retardant-treated materials are required for concealed blocking in roof assemblies.

Acceptable Practices

Common construction practices for support blocking include the following:

- Where carpentry may be subject to deterioration by moisture or insect attack, consider using pressure-preservative-treated blocking material.
- Blocking, shims, hanging strips, furring, and other supporting or attachment members should be both strong and dimensionally stable, kiln-dried to less than 15 percent moisture content.
- Provide blocking and attachment plates and anchors and fasteners of adequate size and number to securely anchor each component in place, accurately located and aligned with other portions of the work.
- Providing support blocking during new construction for future items that may be required, such as grab bars in bathrooms.

Practices to Avoid

- Wall hung cabinet attachment must not be done without proper support blocking.
- Care must be taken not to overtighten screws and strip them of their grip.

Treated Wood Foundations

Description

The construction of treated wood foundations is similar to the construction of standard wood light-framed walls, except that wood foundations use all pressure-treated lumber and additional design and detailing are required due to below-grade loading of the wall. In addition, wood-framed foundations require a good drainage system in order to maintain dry basements and crawl spaces. Drainage systems for wood foundations require a porous backfill material that allows water a direct path to the base of the foundation, where positive drainage carries the water away from the foundations and is collected and quickly removed by sump pump or a gravity system to a storm sewer system.

Assessing Existing Conditions

- Verify with soils engineer if soils and groundwater conditions in the construction area are suitable for a treated wood foundation.
- Soils are grouped by soil type into four categories. Groups I, II, and III are acceptable soil types to use permanent wood foundations; Group IV is unsatisfactory.
- Lumber and plywood must be graded and stamped for use in treated wood foundations, according to American Wood Preservers Association (AWPA) Standard C22.
- Wood foundations are suited to cold climates.

Acceptable Practices

- The footing and basement area consists of a layer of gravel or crushed stone, minimum 4 inches thick.
- Framing of foundations are generally 2 × pressure treated lumber. Rules of thumb suggests 42 inches of backfill 2 × 4s at 12 inches on center; with 64 inches of backfill 2 × 6s at 16 inches on center and with 84 inches of backfill 2 × 6s at 12 inches on center.

- All field-cut ends or drilled holes in lumber shall be field treated with preservative.
- Pressure-treated plywood attached to framing and joints in plywood are caulked and plywood is covered with 6-mil polyethylene film.
- 6-mil polyethylene film is placed over gravel under floor slab or pressure-treated wood-framed floor.
- Treated wood foundations require a sump and a pump, which drains water around the structure to a storm sewer system or to daylight.
- Finish grade around the foundation should be sloped a minimum of ½ inch per foot away from the structure.
- Backfill material must be free of silt, clay, and organic material. The following are size limitations on material:
  - Maximum of 1/2-inch for crushed stone
  - Maximum of 3/4-inch for gravel
  - Minimum of 1/16 inch for sand
- Permeable filter fabric can be placed around the gravel to prevent soil from washing into the drainage area.
- In rainy climates, provide for drainage inside the foundation (under the building footprint). Slope excavation to low point under the building; dig a sump where the top of the pump is below the bottom of the gravel drainage bed under the footings. Minimum depth of sump should be 24 inches deeper than the bottom of the gravel bed under footings.
- Gutters and downspouts should be designed to take water away from the foundations.
- Porches or patios should be sloped away from the building.

Practices to Avoid

- Using wood foundations in wet soil or areas with high water tables.
- Do not backfill against walls below grade until the basement floor is poured (if applicable) and main floor has been framed and sheathed.

Decking

Description

The finished surface of an exterior deck generally consists of either 2 × 4 or 2 × 6 planks of random lengths.

The 2 × lumber can be cedar, redwood, mahogany, pine, or an exotic wood such as Ipe or Meranti. Pressure-treated lumber can also be used as a finished surface for exterior decks, and in many cases is used for the deck structure. Cedar and redwood are probably the most common woods used for exterior decks because of their natural ability to resist decay and their availability. These woods need be maintained yearly with a sealer or protectant to maintain the color or the wood and protect the wood from water damage. Mahogany is harder than cedar or redwood and has a pleasing and regular grain pattern. Exotic woods such as Ipe and Meranti are very hard and strong woods, but can be difficult to work with. These woods are very dense so consequently they will not accept sealers or a protectant.

Pressure-treated wood typically comes incised but for a slight additional cost can be obtained without incising for a better appearance. Regular pressure-treated lumber should be used for the deck structure if that structure is located within 12 to 18 inches of the ground or if concealed from view.

Assessing Existing Conditions

- Ledger board attached to the house should have galvanized metal flashing between sheathing and ledger board and "Z" flashing over the top of the ledger.
- Ledger board should be located so that the minimum distance between the finish deck surface and the finish floor of the home is no less than 1 inch.
- The International Residential Code (IRC R502.2.2) requires that a deck have a minimum of two hold-down tension devices that support lateral loads. The hold-down devices must have an allowable stress capacity of not less than 1,500 pounds.

Acceptable Practices

- Where decks use the house for support, footings should be below the frost line.
- Pressure-treated lumber: fasteners should be galvanized unless in a salt environment such as near the ocean, where Type 304 or 316 stainless-steel fasteners should be used.
- Beams supported by posts shall have a minimum of 1-1/2 inch direct bearing on support posts.
- Joists supporting decking should be spaced at a maximum of 16 inches on center. Twelve inches on center will increase the stiffness of the overall deck.
- Joists should have crown side up.
- Any large knots should be on the top of the joist, where the joist is in compression when loads are applied.
- To increase deck rigidity, double-up rim joist and add solid blocking at 1/3 points of span. This also makes attaching a perimeter guardrail stiffer.
- If deck is not attached to the house, sway bracing should be added to prevent racking of deck structure. Sway bracing can be accomplished with a long galvanized steel strap placed diagonally across the deck structure prior to installing the decking. An option would be to install the decking at a 45-degree angle to the deck joists. Or, if there is enough room under the deck structure, add diagonal bracing from support post to beams and joists, refer to Figure 15.4
- Distance between decking boards will vary, depending on the type of decking being used. For wood decking, 1/8 to 1/4-inch gap is common. For composite decking, follow the manufacturer's recommendations for spacing between decking boards.
- There are three ways to fasten deck boards: nails, screws, or hidden fasteners. Nails are the quickest way to secure decking to structure, but nails tend to pull out as the deck dries and shrinks, and then the decking begins to squeak. Screws come in a variety of colors and styles. Trim-head screws work well, but can create small cracks in the wood due to the screw splitting the wood when installed. Hidden fasteners will eliminate damaging the top of the deck board with a nail of screw. Hidden fasteners are attached to the sides of the decking board, either in a channel milled into the side of the deck board or a groove for a hidden metal biscuit in which a screw or nail is used to attach to hidden fastener to the deck structure.

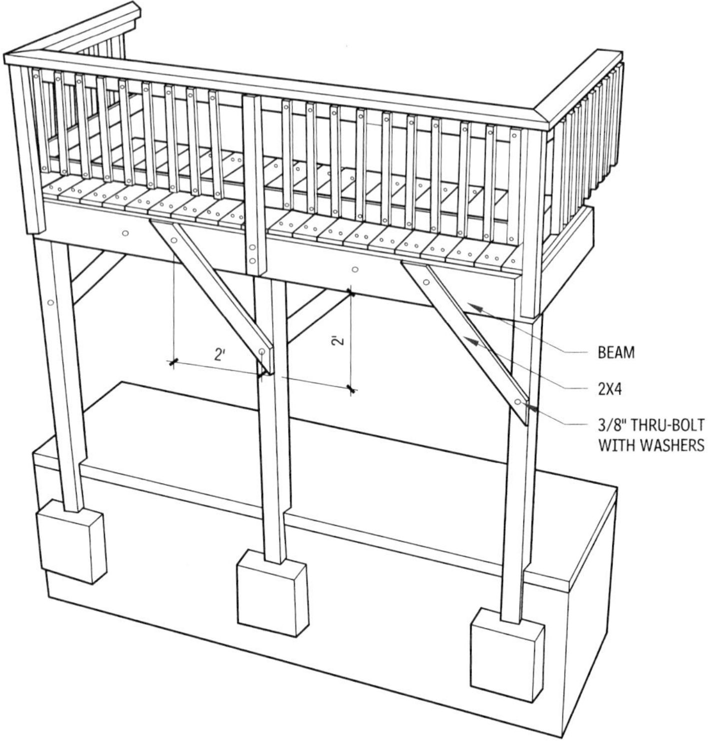

Figure 15.4 Diagonal bracing under deck

Practices to Avoid

- Do not use aluminum fasteners or aluminum framing connectors with pressure-treated lumber.
- Never install a ledger board to the primary structure over the exterior siding. Remove siding and attach ledger board directly to sheathing and rim joist behind sheathing.
- Ledger board cannot be attached to brick veneer. Best practice is for the deck to be freestanding.

Sheathing

Description

Sheathing is used in wall, roof, and flooring applications. Grades of sheathing must be identified as compatible with the type of use intended prior to sheathing installation.

Wall Sheathing

Wall sheathing is part of the home's outer shell and encloses the home as the first material installed as part of the exterior enclosure. It strengthens the walls and is part of the drainage plane. Two materials commonly used for wall sheathing in residential construction are 1/2-inch plywood and 1/2-inch oriented strand board (OSB). Wall sheathing should be wrapped with a weather barrier of building paper or "house wrap" to create a continuous drainage plane.

Gypsum sheathing is available but not commonly used in residential construction, unless required by local authorities having jurisdiction for firewall requirements.

Roof Sheathing

Roof sheathing panels should be installed according to the recommendations of the APA-Engineered Wood Association and local building codes. Typically, 15/32-inch or thicker panels are required in high-wind areas. OSB or plywood can be used although plywood will provide higher nail-head pull-through resistance.

Insufficient fastening can lead to total building failure in a windstorm. Fastener spacing and size requirements for coastal construction are typically different than for noncoastal areas. The highest uplift forces occur at roof corners, edges, and ridgelines. Improved fasteners such as shank nails increase the uplift resistance of roof sheathing.

Composite Nail Base Insulated Roof Sheathing

This type of sheathing has OSB laminated to one face with rigid, cellular polyisocyanurate foam insulation bonded to it, and is also available in a vented product that has spacers made of wood furring strips or blocks adhered to one face. This type of roof sheathing may be needed when ceilings are vaulted or when R-value is desired for colder climates, or in a re-roofing application on a low-slope roof.

Weather Barriers

A house is always vulnerable to the effects of wind, weather, and moisture, particularly when it is exposed during the construction process. If allowed in, moisture can have a devastating effect on many of its internal systems, plus it can lead to mold and mildew issues. A weather barrier of building paper or "house wrap" is an external barrier to protect wall cavities, resist moisture, and reduce air turnover during and after construction. For more information, refer to Chapter 18, "Thermal Protection and Weather Barriers."

Subflooring

Subflooring products used in a house built with a crawl space differ from subflooring used in a house built on a concrete slab. Subflooring panels may be made of plywood, OSB, MDF board, cement board, or masonite-type products. Depending on finished floor material, subflooring panels may be used as the substrate for the flooring material or may be required as a substrate for a floor underlayment, over which the finished floor material is installed.

Subfloor/underlayment combination products (e.g., Sturd-I-Floor) are engineered wood structural panels and may be used, depending on span requirements.

For houses built on a concrete slab, subflooring must be attached to furring strips laid over a vapor barrier to prohibit moisture from the concrete slab coming up through to the finished flooring. Check flooring manufacturer's installation instructions for recommended subfloors and installation methods, since product requirements vary.

Floor Underlayment

Floor underlayment is crucial to the success of the flooring on top of it. Many finished flooring materials require a super-smooth surface underneath them. Without smooth and solid subflooring, the finished floor can fail in a short amount of time. Most finish flooring products have specific recommendations with respect to the type of subfloor the finished flooring material is placed upon.

Cementitious backer panels are typically used as underlayment for ceramic tile and similar materials in a wet environment, such as showers. Because they do not deteriorate when they get wet, they are considered water resistant and are often used as wall sheathing. However, they do not prevent water from penetrating them and affecting materials behind them. For this reason, a water-resistive barrier should be applied either over or directly behind the backer panel if used as sheathing.

Acoustical floor underlayments provide solutions where noise control is a concern. With the trend of installing more engineered hardwood, laminate, and ceramic tile floors instead of carpeting, noise problems are becoming more common. There are many different types of acoustical floor underlayments, including rubber based and wood fiber (cork) and the type used should be in accordance with the finished flooring manufacturer's recommendations.

Roof Underlayment

Roofing underlayment was originally used for temporary protection against the elements, but is now an integral part of a home's overall roof system. Underlayment provides a vital second layer of protection on top of the sheathing to help keep moisture out. It is necessary for roofing manufacturer's warranties and building codes require it to meet standards for fire resistance, wind uplift resistance, puncture resistance, and resistance to wind-driven rain.

The choice of one underlayment over another depends on a number of conditions, including its application, whether it will be used on a steep or low-slope roof, the fire code requirements in place, and in what region the structure is located. Underlayments fall under three basic categories: felts, synthetics, and self-adhering ice-and-water barriers. Check roofing manufacturer's installation instructions for recommended type of underlayment with roofing material.

Structural Sheathing Panels

Wood structural panels include plywood, mat-formed (nonveneer) panels such as OSB and composite panels, which are veneer-faced panels with mat-formed cores. Structural panel grades are generally identified in terms of the veneer grade used on the face and back of the panel (e.g., A-B, B-C, etc.), or rated by a name suggesting the panel's intended end use (e.g., APA-rated sheathing, APA-rated Sturd-I-Floor, etc.). Analysis is done by a qualified structural engineer during design of the house to ensure load requirements are met according to the *APA Span Ratings* provided by the APA, The Engineered Wood Association.

Table 15.1 APA Sturd-I-Wall Construction Recommendations (Siding Direct to Studs and over Nonstructural Sheathing)

Panel Siding Description (All Species Groups)	Nominal Thickness or Span Rating (in.)	Max. Stud spacing (in.)		Nail Size (Use Nonstaining Box, Siding, or Casing Nails)[a,b]	Nail Spacing (in.)	
		Face Grain: Vertical	Face Grain: Horizontal		Panel Edges	Intermediate
APA MDO EXT	11/32 and 3/8	16	24	6d for panels 1/2" thick or less; 8d for thicker panels	6	12
	1/2 and thicker	24	24			
APA-rated siding EXT	16 o.c.	16	24			
APA-rated siding EXT	24 o.c.	24	24			

[a]Verify fasteners when used over foam insulation
[b]Hot dipped galvanized steel nails are recommended for most siding applications.

Assessing Existing Conditions

In order to ensure the proper installation of sheathing, a site visit prior to installation of the exterior finish materials (i.e., siding, brick veneer, or roofing) is required to assess the following conditions:

- Code requirements may differ; therefore, governing codes should be checked prior to site visit.
- Confirm sheathing inspection has previously been passed.
- Determine from the grade mark that sheathing material is designated for the use in which it is installed.
- Determine if sheathing panels meet required thickness, panel span ratings, and nails/fasteners in accordance with International Residential Code tables.
- Confirm wall sheathing horizontal joints are properly flashed before weather barrier is installed.

Acceptable Practices

Ensure plywood or OSB sheathing is stamped EXPOSURE 1. This labeling is a guarantee that waterproof resins and glues were used to bond together the wood. EXPOSURE 1 plywood and OSB are made to withstand repeated rainfall with little or no damage during a normal time frame construction project. To prevent rot and loss of strength, these materials must be allowed to dry and then have permanent protection from moisture. If plywood or OSB that can be permanently exposed to weather and rain is required, purchase products bearing the EXTERIOR stamp or label.

Some OSB panels react differently from plywood if allowed to get wet. When OSB is manufactured, the cut edges are sealed with a special waterproof paint. Carpenters destroy the watertight integrity of OSB each time they make a cut that exposes wood fiber edges. These cut edges are prone to swelling once wet. It is possible to seal these edges once cut, but this may not be done typically since it requires extra time and effort for workers to perform this extra step.

Many flooring problems happen in houses built over crawl spaces. All too often, an underlayment will buckle or warp because of water vapor that escapes from the soil beneath the crawl space and then permeates the subfloor and underlayment. To avoid this issue, cover the soil with a high-performance vapor barrier before installing any underlayment or finished flooring material.

Ensure that existing wood subfloors are dry before installing an underlayment. The moisture content of a wood subfloor should not exceed 15 percent. Use a moisture meter to test for moisture content. Be sure that fasteners used to install the underlayment are driven correctly. The top of the fastener should be flush with the top of the underlayment or slightly below the surface.

Practices to Avoid

- Common mistakes when installing roof sheathing include using the wrong size fasteners, missing the framing members when installing fasteners, overdriving nails, and using too many or too few fasteners.
- Be careful to stagger the seams of roof sheathing.
- Align roof sheathing with edge of roof rather than perpendicular to rafters.

- Attach roof sheathing wrong side up.
- *To avoid resilient floor covering failures* caused by moisture problems from concrete slabs, subsurface-water migration through concrete slabs-on-grade must be eliminated and moisture-vapor transmission through concrete slabs must be minimized.

Shop-Fabricated Structural Wood

Description

Shop-fabricated structural wood consists of laminated veneer lumber (LVL), wood I-joists, shop-fabricated wood trusses and glued-laminated wood beams.

Laminated veneer lumber (LVL) uses multiple lays of thin wood held together with adhesive and with the addition of heat and pressure forms factory fabricated lumber that is stronger, straighter, and more uniform than conventional lumber and has less tendency to warp, twist, bow, or shrink because of its composite nature. LVL is typically used for headers, beams, rimboards, and edge-forming material.

Wood I-joists are engineered composite beam that is made up of a top and bottom flange fabricated with LVL and a vertical web made from LVL, plywood, or oriented strand board. The advantage of these types of beams is that they can span longer distances and don't shrink or twist like conventional lumber.

Shop-fabricated wood trusses are fabricated from a series of pieces of dimension lumber connected together with metal plates. A truss consists of a top and bottom chord, with intermediate webs creating triangular shapes that gives the truss its strength. Trusses can take many shapes, depending on the design requirements of the project.

Glue-laminated beams are beams composed of a series lumber called laminating stock, joined together using adhesive and pressure to form the finished beam. To obtain the desired length required for beams the ends of laminating stock is joined together using a finger or scarf joints. Joints in individual laminations are offset to maintain beam strength. Generally, laminating stock is 1-1/2 inches thick, unless the beam is designed with a sharp curve, then 3/4-inch laminating stock is used. Glue-laminated beams are available in four different grades: premium grade, architectural grade, industrial grade and framing grade.

- *Premium grade* is the highest grade and requires all knotholes and voids to be filled either with wood-tone filler or clear wood inserts of similar grain and color.

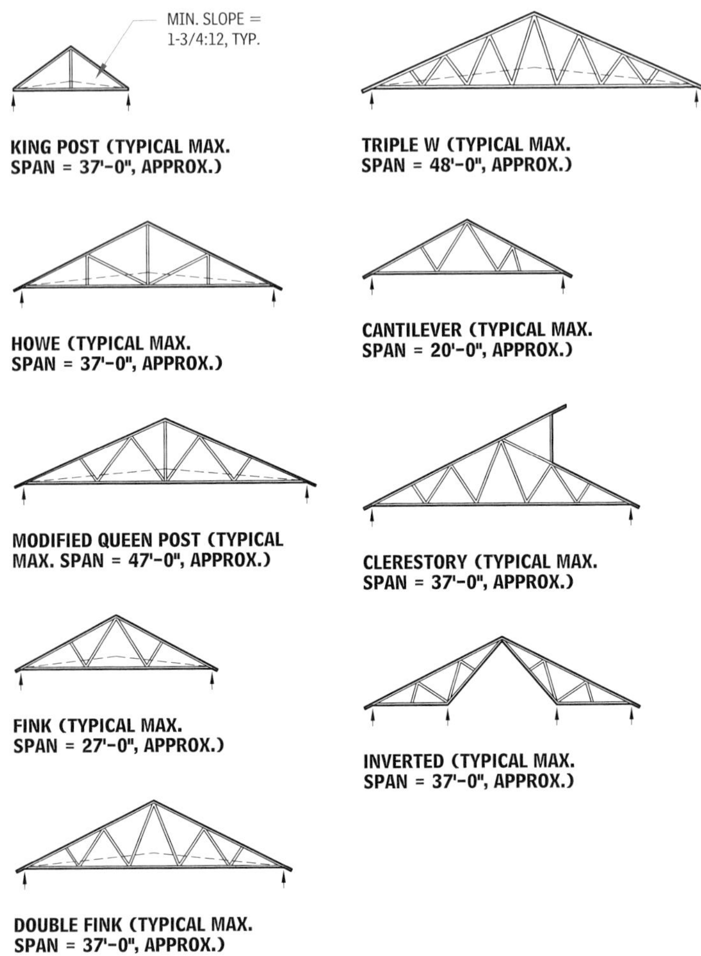

Figure 15.5a Common pitch chord roof trusses

Source: AIA, *Architectural Graphic Standards for Residential Construction*, 2nd ed. Copyright 2010, John Wiley and Sons, Inc.

- *Architectural grade* requires knotholes and voids greater than 3/4-inch wide to be filled with wood-tone filler or clear wood inserts of similar grain and color.
- *Industrial grade* only requires knotholes on the wide face of the beam to be filled.
- *Framing grade* only requires removal of any projections from the wide face of the beam that would make the beam wider that the nominal size. No knotholes are required to be filled.

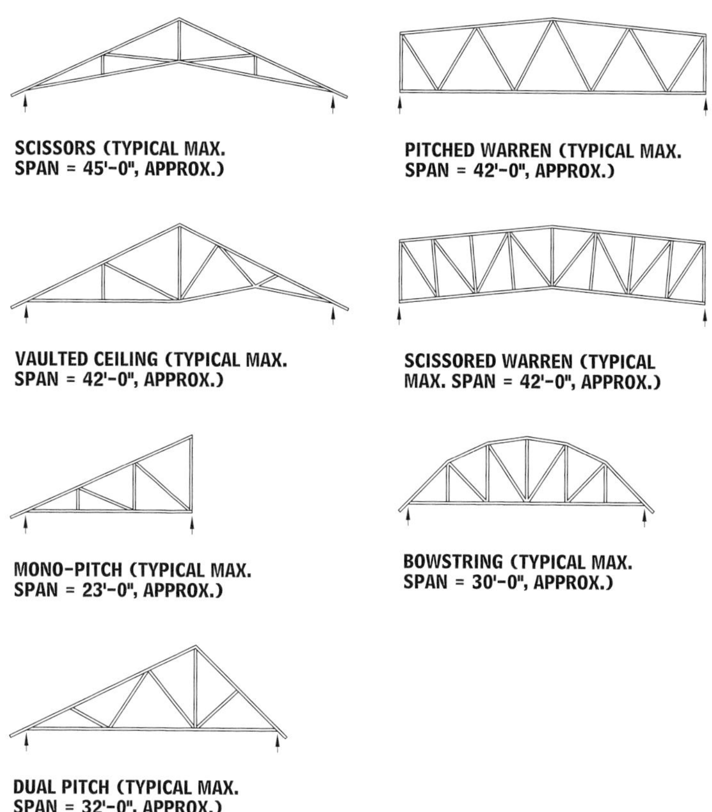

Figure 15.5b Common pitch chord roof trusses

Source: AIA, *Architectural Graphic Standards for Residential Construction*, 2nd ed. Copyright 2010, John Wiley and Sons, Inc.

Acceptable Practices

Wood I-joists:

- Web stiffeners should be placed on both sides of I-joists at locations where a concentrated load will be applied to the I-joist or at the end bearing condition. There should be a 1/8-inch gap between the bottom of the top chord and the top of the web stiffener.
- Load-bearing walls shall align above and below I-joist framing.
- Minimum bearing lengths are 1-3/4 inch for end bearing and 3-1/2 inch for intermediate bearing.
- Ends of I-joists should be restrained either by rim joist or approved blocking.

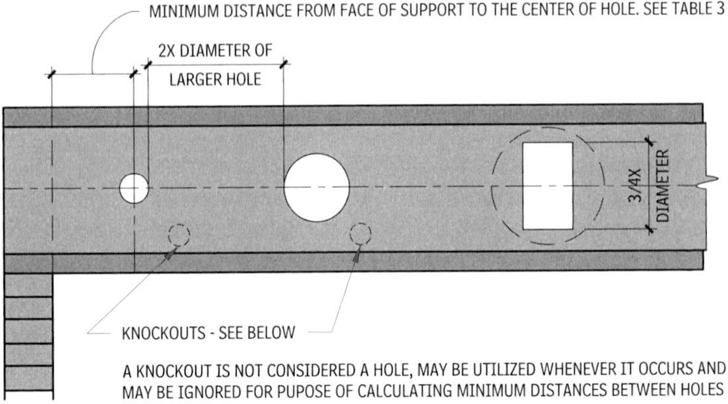

Figure 15.6 I-joists field-cut hole locator
Source: Norbord

- I-joists can be cantilevered to a maximum of 24 inches beyond the bearing wall either by extending the I-joist and attaching a full height plywood stiffener to one or both sides of the joist or by extending the joist and placing a minimum 6-foot-long I-joist next to it. The space between the two webs of the joists must have a filler block between the two joists. Cantilevered joists must be blocked with I-joists at bearing wall.
- Web stiffeners are required at joist hangers that do not laterally support the top flange of the I-joist.

Shop-fabricated wood trusses:

- Shop-fabricated wood trusses must be adequately brace to hold in place until sheathing is installed. Manufacturer's instructions contain requirements for temporary bracing of trusses.
- Non–loadbearing walls should not carry any truss load.
- Permanent lateral bracing must be installed per the truss manufacturer's approved design drawings.
- Trusses 20 feet or less in length may be picked up using a single pick-up point.
- Trusses up to 30 feet in length should be lifted using a cable sling and two pick up points. The pick-up points should be at least half the truss length apart. The angle on the cable sling should be 60 degrees or less.
- Trusses 30 to 60 feet in length should be lifted with a spreader bar and short, cable slings. Cable slings should be "toed-in" to prevent trusses from folding during the lift.
- Trusses over 60 feet in length should be lifted with a strongback that is two-thirds to three-fourths the length of the truss.

Glue-laminated beams:

- Beams that are expected to have a moisture content that remains above 20 percent or are exposed to the elements should be pressure treated.
- Beams should be specified with wet-use adhesive.
- Horizontal holes:
  - Minimum of 4-hole diameters from the top or bottom of beam.
  - Minimum 8-hole diameters from the end of the beam.
  - Maximum hole size 1-1/2 inch diameter or a diameter equal to 1/10 the beam depth, whichever is smaller.
  - Maximum number of holes: 1 hole for each 5 feet of length.
  - Spacing between holes: 8-hole diameters, based on the largest hole.

Practices to Avoid

LVL lumber:

- LVL should not be left exposed to weather.

I-joists:

- Dimension lumber may not be used as rimboard when I-joist is used for floor framing because of shrinkage of dimension lumber.
- I-joists should not be left exposed to weather.
- Notching of I-joists: never notch or cut and remove a top of bottom flange.

Shop-fabricated wood trusses:

- Do not cut, drill into, or damage chords or webs of trusses.
- Do not remove webs for any reason.
- Field repairs should not be made to trusses unless approved by truss manufacturer prior to repair.
- Do not overload a single or group of trusses with building materials or tools.

Resources

WITHIN THIS BOOK

- Chapter 14 Common Work Results for Wood, Plastics and Composites
- Chapter 16 Finish Carpentry

OTHER RESOURCES

- 2009 International Residential Code for One and Two-Family Dwellings. Washington, DC: International Code Council, Inc., 2009.
- American Institute of Architects, *Architectural Graphics Standards*, 11th ed. Hoboken, NJ: John Wiley and Sons, 2007.
- American Institute of Architects, *Architectural Graphic Standards for Residential Construction*, 2nd ed. Hoboken, NJ: John Wiley and Sons, 2010.
- APA—The Engineered Wood Association, www.apawood.org.
- American Institute of Timber Construction (AITC), www.aitc-glulam.org.
- American Wood Council, www.awc.org.
- American Wood Protection Association, www.awpa.com.

Finish Carpentry

Cabinets and Countertops

Description

The Architectural Woodwork Standards: Edition 1 classifies cabinets and countertops into three general categories: Economy grade, Custom grade and Premium grade. These different grades establish finish quality, the quality of materials to be used, and the type of joinery to be used. Cabinets are broken down into basic components, called *surfaces*. The surfaces are as follows:

Exposed surfaces are considered all exterior surfaces exposed to view with cabinet door and drawers closed:

- All surfaces visible when doors and drawers are closed, including knee spaces
- Bottoms of upper cabinets that are over 42 inches above the finished floor
- Cabinet tops that are less than 80 inches above finished floor
- Cabinet tops that are more than 80 inches above finish floor if visible from an upper floor

Exposed interior surfaces are interior surfaces exposed to view in open casework or behind transparent doors:

- Shelving, including edgebanding
- Divisions within the casework
- Interior face of door and drawer fronts
- Interior faces of ends, backs, and bottoms of fabricated elements within open cabinets or elements behind transparent doors, which would include pull-outs
- Top surfaces of fabricated elements that are 36 inches or more above finished floor

Semiexposed surfaces are interior surfaces only exposed when door or drawers are opened.

Concealed surfaces are exterior or interior surfaces that are covered or not normally exposed to view.

- Flat tops of cabinets over 80 inches high, or below a finished floor; unless visible from upper floor
- Toe spaces, unless specified otherwise

There are four common cabinet designs and two different fabrication methods for constructing cabinets. All four cabinet designs can be constructed using either of the fabrication methods. Fabrication of the cabinet body can include the cabinet body, overlaid with a face frame, or the cabinet body with no face frame. The four cabinet designs include flush overlay, reveal overlay, lipped, and flush inset. Cabinets can have three different door styles, flat panel stile and rail, raised panel stile and rail, and flat slab doors.

Countertops come in various forms. The most common countertop is a plastic laminate countertop. Other types of countertops include solid stone, solid surface, tile, and wood.

Plastic-laminate countertops are fabricated using either a particleboard core or a plywood core. Plywood cores should be exterior-grade plywood, with exterior glue, and are used around sink areas and wet areas. Plywood cores are fabricated using a 3/4-inch core with a 3/4-inch drop edge, which gives the appearance that the countertop is 1-1/2 inches thick. Particleboard cores are used all other locations and can be fabricated similarly to the plywood core with the drop edge, or they can be fabricated from a monolithic core that is 1½ inches thick for the depth of the countertop. All Premium- and Custom-grade plastic-laminate countertops should have a low-grade plastic-laminate backer sheet on the opposite side of the core material. For Economy-grade countertops this is not required. The purpose of the backer sheet is to balance out the plastic laminate on the exposed surface of the countertop to prevent warp or twist of the countertop core.

Solid stone and solid surface countertops generally do not require any backer material, unless the stone or solid surface material is cantilevered. Then manufacturers require support of the countertop material, either in the form of plywood, particleboard, or decorative brackets to support the material. Solid surface and stone materials are tooled on the exposed edges by easing the edge or rounding the edge with a router and bit, and then polished to the desired finish.

Tile countertops can be fabricated in three different ways, according to the *Handbook for Ceramic Tile Installation*; TCNA systems C511, C512, and C513. The first system is more traditional. It uses a wood or plywood base on top of the cabinet, to which metal lath is attached. A mortar bed is placed on top of the lath to form a setting bed to which a bond coat of cement paste is used to attach the tile to the mortar bed. The second system uses latex cement mortar or epoxy adhesive over a bonded waterproof membrane to attach tile to two layers of plywood that are attached to the top of the cabinetry. The last system attaches a sheet of plywood and a sheet of cement backer board on top of the cabinet. A bonded waterproof membrane is applied over the top of the cement backer board, to which the tile is thin set to the membrane. Tile countertops are a field-installed countertop.

There are two forms of wood countertops. The first is similar to a butcher-block style top that uses solid wood strips face glued together, usually parallel to the length of the countertop to form the counter surface. The other wood countertop is edge-glued solid wood strips running parallel to the length of the countertop.

Assessing Existing Conditions

In order to ensure that cabinets are fabricated and installed to the desired standard. Verify the following:

Cabinet Finish

Transparent finish wood for exposed surfaces:

- Lumber products must be well matched for grain and color. Lumber cut; plain sawn.
- Premium quality:
  - Panel products can be fabricated with either particleboard or fiberboard cores.
  - Minimum "A" grade per the Hardwood Plywood and Veneer Association (HPVA).
  - Grain shall be well matched for pattern and color.

    Veneer cut: Plain sliced with veneers on any one panel book matched and balanced match.

    Grain pattern shall be well matched across multiple cabinet faces in each room. On Premium-quality cabinetry, cathedral grain shall have the crown pointing up and run the same direction for the entire project.
  - Custom quality: Panel products can be fabricated with either particleboard or fiberboard cores. Veneers shall be as specified by design professional, minimum "A" grade per the Hardwood Plywood and Veneer Association (HPVA), compatible in color and grain.
  - Use one species for the entire project.
  - The use of rotary cut veneers is prohibited.

Transparent finish for other surfaces:

- Interior exposed surfaces for Premium quality: Same lumber and panel species as for exposed surfaces. Veneers shall be minimum "A"

grade per the Hardwood Plywood and Veneer Association (HPVA), well matched for grain pattern and color.
- Interior exposed surfaces for Custom quality: Same lumber and panel species as for exposed surfaces. Veneers shall be minimum "B" grade per the Hardwood Plywood and Veneer Association (HPVA).
- Semiexposed surfaces:
  - Use lumber and panel products that are compatible with products used for exposed surfaces and well matched for grain and color.
  - Vinyl overlay is acceptable for cabinet backs and drawer bottoms, if matched in color to other semiexposed materials.

Opaque finish for all surfaces:

- Premium quality: Use only medium density fiberboard or medium density overlay plywood as substrate.
- Custom quality: Use medium density fiberboard or medium density overlay plywood, close-grain hardwood plywood or solid stock as substrate.

Cabinet Body Construction—Wood Casework:

- Assembly clearances and tolerances flush overlay construction—exposed surfaces.
- Between two doors, 1/8 inch with a maximum variance of $\pm 1/32$ inch.
- Between a door and cabinet edge, 1/16 inch with a maximum variance of $\pm 1/32$ inch.
- Assembly clearances and tolerances inset construction—exposed surfaces.
- Between two doors or between door and face frame, 1/8 inch with a maximum variance of $\pm 1/32$ inch.
- Wood filler not allowed.

Cabinet Joinery

- Cabinet members to be securely fastened together, all joints securely glued.
- Exposed surfaces may not be fastened with staples, screws or T-nails.
- Exposed fasteners shall be plated; black oxide finish is not permitted.

Edgebanding—Transparent Finish

- Exposed edges of Economy grade cabinetry shall be filled and sanded.
- All panel products shall be edge banded.
- Shall be flush with adjacent surface.

- Shall run parallel to the long direction of the edge regardless of grain direction.
- Doors and drawer fronts fabricated from panel products shall be edgebanded on all 4 edges matching exposed face.
- False fronts shall be edgebanded on all four edges matching false front finish.
- Door and drawer front edges showing more than 1/4 inch on the face shall be mitered.
- Bottom edge of upper cabinets shall have edgebanding.
- Top edge of upper cabinets shall have edgebanding, where visible from above.
- Edgebanding shall match exposed surface, where not visible from above fabricators option for edgebanding used.

Edgebanding—Opaque Finish

- Edges of Economy and Custom grade cabinetry can have voids filled and sanded.
- Edges of Economy and Custom grade cabinetry fabricated from medium density fiberboard shall not be edgebanded.
- Premium-grade cabinetry shall be fabricated of medium-density fiberboard shall be edgebanded.

Face Frames

- Face frames shall be securely glued to cabinet bodies; Economy and Custom-grade cabinetry may be face nailed. However, face nailing is not allowed for Premium grade.
- Minimum 3/4-inch-thick solid stock only. Grain shall run horizontally for stiles and vertically for rails.
- Joints shall be one of the following: doweled, mortise and tenoned, screw, or biscuit-joined.
- Exposed corners of Premium-grade cabinetry shall be shoulder-mitered, lock-mitered, spline-mitered, or mitered with a biscuit joint.
- Minimum size of top and bottom face frame members shall be 3/4 inch for Custom- and Premium-grade cabinetry. For Economy grade, minimum 1/2 inch.
- When using flush inset doors, a bottom face frame member is required in Premium grade. For Economy and Custom grade, it is manufacturer's option.
- Bottom edges of aprons shall be smoothly sanded with edges eased. If apron is a panel product, then bottom edge shall be edgebanded.

- End panels shall be minimum 3/4 inch thick. Exposed ends shall have backs and horizontal members rabbeted or plowed into ends.
- Countertops shall extend over the top of end panels.

Cabinet Backs

- Shall be minimum 1/4 inch thick and shall be fabricated of the same material as semiexposed surfaces.
- If back is exposed, must be a minimum of 1/2 inch thick.
- If back is surface mounted to back of cabinet body, is must be screwed to case body, divisions and fixed shelves at a minimum of 4 inches on center; backs are not required to be glued.
- If back is plowed in, it must have a minimum 3/8-inch shoulder and shall be nailed or stapled to case body a maximum 4 inches on center; backs are not required to be glued.
- Stretchers across tops of base cabinets can be solid wood or plywood. They must be a minimum of 3/4 inch thick and 2 inches wide and run across the front and back of base cabinet, except at sink cabinets, which can run front to back. If stretchers are particleboard or MDF they must be at least 3/4-inch thick and 3-1/2 inches wide.
- Wall-hung cabinet bottoms shall be minimum 3/4-inch material and shall be secured to ends, divisions, and back. Wall-hung cabinets shall not exceed 48 inches wide when unsupported. Bottoms shall be of uniform thickness across an elevation, unless concealed behind a face frame.

Cabinet Toe Base

- May be a separate base or integral with cabinet body at fabricator option.
- Shall be minimum 4 inches high and 3/4 inch thick.
- Levelers may be used at manufacturer's option.
- Leveler quantity: Cabinets over 15-1/2 inches deep require four levelers for cabinets up to 37-1/2 inches wide; six levelers for cabinets up to 48 inches wide. Cabinets less than 15-1/2 inches deep require two levelers for cabinets up to 37-1/2 inches wide; three levelers for cabinets up to 48 inches wide.

Shelves—General

- Shelf core shall be minimum 3/4 inch thick.
- Grain or directional pattern shall run the length of the shelf.
- Shelves shall be uniform in thickness across an elevation.

Table 16.1 Minimum Nominal Thickness and Material for Cabinet Components

Components	Materials	Min. Nominal Thickness
Body members (ends, divisions, bottoms, tops)	Panel product	¾ in.
Face frames, rails	Lumber or panel product	¾ in.
Shelves[1]	Lumber	¾ in. for spans up to 36 in.
		1¹⁄₁₆ in. for spans up to 48 in.
	Veneer core plywood	¾ in. for spans up to 36 in.
		1 in. for spans up to 48 in.
	Medium density particleboard or fiberboard	¾ in. for spans up to 32 in.
		1 in. for spans up to 42 in.
Backs	Panel product	¼ in.
Mounting or hanger strips	Lumber or panel product	½ in.
Drawer sides, backs, subfronts	Lumber or panel product	½ in.
Drawer bottoms	Panel product	¼ in.
Drawer fronts	Lumber or panel product	¾ in.
Stile and rail cabinet doors and drawers[2]	Lumber	¾ in.
Frames for glass doors[3]	Lumber	¾ in.
Frameless glass doors	Frameless glass	¼ in.
Flush cabinet doors and drawer fronts[4]	Medium density particleboard or fiberboard	¾ in. up to 30 in. wide by 80 in. high

[1] Consult a woodworking professional for shelf specifications to carry anticipated loads.
[2] Give special consideration to building very wide and/or very tall doors of this thickness; consult manufacturer for guidelines.
[3] Thickness of glass for doors should meet local code.
[4] Use like materials and thicknesses for face of cabinet doors and drawer fronts. Veneer core doors cannot be guaranteed against warping, telegraphing, or delamination.

- Cabinets over 72 inches high and not immediately abutting a structural wall or another cabinet shall have a fixed shelf at approximate mid height.
- Shelves over 36 inches wide shall be fabricated of minimum 1-inch-thick material.

Shelves—Fixed

- Shelves fabricated of particleboard and are 42 inches wide or more in width shall be 1 inch thick.
- Shall be secured to ends, divisions, and back.
- Shelves over 48 inches side shall have a center support.
- For Premium quality, horizontal and vertical shelves or dividers must be same material as other semi-exposed surfaces.
- For Custom quality, hardboard may be used for horizontal or vertical shelves or dividers, but must be tempered and smooth on both sides.

Shelves—Adjustable

- Shelves shall be a maximum of 1/8 inch less than the width of inside of cabinet.
- Shelves shall be a maximum of 1/4 inch less than the depth of the inside of cabinet.
- Shelf supports shall be a maximum of 2 inches on center and between 1 to 3 inches from the front and back of the cabinet.
- Distance between supports shall not exceed 60 percent of the width of the shelf. Provide three shelf supports under each shelf that exceeds 29-3/4 inches in depth.

Drawer Assembly

- Drawers shall be fabricated from the same material throughout the project.
- Drawer fronts shall match cabinet doors. Bottom edges of drawer fronts shall be smoothly sanded with edges eased. If drawer front is a panel product then all edges shall be edgebanded.
- All joints to be securely glued.
    - In flush overlay construction, if drawer subfront is not used drawer sides shall be blind dovetail dadoed to the front.
- Drawer box corner joints:
    - Multiple dovetailed.
    - Lock-joint and nailed.

Table 16.2 Shelf Sizes by Thickness and Finish

Shelf Material	Shelf Finish	Span
Particleboard	With or without low-pressure decorative laminate (LPDL)	At $\frac{3}{4}$" in thickness allows for a maximum of 28" in length
		At 1" in thickness allows for a maximum of 37" in length
	With hardwood veneer on two sides	At $\frac{3}{4}$" in thickness allows for a maximum of 35" in length
		At 1" in thickness allows for a maximum of 46" in length
	With vertical grade high-pressure decorative laminate (HPDL) on two sides with rigid or hard glue line	At $\frac{3}{4}$" in thickness allows for a maximum of 40" in length
		At 1" in thickness allows for a maximum of 53" in length
Medium-density fiberboard (MDF)	With or without LPDL	At $\frac{3}{4}$" in thickness allows for a maximum of 32" in length
		At 1" in thickness allows for a maximum of 43" in length
	With hardwood veneer on two sides	At $3\frac{3}{4}$" in thickness allows for a maximum of 37" in length
		At 1" in thickness allows for a maximum of 49" in length
Veneer core	Douglas fir plywood	At $\frac{3}{4}$" in thickness allows for a maximum of 40" in length
		At 1" in thickness allows for a maximum of 53" in length
Tampered float glass		At $\frac{1}{4}$" in thickness allows for a maximum of 29" in length
		At $\frac{5}{16}$" in thickness allows for a maximum of 35" in length
		At $\frac{3}{8}$" in thickness allows for a maximum of 42" in length
		At $\frac{1}{2}$" in thickness allows for a maximum of 51" in length

- Doweled, minimum two per joint, maximum $1\frac{1}{4}$-inch centers for joints up to 4 inches in length, maximum $2\frac{1}{2}$-inch centers for joints over 4 inches in length.
- Biscuit-joined, minimum two per joint, maximum 3 inches on center. Dowel screws only for Custom drawer boxes.

- Drawer bottoms:
  - Minimum thickness 1/4 inch.
  - Must be plowed into sides, and front/sub-front.
  - Must be minimum 3/8 inch from bottom of drawer box to drawer bottom. Bottom can be plowed into back or mechanically fastened at 4 inches on center.
  - Drawer bottom must be securely glued or glue-blocked.
  - For Custom and Premium construction, softwood plywood and hardboard are not allowed for drawer bottoms.
- Slides shall operate smoothly and be provided with end stops that prevent drawers from being pulled out of cabinet.

Door Assembly

- Maximum cabinet door size is 24 inches wide by 80 inches high by 1-3/8 inch thick.
- Number of hinges—Grade II cabinet hinges:
  - Under 40 inches high—two hinges
  - 40 to 60 inches high—three hinges
  - 60 to 80 inches high—four hinges
  - Over 80 inches high—five hinges with an additional hinge every 18 inches of additional height
- Silencers should be installed on the top and bottom of all hinged cabinet doors.
- Stile and rail doors:
  - Solid lumber stiles and rails shall be minimum 2-1/2 inches wide and 1/4-inch thick.
  - Veneered or overlaid construction with MDF or particleboard cores shall be minimum 3-1/2 inches wide and 3/4 inch thick.
  - Doors over 60 inches high shall have an intermediate rail.
  - Stiles shall run full height of door and top, intermediate and bottom rails shall run between stiles. Grain or directional pattern shall run vertically in stiles and horizontally in rails.
  - Joinery shall be mortise and tenon, dowels, or loose tenon. All glued under pressure.
  - Flat panels shall be minimum 1/4 inch thick; solid lumber panels are not permitted.
  - Raised panels shall be a minimum 1/2 inch thick; solid lumber panels are not permitted.
  - Solid lumber is permitted for rimming panels if mitered and glued under pressure.

  - If glass is used as a flat panel, it must be tempered or laminated safety glass. Tempered glass shall have a permanently etched designation that the glass panel is tempered.
- Flat-panel doors:
  - Grain or pattern shall run vertically and adjacent panels shall have a pleasing match for grain and color.
  - Core shall be covered by veneer, overlay, or rim banding.
  - Premium grade: Solid lumber panel doors are not permitted.
  - Custom and Economy grades: minimum 1/2-inch-thick edge glued solid lumber. Width across grain cannot exceed 13-3/4 inches
- Sliding doors:
  - Minimum thickness for sliding doors 24 inches in height and under shall be 1/4 inch; sliding doors over 24 inches in height shall be 3/4 inch.
  - Vertical edges of sliding doors are considered exposed, top and bottom edges are considered concealed.
  - If a door is 1.5 times as tall as it is wide or if the door is over 34 inches high, then the door shall be mounted using a top track and roller hangers or a metal bottom track with sheaves and top guide.

Cabinet Body Construction—Decorative Laminate Casework

- Exposed surfaces of Economy-grade cabinetry shall be clad with low-pressure decorative laminate (LPDL). Custom- and Premium-grade cabinetry shall be clad with high-pressure decorative laminate (HPDL).
- Exposed interior surfaces of Economy-grade cabinetry shall be clad with LPDL. Custom-grade cabinetry shall be clad with either LPDL or HPDL, manufacturer's option. Premium-grade cabinetry shall be clad with HPDL.
- Exposed interior surfaces of doors and drawer fronts shall be clad in same material as on face of doors and drawer fronts.
- All exposed edges of laminate clad panels shall have edgebanding of matching laminate, PVC, or ABS with radiused edges and corners.
- Semiexposed surfaces, all grades, shall be clad with LPDL, except as noted below.
- Drawers shall be fabricated with a front and false front.

Economy and Custom-grade drawers, including sides, backs and sub-fronts, shall be clad with LPDL. Premium-grade drawers shall be clad with HPDL or LPDL overlay on veneer-core plywood, particleboard, or medium-density fiberboard core. Drawer fabrication shall be as noted under "Drawer Assembly" Acceptable Practices.

Common installation practices for casework include the following:

- Casework shall be square and true within a tolerance not to exceed 1/32 inch difference between top and bottom and 1/16 inch measured diagonally.
- Cabinet toe bases that are not integral to cabinet body construction are not required to be attached to the floor, but shall be attached to cabinet body.
- Prefinished woodwork shall have all nail holes filled and touched up to match finish appearance.
- Equipment cutouts shall be neatly cut out and accurately sized. Cover plates or roses shall completely conceal cutout.
- Anchor or hanging strips:
  - In Custom- and Premium-grade installations, hanging strips are not allowed on the interior of the cabinet. In Economy-grade installations, hanging strips are allowed inside cabinets.
  - If back of hanging cabinet is 1/2 inch thick or thicker, no hanging strips are required.
  - Shall be solid stock, plywood, particleboard, or medium-density fiberboard and be a minimum 1/2 inches thick and 2-1/2 inches wide, securely glued and mechanically fastened.
  - Are required at top and bottom of cabinet.
  - Cabinets over 60 inches high require an intermediate anchor strip. Are not required if cabinet back is 1/2 inch thick or thicker.

Scribing:

- Scribe fillers or molds shall not exceed 1-1/2 inches in width, shall match exposed surfaces, and shall be furnished in maximum available lengths.
- In Premium-grade installations, scribe fillers or molds are not permitted.
- In Custom and Premium installations, end joints of scribing shall be beveled and corners of scribing to be mitered.
- In Custom and Premium installations, color-compatible caulking is permitted, but shall not exceed 1/8 inch in width.
- In Economy-grade installation, scribing is not required.

Closures—Custom and Premium Installations

- Closures are required for all voids or open spaces between cabinets and walls, such as top of tall and upper cabinets and bottom of upper cabinets.

- Nonvisible voids, less than or equal to 1-1/2 inches in width, can use a piece of standard-grade laminate as a closure cap.
- Nonvisible voids, exceeding 1-1/2 inches in width can use a 3/4-inch-thick piece of closure filler as a closure cap.
- At visible voids, a minimum 3/4 inch closure filler shall be provided, matching the adjacent surface.

Countertops

General requirements:

- Custom and Premium-quality countertops shall be of maximum available length.
- Shall be installed plumb, level, and square within 1/8 inch in 96 inches.
- Shall be free of open joints, visible machine marks, cross-sanding, tear-outs, nicks, chips, and scratches.
- Custom and Premium-quality countertops shall be scribed at all flat surfaces.
- Premium-quality countertops shall be scribed at shaped surfaces.
- Countertops shall be fastened to cabinetry using construction adhesive, finish nails, trim screws or pins.

Solid stone countertops:

- Back and end splashes shall be flat-butted and caulked with clear waterproof caulking.
- Unsupported spans shall not exceed 48 inches.
- Maximum cantilever for 3/4 inch material is 12 inches; for 1/2 inch material, 6 inches.
- Scribing of stone countertops is not required.

Plastic-laminate countertops:

- For high-pressure decorative laminate, if no quality standard is identified, installation shall follow the Architectural Woodwork Standards "Custom Grade" unless casework quality standard is identified. Then countertop standard shall be equal to cabinet standard identified.

Solid-surface countertops:

- For solid-surface or stone countertops, if no quality standard is identified, installation shall follow the Architectural Woodwork Standards "Custom Grade."
- Solid-surface fabrication shall be performed by personnel properly trained and approved by solid surface manufacturer.
- Back and end splashes shall be flat-butted and caulked with clear waterproof caulking.

- Solid surface countertops 3/4 inch thick can cantilever a maximum 12 inches beyond support without a subtop. Solid surface countertops 1/2 inch thick can cantilever maximum 6 inches without a subtop.

Wood countertops:

- For wood countertops, if no quality standard is identified, installation shall follow the Architectural Woodwork Standards "Custom Grade."
- If casework quality standard is identified, then countertop standard shall be equal to cabinet standard identified.

Practices to Avoid

Since metal copings are exposed to both view and the natural elements, they must be of enduring quality to ensure performance. Common construction practices to avoid include:

- Using silicone at joints of solid surface material
- Attaching countertops using drywall or bugle-head screws
- Use of exposed fasteners through plastic-laminate countertops

Paneling

Description

Wood paneling includes shop-fabricated wall paneling, fabricated as solid lumber paneling, wood-veneer paneling, and plastic-laminate-faced wood paneling. Wood paneling consists of a series of thin sheets of wood panels framed together by strips of wood, vertical stiles, and horizontal rails.

Wood panels 1 inch thick or less in thickness may be solid lumber panels or made from veneer over plywood or composition boards. The stiles and rails are typically made from solid wood or veneered boards. Rim and lip moldings and other trims are made almost exclusively from solid wood.

Assessing Existing Conditions

In order to ensure the proper installation of wood paneling, you need to verify the following conditions:

- The substrate is recommended to accommodate wood paneling.
- Repair loose or damaged wall studs, and ensure that substrate is tight to its framing.
- The layout has been determined, and panels will fit on the wall and line up around receptacles.
- Check masonry walls for excessive moisture. Walls with moisture must be completely waterproofed with a vapor barrier before they are paneled.

Acceptable Practices

The installation of a wood paneling varies according to what type of wood paneling is being installed and the method of installation. Some of the most common methods for installing paneling include nailing or a combination of nailing and adhesive.

Wood paneling is secured through a combination of nailing and gluing. For instances, where it is difficult to find the studs so that the paneling can be nailed in place, it is recommended that furring strips be installed and the paneling be nailed to them. Furring strips should be level and securely attached to the walls. This can be insured through the use of the level and chalkline. Furring strips should be placed a maximum of 16 inches apart, starting at the top edge of the wall and working downward to the bottom edge. While furring strips can be glued in place, it is preferable to nail them securely into the wall studs. Alternatively, wood paneling can be glued to the existing wall surface. If the latter method is chosen, make sure to follow the instructions for the glue and to pay particular attention to securely gluing the panel's edges.

Common construction practices for wood paneling include the following:

- Solid wood panels will need to be acclimated to the environment a minimum of 24 hours.
- Panels 1/4 inch and thicker can be installed directly over even framing members—studs or furring strips—while panels less than 1/4 inch shall be installed over a substrate.
- Substrate material shall be industrial-grade or moisture-resistant MDF (product class MD) or EFB wheatboard (Industrial Grade particleboard, class M3), complying with the current edition of ANSI standard A208.2, *Medium Density Fiberboard for Interior Use*.
- All paneling may be put up with nails (2-1/2 inch at a 45-degree angle) or with a combination of panel adhesive and nails.
- Adhesive for bonding veneers to substrate shall be PVA, EVA, or PUR type adhesive. Real wood veneer shall be grade A.
- Heavy panels need additional support, with nails 16 to 20 inches apart.
- Leave space between panels to avoid expansion problems.

Practices to Avoid

Common construction practices to avoid include:

- Installing wood paneling on exterior applications.
- Installing wood paneling over substrates that have wall coverings such as wallpaper.
- Extreme humidity inside the house. Humid air must be removed or controlled before installing wood paneling.
- Installing panels less than 1/4 inch thick without a solid backing or directly to framing members.
- Prolonged breathing of vapors when using adhesives.
- Lining joints up, as this creates a week point in the wall; staggering them creates stability.

Stairs and Railings

Description

Most residential stairs are constructed of wood and may be fabricated in the shop, but more frequently they are constructed on site.

The railings that are required for stairs and landings must include handrails and guards. The IRC requires that flights of stairs with four or more risers have a handrail on at least one side.

Assessing Existing Conditions

In order to ensure the proper installation of a stairs and railings, you need to verify the following conditions:

- No single flight may rise more than 12 feet vertically.
- Stairways shall not be less than 36 inches in clear width at all points above the permitted handrail height and below the required headroom height.
- All stairways shall be provided with illumination.

Acceptable Practices

Most residential stairs are designed to the steepest limits permitted by code so as to occupy the least amount of space. However, tread and riser combinations that are less steep may be considered for exterior stairs, grand stairs, or stairs of just a few risers. The most common rule for the comfortable proportioning of stairs in these cases is 2 x Riser height + Tread depth = 25 inches

For a standard straight stair, the 2009 International Building Code requires a minimum tread depth of 10 inches, and a maximum riser height of 7-3/4 inches, with a tolerance of no more than ⅜ of an inch. The minimum headroom shall not be less than 6 feet, 8 inches in height.

Common construction practices for stairs include the following:

- Riser and tread dimensions must be uniform for the entire length of the stair.

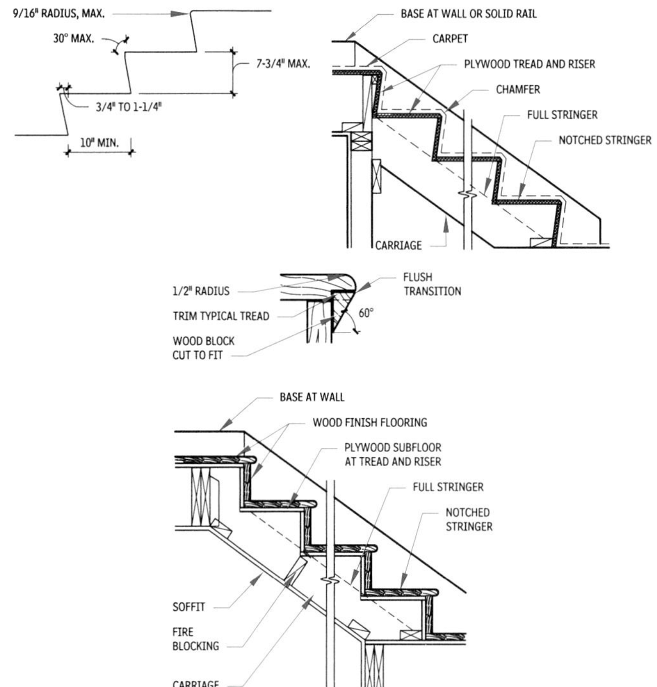

Figure 16.1 Closed riser stairs

Source: AIA, *Architectural Graphic Standards for Residential Construction,* 2nd ed. Copyright 2010, John Wiley and Sons, Inc.

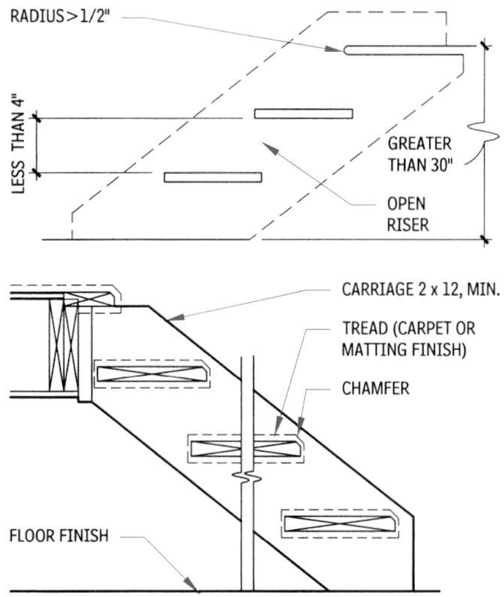

Figure 16.2 Open riser stairs

Source: AIA, *Architectural Graphic Standards for Residential Construction,* 2nd ed. Copyright 2010, John Wiley and Sons, Inc.

- Treads must be slip resistant.
- Carpeting or other stair coverings should be applied securely and should not create a nosing radius greater than permitted by building regulations.
- The IRC allows for open risers in residential construction, but the opening between the treads must be less than 4 inches in diameter.
- Landings must be at least as wide as the stair.
- In each flight, there should be one more riser than tread.

The treads of a spiral stair are typically supported between a center column and an outside stringer, while circular stairs support their treads between an inside and outside stringer. The larger the diameter of a spiral stair is, the more the perceived comfort, ease of use, and safety of the stair will be increased.

Handrails, guardrails, and stairways themselves must meet structural load requirements. There are two types of handrail grips for graspability. Type I includes circular handrails 1¼ inches to 2 inches in diameter, and noncircular handrails with a perimeter dimension between 4 and 6-1/4 inches. Type II handrails have a perimeter dimension greater

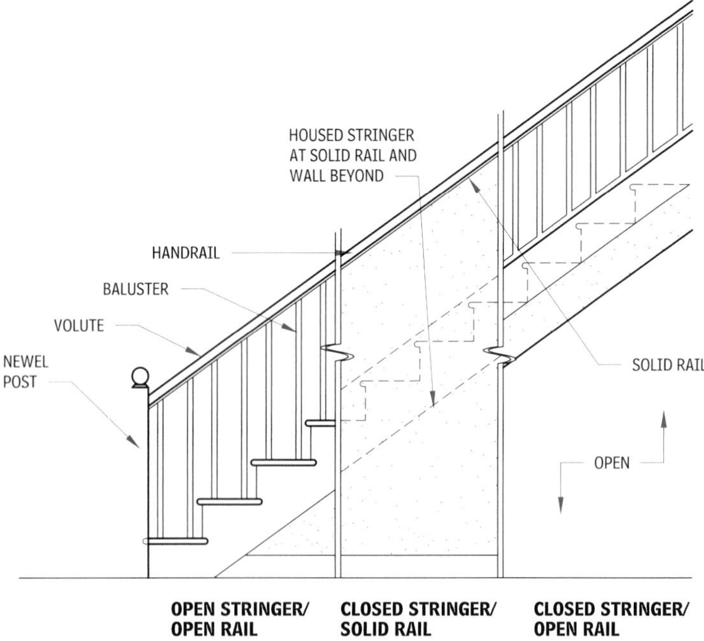

Figure 16.3 Stair elevations

Source: AIA, *Architectural Graphic Standards for Residential Construction,* 2nd ed. Copyright 2010, John Wiley & Sons, Inc.

than 6-1/4 inches, and have a finger recess, the dimension and location of which are dictated by the IRC.

Common construction practices for railings include the following:

- Handrails may project up to 4-1/2 inches into the required stairway width. They must be continuous, and the ends must extend beyond the top and bottom of the stair.
- Handrails need to be installed between 34 and 38 inches above the sloping plane, and guards need to be installed 36 inches above the walking surface.

Stairway doors must swing with the direction of egress travel, and must not obstruct more than half of the required landing width at any point in the swing. When fully open, doors must not strike handrails (including extensions), and must not project more than 7 inches into the travel path.

Wood Trim

Description

Wood trim is, generally, a decorative treatment applied after wall, floor, and ceiling finishes have been installed. It can be made of flat or molded wood from single pieces of wood or built up of several pieces that give a more complex and decorative appearance. There are two types of wood from which wood trim can be fabricated: closed-grained woods and open-grained woods. Closed-grained woods are fast-growing trees, where the annual growth rings are close together and have closed pores. A few examples of close-grained woods are maple, alder, Douglas fir, and poplar. Open-grained woods are slower growing and have predominant open pores. A few examples of open-grained woods are oak, pine, redwood, and cedar.

Interior trim conceals joints between different materials and blocks air infiltration through walls, which typically is greatest at material joints. Interior trim also frames wall and ceiling openings (door and window/skylight trim), defines planar edges (crown and base molding), and acts as a visual divider between dissimilar materials (chair rail).

Assessing Existing Conditions

In order to ensure the proper installation of wood trim, you need to verify the following conditions:

- The gypsum board does not taper in at the edges. This can be resolved by screwing or nailing the board back into the same plane as the main wall.
- If removing existing trim, damaged or in bad condition, examine the wall behind the trim for damage, including mold, mildew, or rodent/pest infestation. These problems should be taken care of before installing new trim.

Acceptable Practices

The Architectural Woodwork Institute differentiates wood trim according to its length: *standing trim* refers to the trims of fixed length

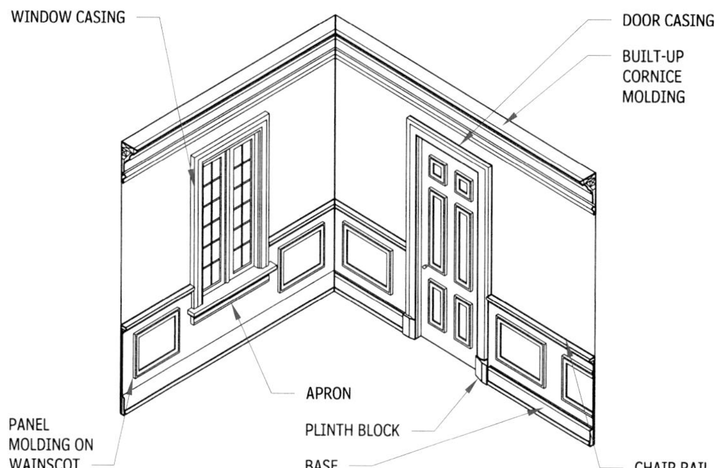

Figure 16.4 Typical wood trim

Source: AIA, *Architectural Graphic Standards for Residential Construction,* 2nd ed. Copyright 2010, John Wiley and Sons, Inc.

delivered to the job site (i.e., door jambs and casings, premachined window stools, etc.); *running trim* refers to the trims of random, longer length delivered to the job site (i.e., baseboard, chair rail, crown molding, etc.).

Casings are used to finish the joint between the window or door head, and jambs and wall finish. Often, a casing used at windows is also used as apron material, with the wide side toward the stool. Stools are used as interior caps on windowsills, and may receive casing from above and apron below. They are specified by width of rabbet and degree of bevel.

Base moldings are used to trim the intersections of a wall or cabinet and the floor. Baseboard may be one piece (with integral base cap) or flat with optional base cap. Separate caps and shoes are flexible and facilitate a close fit to uneven wall and floor surfaces. Crown moldings are applied alone at the joint between the wall and ceiling, or together with other moldings in a built-up cornice, typically toward the top of the cornice assembly, and are measured edge to edge.

Cove moldings are similar to crown molding, but may be smaller in size and have less detail. Cove moldings are also used at inside corners, such as wall to wall or ceiling to wall or as a component of built-up moldings. Often integrated with cornices, picture moldings are used as continuous projecting supports for hanging picture rail hooks. Picture rail hooks are available to fit these profiles. Bed moldings are similar in use and size to cove moldings and may be used at the bottom of built-up cornices and at other vertical-to-horizontal junctures.

Chair rails were originally meant to protect the wall surface from chair backs. Chair rails should be located to align with the chair backs in the room, either alone or atop wainscot paneling.

Half-rounds are used to conceal vertical and horizontal joints. Quarter-rounds are used at inside corners and as base shoes. Base caps are applied at the top of the baseboard, flush against the wall.

Backbands are typically applied as trim at the outer edge of door and window jambs and heads, to form a built-up two-part casing.

Panel moldings are typically used as door and wainscot trim, mitered together and arranged in rectangles.

Common construction practices for wood trim include the following:

- Blocking that receives moldings should be set plumb, level, true, and straight, with no distortion, and should be provided for full surface contact. Attach blocking to substrates with nails, screws, or bolts.
- Woodwork should be stored in a dry, ventilated space. If this is not possible, seal the ends of all pieces as soon as possible. Moldings should be at optimum moisture content at the time of installation and should be allowed to acclimate to project conditions before installation.
- Joints in adjacent and related members should be staggered. Cope at inside corners, and miter at outside corners, to produce tight-fitting joints with full surface contact throughout the length of the joint; use scarf joints (face mitered) for end-to-end joints in trim.
- Blind-nail where possible, and use finishing nails in exposed areas. Predrill as required to eliminate splitting; set exposed nail heads for filling.
- Most flat trimlike baseboards and casing have a ploughed or relieved back, which gives wide trim a degree of flexibility, allowing it to fit snugly against a wall surface.

Practices to Avoid

- Leaving gaps between trim molding that expose the surface below.

Common Work Results for Finish Carpentry

Description

Lumber Production

Commercially marketed lumber includes trees of dozens of species, roughly divided into softwoods, which are the evergreen species, and hardwoods, which are those species that drop their leaves in the fall. The majority of framing lumber comes from the comparatively plentiful

Table 16.3 Hardwoods and Softwoods

Name	Type and Color
African mahogany	Hardwood Pink to reddish brown
African walnut	Hardwood Bronze yellowish-brown with irregular dark lines
Afrormosia	Hardwood Yellow to dark brown
Beech	Hardwood White or pinkish
Douglas fir	Softwood Attractive reddish brown
Elm	Hardwood Light reddish brown
European oak	Hardwood Light to dark brown
Meranti	Hardwood Dark red or yellow
Parana pine	Softwood Pale yellow with attractive streaks
Redwood Scots pine, pine, fir	Softwood Cream to pale reddish brown
Teak	Hardwood Golden brown
Western red cedar	Softwood Dark reddish brown
Whitewood spruce	Softwood Plain creamy white

softwoods. Hardwoods, with their greater range of colors and grain figures, are used primarily for interior finishes, flooring, cabinets, and furniture.

Wood Veneers

Wood veneers are produced in a variety of industry-standard thicknesses. The slicing process is controlled by a number of variables, but the thickness of the veneer has little bearing on the quality of the end product.

Most veneers are taken from large trees, but some are sliced from fast-growing trees, dyed, and reglued in molds to create "grain" patterns. The color of these reconstituted veneers is established during manufacture because the high percentage of glue line resists staining.

The manner in which a log segment is cut with relation to the annual rings of the tree determines the appearance of the veneer. Individual pieces of veneer, referred to as "leaves," are kept in the order in which they were sliced for reference during installation. The group of leaves from one slicing is called a *flitch* and is identified by a number and the gross square feet it contains. The faces of the leaves with relation to their position in the log are identified as the *tight face,* toward the outside of the log, and the *loose face,* toward the inside or heart of the log.

Acceptable Practices

Types of Lumber Cuts

- *Plain sawn:* Boards are created by cutting parallel to the annular growth rings Plain-sawn wood often has interesting grain patterns, often called cathedrals, that are not created by other types of cutting. Since wood expands and contracts in different ways with respect to grain, plain-sawn lumber is typically less stable.
- *Rift sawn:* Boards are created by cutting 30-degree or greater angles to the growth rings, producing narrow boards with accentuated vertical or "straight" grain patterns.
- *Quarter sawn:* Boards are created by first cutting a log into quarters and then creating a series of parallel cuts perpendicular to the tree's rings.

Types of Veneer Cuts

The plain or flat-slicing method is most often used to produce veneers for high-quality architectural woodwork. Slicing is done parallel to a

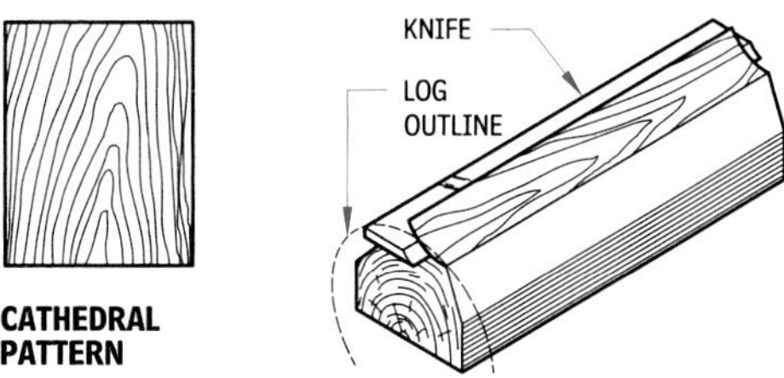

Figure 16.5 Plain-sliced veneer

line through the center of the log. A combination of cathedral and straight-grain patterns results, with a natural progression of pattern from leaf to leaf.

Quarter slicing, roughly parallel to a radius line through the log segment, simulates the quarter-sawing process used with solid lumber. In many species, the individual leaves are narrow as a result. A series of stripes is produced, varying in density and thickness among species. In red and white oak, *fleck* (sometimes called *flake*) is a characteristic of this slicing method.

Rift-cut veneers are produced most often in red and white oak, rarely in other species. Note that rift veneers and rift-sawn solid lumber are produced so differently that a "match" between them is highly unlikely. In both cases, the cutting is done slightly off the radius lines, minimizing the fleck associated with quarter slicing.

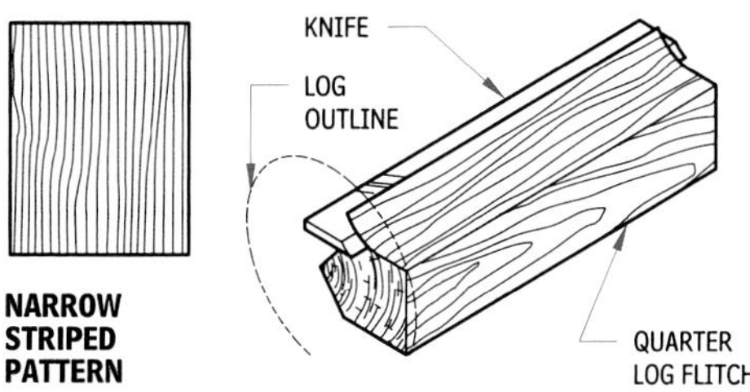

Figure 16.6 Quarter-sliced veneer

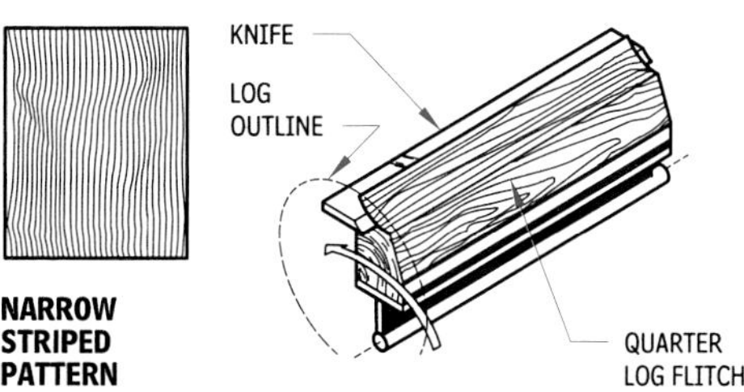

Figure 16.7 Rift-sliced (rift-cut) veneer

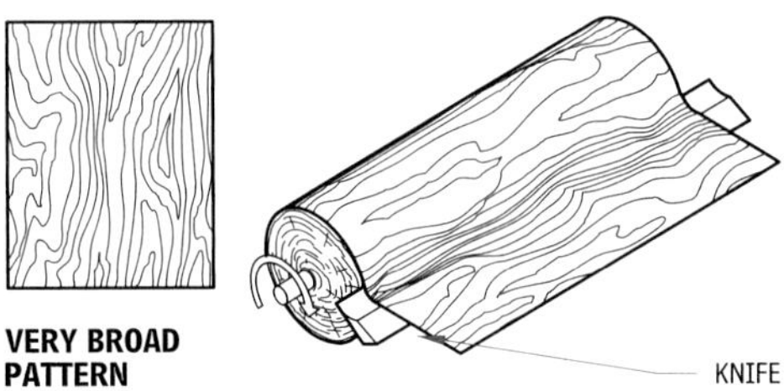

Figure 16.8 Rotary veneer

To create rotary-cut veneers, the log is center-mounted on a lathe and "peeled" along the path of the growth rings, like unwinding a roll of paper. This provides a bold, random appearance. Rotary veneers vary in width, so matching at veneer joints is extremely difficult. Most softwood veneers are cut this way. Rotary-cut veneers are the least useful in fine architectural woodwork.

Matching between Adjacent Veneer Leaves

It is possible to achieve certain visual effects by the manner in which the veneer leaves are arranged. Rotary-cut veneers are difficult to match; therefore, most matching is done with sliced veneers. Matching of adjacent veneer leaves must be specified. Consult an AWS woodworker for choices.

- *Book matching:* Book matching is the most commonly used match in the industry. In it, every other piece of veneer is reversed so that adjacent pieces (leaves) are "opened" like the pages of a book. Because the "tight" and "loose" faces alternate in adjacent leaves, they reflect light and accept stain differently. The veneer joints match, creating a symmetrical pattern that yields maximum continuity of the grain.
- *Slip matching:* In this match method, adjoining leaves are placed (slipped out) in sequence without being turned; thus, all the same face sides are exposed. The grain figure repeats, but joints do not show grain match.
- *Random matching:* In random matching, veneer leaves are placed next to each other in a random order and orientation, producing a casual board-by-board effect in many species. Conscious effort is made to mismatch the grain at joints.
- *End matching:* End matching is often used to extend the apparent length of available veneers for high wall panels and long conference tables. End matching occurs in two types:
  - *Architectural end match:* Leaves are individually book or slip matched, alternating end to end and side to side. Architectural end matching yields the best continuous grain patterns for length as well as width.

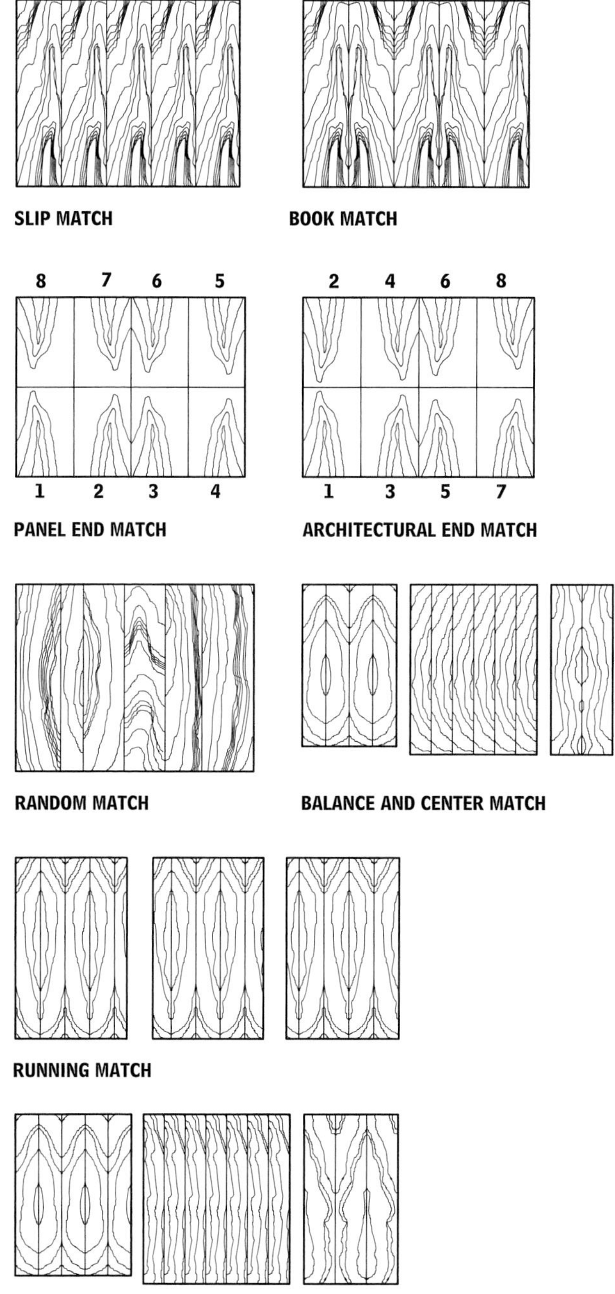

Figure 16.9 Veneer match types

  - *Panel end match:* Leaves are book or slip matched on panel subassemblies, with sequenced subassemblies end matched, resulting in some modest cost savings on projects, where applicable. For most species, panel end matching yields a pleasing, blended appearance and grain continuity.
- *Running matching:* Each panel face is assembled from as many veneer leaves as necessary. This often results in an asymmetrical appearance, with some veneer leaves of unequal width.
- *Balance matching:* In balance matching, each panel face is assembled from an odd or even number of veneer leaves of uniform width before edge trimming.
- *Balance and center matching:* Using this method, each panel face is assembled from an even number of veneer leaves of uniform width before edge trimming. Thus, there is a veneer joint in the center of the panel, producing horizontal symmetry.

Resources

WITHIN THIS BOOK

- Chapter 14 Common Work Results for Woods Plastics and Composites
- Chapter 15 Rough Carpentry

OTHER RESOURCES

- American Institute of Architects, *Architectural Graphics Standards*, 11th ed. Hoboken, NJ: John Wiley and Sons, 2007.
- American Institute of Architects, *Architectural Graphic Standards for Residential Construction,* 2nd ed. Hoboken, NJ: John Wiley and Sons, 2010.
- 2009 International Residential Code for One and Two-Family Dwellings. Washington, DC: International Code Council, Inc., 2009.
- Architectural Woodwork Standards, Architectural Woodwork Institute (AWI), Architectural Woodwork Manufacturers Association of Canada (AWMAC), and Woodwork Institute (WI), 2009.
- Architectural Wood Work Institute, www.awinet.org.
- Architectural Woodwork Manufacturers Association of Canada, www.awmac.com.
- Woodwork Institute, www.woodworkinstitute.com.

Part VI

Thermal and Moisture Protection

Chapter 17

Dampproofing, Waterproofing, and Related Drainage

Dampproofing

Waterproofing

Water Repellants

Underslab and Perimeter Drainage

Dampproofing

Description

Dampproofing is a bituminous material that is commonly used in above- and below-grade applications. Products include hot-applied and cold-applied bituminous dampproofing. Hot-applied products are generally mopped or spray applied, while cold-applied products can be troweled or spray, brush, or roller applied. Dampproofing is designed to only impede water through concrete or masonry substrates. It will not stop the penetration of water through substrates under hydrostatic pressure. Dampproofing is required by the International Residential Code; Section R406.1 to be used when concrete or masonry foundation walls retain earth and enclose interior spaces.

Hot-applied products are intended to be heated before application, so that products can be mopped or sprayed to the desired substrates. There are different types of dampproofing, and each type has different properties. These properties help to determine which type of dampproofing to use. "Type I" hot asphalt is generally used below grade because this type of asphalt is soft and will perform best at lower temperatures. "Type II" asphalt is generally used above grade in locations where temperatures will not exceed 122 °F. This material has good adhesion to substrates and is considered self-healing. "Type III" asphalt is generally used above grade and can be used where substrate temperatures exceed 122 °F, can be left exposed to direct sunlight, and will not sag when applied to vertical surfaces.

Cold applied products consist of cut-back (solvent-based) and emulsified (water-based) asphalt compounds.

Cut-back asphalt dampproofing is generally used below grade where ground water is present because emulsified asphalt dampproofing can re-emulsify when exposed to water. When surfaces are rough or have rock pockets, such as surfaces found on concrete substrates, a trowelable and fibered dampproofing such as a Type I, Class 1 dampproofing, per ASTM D 4586, should be used. When surfaces are smooth, a spray- or brush-applied dampproofing such as a Type I fibered or non-fibered product, per ASTM D 4479, can be used. In addition these two types of cut-back asphalts can be used on damp or wet surfaces; emulsified products cannot.

Cold-applied emulsified asphalts can be fibered (Types I and II asphalt) and nonfibered (Type III asphalt). Products are formulated in accordance with ASTM D 1227. Type I emulsified asphalts are not used because asbestos fibers are allowed in the asphalt product. Each asphalt type has two classes; in the construction industry only Class 1 asphalts containing mineral colloid (clay) emulsifying agents are used because these products will not sag unless exposed to higher temperatures. When surfaces are rough or have rock pockets and VOC content is a concern, a Type II, Class 1 asphalt should be used. When surfaces are smooth and VOC content is a concern, a spray- or brush-applied dampproofing such as either a Type II or Type III, Class 1 asphalt can be used.

Assessing Existing Conditions

In order to ensure the proper installation of bituminous dampproofing, you need to verify the following conditions:

- Substrates are clean of dirt, bond breakers, or substances from previous construction work.
- Masonry foundation walls shall have a minimum 3/8-inch thick parge coat of cement plaster on the exterior face of the wall when enclosing interior spaces.
- Joints in concrete or masonry have been properly sealed and are ready for the application of dampproofing.
- Mortar joints in masonry walls should be cured a minimum of 30 days.
- Dampproofing that will be backfilled against should have a protection board covering material to prevent damage to dampproofing during backfilling.
- Dampproofing should cure a minimum of 24 to 48 hours after application, and backfilling should occur within 7 days after application has been completed.

For dampproofing of cavity walls:

- Verify that dampproofing laps onto all flashings, shelf angles, masonry reinforcement.
- Verify that cavity drainage and ventilation is in place and unobstructed.
- Mortar joints in masonry walls should be cured a minimum of 30 days.

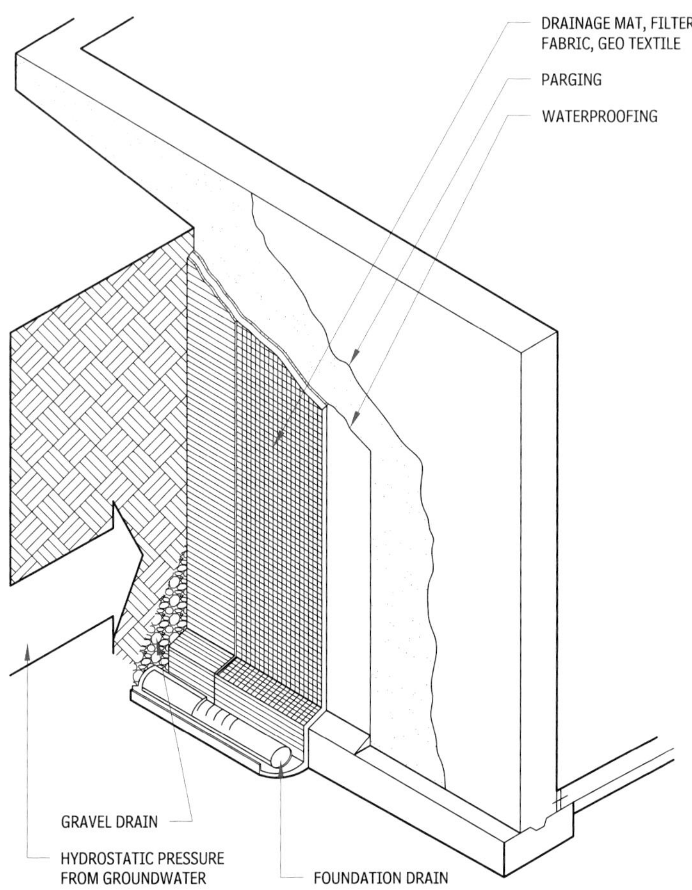

Figure 17.1 Moisture protection
Source: Francis Ching, *A Visual Dictionary of Architecture* John Wiley & Sons.

Acceptable Practices

Common applications for hot applied dampproofing:

- *Type I dampproofing:* Below-grade foundation walls of either concrete of masonry where no habitable spaces are located and the potential for ground water exists
- *Type II dampproofing:* Blind side of planters, retaining walls, or other locations with stable temperatures and substrates that are not exposed to direct sunlight

Common applications for cold-applied cut-back asphalt dampproofing:

- Below-grade foundation walls of either concrete or masonry where no habitable spaces are located and the potential for ground water exists
- Blind side of concrete retaining walls where the potential of ground water exists
- Concrete or masonry backup for stone veneer assemblies or dimension stone cladding
- On the exterior face of the inner wythe of cavity walls

Common applications for cold-applied emulsified-asphalt dampproofing:

- Below-grade foundation walls of either concrete of masonry where no habitable spaces are located and the potential for ground water does not exist
- Blind side of concrete retaining walls where there is no potential of ground water
- Concrete or masonry backup for stone veneer assemblies or dimension stone cladding
- On the exterior face of the inner wythe of cavity walls
- Interior face of exterior above-grade concrete or masonry walls, which will be furred out and finished

Practices to Avoid

When bituminous dampproofing is to be used, avoid the following practices:

- Dampproofing should not be applied to the dry side of below-grade walls nor to both side of a below-grade wall.
- Do not use dampproofing for below-grade walls where interior space is habitable.

Waterproofing

Description

There are many types of waterproofing products: sheet products, cold-fluid-applied products, and cementitious products. In residential construction, waterproofing is only required by the International Residential Code (IRC) Section R406.2 when foundation walls are enclosing interior spaces and there are known severe soil-water conditions or a high water table. The IRC lists eight types of waterproofing systems for use on below-grade foundations:

1. Two felt plies, hot mopped
2. 55-pound roll roofing
3. 6-mil polyvinyl chloride sheet
4. 6-mil polyethylene sheet
5. 40-mil polymer-modified asphalt
6. 60-mil flexible polymer cement
7. 1/8-inch cement-based, fiber reinforced waterproof coating
8. 60-mil solvent-free liquid-applied synthetic rubber

Sheet Waterproofing

The 55-pound roll roofing and six-mil polyvinyl chloride sheets used as waterproofing form an asphalt impregnated glass mat sheet. Sheet shall be attached at the top with a nonrusting flat bar and attached with fasteners to substrate. Seams should overlap a minimum of 4 inches and be sealed with an adhesive recommended by the roll roofing manufacturer.

Six-mil polyvinyl chloride sheets used as waterproofing sheet should be attached at the top with a nonrusting flat bar and attached with fasteners to substrate. Seams should overlap a minimum of 4 inches and be sealed with an adhesive recommended by the manufacturer.

Although bentonite waterproofing is not one of the systems listed in the IRC, it is one of the older and more reliable products on the market. Bentonite waterproofing is a sheet-applied product using sodium bentonite clay as the waterproofing agent, which, when it becomes wet, swells and blocks liquids from penetrating foundation walls. It is important to backfill against bentonite panels as soon as possible after installation because bentonite sheets swell when they get wet; the compression and swelling of the panels is how the bentonite works as a waterproofing system. Other components associated with bentonite waterproofing panels that are a part of the waterproofing system are proper preparation of penetrations through foundation walls to be waterproofed, and installation of waterstops in cold joints prior to the application of bentonite waterproofing panels.

Cold Fluid-Applied Waterproofing

Polymer modified asphalt is applied at total mil thickness of 40 mils using a roller, or by spray applications. Polymer-modified asphalt waterproofing requires special treatment of control joints, cracks, and cold joints in concrete. Control joints and cracks greater than 1/16 inch need to have an asphaltic mastic in combination with a polypropylene film reinforcing applied over the joints and cracks prior to application of waterproofing. Cold joints in concrete should be surface coated with asphaltic mastic prior to the application of waterproof membrane.

Liquid-applied synthetic rubber is spray-applied at a total mil thickness of 60 to 80 mils, achieved in two coats. Form ties must be removed to prevent membrane from being punctured. Concrete walls may be sprayed with membrane 24 to 48 hours after formwork is removed. All voids in mortar joints must be repaired. It is recommended that a protection or drainage panel be applied prior to backfilling.

Cementitious Waterproofing

Flexible-polymer cement can be applied to concrete or masonry walls at a minimum mil thickness of 60 mils. Concrete surface must be cleaned with water and thoroughly saturated with water prior to application of waterproofing. Inside corners and corners where the foundation wall meets the footing must be coved 2 inches using manufacturer recommended patching compound mixed to a mortar consistency. Allow coved areas to cure prior to application of waterproofing. Apply flexible polymer cement in 2 equal coats using a trowel or spraying apparatus to a minimum of 60 mil thickness.

Cement-based, fiber-reinforced waterproof coating can be applied to concrete or masonry walls to a minimum thickness of ¼ inch. Waterproofing is a cementitious coating enhanced with polypropylene fibers and polymers for flexibility. Polypropylene fibers help to prevent cracking of cementitious material.

Assessing Existing Conditions

In order to ensure the proper installation of waterproofing, verify the following conditions.

General conditions:

- Substrates are clean of dirt, bond breakers, or substances from previous construction work.
- Concrete and masonry surfaces must be smooth and free of contaminants such as curing compounds, form release agents, and evaporation retarders.
- All fins, or projections on concrete or masonry surfaces, have been removed.
- Sealants used in control joints of concrete or masonry walls are cured.
- Mortar joints in masonry walls should be cured a minimum of 30 days.
- Voids and honeycomb pockets in concrete walls must be filled with waterproofing manufacturer-approved product; product shall be fully cured prior to application of waterproofing.

Sheet Waterproofing:

- For bentonite waterproofing, confirm that waterstops were installed at all concrete cold joints.
- For bentonite waterproofing, verify that transitions between horizontal and vertical planes, plumbing, mechanical and electrical penetrations, and form ties have been prepared with bentonite mastic, prior to installation of bentonite sheets.

Cold fluid-applied waterproofing:

- If liquid-applied synthetic rubber is to be used on concrete masonry units, if cells are to be grouted, cells must be grouted and cured for seven days prior to application of membrane.

Cementitious waterproofing:

- Inside corners and corners where the foundation wall meets the footing must be coved 2 inches using manufacturer-recommended patching compound mixed to a mortar consistency. Allow coved areas to cure prior to application of waterproofing.
- Concrete surface must be cleaned with water and walls thoroughly saturated prior to application of waterproofing.

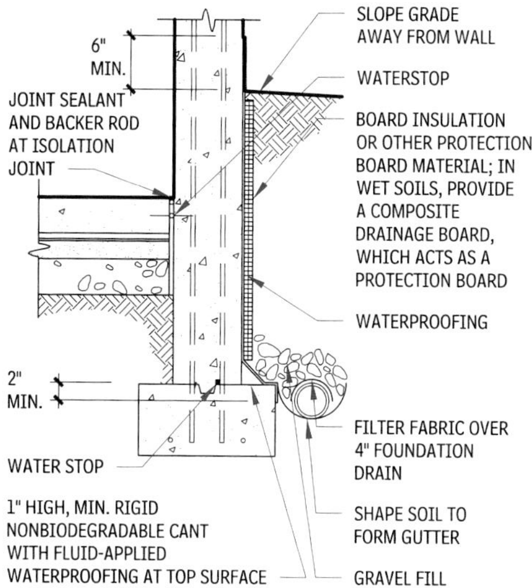

Figure 17.2 Waterproofing at footings
Source: AIA, *Architectural Graphic Standards,* 11th ed. Copyright 2007, John Wiley & Sons, Inc.

Acceptable Practices

Some practices to follow at the completion of waterproofing systems:

- Cementitious waterproofing systems are generally moisture cured and covered with polyethylene sheeting.
- Protect waterproof systems with protection panels, which can be heavy building felt or drainage panels. Drainage panels vary by manufacturer, but can be a formed plastic, three-dimensional panel that allows water to drain vertically to the top of the footing and into a perimeter drainage system. Generally in waterproof coatings, the protection or drainage panels are installed prior to the coating fully curing, and the coatings act as an adhesive to hold protection in place while backfilling.
- Fluid-applied waterproofing coatings are generally cured for 24 hours, then backfill can be placed against waterproofing system.

Practices to Avoid

When waterproofing is required to be used, avoid the following practices:

- Avoid the use of 6-mil polyethylene sheeting for waterproofing. It has been shown to disintegrate when exposed to continual dampness and is easily punctured.

- Do not penetrate waterproofing systems after waterproofing work has been completed.
- Waterproofing systems should not be installed during heavy rain or snow.
- Do not apply cementitious waterproofing in direct sunlight.

Underslab and Perimeter Drainage

Description

Perimeter drainage is a drainage system located at the base of the perimeter footings of the structure. The purpose of the drainage system is to quickly and easily move water from around the perimeter foundations and away from the structure. When water tables are so high that a perimeter drainage system does not have the capacity to remove the water quickly enough, then an underslab drainage system can be included to supplement the perimeter drainage system. Underslab drainage is not required by the International Residential Code (IRC), but is mentioned here as a suggestion to supplement perimeter drainage in extreme cases. Perimeter drainage is required by code when foundation walls are enclosing interior spaces below grade, according to the IRC; Section R405.

The components of a perimeter drainage system (underslab drainage has the same components) are:

- Pipe: Precast concrete drainage tiles, plastic perforated pipe, or crushed stone drains
- Crushed stone or coarse sand
- Filter membrane such as a perforated geotextile fabric
- Method of removing the water, either by gravity, pump, or stormwater system

Assessing Existing Conditions

In order to ensure an adequate perimeter drainage system, you will need to verify the following. When underslab drainage is required, modify the following as noted:

- Bottom of pipe or drainage tile shall be at the bottom of the perimeter footing. For underslab drainage pipe, it is approximately 14 to 16 inches below basement finished floor level.
- Filter membrane shall wrap around the crushed gravel or coarse sand and pipe or drainage tile. For underslab drainage, place a layer of filter membrane on top of undisturbed soil under drain field.

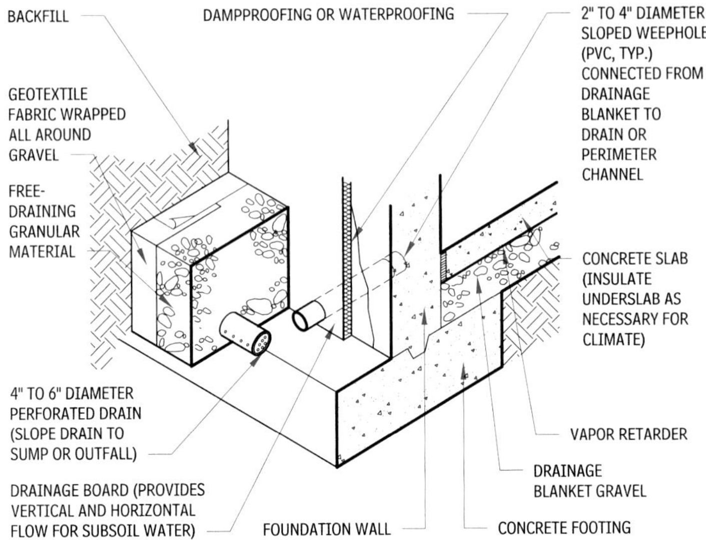

Figure 17.3 Typical perimeter drain
Source: AIA, *Architectural Graphic Standards for Residential Construction,* 2nd ed. Copyright 2010, John Wiley & Sons, Inc.

Allow extra filter membrane at perimeter to lap under filter membrane placed on top of drainage field.

- Pipe or drainage tile shall sit on a bed of crushed gravel or coarse sand, minimum 2 inches deep. Pipe should slope to drain. At underslab drainage system—generally perforated pipe or drainage tiles—is placed 12 to 24 inches on center, forming a drain field under the structure. The spacing of the pipe is determined by the amount of water expected. Connect all pipes together at a one end of the drain field using unperforated pipe. Run unperforated pipe to location where water is to be removed.
- If drainage tiles are used, the top of the drainage tile at each joint shall be protected with strips of building paper.
- Perforated pipe shall be placed with pipe perforations down.
- Cover pipe or drainage tile with minimum 6 inches of crushed gravel or coarse sand and cover with filter membrane. At underslab drainage, place 6 inches of crushed gravel or coarse sand over entire drainage field and cover entire top surface of drainage field with filter membrane and lap over extra material under drainage field.
- Verify that water from drainage system is removed, either by mechanical means, gravity, or stormwater system.

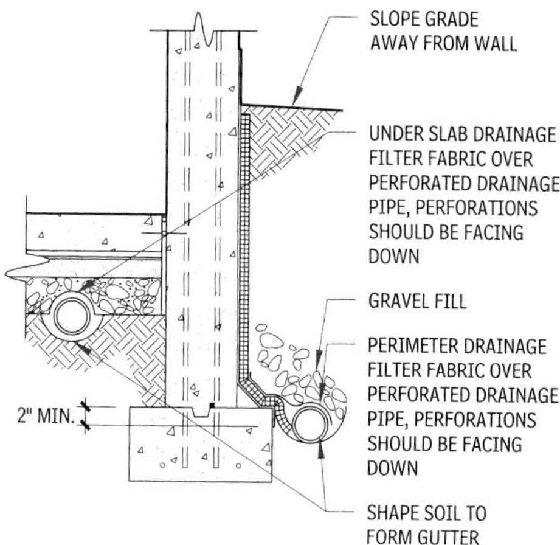

Figure 17.4 Membrane waterproofing

Source: AIA, *Architectural Graphic Standards for Residential Construction,* 2nd ed. Copyright 2010, John Wiley & Sons, Inc.

If crushed stone drains are used, verify the following:

- Crushed stone drains shall extend a minimum of 12 inches from face of footing and minimum 6 inches above top of footing.
- Crushed stone drains should be wrapped in perforated filter membrane on all sides.
- Crushed stone drains shall have a way to collect the water and remove by mechanical means, gravity, or stormwater system.

Acceptable Practices

When establishing if perimeter or underslab drainage is required:

- If site soil conditions are well-drained or composed of sand-gravel mixture and are classified as Group I soils in accordance with the Unified Soil Classification System; IRC table R405.1, perimeter or underslab drainage may not be required.

Water Repellants

Description

There are many different uses for water repellants in the construction industry, as well as many different types of water repellants to choose from. It is not very common to see water repellants used in residential construction; however, the two types that will be discussed are both very common in the industry, yet very different. Both are applied topically; one is applied to brick, concrete, or stone and the other is applied to the face of wood.

Water repellants for brick, concrete, or stone should be topically applied, penetrating, and breathable. A breathable product allows any trapped moisture inside the wall system to escape if necessary. Water repellants for brick, concrete, or stone are applied to prevent water penetration into the surface of the building material. The prevention of water penetration into surfaces is important because it can prematurely degrade surfaces through freeze and thaw cycles, can create mold or mildew on or behind surfaces, can stain surfaces, or can be a primary cause of efflorescence. Potential sources of water on building surfaces are from wind-driven rain and lawn sprinklers.

Water repellants for wood are used for wood decks or fences that are not painted or finished in any way. Water repellants for wood are applied using a brush, roller, by dipping, or spray. A water repellant is generally used to protect the wood from UV rays, staining, or discoloration of wood, and from water damage. It helps prolong the life of wood exposed to the elements.

Assessing Existing Conditions

Follow these guidelines for water repellants on brick, concrete, or stone surfaces:

- Surface should be clean, and free of dirt, dust, oils, and other contaminants.
- All sealant joints in areas where water repellants are to be applied should be fully cured.

- Surfaces that are not to receive water repellant should be covered or protected from overspray.
- If efflorescence is present, it must be removed prior to application of water repellant.

Follow these guidelines for water repellants on wood surfaces:

- Surfaces must be dry for at least 48 hours prior to application.
- Most water repellants cannot be applied to hard or dense woods such as Ipe.
- Wood surfaces should be cleaned and stains removed prior to application of water repellant.
- Surfaces that are not to receive water repellant should be cover or protected from overspray.

Acceptable Practices

Water repellants on brick, concrete or stone surfaces:

- Test surfaces where water repellant is to be applied and let thoroughly dry to make sure that treatment is visually acceptable.
- Apply in two coats.

Water repellants on wood surfaces:

- Allow pressure-treated lumber to acclimate to environment for minimum 30 days prior to treatment.
- Apply in one coat.
- On new deck or fence surfaces, apply water repellant to cut ends of lumber that could be concealed after installation.

Practices to Avoid

Water repellants on brick, concrete, or stone surfaces:

- Application to surfaces that are below 40° F or above 95° F.
- Do not apply during windy weather.

Water repellants on wood surfaces:

- Temperature shall not be below 50° F for a minimum of 48 hours after application.

Resources

WITHIN THIS BOOK

- Chapter 7 Cast-In-Place Concrete
- Chapter 9 Unit Masonry
- Chapter 18 Thermal Protection and Weather Barriers
- Chapter 21 Flashing and Sheet Metal Specialties
- Chapter 31 Plumbing

REFERENCE STANDARDS

- ASTM D 1227—Standard Specification for Emulsified Asphalt Used as a Protective Coating for Roofing
- ASTM D 4479—Standard Specification for Asphalt Roof Coatings—Asbestos-Free
- ASTM D 4586—Standard Specification for Asphalt Roof Cement—Asbestos-Free

OTHER RESOURCES

- American Institute of Architects, *Architectural Graphics Standards*, 11th ed. Hoboken, NJ: John Wiley and Sons, 2007.
- American Institute of Architects, *Architectural Graphic Standards for Residential Construction,* 2nd ed. Hoboken, NJ: John Wiley and Sons, 2010.
- 2009 International Residential Code for One and Two-Family Dwellings. Washington, DC: International Code Council, Inc., 2009.

Chapter 18

Thermal Protection and Weather Barriers

Thermal Insulation

Exterior Insulation and Finish System

Air and Moisture Barriers

Thermal Insulation

Description

Thermal insulation is used in residential construction to conserve energy by slowing the transfer of heat between exterior and interior spaces. Types of thermal insulation include board, blanket, loose-fill, or spray applied, which are rated according to their ability to resist heat flow. Resistance to heat flow is reported based on the total thickness of a material known as thermal resistance (R-value) or by unit thickness known as thermal resistivity (ρ-value). The higher the value, the better the insulation will perform. The IRC requires insulation of building envelope components, such as walls, ceilings, and floors, to meet the minimum R-values listed in Table N1102.1 for each climate zone. Choosing the type of insulation to use depends on space available and accessibility to the area to be insulated, as well as consideration of the materials ability to maintain its thickness or its compressive strength.

Board, or rigid, insulation is made from fibrous materials or plastic foams and is often used for foundations or as an insulating wall sheathing. Boards provide a greater R-value in less thickness, they are typically available in 4 by 8 foot sheets, resulting in fuller coverage with fewer seams where heat loss can occur. Blanket insulation is made from mineral fibers, including fiberglass or rock wool. It is available rolled in widths to fit the spacing of wall studs and attic or floor joists. Both blanket and board insulation can be hand-cut to fit smaller areas and where obstructions exist. Some materials are available faced with a reflective foil to reduce thermal transmittance by radiation or a vapor retarder in place of a separate sheet to control condensation.

Loose-fill and spray-applied insulation often require special equipment and a professional installer. Loose-fill fibers or fiber pellet insulation, made from cellulose, fiberglass, or rock wool, is blown into the space. It can be used in wall cavities, on unfinished attic floors, and for filling irregularly shaped areas and around obstructions. Spray-applied insulation is sprayed into place as an open- or closed-cell foam made of polyisocyanurate or polyurethane. Open-celled foam has a lower R-value but allows easier movement of water vapor through the material than closed-cell foam. Closed-cell foams are commonly used where space is limited and the required thickness to achieve an open-cell R-value is not possible. Spray applied foam is similar to loose-fill in that it can fill irregular areas, but since it foams in place, it will not settle and can be applied to overhead and open vertical surfaces as well.

The effectiveness of an insulating material depends on how it is installed. It is important to detail insulated locations to show access to spaces, methods of securing the insulation in place and the sequencing of other materials. Compressed materials and gaps in insulation result in decreased R-values. When insulation is part of a rated system, verify that materials are acceptable to authorities having jurisdiction.

Assessing Existing Conditions

- Insulation is properly installed to achieve required R-value.
- Thickness of insulation will fit into space without compression.
- A continuous barrier exists between the inside conditioned space and outside. Joints and ruptures in vapor-retarder facings are taped, and each continuous area of insulation is sealed to ensure airtight installation.
- Widths and lengths of insulation fill the cavities formed by framing members. Ends where more than one length is required are firmly butted together.
- Perimeter board insulation extends a minimum of 24 inches below exterior grade and 24 inches under slab from exterior walls.
- Insulation is cut around obstructions and voids are filled.
- Units are bonded to substrate with adhesive, or mechanical anchorage provides permanent placement and support of units.
- Thermal insulation installed in concealed spaces has flame-spread index of 25 and smoke-developed index of 450.
- A 3-inch clearance is provided around recessed light fixtures.

Acceptable Practices

Homes that are well insulated use less energy to condition spaces, maintain a more constant comfortable temperature, and require less maintenance than those with overburdened mechanical conditioning systems. The key to an effective thermal system is complete insulation coverage and proper installation.

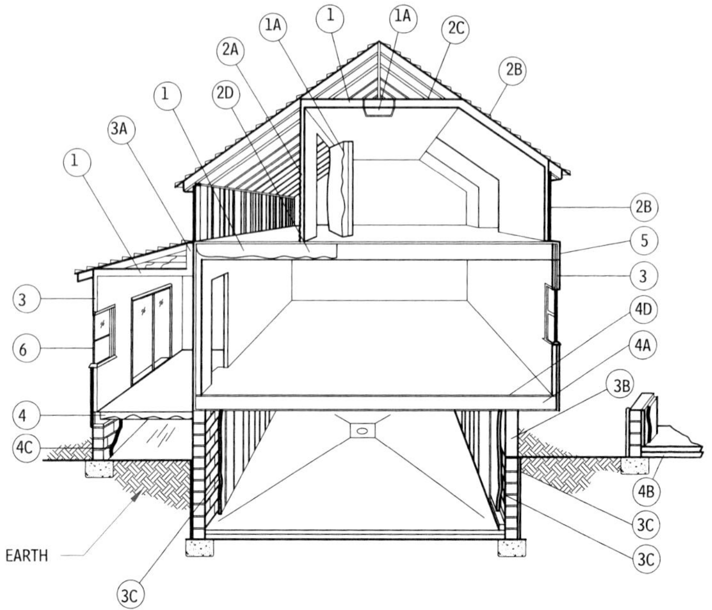

Examples of Where to Insulate

1. In unfinished attic spaces, insulate between and over the floor joists to seal living spaces below.
   1A attic access door.

2. In finished attic rooms with or without dormer, insulate...
   2A between the studs of "knee" walls;
   2B between the studs and rafters of exterior walls and roof;
   2C ceilings with cold spaces above;
   2D extend insulation into joist space to reduce air flows.

3. All exterior walls, including...
   3A walls between living spaces and unheated garages, shed roofs, or storage areas;
   3B foundation walls above ground level;
   3C foundation walls in heated basements, full wall either interior or exterior.

4. Floors above cold spaces, such as vented crawl spaces and unheated garages. Also insulate...
   4A any portion of the floor in a room that is cantilevered beyond the exterior wall below;
   4B slab floors built directly on the ground;
   4C as an alternative to floor insulation, fountation walls unvented crawl spaces;
   4D extend insulation into joist space to reduce air flows.

5. Band joists.

6. Replacement or storm windows and caulk and seal around all windows and doors.

Figure 18.1 Spaces in residential construction recommended to receive insulation
Source: Oak Ridge National Laboratory

Common installation practices include the following:

- Board insulation installed on concrete substrates by adhesively attached, spindle-type insulation anchors
- Spindle standoffs to create required cavity widths between board insulation and concrete substrates
- Spray insulation applied after completion of pipes, ducts, conduits, wiring, and electrical outlets and items not indicated to receive insulation are masked

Table 18.1 Insulation and Fenestration Requirements by Component

Climate Zone	Fenestration U-Factor	Skylight U-Factor	Glazed Fenestration SHGC	Ceiling R-Value	Wood Frame Wall R-Value	Mass Wall R-Value[a]	Floor R-Value	Basement[b] Wall R-Value	Slab[c] R-Value and Depth	Crawl Space[b] Wall R-Value
1	1.2	0.75	0.35	30	13	3/4	13	0	0	0
2	0.65	0.75	0.35	30	13	4/6	13	0	0	0
3	0.50	0.65	0.35	30	13	5/8	19	5/13[e]	0	5/13
4 except marine	0.35	0.6	NR	38	13	5/10	19	10/13	10,2 ft	10/13
5 and marine 4	0.35	0.6	NR	38	20 or 13 + 5[d]	13/17	30f	10/13	10,2 ft	10/13
6	0.35	0.6	NR	49	20 or 13 + 5[d]	15/19	30g	10/13	10,4 ft	10/13
7 and 8	0.35	0.6	NR	49	21	19/21	30g	10/13	10,4 ft	10/13

[a]Second R-value applies when more than half the insulation is on the interior

[b]First R-value applies to continuous insulation, the second to framing cavity insulation; either insulation meets the requirement

[c]R-5 shall be added to the required slab edge R-Values for heated slabs. Insulation depth shall be the depth of the footing or 2 feet, whichever is less, in zones 1 through 3 for heated slabs.

[d]13+5 means R-13 cavity insulation plus r-5 insulated sheathing. If structural sheathing covers 25% or less of the exterior, R-5 sheathing is not required where structural sheathing is used. If structural sheathing covers more than 25% of exterior, structural sheathing shall be supplemented with insulated sheathing of at least R-2

[e]Basement wall insulation is not required in war-humid locations as defined by the IRC

- A second layer of batt insulation in attic floors laid perpendicular to the first to cover the tops of joists and reduce thermal bridging through the frame
- Installation of eave ventilation troughs between roof framing members in insulated attic spaces at vented eaves
- Continuous insulative sheathing over the outside wall of metal framed in addition to insulation between the studs to resist thermal conduction
- Blankets with facings stapled or taped to the studs, where cavity heights are greater than 96 inches or blankets do not completely fill the cavity, to hold insulation in place until the wall facing is installed
- Mechanically supported unfaced blankets where cavity heights exceed 96 inches
- Replacing air with argon in special closed-pore foam insulations to achieve higher R-values
- Insulation of basement walls rather than basement ceilings, since multiple penetrations through the floor could decrease the floors thermal resistance

Practices to Avoid

- Compression of insulation by placing denser insulation on top of lighter insulation. In attics, it is acceptable to place denser blanket insulation on top of loose-fill insulation to reduce air circulation.
- Compression of insulation by placing blanket insulation into a thinner cavity than their thickness.
- Compression of insulation by stuffing blanket insulation behind pipes or wires. Blankets should be cut through their depth and tucked over and under the pipe or wire.
- Extended exposure of gas-filled foam plastic insulation to air, which dilutes the gas and reduces resistance to heat flow.
- Voids in insulated surfaces, such as floor-to-window and partition-to-exterior wall junctures where there are close-spaced wall studs.
- Contact of insulation with heat-producing equipment such as recessed lighting fixtures where heat can build up and cause a fire.
- Covered vents where proper ventilation must be maintained to avoid overheating and moisture build-up. Moisture trapped within insulation can lead to mildew, corrosion, or decay.
- Placement of a radiant barrier on the attic floor where it will get covered with dust and not work efficiently.
- Use of low-density loose fill, which will settle and give a reduced R-value.

Exterior Insulation and Finish System

Description

Some homes are built with an exterior insulation and finish system (EIFS), which combines foam plastic insulation with a two-layer synthetic coating that gives a stucco-like appearance. Sometimes this is called synthetic stucco. In the past, quality-control problems where poor EIFS construction led to water leaks into the wall assembly. Newer versions of EIFS have been designed to be more robust and to allow any water entering through a construction defect to drain harmlessly out of the wall. This system can be used to finish wood-framed, metal-framed, and masonry walls. It offers special advantages for the metal-framed and masonry walls because the continuous external insulation layer optimizes the thermal performance of both of those two wall systems.

Assessing Existing Conditions

There are two types of EIFS systems: barrier or conventional EIFS, and water-managed or drainable EIFS. Drainable EIFS is the preferred system and is most widely accepted by residential building codes.

In a typical barrier type application, the extruded polystyrene insulation (EPS) or polyisocyanurate foam board is attached with either adhesive or mechanical fasteners to the exterior sheathing substrate. A fiberglass reinforced mesh is then applied to the EPS board and fully embedded in a basecoat of EIFS material as it is applied. After the basecoat is cured (usually 24 hours), a flexible, acrylic-modified finish coat in the desired color and texture is applied, which gives the wall its stucco appearance. Typical thickness from EPS board to the finished surface is approximately 3/8-inch thickness.

Water-managed or drainable EIFS installations consist of an insulation board attached with special mechanical fasteners or adhesives to a metal, plastic, or glass fiber mesh, creating a drainage plane. Alternatively, a grooved foam board can allow drainage.

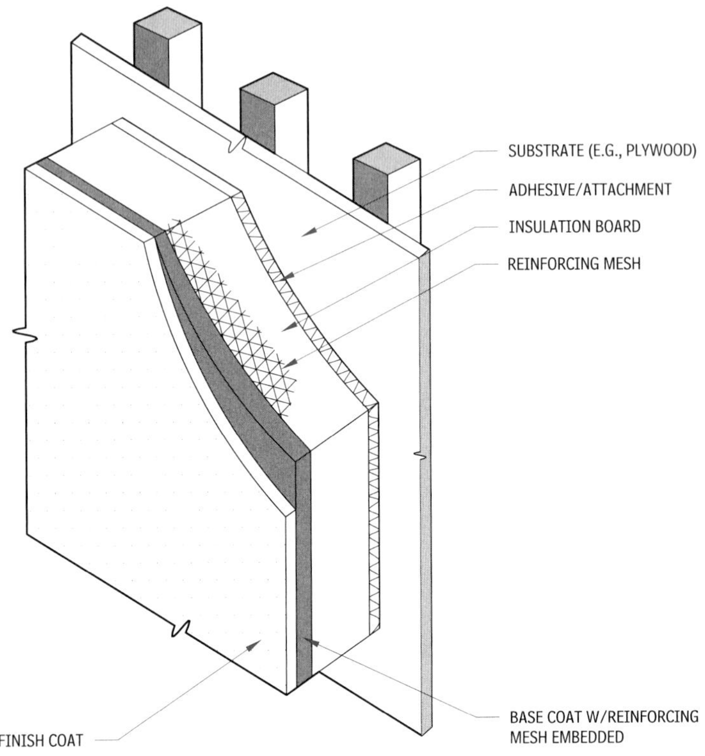

Figure 18.2 Barrier EIFS system

For both systems, OSB plywood and exterior-grade gypsum sheathing are the most common substrates. Also in both, the mesh covers a weather restive barrier such as building paper or house wrap, which, in turn, covers the sheathing or substrate.

Provisions should be made to ensure that the EIFS system can be properly terminated above grade and that the required flashing is in place. Periodic maintenance should include thorough checking of the flashing and sealing to ensure that the building envelope remains watertight. Damaged or missing flashing should be repaired or replaced immediately; likewise, cracked or deteriorated sealants should immediately be repaired, or removed and replaced.

Some state and local building codes ban or restrict the use of EIFS; some codes require third-party installation inspections. Also know that some mortgage lenders and insurers will not finance or insure houses with EIFS due to previous problems.

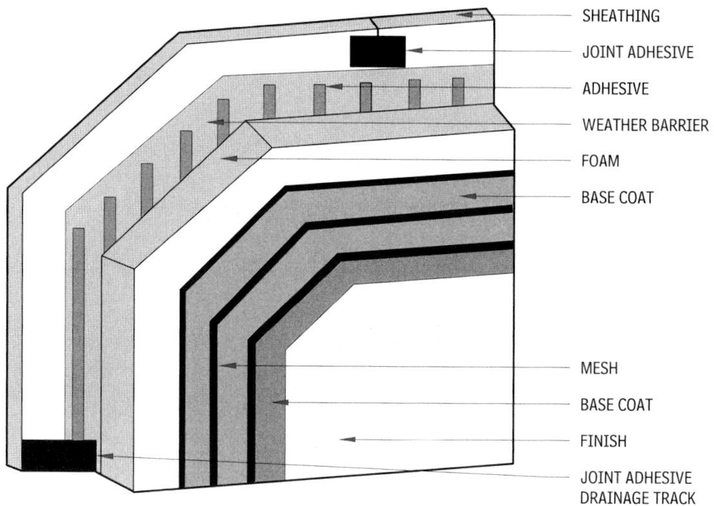

Figure 18.3 Drainable EIFS system

Acceptable Practices

Exterior insulation and finish systems should be installed only by experienced applicators that have completed an EIFS manufacturer's training program. Manufacturers who are members of EIFS Industry Members Association (EIMA) provide extensive specifications, training manuals and training programs for all applicators using their products. To ensure long-term performance of EIFS, EIMA recommends the following for all installations:

- Selection of an EIMA member manufacturer who can provide technical support, documented product and system test results, as well as building code compliance information.
- Selection of a knowledgeable, experienced applicator who has current approval of the manufacturer.
- A minimum temperature of 40 °F and rising during installation and 24 hours thereafter is recommended.
- Examination of the substrate for proper tolerances, cleanliness, and secure fastening.
- All openings shall be properly flashed. Individual windows that are ganged to make multiple units shall have continuous flashing and/or joints between them and shall be fully sealed.

- Provisions should be made to ensure the EIFS system can be properly terminated above grade and at patios, decks, landings, etc., and the required flashing is in place.

  At terminations/foundation, provide adequate clearance so EIFS system can terminate above grade.

  All terminations require back wrapping, unless a starter track with weepholes is used. The reinforcing mesh is continued onto the back side of the insulation board a minimum of 2½ inches.
- When the system terminates against a dissimilar material, such as wood or concrete, the system should be held back a minimum of ¾ inch to allow for an expansion joint and caulking. In wood-framed construction, expansion joints are installed at each floor line to allow for framing shrinkage; minimum of ¾ inch is recommended.
- Expansion joints should be included at areas where there is a change in substrate that could result in differential movement, at areas with significant movement, as expansion joints in the substrate or building; minimum of ¾ inch is recommended.
- Terminations at penetrations require back wrapping with reinforcing mesh and base coat. The insulation board must be held back from the opening a minimum of ½ inch for proper sealant installation.
- If there is a question as to whether the finish is EIFS or real stucco, remember that EIFS is relatively light and sounds hollow when tapped. Real stucco is relatively heavy and feels and sounds solid when tapped. If you are still unsure, employ a qualified inspector.

Practices to Avoid

- Avoid poor-quality windows and/or improper flashing and sealing. It is imperative that windows, doors, roofs, deck-to-house attachments, and all other exterior wall penetrations and areas of transition between materials are properly flashed and sealed.
- Avoid using non-drainable wall assembly that does not encourage drainage.
- Avoid conditions that may ultimately affect the performance of EIFS by mix coatings only as recommended by EIFS manufacturer and applying coatings at the correct/recommended thickness.

Air and Moisture Barriers

Description

Weather barriers include materials that resist moisture and materials that provide a barrier to air infiltration or loss. Confusion about weather barriers is common. Air barriers that control the vapor form of moisture can also be vapor barriers. Vapor barriers that are properly sealed and flashed can control bulk water and also be a water-resistive barrier. In other words, an air barrier, vapor barrier, and water-resistive barrier can be achieved with one or multiple products. The terms *water-resistive barriers* and *weather barriers* are both used in model codes to refer to the same product, and *vapor retarder* is often used interchangeably with *vapor barrier*. For the sake of this topic, weather barriers include air barriers, vapor barriers, and water-resistive barriers. It is important to understand the function of each to properly choose barriers and design weather-barrier assemblies to work as needed.

Air Barriers

Air flows from higher to lower pressures, and thus, conditioned air within a building under wind, stack, and fan pressures will travel out. Air barriers block pollutants such as water vapor, dust, odors, and insects, as well as control air flow. Air barrier materials are rated by air permeance, which is the rate of airflow through a unit area of a material driven by unit static pressure difference (Pa) across the material. The Air Barrier Association of America (ABAA) defines air barrier materials as those with an air permeance no greater than 0.02 L/(s•m^2) at 75 Pa pressure difference when tested in accordance with ASTM E 2178—unmodified. Hundreds of materials meet this requirement, and rigid materials such as gypsum board, concrete, plywood, metal liners, and glass are used as air barriers. Other materials designed as air barriers include self-adhering sheets and fluid-applied membranes, as well as spray applied foam materials. When selecting an air barrier material, it is important to consider its performance characteristics. A materials tensile strength, adhesion compatibility and puncture resistance can ensure a successful installation and longer life.

An air barrier material alone will not produce an airtight building. Air barrier materials and components, such as doors and windows, wall, roof and ground separation air barrier assemblies, are tied together to provide a continuous plane of air tightness for the whole envelope called an air barrier system. Air barriers systems can be located anywhere in the building envelope. While several materials that qualify as an air barrier material may be used, where and how they are connected determines the location of the actual air barrier or pressure boundary, where 50 percent or more of the air pressure drops. In many cases, the pressure boundary is also a gas, fire, and smoke barrier and needs to meet specific code requirements.

Moisture and Water-Resistive Barriers

Moisture trapped within a wall can lead to mold growth or corrosion of building materials. An effective envelope manages moisture by preventing entry, removing moisture that enters and allowing wet areas to dry out through ventilation. While an air barrier may also be considered a vapor barrier in that it can be used to restrict the flow of moisture present in air, if it is too impermeable it may also trap moisture. Vapor barriers and water-resistive barriers are different from air barriers in that they allow moisture in *and* out of a building envelope.

Vapor barriers are most commonly used on the warm side of insulation to prevent condensation where warm moist air contacts a cold surface. Common vapor barrier materials include polyethylene plastic. Environmental conditions influence the location of the dew point in a wall assembly, which determines the proper placement for a vapor barrier. Unlike air barriers, a vapor barrier does have to be continuous or sealed; such gaps, however, may allow more vapor diffusion than desirable. How much water vapor resistance needed is determined by how easily water vapor can escape an assembly and the thermal resistance of the sheathing. The higher the water-vapor transmission rate, the easier it is for vapor to pass through the barrier and the less likely it is for vapor to be trapped in the wall cavity.

Water-resistive barriers are used as a drainage layer installed between the exterior sheathing and siding. When used with flashing, they form a shingled assembly to direct water and protect building materials from water penetration. Water-resistive barriers include housewraps and tar or felt building paper. Housewraps are typically polyolefin sheets with very small holes that vent water vapor but resist bulk water penetration. Differences in the size and density of the holes result in different air and vapor permeance. Building papers' resistance to water penetration depends on its construction as well. The most common building paper is 15# felt. Its permeance falls between most nonperforated and perforated housewraps.

Assessing Existing Conditions

In order to ensure the proper installation of air, vapor, and water-resistive barriers, verify the following conditions:

- Air permeance of air barrier materials is appropriate.
- Air barrier and surrounding materials are compatible.
- Substrate has been properly prepared.
- Air barrier is continuous.
- Edges and joints at penetrating pipes, conduit, electrical boxes, etc. are sealed.
- Vapor barrier occurs at proper location.
- Vapor barrier is firmly attached.
- Water-resistive barrier is acceptable to authorities having jurisdiction.
- Water-resistive barrier is lapped high over low for shingled effect and integrated with other flashings.
- Water-resistive barrier fasteners have plastic washers and are spaced per code (12–18 inches).
- Water-resistive barrier is installed with no wrinkles.
- Water-resistive seams are taped if used as an air barrier.

Acceptable Practices

Weather-resistive barriers need to be integrated with the buildings structure, insulation, and other system components, to function properly. Consideration must be given to how to construct a barrier and ensure its continuity. Differential movement, compatibility of materials, and support of weather barriers are particularly important to detail at foundations and walls, wall openings, walls and roofs, changes in wall construction, over unconditioned spaces, control joints, and enclosure penetrations.

Common construction practices for weather barriers include the following:

- Spray-applied urethane foams can perform as an air and vapor barrier as well as a drainage plane and for thermal protection. They are often also used to support sheet membranes.
- Testing of air barrier assemblies to ensure quality installation.
- Use of kraft paper or foil-backed insulation as a vapor barrier.
- Water-resistive barriers with sealed seams for use as an air retarder.
- Sealed rigid foam sheathing used as a weather-resistive barrier.
- Self-adhesive flashing using butyl rubber is more expensive than rubberized asphalt, but it is more adhesive at cold temperatures, and it does not soften and run as readily at high temperatures.

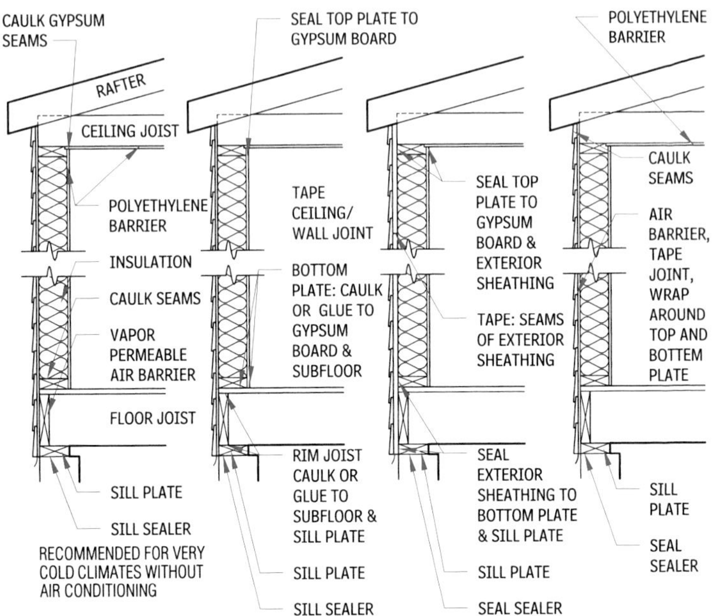

Figure 18.4 Common approaches to air barriers

Practices to Avoid

It is important to ensure that a weather barrier is installed to function properly over the life of a building. Damaged areas due to weather barrier failure can be extensive and costly, since they are often installed under other building materials or part of a complex assembly.

- Do not conceal tears or punctures in vapor retarder.
- Avoid using vapor controlling materials that are less permeable than required, which could trap moisture.
- Avoid using vapor barriers on both sides of a wall.
- Building papers or felts must not be left uncovered or subject to wind damage.
- Using untreated wood siding releases tannins that lessen the water repellency of building wraps.
- Do not use building wraps fasteners without tape to seal the holes. In high temperatures, fastener holes tend to stretch and allow air and moisture in.
- Asphalt-saturated building paper is self-sealing and can form a vapor barrier and trap moisture, so it should be avoided.

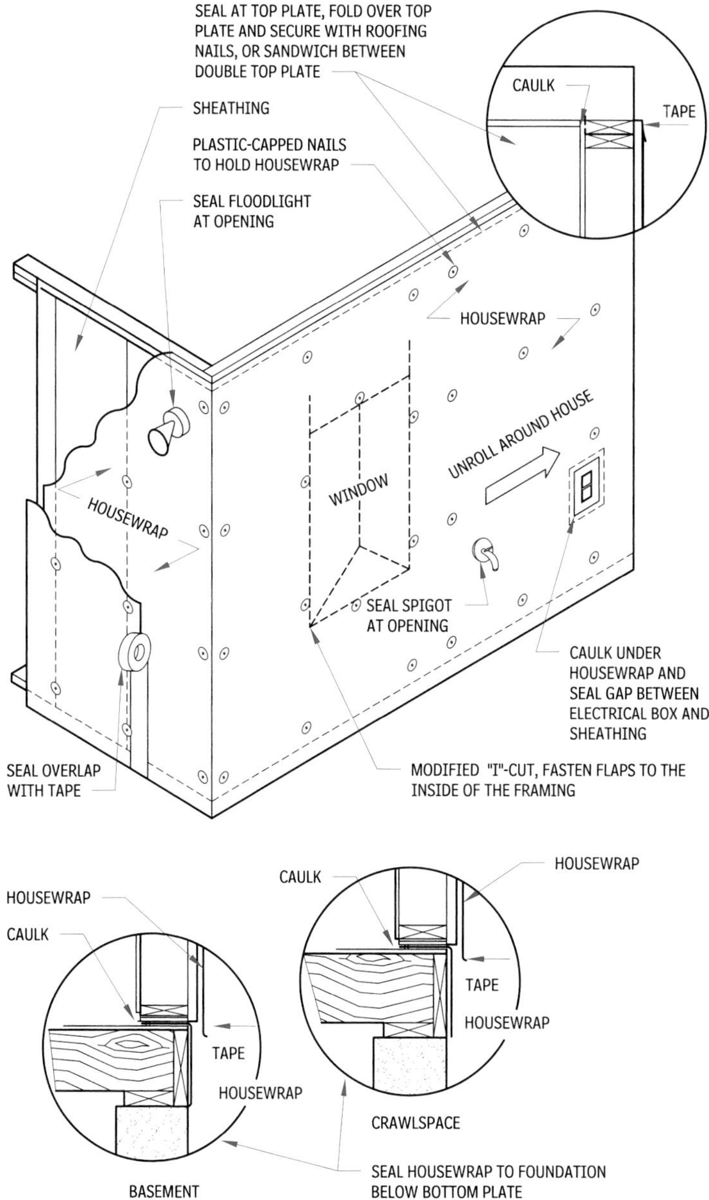

Figure 18.5 Weather barrier installation details.

- Do not use building paper as an air barrier because the seams are merely lapped rather than sealed.
- Flashing that forms a pan can trap moisture. Flashing should shed water to the outside of the building.
- Self-adhesive flashing using butyl rubber must not be used in contact with asphalt.

Resources

WITHIN THIS BOOK

- Chapter 1 Construction Information
- Chapter 2 Common Building Code Requirements
- Chapter 17 Dampproofing, Waterproofing, and Related Drainage
- Chapter 20 Exterior Wall Covering

REFERENCE STANDARDS

- ASTM C 1015—Standard Practice for Installation of Cellulosic and Mineral Fiber Loose-Fill Thermal Insulation
- ASTM C 1320—Standard Practice for Installation of Mineral Fiber Batt and Blanket Thermal Insulation for Light Frame Construction
- ASTM E 1677—Standard Specification for an Air Barrier Material or System for Low-Rise Framed Building Walls
- ASTM E 2178—Standard Test Method for air Permeance of Building Materials
- ASTM E2357—Standard Test Method for Determining Air Leakage of Air Barrier Assemblies

OTHER RESOURCES

- 2009 International Residential Code for One and Two-Family Dwellings. Washington, DC: International Code Council, Inc., 2009.
- American Institute of Architects, *Architectural Graphics Standards*, 11th ed. Hoboken, NJ: John Wiley and Sons, 2007.
- American Institute of Architects, *Architectural Graphic Standards for Residential Construction*, 2nd ed. Hoboken, NJ: John Wiley and Sons, 2010.
- National Association of Home Builders (NAHB) Research Center; Quality Plan for the Installation of EIFS.
- EIFS Industry Members Association (EIMA), www.eima.com.
- EIFS Council of Canada, www.eifsocouncil.org.

Chapter 19

Roof Covering

Shingles and Shakes

Roof Tiles

Vegetated Roofing

Metal Roofing

Membrane Roofing

Shingles and Shakes

Description

Wood shingles and shakes are used both as roof coverings and wall claddings. For roof applications, they are commonly used on sloped-roof shapes such as gable, hip, gambrel, and mansard. Because the application for wall shakes and shingles is so similar to the roof application, this discussion will include both wall and roof shingles and shakes.

The terms *shingles* and *shakes* are sometimes used interchangeably but are, in fact, different products:

- Wood shingles are sawn on both faces from wood blocks and tapered from butt to tip and have a relatively smooth surface.
- Manufacturers offer a wide range of fancy-butt shingles, including a semi-round shape known as the fish scale, a pointed butt to provide a diamond-shaped finish, and arrow, half-cove, hexagonal, octagonal and diagonal shapes.
- Wood shakes are split from wood blocks, typically being split on the exposed face and sawn on the concealed back (turned away from the weather), or sawn on both faces.
- Shakes may be used on both roofs and walls.

Dimensions

Wood shingles and shakes are produced in several different widths, lengths, and thicknesses. As a rule, the thicker the shake, the better the application.

Width: Wood shingles and shakes are produced in random widths ranging from 4 inches minimum to 14 inches maximum. Fancy-butt shingles, available in approximately nine different butt profiles, are 5 inches wide.

Length: Wood shingles are produced in three lengths, 16, 18, and 24 inches. Fancy-butt shingles are 18 inches long. Wood shakes are generally produced in two lengths, 18 and 24 inches. Rebutted and rejointed shakes, reflecting their shingle origins, are also produced in three lengths, 16, 18, and 24 inches.

Thickness: As shingle length increases, butt thickness increases. Traditionally, shingle thickness is based on the combined butt thickness of a number of shingles, as in the following examples:

- 2 inches thick for five 16-inch long shingles
- $2\frac{1}{4}$ inches thick for five 18-inch long shingles
- 2 inches thick for four 24-inch long shingles

Wood Types

Almost all wood shingles and shakes are made from western red or eastern white cedar or cypress because of their natural resistance to deterioration from moisture and insects, but other woods that have been preservative treated are available, depending on project location. Some treatments retard both decay (preservatives) and weathering (finishes). Realistic wood-shingle replicas in alternative materials are available.

Shingles made from western red cedar are bonded to plywood panels. Confirm availability for project location, since these panels are currently produced only by manufacturers located on the West Coast of the United States.

Fire-Retardant Treatment

Fire-retardant-treated wood shingles and shakes require classification markings from FM Global, Underwriters Laboratories (UL), or another testing and inspecting agency acceptable to authorities having jurisdiction. Fire-retardant treatment eliminates the possibility of preservative treatment because both treatments cannot be used together.

ASTM or UL classification is based on the degree of external fire resistance:

- *Class A:* Effective against severe fire exposure; generally cannot be achieved without considerable attention to the construction beneath the fire-retardant-treated shingles and shakes.
- *Class B:* Effective against moderate fire exposure; can be met with some additional attention to roof construction by pressure-impregnated, fire-retardant-treated shingles and shakes.
- *Class C:* Effective against light fire exposure; can be met with some additional attention to roof construction by pressure-impregnated, fire-retardant-treated shingles and shakes.

Assessing Existing Conditions

In order to ensure the proper installation of shingles and shakes as roof covering or wall cladding, verify the following before installation:

- Confirm local building code requirements for fire resistance are met. The IRC does not indicate fire-resistance requirements for wood shingles and shakes.
- For shingles or shakes used as roof covering, confirm that underlayment, weather resistive barrier, ice barrier, sheet waterproofing, sheathing, minimum offsets, flashing, double starter course, and other assembly materials are installed in compliance with the IRC requirements.

Acceptable Practices

In the installation of shakes and shingles, quality assurance of materials is essential. Products made under the grading and manufacturing requirements of the Cedar Shake and Shingle Bureau are labeled to assure end users of a high level of quality and performance.

Table 19.1 How to Read a Certi-label

1. The "Certi" Brand Name—Your Quality Assurance
2. Product Grade
3. Product Type
4. Independent, Third-Party, Quality Control Agency
5. This Number Shows Compliance with Total Quality Manufacturing System
6. Mill Name, Location, and Phone Number
7. Industry Product Description

8. Product Dimensions
9. Cedar Bureau Label Number
10. Building Code Compliance Numbers
11. Product Performance Tests Passed
12. Label Identification Number
13. UPC Code
14. Coverage Chart and Recommended Exposure
15. Application Instructions on Reverse Side

Source: Cedar Shake and Shingle Bureau

- For cedar roof preservatives, use only a product that is labeled as a cedar roof treatment product, is a water repellent, UV inhibitor, and/or EPA registered wood preservative.
- Surface treatment of the roof with a commercial treating solution containing zinc or copper napthanate, in solution form, works to preserve a cedar roof and to retard future surface growth.
- Zinc or copper strips nailed at the ridge cap can be used to control moss for the first few courses below the ridge cap.
- Use of a fungicide/preservative treatment is recommended.
- Semitransparent penetrating oil-based stains are the most effective finishes for roofs. The stain should contain a wood preservative and a water repellent.
- Providing airspace between the shingles and the felt-covered sheathing improves drying.

Practices to Avoid

Common construction and maintenance practices to avoid for quality performance and appearance of shingles and shakes include the following:

- Never seal wood shingle or shake roofs. Sealing the roof will lock in moisture that would otherwise naturally evaporate during normal weather conditions.
- Do not allow needles, branches, leaves, dirt, or moss to accumulate on shingle/shake roofs. Wood needs to breathe, and therefore accumulation of debris and dirt will retain moisture that could harm wood and affect its lifespan.
- Film-forming finishes, such as paint, solid-color stains, or varnish, should never be used on roofs. Such finishes do not tolerate shrinking and swelling and will crack, providing a site for water to enter; the areas of intact film will later restrict moisture release.

Roof Tiles

Description

Tile roofs can be long-lasting and durable, if they are well detailed and constructed. The most common roofing tiles are available in either clay or concrete, and come in a large number of profiles, sizes, colors, and textures. All tiles absorb moisture and, generally, the more porous the material, the less strong and durable the tile. Concrete tile is generally more porous than clay, and may require a sealer.

Assessing Existing Conditions

In order to ensure the proper installation of a roof tiles, verify the following conditions:

- The structure needs to be able to support tiles adequately.
- A proper weather barrier is applied in areas of high rain, wind-driven rain, or in cold climates for protection against ice dams.
- For high-wind areas, refer to *The Concrete and Clay Tile Installation Manual,* published by the Florida Roofing, Sheet Metal, and Air Conditioning Contractors Association and the Roof Tile Institute.
- Coordinate roof tiles installation with flashing and gutter installation.

Acceptable Practices

Tile is made from two basic materials, clay and concrete:

- *Clay:* Clay tiles are formed from natural material, so color uniformity is dependent on the uniformity of the raw clay, unless it is glazed. Unglazed tile weathers only slightly, over time. Glazed tiles are available in a larger number of colors, including bright blues, greens, reds, and oranges. One of the advantages of clay tiles that have kept them a staple for centuries is the ability of clay to insulate, keeping inside temperatures warm in winter and cool in summer. Combined with a natural ability to reflect, instead of absorb, heat from the sun, clay tiles can reduce the energy required to maintain comfortable temperatures in a home.

- *Concrete:* Concrete tiles are pressed in molds, under high pressure. The synthetic oxide compounds color the surface. Tiles are sometimes painted, which may fade with time. Although concrete tiles don't last as long as clay tiles, they do share a majority of the same advantages, such as insulation, durability, and weather resistance.

Tiles are typically available in three profiles: flat, barrel, and S-shaped. Barrel and S-shaped tiles are also called mission tiles.

- *Flat:* These are approximately 10 by 13 inches up to 13 by 20 inches. Flat tiles may be very simple, requiring a doubled shingled overlap, or may be interlocking, with approximately a 3-inch head overlap. Tiles may be fluted on the back to reduce weight or lugged to hang on battens.
- *Barrel:* Barrel tile sizes are typically 16 by 8 inches, 19 by 10 inches, or 18 by 12 inches, punched for one hole.
- *S-shaped:* These tiles are approximately 10 by 13 inches, up to 13 by 20 in. S-shaped tiles are essentially the pan and cover portions of barrel tiles in one piece.

Practices to Avoid

- Avoid installing clay roof tiles on a high-sloping roof without proper fasting system.
- Avoid using concrete roof tiles with surface color coats in areas where freeze/thaw cycles exceed 30 per year.

Vegetated Roofing

Description

There are two types of vegetated roofs—an extensive roof and intensive roof. Extensive roof systems are lightweight, low maintenance, and intended for appearance purposes. Extensive systems are lightweight because the growing media is thin and the drought-resistant plants that are used require little if any water, which is how an extensive system is low maintenance. The extensive assembly consists of a waterproofing system, insulation, water-retention system, growing media, and plants. The extensive system is very light, weighing little more than a traditional ballast roof, which makes this system a good choice for existing roofs or new construction.

Intensive roof systems incorporate plantings that require regular maintenance and generally are designed to be occupied. An intensive system is broken down into two different systems, shallow-intensive and intensive. A shallow-intensive system is considered to be a lightweight assembly, but has a deeper soil depth than extensive systems. Shallow-intensive systems generally incorporate sod lawns and perennials. An irrigation system may be required. The intensive assembly consists of a waterproofing system, insulation, water-retention system, growing media, and plants. However, in this system the water-retention system is intended to assist the irrigation system with the irrigation of the assembly. The growing medium in intensive assemblies are generally 6 to 36 inches deep, which require additional building structural support. Thus, vegetated roofs are used primarily in new construction.

There are options for the waterproofing systems for these assemblies:

- Hot-applied asphalt waterproofing system
- Sheet waterproofing system
- Built-up roof assembly (commonly called an inverted roof assembly)
- Single-ply roof assembly (commonly called an inverted roof assembly)

The most common waterproofing system used for intensive vegetated roof assemblies is the hot-applied asphalt waterproofing system. For the extensive vegetated roof assembly, the most common waterproofing systems used are single-ply or built-up roof assemblies, because these extensive assemblies don't have constant traffic, just occasional maintenance traffic.

Assessing Existing Conditions

In order to ensure a successful vegetated roof assembly, you need to verify the following conditions:

- The waterproofing system work has been completed and a flood test has been done prior to installation of vegetated roofing materials.
- Roof drains should have metal covers to prevent planting materials or growing medium to clog drains.
- Roof edges should have edge restraints to prevent growing medium from clogging gutters.
- Waterproofing system should extend a minimum of 6 inches above top of finish growing surface. In some instances, waterproofing membranes are required to be protected from UV due to degradation of waterproofing membrane. Verify that all flashings are in place where waterproofing membrane is exposed to the elements.

Acceptable Practices

When choosing a vegetated roof assembly, because of all the individual components associated with this assembly, it is a good idea to incorporate an test prior to the placement of overburden. This will allow any leaks in the waterproofing system to be easily found and repaired, with a minimal amount of vegetated roofing components removed.

Provide the following in vegetated roof assemblies:

- Create work areas around mechanical equipment, either gravel or unit pavers.
- Provide pathways within the vegetated roof to allow for maintenance of plantings.
- Include a pathway at the perimeter of the vegetated roof for access to building perimeter assemblies for service or repair.
- Install edge restraints between paved areas and planting areas.
- Have a provision for water on the roof. Generally for a minimum of the first year, even extensive systems require watering and maintenance to establish plantings.

Practices to Avoid

- Avoid waterproofing systems with insulation below the waterproofing membrane. Because board insulation can flex when walked on, this flexing can place a strain on the waterproofing membrane and cause failure.
- Avoid plantings up to the roof edge. Allow a minimum of 12 inches from edge of roof.

Metal Roofing

Description

Metal roof panels come in many different shapes and vary by manufacturer. Panel width can vary as well and can be anywhere between 12 inches to 36 inches wide. With narrower panels, 12 to 16 inches wide, it is acceptable to have small or no striations, pencil ribs, or corrugations between panel seams. With wider panels, 18 to 36 inches, it is wise to have intermediate striations, pencil ribs, or corrugations to help to prevent "oil-canning" or buckling of panels.

There are three types of fastening systems for metal roof panels: surface fasteners, concealed clip, and integral flange attachment. Surface fasteners have neoprene washers at the base of the head of the fastener and fasten the metal panel to the substrate through the face of the panel. The neoprene washers prevent water from penetrating the face of the metal panel. Concealed clips are individual clips that are spaced at a distance recommended by the manufacturer; the clips are located at each seam and are concealed between each panel. The advantage of the concealed clip design is that the clips allow the panel to expand and contract with the changing temperature of the metal panel; therefore "oil-canning" is not as big of a problem as with the surface fasteners. The integral flange attachment method for metal panels incorporates the attachment of the metal panel into a flange of the metal panel, usually at each seam. The next panel overlaps the integral flange and attaches to the previous panel by snapping the two panels together. The attachment flanges generally are fabricated with slotted holes at a predetermined distance, which allows for panel movement.

Assessing Existing Conditions

For roof assemblies in general, the following conditions should be verified:

- Commonly minimum roof slope for metal roofing is 3:12. However, certain metal roof profiles can go as low as 0.25:12. Verify minimum roof slope meets manufacturers requirements.

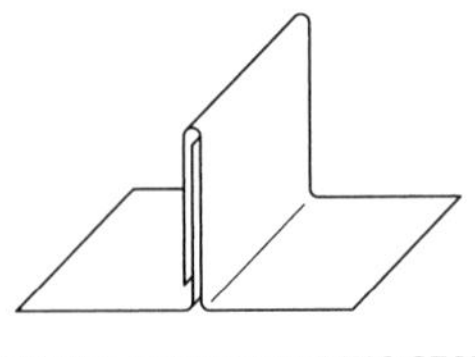

SINGLE-LOCK STANDING SEAM

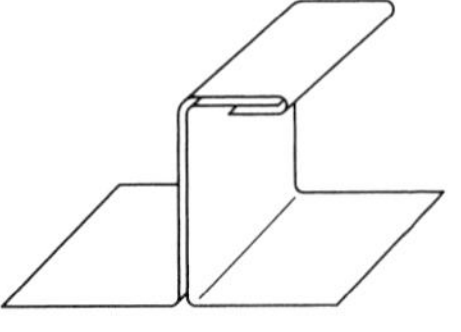

OPEN STANDING SEAM

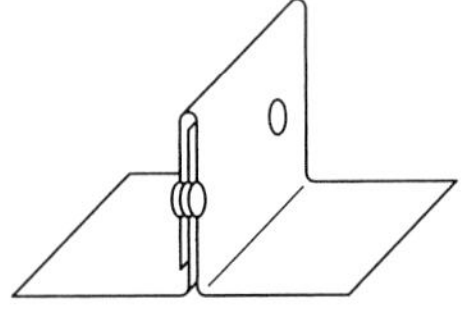

SINGLE-LOCK STANDING SEAM, BUTTON PUNCHED

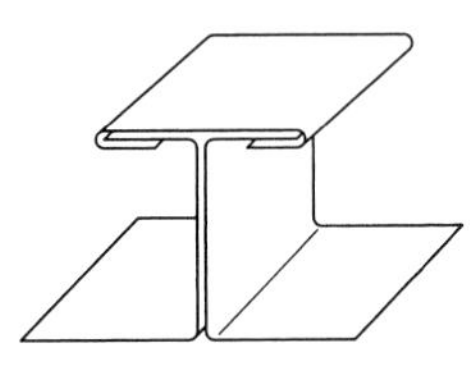

CAPPED STANDING SEAM

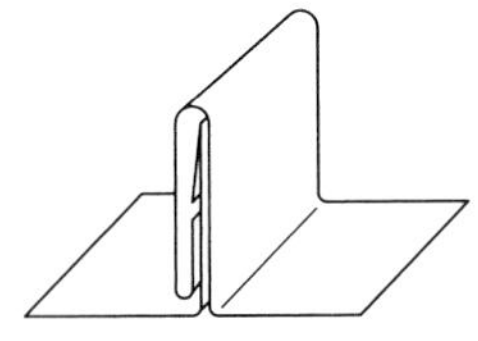

STANDING SEAM WITH SNAP LOCK

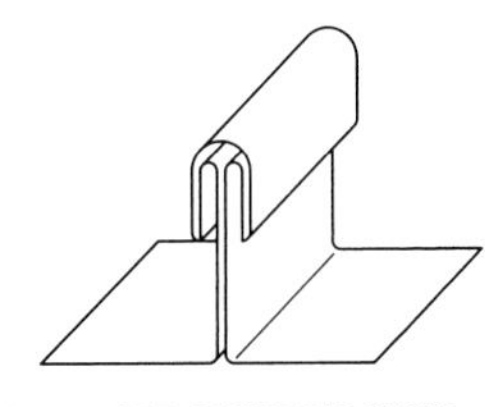

SNAP-CAP STANDING SEAM

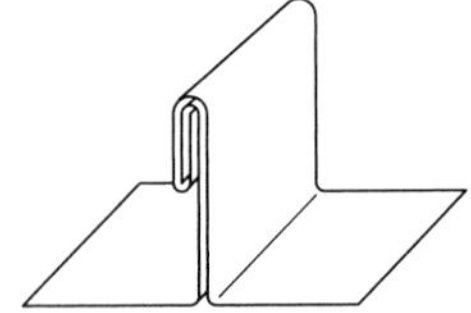

DOUBLE-LOCK STANDING SEAM

Figure 19.1 Standing Seams

Source: AIA, Architectural Graphic Standards for Residential Construction, 2nd ed. Hoboken, NJ: John Wiley & Sons, 2010

- Verify that roof slopes evenly to all drains.
- All penetrations through roof and rooftop equipment should be installed and complete, ready for installation of roofing system.
- Most manufacturers recommend a minimum of 30-pound felt underlayment to be installed under metal panels and on top of roof sheathing, verify manufacturer's requirements to maintain roof warranty.
- In climates with heavy wind, snow, or ice, it is recommended by the manufacturer to install a self-adhering 40-mil rubberized asphalt underlayment instead of roofing felt. This underlayment

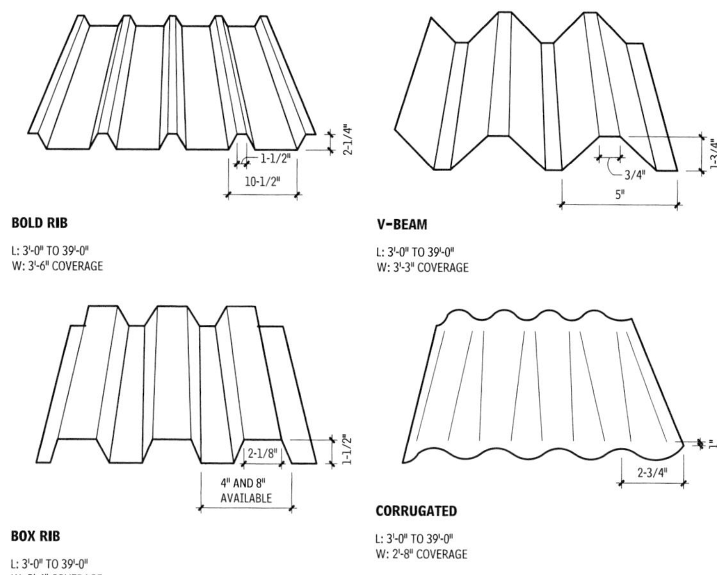

Figure 19.2 Corrugated or Formed Metal Roofing Panels
Source: AIA, Architectural Graphic Standards for Residential Construction, 2nd ed. Hoboken, NJ: John Wiley & Sons, 2010

should be rated for high temperatures as well, due to the fact that it is under a metal roof. These products help to prevent roof leaks due to ice dams forming at eaves, valleys, or where a vertical surface intersects the roof slope. It also helps prevent leaks due to heavy winds.

Acceptable Practices

When installing metal roofing, the following are suggested guidelines:

- There should not be any moisture on the substrate.
- Metal roofing manufacturers can provide all necessary flashings and boots associated with the metal roofing systems so that colors match including those associated with skylights, roof dormers, chimneys.
- If roofing is installed in a snowy climate, "snow guards" can be attached to the metal roofing. This prevents snow from sliding off the metal roofs and damaging gutters, or even causing personal injury. At a minimum, snow guards should be installed over entrances and garage doors.

Practices to Avoid

Avoid the following practices in metal roofing assemblies:

- Do not install damaged materials.
- Avoid having end-to-end metal panel joints between ridge and eave. If unavoidable and manufacturer does not provide a standard detail, refer to the *Architectural Sheet Metal Manual*, section "Common Lock, Hook Seam or Clinch Lock Joint," from the Sheet Metal and Air Conditioning Contractors' National Association (SMACNA).
- At metal roofs attached with concealed clips, do not attach at both the ridge of the roof and eave. Panels should only be attached at the ridge; the eave should have a sliding joint to allow for panel movement.
- Do not leave metal panel cutting on roof. These can damage roof finish.
- Avoid snow guard systems that attach directly through metal panel to roof substrate. The best snow guards will attach to the standing seams of the metal panels.

Membrane Roofing

Description

There are two types of membrane roofs: built-up membranes and single-ply membranes. Built-up roofing is composed of a series of reinforced roofing felts coated with asphalt. If the built-up roof system uses adhesive between roofing felt layers, it is considered a cold-applied system. If the built-up roof system uses hot asphalt to bond the felts together, then the system is called a hot-applied system. There are three different surfaces that are typically used as the finished surface of the built-up roof:

1. The surfacing can be a mineral cap sheet, which is a ply sheet with mineral granules factory applied over the surface of a ply sheet
2. The surfacing can be a smooth surface where the last ply has a flood coat of asphalt applied over the top surface of the entire roof.
3. The surfacing can have a layer of ballast installed in a flood coat of asphalt or adhesive over the entire roof. Ballast is generally stone broadcast into the asphalt or adhesive flood coat.

Single-ply membranes come in three types and there are three different installation methods common to all three types of single-ply membranes. The three types of single-ply membranes are polyvinyl-chloride (PVC), thermoplastic–polyolefin (TPO), and ethylene propylene diene monomer (EPDM) roof membranes. Single-ply membranes can be installed by mechanically fastening each membrane sheet to the roof substrate, adhesive attached to the roof substrate by using adhesive under the entire membrane sheet, or by the use of ballast where the membrane is loose laid on the roof surface, fastened at the perimeter of the building, and the ballast is used to hold the system in place. PVC and TPO membranes come in various colors; EPDM membranes come only in black.

Assessing Existing Conditions

For roof assemblies in general, the following conditions should be verified:

- Review manufacturer's specifications and details prior to visiting jobsite. In order to obtain the desired roofing warranty, manufacturers have specific suggested details and specific products that must be used.

- Verify that roof slopes are a minimum of 1/4 inch per foot and that roof slopes evenly to all drains.
- All penetrations through roof and rooftop equipment should be installed and complete, ready for installation of roofing system.

For built-up roof assemblies, the following conditions should be verified:

- Pressure-treated or fibrous cant strips should be installed at all locations where the horizontal plane of the roof intersects a vertical plane.
- If insulation is to be placed on top of the roof deck, verify that pressure-treated nailers have been installed at the perimeter of the roof area and at openings in roof deck. The height of the nailers should match the height of the insulation.

For single-ply roof assemblies, the following conditions should be verified:

- If insulation is to be placed on top of the roof deck, verify that nailers have been installed at the perimeter of the roof area and at openings in roof deck. Nailers cannot have any oil-based preservatives such as creosote. These types of preservatives are not compatible with single-ply membranes. The height of the nailers should match the height of the insulation.

Acceptable Practices

When installing a built-up roof, the following are suggested guidelines:

- There should not be any moisture on the substrate to which asphalt is to be applied. Moisture can cause poor adhesion of the mopping asphalt.
- Begin application of roofing at low point of roof.
- If built-up roofing is to be placed directly on the roof deck, then a mechanically attached layer of sheathing paper (slip sheet) is required.

When installing built-up roofing in cold weather (temperatures below 45° F), special care should be taken. Check the following:

- It is best to store roofing products in a heated space prior to installation.
- Rolled materials should be pre-cut to length and allowed to flatten.
- Check asphalt temperature at the mop or asphalt spreader to make sure the asphalt is at the correct temperature. The correct temperature of the asphalt is dependent on the type of asphalt being used on the project.
- If a cold-applied system is being installed, the roofing adhesive can only be used if the temperatures is above 40° F.

Table 19.2 Types of Asphalt/Cap Sheet Roofs

	Incline in Inches	Types of Asphalt (Min.)
Cap Sheet Roofs	0–½	Type II
	½–3	Type III
	3–6	Type IV
Smooth-Surfaced Roofs	0–1	Type II
	1–3	Type III
	3–6	Type IV
Gravel-Surfaced Roofs	0–½	Type II
	½–3	Types III

When installing a single-ply roof, the following are suggested guidelines:

- Begin application of roofing at low point of roof.
- All seams are lapped and sealed. A sealed seam is achieved through the use of either an adhesive or through hot air welding. Typically, hot air welding of seams is used in TPO membranes, adhesive seams are used in PVC membranes, and butyl-based seam tapes are used for EPDM membranes. With both adhesive seams and seam tapes, seams must be properly cleaned prior to application with a membrane cleaner recommended by roofing manufacturer.
- Minimum temperature for application of adhesives is 40° F.
- If single-ply roofing is to be placed directly on a wood or plywood roof deck, then a mechanically attached layer of sheathing paper (slip sheet) is required.

Practices to Avoid

Avoid the following practices in built-up roofing assemblies:

- Do not install damaged or wet materials.
- Asphalt should not be overheated. This will damage the asphalt by dropping the softening point. A slight oiliness to the asphalt is a symptom.
- Different asphalt grades should not be mixed together or diluted with any material.

Avoid the following practices in single-ply roofing assemblies:

- Do not install damaged or wet materials.
- Single-ply roofing membranes should not be placed in contact with coal tar pitch or asphalt products of any kind.

Resources

WITHIN THIS BOOK

- Chapter 17 Dampproofing, Waterproofing, and Related Drainage
- Chapter 18 Thermal Protection and Weather Barriers
- Chapter 20 Exterior Wall Covering

REFERENCE STANDARDS

- ASTM E 108—*Test Methods for Fire Tests of Roof Coverings*
- UL 790—*Tests for Fire Resistance of Roof Covering Materials*

OTHER RESOURCES

- 2009 International Residential Code for One and Two-Family Dwellings. Washington, DC: International Code Council, Inc., 2009.
- American Institute of Architects, *Architectural Graphics Standards*, 11th ed. Hoboken, NJ: John Wiley and Sons, 2007.
- American Institute of Architects, *Architectural Graphic Standards for Residential Construction*, 2nd ed. Hoboken, NJ: John Wiley and Sons, 2010.
- Cedar Shake and Shingle Bureau, www.cedarbureau.org.
- *Exterior and Interior Wall Manual.* Sumas, WA: Cedar Shake and Shingle Bureau, 2004.
- The National Roofing Contractors Association's (NRCA) *The NRCA Roofing and Waterproofing Manual.*
- *New Roof Construction Manual.* Sumas, WA: Cedar Shake and Shingle Bureau, 2010.
- SMACNA, *Architectural Sheet Metal Manual,* 6th ed. Chantilly, VA: Sheet Metal and Air Conditioning Contractors' National Association, Inc., 2003.

Chapter 20

Exterior Wall Covering

Panel Siding

Board Siding

Stucco

Panel Siding

Description

Panel siding, also called sheet siding is available in rough-sawn plywood, smooth-sided plywood, fiber-cement panels, and engineered or composite wood (OSB, pressed hardboard and veneered plywood) panels. Newly available are faux wood, stone, and brick siding panels made of high-density polyurethane and molded to resemble wood, stone, or brick veneer.

The most common panel size is 4 by 8 feet, but sheets 10 and 12 feet long are available in some products and can be utilized to help minimize the number of horizontal butt joints. Panel siding sheets typically have shiplap edges so that one piece laps onto its neighboring sheet, and can be applied horizontally or vertically.

Wood and pressed hardboard panel siding is generally field painted or stained; fiber-cement can be either factory primed for field finishing, or factory painted in a variety of patterns and colors.

Prior to installation of all siding types, a weather-resistant barrier must be installed to prevent moisture/condensation from forming behind the siding, which could lead to rot or mold of wall assemblies.

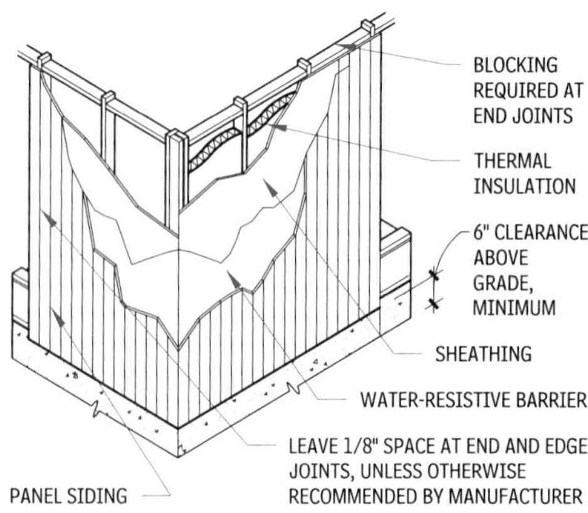

Figure 20.1 Vertical panel siding
Source: AIA, *Architectural Graphic Standards for Residential Construction,* 2nd ed. Copyright 2010, John Wiley and Sons, Inc.

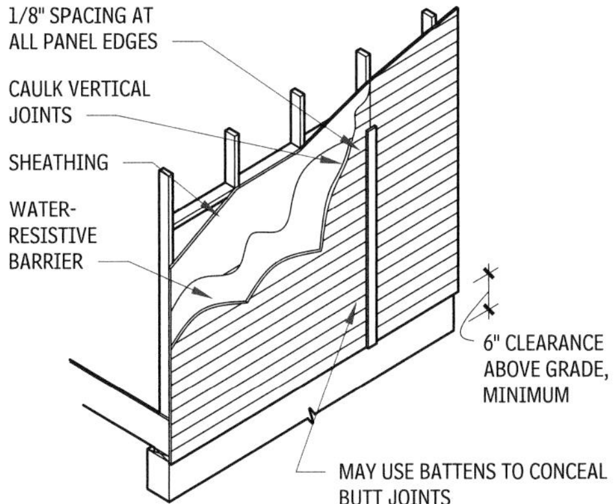

Figure 20.2 Horizontal panel siding
Source: AIA, *Architectural Graphic Standards for Residential Construction,* 2nd ed. Copyright 2010, John Wiley and Sons, Inc.

Rough-sawn plywood, commonly known as Texture 1–11 (or T1–11), is available with either 4-inch or 8-inch parallel grooves and shiplapped edges.

Smooth-sided panels are often used to create a faux board-and-batten look. Alternatively, the joint between panels can be covered with a single batten.

Fiber-cement siding is available in panels or boards. It is noncombustible and resists damage from exposure to moisture, humidity, salt air, and termite infestation. A variety of styles, widths, patterns, textures, and colors are available. Features of fiber-cement siding are minimal maintenance requirements and long (commonly 50 years) warranty terms. Refer to "Board Siding" later in this chapter for additional information on fiber-cement siding.

Engineered or composite wood (OSB, pressed hardboard, and veneered plywood) panels are bonded together with special resins and are typically treated with fungus repellents and insecticides. These products often stand up to moisture, mildew, and termites, sun damage, abrasion, and chemicals better than solid wood siding. However, engineered siding materials must be completely sealed with several coats of paint or stain at all edges to avoid water absorption.

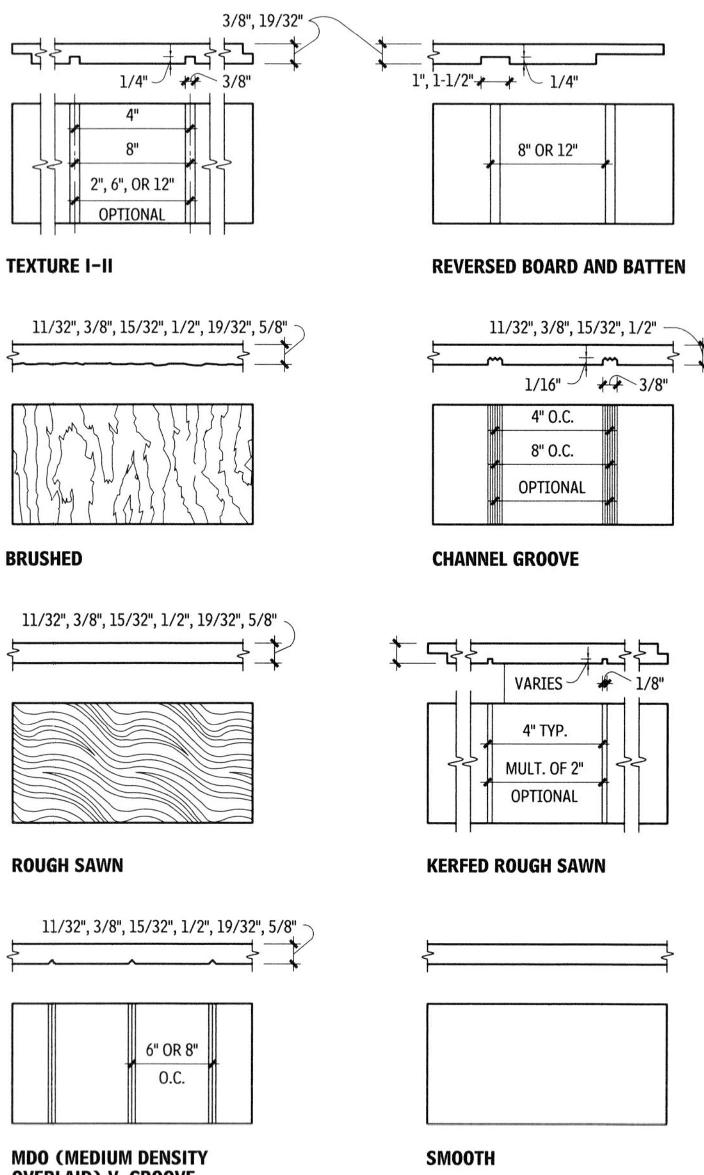

Figure 20.3 Plywood siding

Source: AIA, *Architectural Graphic Standards for Residential Construction,* 2nd ed. Copyright 2010, John Wiley and Sons, Inc.

Assessing Existing Conditions

In order to ensure the proper installation of siding, you need to verify the following conditions:

- Ensure siding is the proper minimum thickness and is attached in compliance with the IRC.
- IRC requires weather-resistant siding attachment and minimum material thickness requirements but does not reference the recommendations in AAMA 1402. Verify the requirements of authorities having jurisdiction.
- IRC requires fiber-cement siding to comply with ASTM C 1186, *Specification for Flat Non-Asbestos Fiber-Cement Sheets.*
- Ensure siding is installed directly over the wall sheathing with an appropriate weather-resistant barrier (building paper or house wrap), according to IRC requirements and in accordance with siding manufacturer's written installation instructions.

Table 20.1 Weather-Resistant Siding Attachment and Minimum Thickness

Siding Materials		Nominal Thickness[a]	Joint Treatment	Water-Resistive Barrier Required
Horizontal Aluminum	Without Insulation	0.019"[b]	Lap	Yes
		0.024"	Lap	Yes
	With Insulation	0.019"	Lap	Yes
Anchored Veneer: Brick, Concrete, Masonry, or Stone		2"	N/A	Yes
Adhered Veneer: Concrete, Stone, or Masonry[c]		N/A	N/A	Yes
Hardboard Panel Siding-Vertical[d]		7/16"	N/A	N/A
Hardboard Lap-Siding-Horizontal[d]		7/16"	End joint cover or caulk	Yes
Steel		29 ga.	Lap	Yes
Particleboard Panels		3/8" to 1/2"	N/A	Yes
		5/8"	N/A	Yes

(*continued*)

Siding Materials	Nominal Thickness[a]	Joint Treatment	Water-Resistive Barrier Required
Wood Structural Panel Siding [e](exterior grade)	3/8" to 1/2"	End joint cover or caulk	Yes
Wood Structural Panel Lap-Siding	3/8" to 1/2"	End joint cover or caulk	Yes
Vinyl Siding[f]	0.035"	Lap	Yes
Wood, Shiplap	19/32" Average		
Wood, Bevel	7/16"	Lap	Yes
Wood, Butt Tip	3/16"	Lap	Yes
Fiber Cement Panel Siding[g]	5/16"	Joint cover or caulk	Yes
Fiber Cement Lap-Siding[g]	5/16"	Lap[h]	Yes

a. Based on stud spacing of 16 inches on center.
b. Aluminum (0.019 inch) shall be unbacked only when the maximum panel width is 10 inches and the maximum flat area is 8 inches.
c. Adhered masonry veneer shall comply with the requirements in Section 6.1 and 6.3 of ACI 530/ASCE 5/TMS-402.
d. Hardboard siding shall comply with CPA/ANSI A135.6.
e. 3/8 inch plywood shall not be applied directly to studs spaced more than 16 inches on center when long dimension is parallel to studs. Plywood 1/2 inch or thinner shall not be applied directly to studs spaced more than 24 inches on center. The stud spacing shall not exceed the panel span rating provided by the manufacturer unless the panels are installed with the face grain perpendicular to the studs or over sheathing approved for that stud spacing.
f. Vinyl siding shall comply with ASTM D 3679.
g. Fiber cement panels to comply with ASTM C 1186, Type A, minimum Grade II.
h. Siding without tongue-and-groove end joints shall be caulked.

Acceptable Practices

- Comply with siding manufacturer's written installation instructions applicable to products and applications indicated, unless more stringent local code requirements apply.
- T1–11 plywood panel siding can buckle, warp, or even come apart if it is not installed correctly and kept well sealed. The least expensive types must be sealed with primer and two or more coats of exterior paint and attached with nails every 16 inches. Higher-end products are thicker, use better wood and glue, and come with a first coat of sealer.

- Stain-grade plywood panels have no football-shape patches as lower grades commonly do. Typically, these panels have vertical grooves (the panels should be installed upright, so water will not sit in the grooves). The grooves may be evenly or variably spaced.
- For vertical applications, siding should be nailed to horizontal blocking lines or furring strips. Install fasteners for vertical vinyl siding and related accessories no more than 12 inches on center.
- Siding should be thought of as a rainscreen rather than a weather-resistant barrier. Siding sheds water but does not completely prevent water penetration. Siding must be backed up with a wind- and water-resistant barrier to prevent water entry into the wall, and it must be detailed to allow water and water vapor to freely drain and flow from behind it. Flashing details, end conditions at trim and windows, endlaps, and bottom (starter) details are critical to proper weather performance.
- Butt joints between boards placed vertically should be staggered and made on studs. Fit siding snugly to other pieces and to trim.
- Corner boards are a popular alternative to mitered corners. They are often 3/4 inch or 1-1/4 inch material, depending on the thickness of the siding. Width is a matter of taste and proper proportion. Corner boards are applied to the sheathing, with the siding fitting tightly against the narrow edge of the boards. Joints should be filled with caulking compound when siding is applied. Trim boards can be used to cover butt jointed siding.
- At inside corners, siding is frequently butted against a trim strip. It can also be butted against adjoining walls, with a trim strip used to cover the joint.
- At outside corners, some builders choose mitered corners for a professional-looking finish. Mitered corners are most common on horizontally applied siding, and they must fit tightly for the full depth of the miter. To maintain a tight fit, the siding should be properly seasoned before installation and protected from the weather at the job site. The ends are often set in caulking compound when siding is applied.

Practices to Avoid

- Do not use unfinished/unsealed wood.
- Do not reduce the siding overlap recommendations. Doing so could result in damage from wind-driven water.

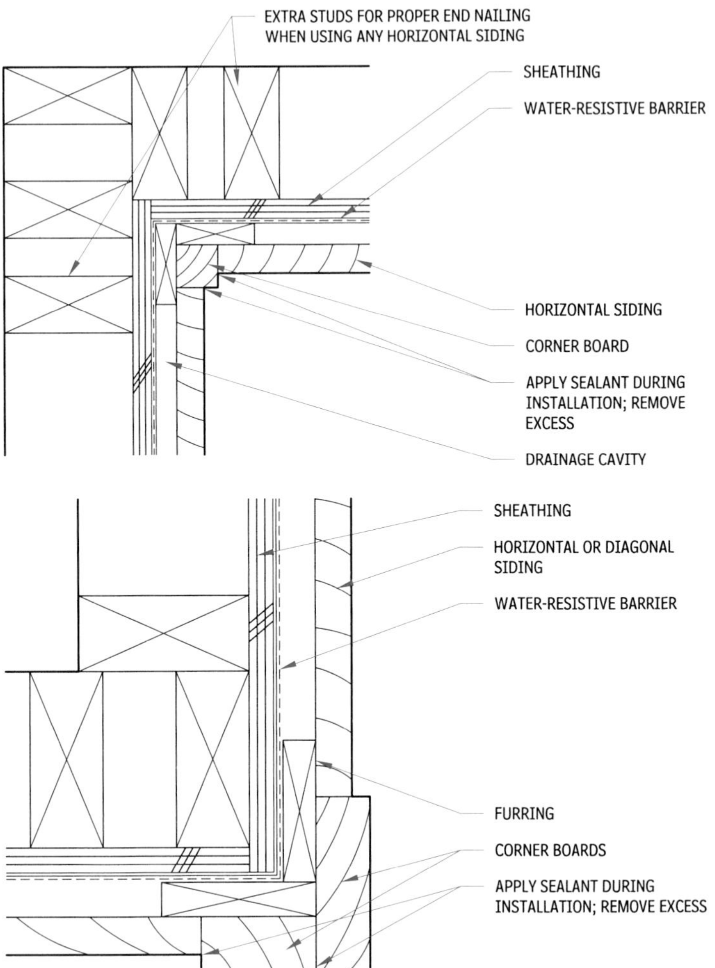

Figure 20.4 Corner board joints

Source: AIA, *Architectural Graphic Standards for Residential Construction,* 2nd ed. Copyright 2010, John Wiley and Sons, Inc.

Board Siding

Description

Wood, vinyl, aluminum, fiber-cement, and hard board or plank sidings are commonly used on the exterior walls of residential and light commercial projects and are available in many different horizontal and vertical profiles. Wood siding is the traditional board siding material, while vinyl, aluminum, fiber-cement, and hard board sidings have become widely used in recent years because of lower cost, ease of installation, and less maintenance. Manufacturers of these alternatives to wood siding offer an assortment of smooth and textured panels, matching soffits, trims, and decorative accessories in various sizes to simulate the different types and sizes of wood siding. Aluminum and vinyl sidings offer a wider variety of patterns than fiber-cement siding.

Aluminum siding was popular some years ago but lost some of its appeal when vinyl siding became available. One drawback for aluminum siding is its baked-on enamel finish, which is easily scratched. Vinyl siding is extruded with integral color, so marring the finish is not typically an issue. Aluminum siding, however, is still commonly used for trim pieces because of its flexible properties and is easily custom bent, while vinyl must be extruded or molded into shape as it is manufactured.

Vinyl siding is made from a PVC plastic resin that is heated until molten and then extruded into sheets of siding panel profiles. The sheets are then embossed with a brushed or wood-grain pattern. Thickness or gauge of the vinyl is the key to its durability and cost. Premium brands are available in up to 0.055 inch thickness; most typically used being 0.040 to 0.045 inches thick. Vinyl siding is available in a range of light to medium colors; darker colors tend to fade from UV exposure and are not generally available.

Fiber-cement siding is composed of cement, sand, and cellulose fiber that has been autoclaved to increase its strength, dimensional stability, and impact resistance. This product is generally noncombustible, resists damage from exposure to moisture, humidity, salt air, and termite infestation, and some manufacturers offer a 50-year warranty. Planks are available in 5-1/4-inch to 12-inch widths and 5/16-inch and 7/16-inch thickness, and can be purchased in a variety of factory-primed or factory-finished colors, patterns, and textures.

Hard board siding, commonly known as "Masonite," is constructed from a mixture of wood fibers, wax, and other resins, manufactured through a process of heat and pressure, fusing the components into a smooth strong board. Hard board siding is also available in a variety of factory-primed or factory finished colors and patterns and can be a low-cost siding alternative with field painting most typical.

Wood or clapboard siding is available in several face profiles, including bevel, board and batten, lap/channel, tongue and groove, and wavy-edge bevel. Special shapes, such as scallop edge, are available from some manufacturers, and now available is also knotty pine or cedar wood siding, made to resemble quarter or half logs and hand-hewn logs.

Siding Profiles

Bevel or clapboard siding is a type of siding made from wedge-shaped boards that are designed to overlap with each other. When bevel siding is applied, it is layered like shingles, with the thin side of each board lying under the thick edge of the board on top. Spacing for the siding should be laid out beforehand. The number of board spaces between the soffit and bottom of the lowest piece of siding at the foundation should be such that the overlap is in accordance with IRC or other code requirements. The wider the siding, the greater the overlap can be. Red cedar has been a popular choice for centuries because it is naturally weather and pest resistant, but other soft and hard woods, such as pine and fir, can be used as well.

Board-and-batten is a vertical pattern created using boards and battens of various widths for a range of effects. Although for good appearance most builders strive for the widest boards and narrowest battens, the battens must be sufficiently wide to adequately overlap boards. For nominal 6-inch boards spaced 1/2 inch apart, battens should overlap by at least 1/2 inch. With wider boards, increase battens, overlap proportionately. Although there are no set widths for board and batten siding, an attractive combination is 1″ × 3″ battens with 1″ × 10″ boards. Siding should be nailed to horizontal blocking lines or to furring strips. The battens are *not* nailed to the boards. Instead, the nails go through the gaps between the boards and into the furring strips. This lets the boards flex, and it also reduces the chance that the nails will split the wood either of the boards or of the battens.

Lap or channel sidings can be installed horizontally or vertically. For horizontal applications, start with the bottom course and work up with channels pointing upwards. Allow a 1/8-inch expansion gap between pieces if the siding is air- or kiln-dried. Do not nail through overlaps. For siding up to 6 inches wide, use one nail 1 inch up from the lap. Face nail with two nails per bearing for 8-inch patterns and wider, keeping nails 2-1/2 to 3 inches apart to allow for dimensional movement without splitting.

Tongue-and-groove siding can be installed horizontally or vertically. In horizontal application, start at the bottom and work up with the grove edges facing downwards to ensure a weather-tight wall. Siding up to 6-inches wide can be blind nailed with one siding nail per bearing toe-nailed through the base of each tongue. Wider siding should be face nailed using two nails per bearing. Ring shank nails must penetrate 1-1/4 inches into solid wood.

Shiplap is a profile with a top edge that is always thinner than the bottom edge and most shiplap boards are about 6 inches wide. When horizontally applied, the rabbeted or shiplap edge overlaps to ensure a tight installation against weather and self-aligns one board to another.

Simple drop/English siding is a profile that is tongued and grooved or rabbeted and overlapped so that the lower edge of each board interlocks with a groove in the board immediately below it.

Assessing Existing Conditions

In order to ensure the proper installation of board siding, you need to verify the following conditions:

- Ensure siding is the proper minimum thickness and is attached in compliance with the IRC.
- IRC requires weather-resistant siding attachment and minimum material thickness requirements but does not reference the recommendations in AAMA 1402. Verify the requirements of authorities having jurisdiction.
- IRC require fiber-cement siding to comply with ASTM C 1186, *Specification for Flat Non-Asbestos Fiber-Cement Sheets.*
- On new construction, siding is installed directly over the wall sheathing with an appropriate weather-resistant barrier (building paper or house wrap). On older homes, vinyl can sometimes be installed over the home's current siding. Keep in mind that vinyl needs to be nailed into solid wood, so if the home has aluminum siding or older vinyl siding, these will probably have to be removed. Going over existing wood siding or stucco is possible, although it's sometimes necessary to install vertical furring strips first.

Acceptable Practices

- Comply with siding manufacturer's written installation instructions applicable to products and applications indicated, unless more stringent local code requirements apply.
- Install fasteners for aluminum siding and fiber cement siding, and related accessories no more than 24 inches on center.
- For aluminum or vinyl siding, center nails in elongated nailing slots without binding siding to allow for thermal movement.
- Install fasteners for horizontal vinyl siding and related accessories no more than 16 inches on center.
- For vertical applications, siding should be nailed to horizontal blocking lines or furring strips. Install fasteners for vertical vinyl siding and related accessories no more than 12 inches on center.
- Aluminum and vinyl sidings have high coefficients of expansion, so provisions must be made in detailing and installation to accommodate this expansion. Although long-length panels help eliminate end joints, they should not be used unless special care is taken to accommodate the additional expansion. Longer panels will require deeper pockets at J-beads, and other trim and will require longer nailing slots.
- Where aluminum siding will contact dissimilar metals, protect against galvanic action by painting contact surfaces with primer or by applying sealant or tape or installing nonconductive spacers.
- Hard board siding is delivered with its face primed with some sort of paint, but the reverse side is left bare. It is a good idea to "prime" the reverse side of the siding before it is installed. When repainting hard board siding, pay particular attention to the bottom edge. Make sure you reach under and thoroughly coat it. Priming or otherwise sealing the reverse side of *any* composite or wood siding will help preserve it.
- Siding should be thought of as a rain screen rather than a weather-resistant barrier. Siding sheds water but does not completely prevent water penetration. Siding must be backed up with a wind- and water-resistant barrier to prevent water entry into the wall, and it must be detailed to allow water and water vapor to freely drain and flow from behind it. Flashing details, end conditions at trim and windows, endlaps, and bottom (starter) details are critical to proper weather performance.
- Fiber-cement siding should be cut with a blade designed specifically for fiber-cement dust reduction. For finishing, although fiber-cement products come either primed or unprimed, priming and painting in the factory are recommended. An alkaline-resistant

primer is required, and manufacturers generally recommend using a 100 percent acrylic topcoat.

- Comply with siding manufacturer's guidelines and layout recommendations for using a starter strip when beginning siding installation.
- The rows, or courses of siding, should line up all the way around the house, around every corner. The courses of siding should be level. However, if the house has settled or there are parts of the house that aren't perfectly level (such as soffits), it might be better have the siding be parallel to the house (even if this means the siding won't be perfectly level).
- Houses that change levels—such as walk-outs or split-levels—pose particular layout challenges. If you start with a full course along the bottom in one area, as the level changes up or down, you may end up with less than a full course along the bottom in other areas. In this case, you'll want to pick the most prominent, visible area of the house and start with a full course there, and let the cuts fall where they may in other.
- Vinyl siding can be cut with inexpensive hand tools. Large-bladed tin snips can be used to cut the pieces of siding to length. Smaller aviation snips are best for cutting trim pieces to precise lengths and shapes.
- Vinyl siding and accessories come with slots to nail through. When you nail, you don't drive the nail tight. Some manuals recommend a 1/32-inch gap between the head of the nail and the siding. If, after you've nailed it, the piece of vinyl will slide back and forth, then you're OK. If not, you've pinned it too tight to the house.
- Butt joints between boards should be staggered and made on studs. Fit siding snugly to other pieces and to trim.
- Corner boards are a popular alternative to mitered corners. They are often 3/4 inches or 1-1/4 inches material depending on the thickness of the siding. Width is a matter of taste and proper proportion. Corner boards are applied to the sheathing with the siding fitting tightly against the narrow edge of the boards. Joints should be filled with caulking compound when siding is applied. Trim boards can be used to cover butt jointed siding.
- At inside corners, siding is frequently butted against a trim strip. It can also be butted against adjoining walls with a trim strip used to cover the join.
- At outside corners, some builders choose mitered corners for a professional-looking finish. Mitered corners are most common on horizontally applied siding and they must fit tightly for the full depth of the miter. To maintain a tight fit, the siding should be properly seasoned before installation and protected from the weather at the job site. The ends are often set in caulking compound when siding is applied.

Practices to Avoid

- Aluminum siding has high coefficients of expansion and will oil-can if fasteners are driven too tight or located improperly.
- Try to avoid having thin pieces of siding under windows, doors, or soffits.
- Do not reduce the siding overlap recommendations of siding manufacturer's installation instructions. To do so could result in damage from wind-driven water.

Stucco

Description

Stucco, also known as an exterior application of portland cement plaster, is a weather-resistant surfacing material that can be applied in a variety of textures and colors to flat, curved, or built up shapes for unlimited design options. Stucco resists wind and rain penetration, but it is not waterproof. Moisture can pass through it, and thus careful selection of materials and proper detailing of stucco assemblies is important. Stucco is often confused with exterior insulation finish systems (EIFS), or synthetic stucco, which is an exterior wall-cladding system that manages water using foam plastic insulation, covered by a reinforced base coat and a textured protective finish coat. EIFS is discussed separately within this book in Chapter 18.

Materials used for stucco need to comply with ASTM C926 and ASTM C1063 per IRC requirements. Typical materials include portland, masonry, plastic, and blended hydraulic cements, mixed with lime, sand, and water. In some cases, additives may be used to control set time, cracking, strength, and workability. Stucco can be applied by hand or spray application and is categorized by the type of cement binder used, number of coats, and the total thickness of the application. Local codes and Table 10.2 of ASTM C926 determine the thickness and number of coats required for the substrate and supports used. Most often, three coats are required. The first is a scratch coat, followed by the brown coat for leveling, and finally a finish texture coat. Coats are required by code to harden and dry, often up to a week, before the next application. One-coat stucco applications, which use preblended products, are faster, thinner, lighter, and more flexible but show irregularities of the substrate surface and are not yet recognized by local codes.

Stucco can be applied over metal lath or solid substrates such as concrete and unit masonry to form an assembly. Solid substrates are more rigid, but residential construction most commonly uses assemblies with metal lath over wood or metal studs and sheathing. Metal lath comes in different configurations and weights as expanded-metal or wire-fabric, and is required to be corrosion resistant. Local codes and ASTM C1063 use supporting members to determine the type, weight, and spacing of lath required. Metal lath can be mechanically fastened or wire tied to supports and should be furred 1/4 inch from the sheathing substrate to permit the stucco to completely embed the lath. One or two layers of a weather-resistive barrier, such as netting, film, kraft paper, or felt, are typically required behind the lath by local code. Some manufacturers offer lath with a paper backing already applied. Selection of the weather-resistive barrier should be done with caution since heavier types could trap moisture within the wall. Two layers are often used to ensure drainage where the plaster is adhered to the first layer.

Regardless of the substrate, stucco assemblies should be structurally sound and able to withstand stresses that could cause movement and cracking of the plaster. Corrosion-resistant accessories, such as foundation weep screeds, corner reinforcements, control joints, and expansion joints, should be used to help direct water and form an aesthetically pleasing and sound wall. Control joints prevent random stucco cracking by relieving expansion and contraction stresses. Control joints should be located at floor lines, dissimilar materials, framing material changes, and changes in building height or shape, as required by ASTM C1063. Finally, sealants should be used to protect all exposed edges of assemblies.

Stucco does not require additional finishing once the finish coat hardens. Tinting or aggregates achieves the final color desired, or it can be painted. Stucco applications are truly an expression of art, varying in texture and color. Although factory-prepared finishes produce textures and patterns that can be reliably reproduced, a sample panel is always recommended.

Assessing Existing Conditions

In order to ensure the proper installation of stucco, verify the following conditions:

- Substrate is structurally sound and supported per code requirements (Table 4.1 of ASTM 1063).

- Solid substrates are prepared properly, clean, and free of debris, moistened and "roughed" at ceilings and vertical surfaces. A bonding compound has been applied.
- Blocking is provided at perimeter of substrate materials where required.
- Non-bearing substrates are structurally isolated to prevent transfer of movement.
- Weather-resistive barrier meets code requirements and is installed shingle style to shed moisture.
  - Over wood based sheathing the IRC requires the equivalent of at least two layers of FS UU-B-790, Type I, Grade D (vapor-permeable) paper.
  - Over non-wood-based sheathing, the IRC requires at least one layer of No. 15 felt, complying with ASTM D226, Type I.
- Metal lath is properly oriented with a 1/4-inch space between the sheathing and fastened with code-approved nails or staples spaced 6 inches maximum.
- Accessories are zinc or PVC for corrosion resistance and anchored per code requirements.
- Control joints are located per ASTM C1063, as follows:
  - Vertical surfaces are delineated into 144-square-foot areas maximum.
  - Horizontal and nonvertical surfaces are delineated into 100 sq. ft. areas maximum.
  - Delineated areas do not have length-to-width ratios greater than 2.5:1.
  - Control joints are not spaced more than 18 feet apart.
- Foundation weep screeds are used to terminate stucco at the bottoms of walls a minimum of 4 inches above grade or 2 inches above paved surfaces.
- Weather-resistant sealant is used at accessories to prevent moisture penetration.

Acceptable Practices

Stucco should be selected based on both appearance and performance requirements. Proportioning and mixing directly affect the final quality and life-span of hardened portland cement plaster, which needs to resist impact and abrasion, weather, such as wind, rain, freezing and thawing, and aggressive chemicals from acid rain and soils. Use fresh and clean materials to promote proper application (adhesion, cohesion, and workability) and hardening properties, and maintain constant proportioning and mixing throughout the application.

Common construction practices for stucco include:

- Use of base and finish coats with a higher compressive strength where abrasion and impact resistance is needed
- Use of lower-strength (less costly) coats on ceilings or areas of low abuse
- Perlite aggregates to reduce weight or improve sound absorption, insulation, or fire resistance
- Fiber additives to strengthen plaster and reduce cracking
- Acrylic polymers to improve flexibility and reduce cracking
- Air-entraining agents to improve freeze-thaw resistance
- Pretesting of materials with air-admixtures to avoid adverse affects
- Sulfate-resistant additives where in contact with soil, or if aggregates contain aggressive materials
- Use of rough textures to discourage touching or to hide texture inconsistencies and cracks
- Use of smooth textures to avoid accumulation of surface dirt and reduce maintenance costs
- Use of preblended mixes for more consistent proportioning and quality control and better compatibility with finish coats

Practices to Avoid

The life of stucco is primarily determined by the environment in which it is installed. To avoid accelerated deterioration of stucco, it is important to avoid the following conditions:

- Do not allow any chemicals from air, water, or substrate—such as salts, acids, sulfates, chlorides, and carbonates that are in imbalance with plaster—to sit on the surface, or it will dissolve the plaster materials.
- Do not allow water or moisture to percolate through plaster coating, or delamination may occur.
- Do not allow uneven exposure to weather or uneven hydration, or discolorations may develop.

- Do not install top coats over smooth, contaminated, dry or excessively wet base coats or debonding of plaster coats may occur.
- Do not use perlite aggregates in base coats since they are more absorptive than others and therefore will perform poorly in freeze thaw situations.
- Do not allow sand for mixing to sit exposed or where it could absorb additional moisture, which could disproportion a plaster blend.
- Do not use calcium chloride as an accelerating admixture with metal lath substrates, or it could cause the lath to corrode.
- Do not use stucco below grade.
- Do not use stucco as a parapet coping or for other nonvertical weather exposed surfaces.

Resources

WITHIN THIS BOOK

- Chapter 7 Cast-in-Place Concrete
- Chapter 9 Unit Masonry
- Chapter 18 Thermal Protection and Weather Barriers
- Chapter 21 Flashing and Sheet Metal Specialties

REFERENCE STANDARDS

- ASTM C 926—Standard Specification for Application of Portland Cement-Based Plaster
- ASTM C1063—Standard Specification for Installation of Lathing and Furring to Receive Interior and Exterior Portland Cement-Based Plaster
- ASTM C1186—Specification for Flat Non-Asbestos Fiber-Cement Sheets
- ASTM D226—Standard Specification for Asphalt-Saturated Organic Felt Used in Roofing and Waterproofing
- ASTM D3679—Standard Specification for Rigid Poly (Vinyl Chloride) (PVC) Siding
- ASTM F 1667—Standard Specification for Driven Fasteners: Nails, Spikes, and Staples

OTHER RESOURCES

- 2009 International Residential Code for One and Two-Family Dwellings. Washington, DC: International Code Council, Inc., 2009.

- American Institute of Architects, *Architectural Graphics Standards*, 11th ed. Hoboken, NJ: John Wiley and Sons, 2007.
- American Institute of Architects, *Architectural Graphic Standards for Residential Construction*, 2nd ed. Hoboken, NJ: John Wiley and Sons, 2010.

Chapter 21

Flashing and Sheet Metal Specialties

Flashing

Description

Flashing is an integral component found at numerous locations in all construction to prevent water from entering the wall cavity or the dwelling's structural components. This corrosion-resistant sheet product is applied in a shingle-fashion and directs moisture to the exterior of the building element. Although flashing can be manufactured from several materials, the flashing that is exposed to sunlight is generally sheet metal, in prefinished or natural finish. Non-exposed flashing can be copper-coated kraft paper or a self-adhered membrane with a metal drip edge.

Assessing Existing Conditions

The building code requires flashing at the following locations:

- Exterior window and door openings
- Intersection of chimneys or other masonry construction with frame or stucco walls, with projecting lips on both sides under stucco copings
- Under and at the ends of masonry, wood, or metal copings and sills
- Continuously above all projecting wood trim
- Where exterior porches, decks or stairs attach to a wall or floor assembly of wood-frame construction
- Wall and roof intersections
- Built-in gutters
- Roof tiles, shingles, and vents
- EIFS, fiber-cement siding, copings, roof, valleys, and chimneys

Acceptable Practices

Flashing is necessary at any location where a horizontal component interrupts a vertical element or where water might collect. This is particularly true at wood features, which may be susceptible to rot.

Given the numerous locations and applications of flashing and counterflashing, it is difficult to attempt to describe all the conditions and details for this subject matter. SMACNA, *Architectural Sheet Metal Manual* is the most widely used standard for metal flashing includes design and construction guidelines and details. It applies to multiple metal types typically, while other trade groups concentrate on specific metals.

Flashing, when installed as a part of a cavity drainage system, should be extended to exterior of the wall or building element. The path of travel for moisture must be clean and clear. Flashing should extend to the exterior of the wall with end dams to ensure water is not lost to the cavity once captured by the flashing. The recommended minimum thicknesses of flashing will vary, depending on the application.

Exposed flashing

- Galvanized steel: 26 gage
- Copper: 16 ounces
- Stainless steel: 26 gage
- Aluminum: 0.032 inches

Nonexposed flashing

- Copper-coated kraft paper: 5 ounces
- Self-adhering membrane: Complying with AAMA 711

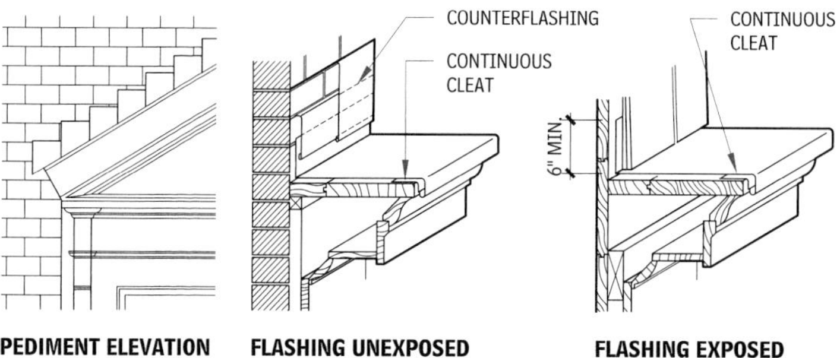

Figure 21.1 Wood pediment flashing
Source: AIA, *Architectural Graphic Standards for Residential Construction*, 2nd ed. Copyright 2010, John Wiley and Sons, Inc.

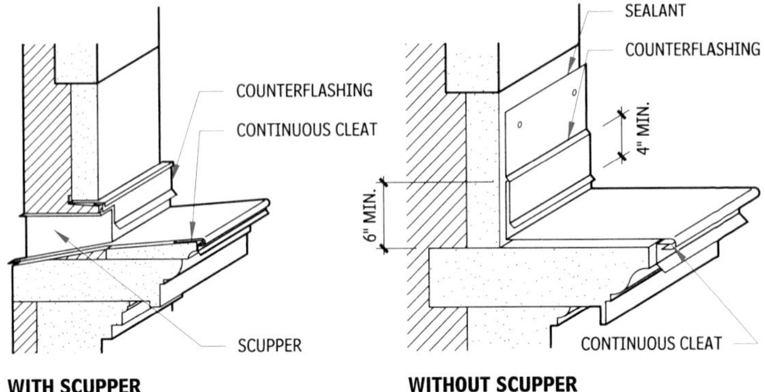

Figure 21.2 Stone ledge flashing
Source: AIA, *Architectural Graphic Standards for Residential Construction,* 2nd ed. Copyright 2010, John Wiley and Sons, Inc.

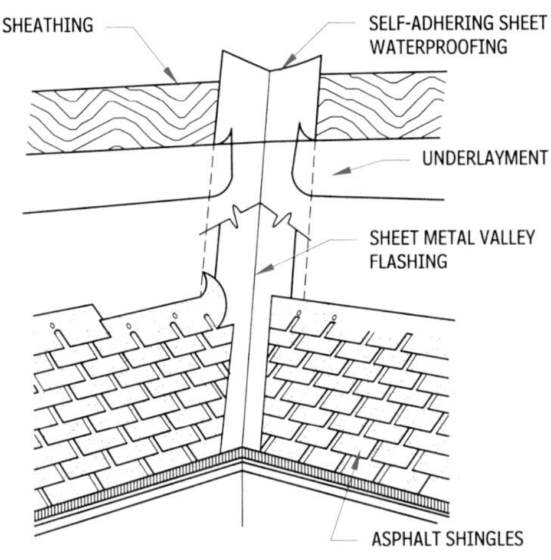

Figure 21.3 Roof valley flashing
Source: AIA, *Architectural Graphic Standards for Residential Construction,* 2nd ed. Copyright 2010, John Wiley and Sons, Inc.

Practices to Avoid

- Contact of dissimilar metals including screws or dissimilar metal down-stream from water flow.
- Caulking is no substitution for good flashing and can actually hold moisture inside of walls.
- "Fish-mouths," or reverse lapping of flashing.
- Mechanical fastening of flashing at both ends, which prevents thermal movement.

Metal Coping

Description

Parapet walls and the exposed top surface of masonry walls must be properly coped to prevent moisture from entering the wall. This location is extremely vulnerable to water intrusion. A coping may be constructed from various materials, including precast concrete, stone, and masonry—however, extruded metal is the most common. Metal copings may be field formed or manufactured. Field forming is the most common type of forming process for residential construction due to cost.

Regardless of material, the purpose of a coping is to waterproof the top of a wall exposed to weather. The coping design is a synthesis of functional, technical, and aesthetic considerations. The choice of materials, design, and installation must all work together to ensure the final construction meets the needs of the application.

Assessing Existing Conditions

In order to ensure the proper installation of a metal coping, you need to verify the following conditions:

- Treated wood blocking is securely anchored to top of wall.
- Underlayment installed on top of wood blocking to act as a secondary weather barrier.
- Coping has adequate lap at front and back of wall.
- Coping is sloped to the back of wall to prevent standing water.
- Coping joints are adequately lapped at joints.
- Provisions for thermal movement (joints and attachment) have been made to ensure that coping is allowed to move in changing temperatures.
- Corners have watertight seams.

Acceptable Practices

In the installation of a metal cap on the top of a wall, consideration must be given to the thermal movement (expansion and contraction of metal) of the coping. Aesthetic considerations are also necessary in choosing a joint type. SMACNA, *Architectural Sheet Metal Manual* is the most widely used standard for metal copings and includes design and construction guidelines and details. It applies to multiple metal types typically used for metal copings, while other trade groups concentrate on specific metals.

Common construction practices for metal copings include the following:

- Joints may be low profile or standing seam type, to meet the aesthetic desires for the construction.
- Single lap joint width: 4 inches minimum.
- Backup plate width: 12 inches.
- Cover plate width: 6 inches minimum.
- Lay out the coping sections to minimize the number of joints.
- Sheet metal for copings generally comes in 10-foot sections. The length of the coping section, joint type, and spacing of joints are important considerations in the aesthetic appearance of the coping.

Practices to Avoid

Since metal copings are exposed to both view and the natural elements, they must be of enduring quality to ensure performance. Avoid these common construction practices:

- Contact of dissimilar metals including screws. Refer to topic on "Galvanic Action" in Chapter 11.
- Don't use field-formed corner units, as these are best shop fabricated to ensure watertight seams at corners.
- Metal copings on walls should not serve as guardrails, as the metal coping can get hot and burn the skin.
- Fasteners should not be exposed on the exterior face side of metal coping.
- Nonslotted holes do not allow for thermal movement of the coping and will pull out fasteners.
- Nails for fasteners, Screws provide better attachment and adjustment for thermal movement.

Gutters and Downspouts

Description

The design and construction of a roof drainage system is critical to prevent water intrusion into the dwelling and the structure, interiors construction, and contents. The most common components of a residential roof drainage system are the gutters and downspouts. The sizing of downspouts and gutters is based on roof drainage area, roof slope, and rainfall intensity (by location). Tables 21.1 and 21.3 will assist in selection of appropriate gutter and downspout size. Gutter and downspout sections can be formed in the field, shop, or manufactured from a variety of metal materials, including galvanized steel, copper, aluminum, and stainless steel. They can be prefinished from coated-coil stock, finished in the field, or left natural. Gutters may be hanging gutters or built-in gutters, but this topic will only discuss hanging gutters. Hanging gutter designs include rectangular, half-round, or ogee. Rectangular gutters are manufactured in numerous styles or profiles.

Assessing Existing Conditions

When reviewing the installation of gutters and downspouts, you need to verify the following conditions:

- Size and configuration of the gutters and downspouts are in compliance with design documentation to ensure they will hold the water from the roof.
- Spacing of expansion joints in hanging gutters are installed to allow for thermal movement.
- Attachment of gutters to roof or fascia is adequate to support weight of full gutter.
- Front edge of gutter is lower that back edge to ensure that if the gutter overflows, water is not directed back into the construction.
- Spacing of hangers on downspouts are adequate to ensure support of downspouts.

Acceptable Practices

The installation of a roof drainage system must consider the thermal movement (expansion and contraction of metal) of the gutters and downspouts. SMACNA, *Architectural Sheet Metal Manual,* is the most widely used standard for gutters and downspouts and includes design and construction guidelines and details. It applies to multiple metal types typically, while other trade groups concentrate on specific metals.

Gutters and downspouts are formed in a variety of metals, shapes, sizes, and hanger types. The major acceptable practice issues regarding gutters are gutter design (material and shape), size, support, and thermal expansion. Gutters may be level with edge of roof line, but it is preferred that they slope to downspouts.

In general, downspouts are round or rectangular in shape. Downspouts with open or semi-open faces are recommended for locations susceptible to icy conditions. Downspout hangers may be manufactured or shop-fabricated. Shop-fabricated hangers are fabricated in the same material as the downspout, from 1/16-inch-minimum flat stock material. Fasteners can include screws, bolts, and blind rivets.

Common construction practices for gutters include:

- The front edge of hanging gutters on sloped roofs should be in line with the roof slope.
- The front edge of hanging gutters on flat roofs should not less than 1 inch below roof edge.
- Ratio of gutter depth to depth: 3 to 4.
- Joints in gutters should be lapped 1 inch in direction of flow and riveted on 2 inch centers or soldered if metal can be soldered.
- Gutters can be supported by straps (24 in. oc), spike, and ferrule (24 in. oc), or brackets (36 in. oc).
- Gutter accessories include:
  - Gutter baffles are recommended valley locations to prevent water from "shooting" over gutter in heavy intensity rain.
  - Gutter screens or downspout strainers are recommended in locations where gutters are subject to clogging from leaves.

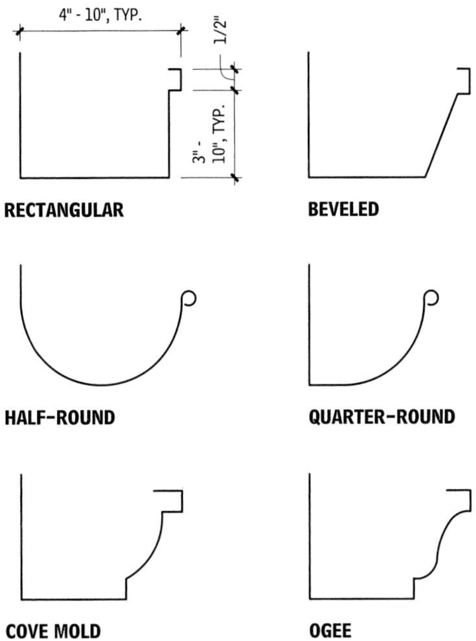

Figure 21.4 Gutter shapes
Source: AIA, *Architectural Graphic Standards,* 11th ed. Copyright 2007, John Wiley and Sons, Inc.

Table 21.1 Roof Gutters Maximum Roof Area for Gutters

Diameters of Gutter	Cross-section Area	Level		1/8 in. per ft. Slope		1/4 in. per ft. Slope	
	in.^{2}	ft.^{2}	gpm	ft.^{2}	gpm	ft.^{2}	gpm
3 inches	3.5	680	7	960	10	1360	14
4 inches	6.3	1440	15	2040	21	2880	30
5 inches	9.8	2500	26	3520	37	5000	52
6 inches	14.1	3840	40	5440	57	7680	50
7 inches	19.2	5520	57	7800	81	11040	115
8 inches	25.1	7960	83	11200	116	14400	165
10 inches	39.1	14400	150	20400	212	28800	299

Table 21.2 Recommended Minimum Gages for Gutters

Girth	Galvanized Steel	Copper	Aluminum	Stainless Steel
in.	ga.	oz	in.	oz
up to 15	26	16	0.032	28
16–20	24	16	0.04	26
21–25	22	20	0.051	24
26–30	20	24	0.063	22
31–35	18	24		20
Over 35	16			18

Common construction practices for downspouts include:

- Spacing of hangers: 10 feet max.
- Spacing of top hanger to gutter: 2 feet. max.
- Spacing of bottom hanger to elbow/end of downspout: 2 feet. max.
- Setting a downspout 1/2 inch away from wall may increase the service life of the downspout.

Practices to Avoid

- Contact of dissimilar metals including screws. Refer to topic on "Galvanic Action" in Chapter 11.
- Downspout fasteners with long penetrations can increase clogging of the downspout.

Table 21.3 Dimensions and Minimum Gages of Standard Downspouts

	Area	Nominal Size	Actual Size	Galvanized Steel	Stainless Steel	Aluminum	Copper
TYPE	$in.^2$	in.	in.	ga.	ga.	in.	oz
Plain Round	7.07		3	26	28	0.025	16
	12.57		4				
	19.63		5				
	28.27		6				
Corrugated Round	5.91	3		26	28	0.025	16
	11.01	4					
	17.72	5					
	25.97	6					
Plain Rectangular	3.94	2	$1\frac{3}{4} \times 2\frac{1}{4}$	26	28	0.025	16
	6	3	2×3				
	12	4	3×4				
	20	5	$3\frac{3}{4} \times 4\frac{3}{4}$				
	24	6	4×6				
Rectangular Corrugated	3.8	2	$1\frac{3}{4} \times 2\frac{1}{4}$	26	28	0.025	16
	7.73	3	$2\frac{3}{8} \times 3\frac{1}{4}$				
	11.7	5	$2\frac{3}{4} \times 4\frac{1}{4}$				
	18.75	5	$3\frac{3}{4} \times 5$				

Scuppers

Description

The design and construction of a roof drainage system is critical to prevent water intrusion into the dwelling. Flat roofs with parapet walls may incorporate scuppers into their design as a primary means of roof drainage or as overflow devices. In either case, the scupper must be sized according to the anticipated water capacity, based on the intensity of rainfall, and the contributing roof area to the scupper.

Scuppers may be manufactured with parapet wall sleeves and may have ornamental downspout outlets or, more typically, they are constructed of sheet metal. As with any penetration of a wall, scuppers must be constructed to ensure water tightness as well as capacity to drain water from the roof.

Assessing Existing Conditions

Roof drainage scuppers

- Located level with roof surface.
- Scupper size is capable of accepting the water capacity of the contributing roof area.

Overflow scuppers

- Located 2 inches above lowest point of roof.
- Minimum opening height of 4 inches.
- Size to accommodate three times the capacity of the roof drain that it serves

General

- Ensure that all joints are soldered except aluminum construction.
- Conductor head, if used, should be 2 inches wider that scupper.

Acceptable Practices

SMACNA, *Architectural Sheet Metal Manual* is the most widely used standard for scuppers. It includes design and construction guidelines and details. It applies to multiple metal types typically, while other trade groups concentrate on specific metals. Sizing of scuppers for overflow drains, also referred to as secondary (emergency) drains, must comply with the *International Plumbing Code*. This code provides charts for horizontal piping size, which can be converted to area for scuppers.

Recommended thickness of scupper materials are as follows:

- Galvanized steel: 24 gage
- Aluminum: 0.032 inches
- Copper: 16 ounces
- Stainless steel: 26 gage

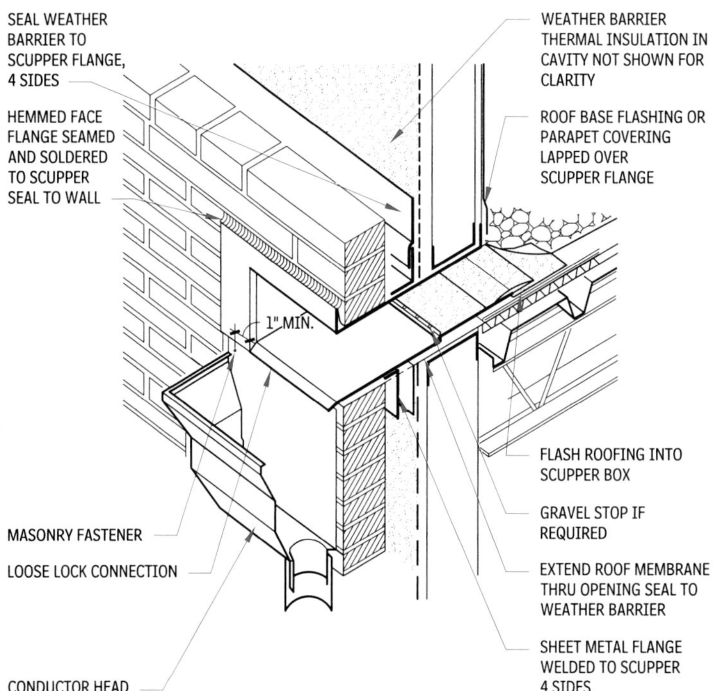

Figure 21.5 Scupper and conductor head at parapet wall
Source: AIA, *Architectural Graphic Standards,* 11th ed. Copyright 2007, John Wiley and Sons, Inc.

Practices to Avoid

- Contact of dissimilar metals including screws.
- In areas subject to leaf debris, screens may need to be installed on primary roof drainage scuppers and inspected periodically for cleaning.

Resources

WITHIN THIS BOOK

- Chapter 11 Common Work Results for Metals
- Chapter 19 Roof Covering
- Chapter 20 Exterior Wall Covering
- Chapter 31 Plumbing

REFERENCE STANDARDS

- AAMA 711—Voluntary Specifications for Self Adhering Flashing Used for Installation of Exterior Wall Fenestration Products

OTHER RESOURCES

- 2009 International Plumbing Code. Washington, DC: International Code Council, Inc., 2009.
- 2009 International Residential Code for One and Two-Family Dwellings. Washington, DC: International Code Council, Inc., 2009.
- American Institute of Architects, *Architectural Graphics Standards*, 11th ed. Hoboken, NJ: John Wiley and Sons, 2007.
- American Institute of Architects, *Architectural Graphic Standards for Residential Construction*, 2nd ed. Hoboken, NJ: John Wiley and Sons, 2010.
- Copper Development Association, Inc., *Copper in Architecture—Design Handbook*, www.copper.org.
- SMACNA, *Architectural Sheet Metal Manual,* 6th ed. Chantilly, VA: Sheet Metal and Air Conditioning Contractors' National Association, Inc., 2003.

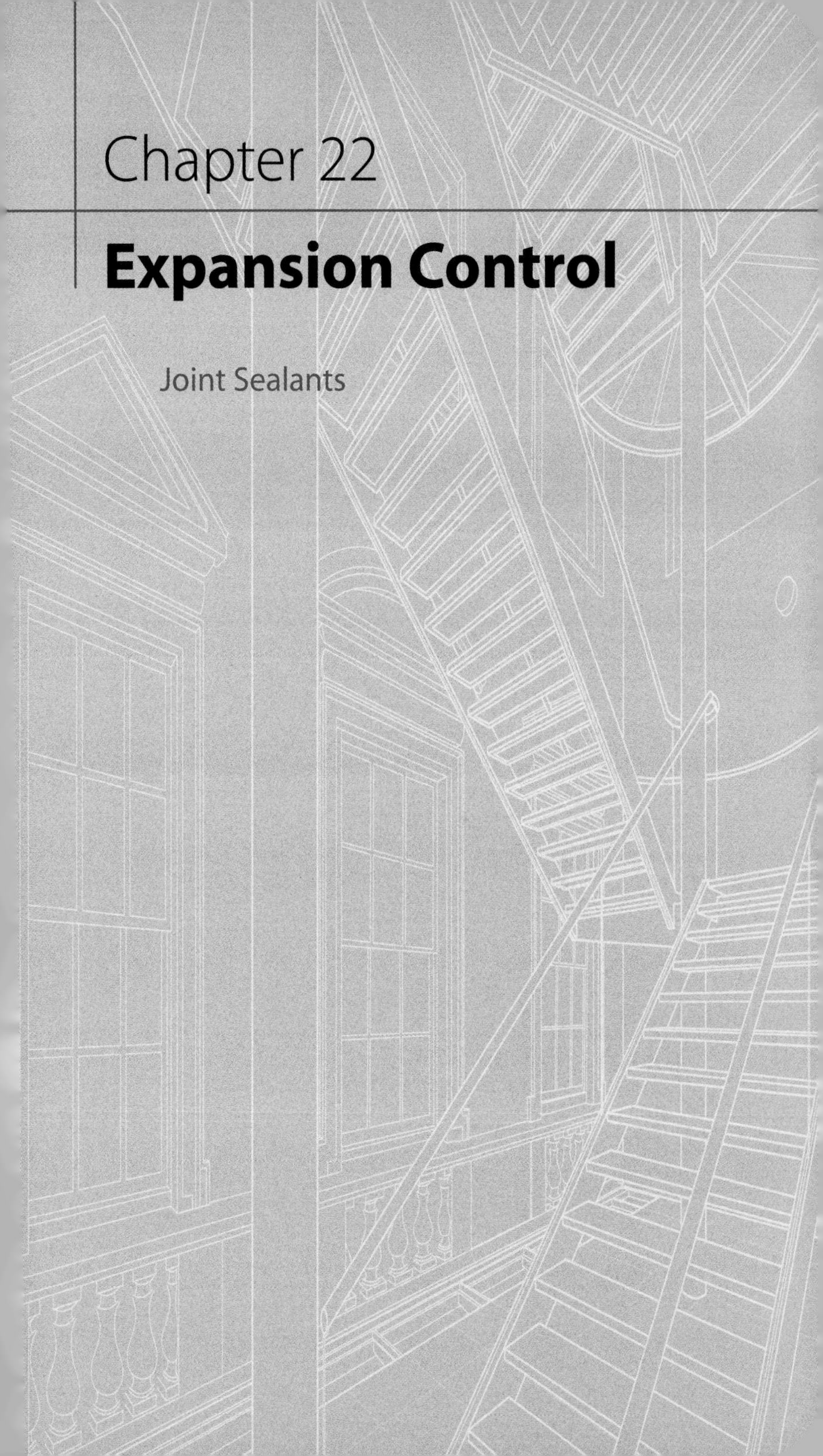

Chapter 22

Expansion Control

Joint Sealants

Joint Sealants

Description

Joint sealants are used to seal openings between two or more substrates to prevent air, water, and other environmental elements from entering or exiting a structure while permitting limited movement of the substrates. Specialty sealants are used in special applications, such as for bathrooms/kitchens, rooftops, fire stops, and electrical or thermal insulation applications.

The terms *caulk* and *sealant* are sometimes used interchangeable, but there is a difference. Sealants are designed to seal an interface that has movement. Caulks are designed to fill a gap.

Assessing Existing Conditions

In order to ensure the proper installation of joint sealants, you need to verify the following conditions:

- Determine the substrates to be sealed and performance needs. Existing joints in high-traffic areas or with more joint movement may need to be replaced sooner.
- The sealant's movement capabilities will coordinate with the joint design.
- Exterior sealants can cope with exposure to ultraviolet light, ozone, heat, water, temperature extremes, air pollution, and cleaning chemicals.
- Interior seals can cope with exposure to mildew, paint, and cleaning chemicals.

Acceptable Practices

Joint sealants come in a wide variety, depending on their purpose, application, and properties.

- Latex (water-based, including EVA, acrylic):
    - Interior and exterior uses (not used for exterior applications on high rise construction or for applications undergoing cyclic movement greater than ±25 percent).

    - Premium products rated for movement meet ASTM C920, Classes 12-1/2 and 25. Products not rated for movement meet ASTM C834.
    - Excellent paintability (with latex paints).
    - Sealants exhibit some shrinkage after cure.

- Acrylic (solvent-based):
    - Used mainly for exterior applications for perimeter sealing; low movement joints.
    - Generally have a maximum of plus or minus 7.5 percent movement (ASTM C1311).
    - May need special handling for flammability and regulatory compliance.
    - Can be painted.
    - Short open time; difficult to tool.
    - Exhibits some shrinkage after cure.

- Silicones:
    - Structural sealant glazing of glass to metal framing systems.
    - Excellent joint movement capabilities (ASTM C920, Classes 25, 35, 50, and 100/50).
    - Excellent UV resistance and heat stability.
    - Good adhesion to many substrates, especially glass; a primer is recommended on some substrates, particularly cementious substrates.
    - Most formulations are not paintable; however, there are a few that are paintable.
    - May stain some types of porous materials such as concrete and natural stone.

Most residential sealants are a blend of two or more materials, and are used in specific applications. Always check material labels carefully, as they commonly describe the type of application it is best used for and other important information.

Use a sealant backing or bond breaker tape to eliminate "three-sided adhesion." The sealant should bond only to the substrates that will be moving. Installer should always prime substrate before insertion of the sealant backing. A sealant backing is used when joints are deeper than required, which is usually 1/4-inch deep. The most common backing materials are closed-cell sealant backing made from a polyethylene foam, open-cell backing made from a urethane foam, bicellular backing, which is composed of both open- and closed-cell polyethylene or polyolefin foam, and bond breaker tape made from self-adhesive polyethylene or Teflon materials.

There are three common types of joints, all of which have different applications of joint sealant. The butt joint has a minimum joint width of 1/4 inch, and the joint depth shall be a minimum of 1/4 inch and maximum joint width of 1/2 inch and should be approximately half of the joint width. A fillet or angle joint is used when two substrates meet at an angle. A 1/4 inch minimum joint depth and a 3/8-inch sealant/surface contact are recommended. Lap joints are used to seal metal to metal and have the same joint requirements as a butt joint. The type of joint most commonly used in restoration is the bridge joint, in which a sealant is applied over bond breaker tape, over the existing joint sealant. A minimum ¼ inch of surface contact and thickness is recommended.

Practices to Avoid

- Avoid installing joint sealant where substrate has not been cleaned or has materials that would compromise adhesion, such as dust or dirt.
- Avoid using sealants that have reached the end of their package shelf life.
- Avoid leaving gaps in joints cause by uneven sealant flow.
- Avoid using rigid joint filler or sealant backing in joints that will experience movement.
- Avoid using braided sealant backing to compensate for a joint opening that is too large for it.
- Avoid puncturing closed-cell sealant backing materials.
- Avoid using joint sealant in rooms that are not well ventilated.

Resources

WITHIN THIS BOOK

- Chapter 7 Cast-In-Place Concrete
- Chapter 8 Common Work Results for Masonry
- Chapter 9 Unit Masonry
- Chapter 10 Stone Assemblies
- Chapter 18 Thermal Protection and Weather Barriers
- Chapter 20 Exterior Wall Covering
- Chapter 21 Flashing and Sheet Metal Specialties

REFERENCE STANDARDS

- ASTM C1193—Standard Guide for Use of Joint Sealants
- ASTM C1472—Standard Guide for Calculating Movement and Other Effects When Establishing Sealant Joint Width

OTHER RESOURCES

- 2009 International Residential Code for One and Two-Family Dwellings. Washington, DC: International Code Council, Inc., 2009.
- American Institute of Architects, *Architectural Graphics Standards*, 11th ed. Hoboken, NJ: John Wiley and Sons, 2007.
- American Institute of Architects, *Architectural Graphic Standards for Residential Construction*, 2nd ed. Hoboken, NJ: John Wiley and Sons, 2010.
- Sealant Waterproofing and Restoration Institute, www.swrionline.org.

Part VII

Openings

Chapter 23

Doors and Frames

- Swinging Doors
- Sliding Doors
- Folding Doors
- Door Hardware Functions
- Door Hardware Finishes
- Attic Access

Swinging Doors

Description

Swinging doors are hung in frames and can be prehung (assembled in the factory) or hung on the jobsite. In residential construction, doors are generally prehung. Prehung exterior doors are generally provided with the door, frame, hinges, weatherstripping, and threshold. Prehung interior doors are generally provided with the door, frame, and hinges.

Swinging doors are available in four materials: wood, fiberglass, metal, and aluminum storm doors. There are three basic types of frames: wood frames, metal frames, and aluminum clad frames. In single-family residential construction, wood frames and aluminum clad frames are the most common.

If swinging doors have glass panels, the glass panels must be tempered per the International Residential Code (IRC) R308.4.

Door Materials

Swinging doors come in wood, fiberglass, metal, and aluminum storm doors.

Wood

Typical thicknesses of wood doors are 1-3/4 inches for exterior doors and 1-3/8 inch thick for Interior doors. There are three types of swinging wood doors:

- *Flush:* Generally made up or either five or seven plies of hardwood, including a decorative hardwood veneer on the exposed faces of the door.
- *Stile and rail:* Consist of vertical stiles and horizontal rails fabricated with flat panels, glass panels, or raised panels inserted between the stiles and rails.
- *Molded hardboard doors:* Similar to flush doors in their construction, but the faces of the door are hardboard. The door is then routed to simulate the appearance of a stile and rail door.

Flush wood and molded hardboard doors are available in solid core and hollow core.

Fiberglass Doors

Fiberglass doors are fabricated using wood stiles and top and bottom rails with polystyrene foam-insulating core. The insulating core is machine cut to the desired shape and pattern of the door style; then fiberglass is applied to the inside and outside faces of the door. The standard thickness for fiberglass doors is a nominal 1-3/4 inch thick.

Metal Doors

Metal doors are available in flush and embossed panel doors.

Flush metal doors incorporate a full steel sheet for the faces of the door, generally with seams on the lock and hinge edges of the doors.

Embossed panel doors are fabricated similarly to flush panel doors except that the steel face sheets are stamped to simulate a stile and rail door.

Typical cores for metal doors:

- Kraft-paper honeycomb when an uninsulated door is required
- A polystyrene or polyurethane core when an insulated door is required.

Flush and embossed metal doors are also available with a glass lite in the upper portion of the door. This is referred to as a *half glass* door. Glass sizes vary between manufacturers, generally having a top rail between 6 and 7 inches high; the distance from the sides of the door and the glass lite match the top rail.

Storm Doors

Storm doors are fabricated from tubular aluminum and are similar in design to a stile and rail door. Storm doors typically have a glass lite that is available in three styles:

- Full lite vision panel where the vision panel can be removed and replaced with a screen for ventilation
- Full lite operable vision panel
- Half lite operable vision panel

Finishes are generally baked-on enamel-finish coat, in a variety of colors.

Frames

Wood frames are generally fabricated from solid stock lumber or from particleboard with all exposed surfaces veneered.

Wood frames are fastened to the opening at three equally spaced locations on each side of the opening with either manufacturer supplied clips or by fastening directly through the door frame to the wall framing.

Assessing Existing Conditions

- Doors should swing freely without binding, and properly hung doors should not move when released in any position.
- Doors should maintain a consistent distance on all sides of the frame, 1/8-inch sides and top and minimum 3/8 inch from finished floor.
- If a swinging door has glass panels, verify that the glass panel is tempered. Tempered glass is required to have a permanent, etched designation visible after the glass is installed per IRC R308.1.

Check door for warp and verify frame is plumb and square. If door does not latch properly or the door hits the top of the frame but not the bottom of the frame, check the following:

- To check a door for warp, place a string line at opposite corners of the door; a door is considered to be defective if the warp is equal to or greater than 1/4 inch for a 1-3/4-inch-thick door.

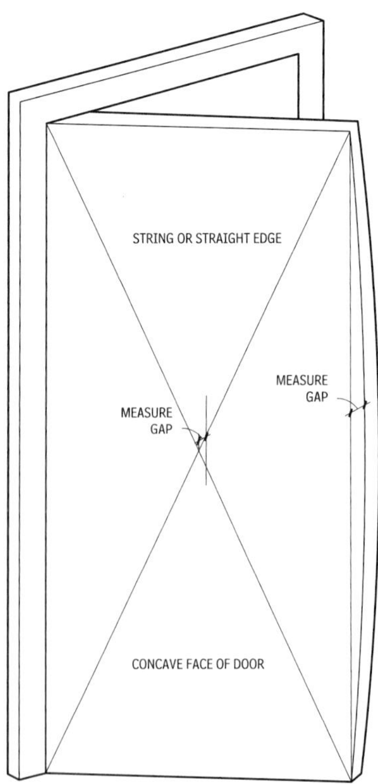

Figure 23.1 Door warp

- To check if a frame is plumb, obtain a carpenters level and check to see that both vertical jambs are plumb.
- To check a frame for square, obtain a carpenters square and check both corners where the vertical jamb meets the head of the frame. A frame should not be more than 1/16 inch out of square.
- Verify door manufacturer's warranty for door warp. Industry standard and most door manufacturers' warranties state that before a door can be considered defective due to door warp, it must hang in the opening for at least one year; the one-year minimum is because in some cases the door warp is caused by the door becoming acclimated to the environment in which it is located.

Acceptable Practices

Door Handing

Doors and door frames are handed. The proper hand of a door is determined by the side of the door that the key is on. If the door is a passage door, with no lock then the handing is determined by what is considered "outside" and "inside."

Installation

Each dwelling unit must have a minimum of one egress door. An egress door is identified as follows:

- Minimum 32 inches clear width from face of frame stop to face of door when open 90 degrees to the opening.
- Minimum 78 inches high from top of threshold to face of frame stop.
- Door must be openable from inside dwelling without the use of a key or any special knowledge or effort.

Doors in dwelling units accessible to the physically handicapped shall meet the following requirements:

- Minimum 32 inches clear width from face of frame stop to face of door when open 90 degrees to the opening.
- Doors not requiring passage of wheelchair, such as shallow closets, may have the clear opening width reduced to 20 inches minimum.
- Changes in floor level, such as the threshold at the entry door, may not exceed ½ inch. Other changes in level shall be beveled with a slope not greater than a ratio of 1:2.

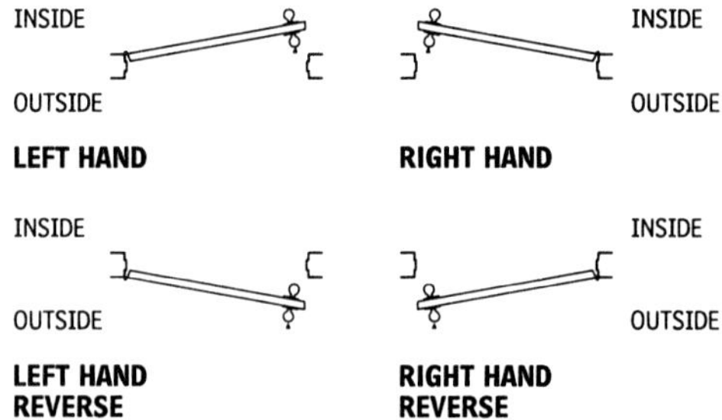

Figure 23.2 Door handing
Source: AIA, *Architectural Graphic Standards,* 11th ed. Copyright 2007, John Wiley and Sons, Inc.

Practices to Avoid

- To prevent door warp, door should not be stored in a standing position or leaned against each other in the standing position. Excessive moisture or heat, while in the standing position, can cause the door to warp.
- Avoid the storage of doors in direct sunlight. Excessive heat on a door can cause the door to warp.
- Avoid the installation of additional hardware items to the door. Hardware items such as a peephole or door knocker, if installed on the door, can void the manufacturer's warranty.

Sliding Doors

Description

Exterior residential sliding doors are commonly horizontal sliding glass patio doors and surface-mounted horizontal sliding doors, which can be solid doors, or a stile and rail door with glass infill panels.

Interior sliding doors are commonly bypassing doors, surface-mounted horizontal sliding doors, pocket doors, and accordion sliding doors.

Sliding doors' basic components include a top track, trolleys (minimum two per operating leaf), locking mechanism, bottom track or stay roller, and an operating handle or pull.

Materials used for exterior doors include aluminum, vinyl, and vinyl- or aluminum-clad wood frame. Commonly used materials for interior sliding doors include solid-core or hollow-core wood doors, aluminum stile and rail doors with glass infill, wood stile and rail doors with flat panel, and raised panel or glass infill panels. If sliding doors have glass panels, the glass panels must be tempered per the International Residential Code (IRC) R308.4.

Exterior patio doors are fabricated with a series of fixed panels and operating panels. The number of panels depends on the size of the opening. Maximum frame width can reach up to 188 inches. Maximum panel size is nominally 48 inches. In most situations, there is one fixed panel and one operating panel. The operating panel is toward the outside of the door assembly. The glazing is installed from the inside of the door for security purposes.

Exterior surface-mounted sliding doors are used where large, unobstructed openings are required. These doors are difficult to weatherstrip so are generally used in unconditioned spaces such as garages, carports, barns, or workshop areas.

Interior sliding doors are generally field fabricated by using track and trolley hardware sets and blank doors that match the swinging doors in the project. The only exception is the accordion sliding doors, which have multipaneled hinged units fabricated from wood, metal, or plastic. Typically openings are trimmed out with a wood casing. The track is then attached to the casing and either the track has a fascia piece as part of the track assembly or a hardwood fascia can be attached to the casing to conceal the track.

Assessing Existing Conditions

- Doors should operate freely without binding. If doors are hung properly, the door in any position should not move when released.
- Verify that all hardware is installed and working correctly and that all bumpers and door guides are installed correctly to protect the door and to provide quiet operation.
- Surface-mounted sliding doors should have a stay roller to prevent the door, when moved, from being pulled away from the wall.
- Surface-mounted sliding doors should have a built-in stop to prevent over-travel of the door and personal injury.
- Locks should latch properly and work with minimal effort.
- If a sliding door has glass panels, verify that the glass panel is tempered. Tempered glass is required to have a permanent, etched designation visible after the glass is installed, per IRC R308.1.

Acceptable Practices

- Wood doors should not be delivered to the jobsite until the humidity level in the finished space is maintained at a relative humidity of 30 to 50 percent.
- To prevent damage to wood sliding doors, storage and handling is very important. To prevent damage to wood veneers and finish, doors should be stored flat on the floor and elevated off the floor with the use of 2x material located at quarter points along the door height.
- Cover doors with plastic sheeting to prevent dust and dirt from collecting on the top surface. Allow air to circulate around doors and sheeting.
- In bathrooms or utility rooms, verify that there is an operable window or exhaust fan. Excessive moisture within a room can cause wood sliding doors to warp.
- Exterior door frames shall be secured to the supporting structure in accordance with IRC R612.8. Door frames must be secured to supporting structure with manufacturer's supplied attachment clip or flange or directly attached to supporting structure through door frame.

Folding Doors

Description

Exterior folding doors are commonly used where large unobstructed openings are desired. These doors are fabricated of wood or aluminum with glass vision panels. Typical finishes are painted aluminum, anodized aluminum, painted wood, or stained wood with a transparent finish. Wood folding doors have the option of an exterior finish of aluminum cladding.

Folding doors' basic operating components include a top track, trolleys, locking mechanism, bottom track or top and bottom pivots, and an operating handle or pull.

Interior folding doors are bifolding doors that are commonly used for closets, linen closets, coat closets, and laundry closets. Materials used for interior folding doors include solid-core or hollow-core wood doors or wood stile-and-rail doors with flat panel, or raised panels. Doors are generally field fabricated by using track and trolley hardware sets. Typically, the opening is trimmed out with a cased opening. The track is then attached to the casing, and either the track has a fascia piece as part of the track assembly or a hardwood fascia can be attached to the casing to conceal the track.

Assessing Existing Conditions

- Exterior folding doors require slab block out for sill condition.
- Where accessibility is an issue, verify that sill condition does not exceed 1/2 inch in height.
- Verify that hard surfaces on exterior side of folding doors slope away from door minimum 1/4 inch per foot.
- Verify that flexible flashing and weather barrier at openings are properly lapped to shed water to outside of building.
- Sheet metal drip flashing at head condition should be provided to prevent water penetration into building.
- Operate locks on exterior folding doors to verify that they latch properly and work with minimal effort.

- Interior folding doors used as a laundry closet shall have louvered doors or a louver in the wall or above the closet doors for makeup air, per International Residential Code (IRC) G2439.4 for gas appliances only.

Acceptable Practices

- Exterior wood doors should have the final finish on doors as soon as possible after installation to prevent door warp from excessive moisture. Verify that top and bottom of door has been finished.
  Interior wood doors should not be delivered to the jobsite until the humidity level in the finished space is maintained at a relative humidity of 30 to 50 percent.
- To prevent damage to folding doors, storage and handling is very important. To prevent damage to wood veneers and finish, doors should be stored flat on the floor and elevated off the floor with the use of 2x material located at quarter points along the door height.
- Cover doors with plastic sheeting to prevent dust and dirt from collecting on the top surface. Allow air to circulate around doors and sheeting.
- Interior bifold doors should maintain a consistent distance on all sides of the frame, 1/4-inch sides, and minimum 1/16 inch between door leaves.

Door Hardware Functions

Description

There are four basic door hardware elements that are provided with doors: door hinges, lockset or passage set, and for exterior doors, weatherstripping and thresholds.

There are various types of door hinges in residential construction; the most common type used is called a plain bearing hinge. Doors in residential construction get relatively low usage and therefore, a plain bearing hinge is adequate to hang the door. Plain bearing hinges are the least expensive hinges. Plain bearing hinges use metal-on-metal contact to swing the door; there are no bearings of any sort used in the fabrication of plain bearing hinges. In residential construction, generally five-knuckle, radiused corner hinges are used. Five-knuckle hinges are used because there is more surface area between knuckles to distribute the load of the door. Radiused corner hinges are used because the door and frame can be prepped for the hinge by a machine; door preparation does not require the use of any hand tools.

The quantity and size of the hinges required to hang a door is dependent on the weight of the door. Generally, the size for an entry door in a residence, 36 by 80 inches, three hinges sized 4-1/2 by 4-1/2 inch are required. For interior doors, generally two hinges sized 3-1/2 by 3-1/2 inch are adequate for 1-3/8-inch thick interior door up to 36 inches wide.

Table 23.1 Recommended Hinge Sizes

Door Thickness	Door Width	Hinge Height	Hinge Thickness
1⅜ in.	Up to 36 in.	3½ in.	0.123 in.
1⅜ in.	More than 36 in.	4 in.	0.130 in.
1¾ in.	Up to 36 in.	4 ½ in.	0.134 in.
1¾ in.	36–48 in.	5 in.	0.134 in.
1¾ in.	More than 48 in.	6 in.	0.160 in.
2–2 ½ in.	Up to 42 in.	5 in.	0.190 in.

If an exterior door swings to the outside, the hinges are then located on the exterior side of the residence. In these situations, a hinge fabricated of stainless steel or solid brass should be used so that the hinge will not rust. In addition, at least one hinge should be prepped with a nonremovable pin (NRP). Prepping a hinge to have a nonremovable pin will prevent the hinge pins from being removed from the hinges and the door removed from the frame. Generally, the hinge with the nonremovable pin is the center hinge.

The next door hardware element is the lockset for the door. There are four basic door hardware locking functions in residential construction. The four functions are passage set, privacy lock, entrance lock, and storeroom lock. In addition, there are auxiliary locks, more commonly called deadbolts, which come in three functions: single cylinder, double cylinder, and thumbturn only. Also available for locksets and auxiliary locks are electronic keypads. The electronic keypads are integrated into the lockset or auxiliary lock design and require no special door preparation to install.

The four basic locking functions for bored locksets are as follows: the passage set has no capability of locking; inside and outside knobs or levers turn freely; the privacy lock has push-button locking from the inside, with emergency unlocking from the outside with the use of a special key or tool; the entrance lock has a keyed cylinder on the outside, which can lock or unlock the lever on the outside and a push button that can either be pushed in or pushed in and turned to lock the outside knob or lever. The storage lock has a keyed lever on the outside, the lever is always rigid and always requires the use of a key to gain access through the door. The inside lever is always active, allowing the occupants to exit from the inside at all times. Locksets with electronic keypads are battery operated, so no special door preparation is required. Electronic keypads can hold up to 19 different user codes, and they still have key operation. In addition, these types of locksets have an option to automatically relock the door after five seconds or can remain unlocked until the lockset is manually relocked.

The three functions of the auxiliary lock are: the single cylinder auxiliary lock has a keyed cylinder on the outside for locking and unlocking the auxiliary lock; the inside has a thumbturn and allows the door to be locked or unlocked without a key; the double cylinder auxiliary lock has keyed cylinders on the inside and outside of the auxiliary lock, which would require the use of a key to lock or unlock either side of the door. The thumbturn-only auxiliary lock has only a thumbturn on the inside of the door, which allows locking or unlocking of the door from the inside. There is no capability of unlocking the door from the outside. Deadbolts with electronic keypads are battery operated, so no special door preparation is required. Electronic keypads can hold up to 19 different user codes and they still have key operation.

Locksets come in two different types, bored locksets and mortise locksets. Generally, mortise locksets are used on exterior doors in high-end construction and bored locksets are used for interior doors. In standard residential construction, a bored lockset accompanied by an auxiliary lock (deadbolt) is commonplace for exterior entry doors.

Generally, mortise locksets combine the latching mechanism and the deadbolt in the rectangular-shaped case, thus eliminating the need for an auxiliary lock (deadbolt) as is used with a bored lockset. There are two types of bored locksets—a tubular lockset and a cylindrical lockset. Tubular locksets have latchbolt assemblies that extend through the lock body when installed on the door. Cylindrical locksets have a latchbolt assembly that interlocks with one side of the lock chassis. Tubular locksets are commonly used for interior doors and cylindrical locksets for exterior doors.

For exterior doors, weatherstripping and thresholds are provided to help reduce the amount of wind blown through the perimeter of the door and frame. Thresholds help to prevent wind-driven rain from passing under the door. If the entry door is pre-hung, generally the threshold and weatherstripping come as part of the door assembly. Commonly, the door weatherstripping is inserted into a saw-cut strip in the stop on the frame of the door. The weatherstripping is held in place through a friction fit when the door is in the open position. This type of weatherstripping does not require any mechanical fasteners and can be installed quickly by the door installer. The weatherstripping is a foam product with a UV stable polyethylene cover to prevent tearing of the foam. The friction fit that secures the weatherstripping to the door frame is fabricated of a rigid PVC material. In addition, a vinyl door bottom or shoe is added to the bottom of the door. The door bottom and threshold work together to prevent wind and wind-driven rain from passing under the door.

Assessing Existing Conditions

- Hardware should not bind if properly installed. Turn levers to ensure locksets are properly installed, operating with minimal effort, and that latchbolts do not stick in the retracted position when retracted.
- Open and close all doors to ensure that the doors latch when closed.

- Test auxiliary locks to ensure that deadbolt extends completely out when door is closed. There should be no binding of deadbolt or difficulty in extending the deadbolt with the key when the door is closed.
- Check that door has been properly installed and hung; proper tolerances between door and frame for single doors should be 1/8 inch between door and frame. If distance exceeds 1/8 inch, the latchbolt may not adequately secure the door.
- If extra-thick door trim is used, use an extended lip strike to protect the door trim and allow the door to close and latch more easily.

Acceptable Practices

- Locksets at exterior doors should be supplied with a deadlocking latchbolt.
- Auxiliary locks (deadbolts) for added security should be supplied with a minimum 1 inch throw and hardened steel deadbolt.
- Locksets and auxiliary locks (deadbolts) at exterior doors should be provided with 1/8-inch-thick solid-steel door reinforcer, mortised into door jamb and secured using 3-inch-long screws screwed into wall studs.

Practices to Avoid

Door hardware is strictly regulated by building codes; some common hardware issues to avoid:

- In certain jurisdictions the use of double cylinder auxiliary lock are prohibited due to the exiting requirements.
- Swinging doors accessible by the physically handicapped cannot have more than a 1/2-inch elevation change between the outside finished surface and the inside finish floor.

Door Hardware Finishes

Description

Door hardware comes in many different finishes. There are four basic types of finishes, natural finish, plated finish, coated finish, and anodized finish.

Natural finishes are obtained when raw materials are buffed or polished to achieve the final finish. Natural finishes include polished or satin brass or stainless steel, and mill finish aluminum.

Plated finishes are generally the most expensive and each plated finish has its own physical characteristics that help determine which plated finish is the most appropriate for the particular situation. Plated finishes can be electrically deposited on the surface of a base metal or chemically deposited on the base metal. The base metal is the material that the door hardware component is fabricated from and can be fabricated from brass, bronze and nickel. Once the component is fabricated, the component is plated. Brass is the best base metal to use if the component is to be plated, because the plating process bonds the best to brass.

Coated finishes can be either spray applied or dipped, then the coating is baked on, or a coated finish can be powder coated. Spray applied or dipped coatings are generally lacquer or polyester coatings. Lacquer coatings are the most durable and are generally clear and applied to a plated finish to prevent oxidation of the finish. Powder-coated finishes offer a very-high-quality finish, but hardware items that are powder coated are limited in what base metal can be used because of the high heat required to bake the coating to the base metal.

Anodized finishes are applied to aluminum available in two types: anodized or color-anodized. Anodized finishes are very hard and corrosion-resistant and result in a long-lasting, permanent, and chemically stable surfaces. Anodized finish color is clear. Colored anodized finishes include light bronze anodized, medium bronze anodized, dark bronze anodized, black anodized, and champagne anodized.

Hardware finishes can give a home's look a particular style. Finishes such as brushed finishes like satin nickel, satin chrome has a soft, yet contemporary feel. Matte black, oil-rubbed bronze, or aged bronze have an old-world feel and are designed to age with wear, providing a timeless look. Antique pewter and antique brass offer an elegant, yet old-fashioned look. Bright brass has a classic look and is one of the most common finishes found in homes. Satin bronze is soft and luxurious. Satin bronze adds elegance and a tradition look for hardware.

Assessing Existing Conditions

In order to ensure the correct hardware finish has been supplied and that the hardware finish will not show premature aging, verify the following:

- If door is not properly hung, excessive wear on hardware could result.
- Door stops should be located such that the door or other hardware makes contact with the door stop prior to coming in contact with other surfaces.

Acceptable Practices

The following are suggestions for maintaining hardware finish quality by protecting the finish from abrasion or abuse:

- All doors should have an acceptable method of stopping the door prior to contact with hard or rough surfaces.
- Door stops should have soft or rubber surfaces when coming in contact with hardware finishes.
- Door hardware that will have high usage or are highly abused should be fabricated of solid material and have a natural finish like stainless steel, lacquered brass, or anodized aluminum.

Practices to Avoid

Since hardware finishes are susceptible to abuse, which can cause premature deterioration of the hardware finish, the following practices should be avoided:

- Metal-on-metal contact of door hardware finishes should be avoided; this can cause premature wear to hardware finishes.
- Do not use paint-removing solvents, acids, or other strong caustic cleaning solutions to clean door hardware.

Table 23.2 Comparative Finish Designations

		Finish Code—Base Material				
U.S.	Description	Steel	Brass	Bronze	Stainless	Aluminum
US3	Bright brass	632	605	—	—	—
US4	Dull brass	633	606	—	—	—
US5	Dull brass, oxidized (antique brass)	638	609	—	—	—
US9	Bright bronze	637	—	611	—	—
US10	Dull bronze	639	—	612	—	—
US10B	Antique bronze, oiled	—	—	613	—	—
US14	Bright nickel plated	645	618	618	—	—
US15	Dull nickel plated	646	619	619	—	—
US19	Flat black	622	—	—	—	—
US26	Bright chromium	651	625	625	—	—
US26D	Dull chromium	652	626	626	—	—
US28	Anodized dull aluminum	—	—	—	—	628
US32	Polished stainless steel	—	—	—	629	—
US32D	Dull stainless steel	—	—	—	630	—

- Door hardware should not be installed on doors that do not have a final finish applied to door surface.
- Prior to refinishing doors or frames all door hardware should be removed from door. Hardware should only be reinstalled after finish has had time to adequately dry.

Attic Access

Description

Attic access is required by the International Residential Code (IRC) R807.1 when the attic area exceeds 30 square feet and has a vertical height of at least 30 inches. Access to the attic should be provided in a hallway or easily accessible location. Openings to attics can be in the form of a pull-down hatch with ladder, scuttle hole with no ladder, or access through a knee wall in an upstairs attic room. Minimum rough opening size of scuttle hole or access opening is 22 inches by 30 inches for attic spaces not housing heating or cooling appliances. If attic spaces are housing heating and cooling appliances, the size of the attic access shall be large enough to remove the largest appliance, but not less than 22 inches by 30 inches. Refer to IRC R1305.1.3. The ideal location for attic access is in the garage or in an unconditioned area of the house, because then there is no need to worry about weatherstripping and insulating the opening to the attic.

Assessing Existing Conditions

In order to ensure adequate and usable attic access, verify the following:

- Verify location of attic access and that there are adequate clearances to allow access using pull-down ladder, or adequate room for user-supplied ladder.
- Check framing to verify that perimeter of opening is blocked out with framing matching ceiling joists height. If ceiling insulation is thicker than the height of the ceiling joists, provide insulation damns to prevent insulation from falling in access opening.
- If attic access is located within a conditioned space, confirm that access cover has been insulated and that weatherstripping is in place around opening.
- All perimeter gaps in framing around attic access should be sealed with spray foam insulation to maintain the air/thermal barrier.

Acceptable Practices

- If attic access must be located in conditioned space and a pull-down stair is to be provided, provide insulated cover over pull-down stair to help prevent drafts at attic access.
- Insulate access doors, where access to attic is through knee wall, with rigid insulation, R-19 minimum. In addition, weatherstrip doors and provide threshold with weatherstripping or door bottom.

Practices to Avoid

Things to consider for attic access:

- Attic access pull-down ladders that run perpendicular to ceiling joists, requiring blocking out of ceiling
- Attic access that is not insulated

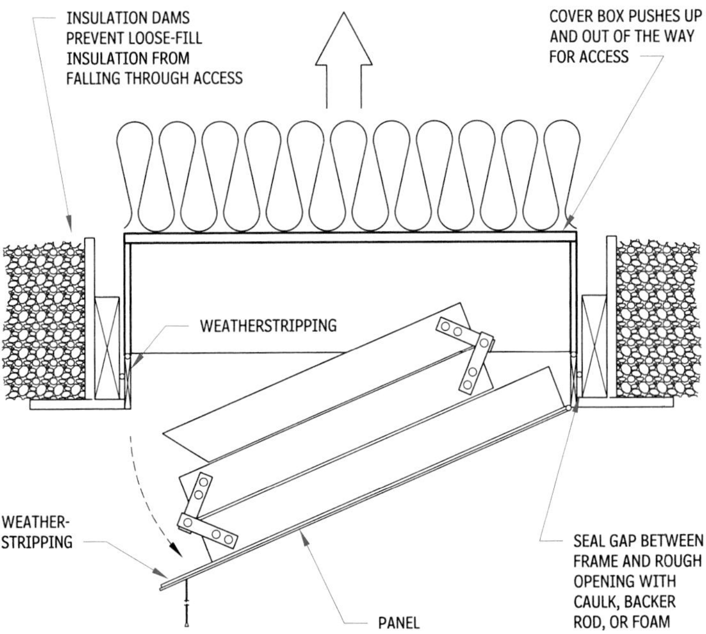

Figure 23.3 Pull-down attic staircase
Source: Southface

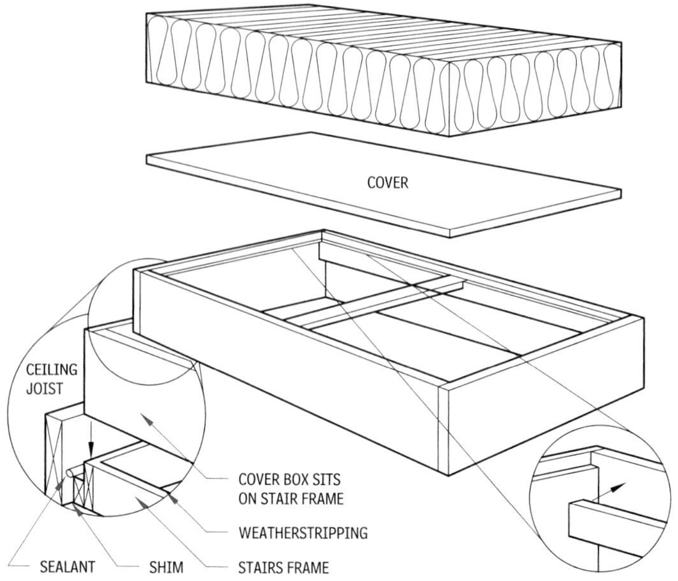

Figure 23.4 Insulated attic stairs cover box
Source: Southface

Figure 23.5 Access door in knee wall
Source: Southface

Resources

WITHIN THIS BOOK

- Chapter 2 Building Code Requirements
- Chapter 3 Accessibility Guidelines
- Chapter 12 Cold-Formed Metal Framing
- Chapter 15 Rough Carpentry
- Chapter 20 Exterior Wall Covering
- Chapter 27 Gypsum Board

REFERENCE STANDARDS

- ANSI/BHMA A156.2—Bored and Pre-assembled Locks and Latches
- ANSI/BHMA A156.5—Auxiliary Locks and Associated Products
- ANSI/BHMA A156.13—Mortise Locks and Latches
- ANSI/BHMA A156.18—American National Standard for Materials and Finishes

OTHER RESOURCES

- 2009 International Residential Code for One and Two-Family Dwellings. Washington, DC: International Code Council, Inc., 2009.
- American Institute of Architects, *Architectural Graphics Standards*, 11th ed. Hoboken, NJ: John Wiley and Sons, 2007.
- American Institute of Architects, *Architectural Graphic Standards for Residential Construction*, 2nd ed. Hoboken, NJ: John Wiley and Sons, 2010.
- Builders Hardware Manufacturers Association (BHMA), www.buildershardware.com.

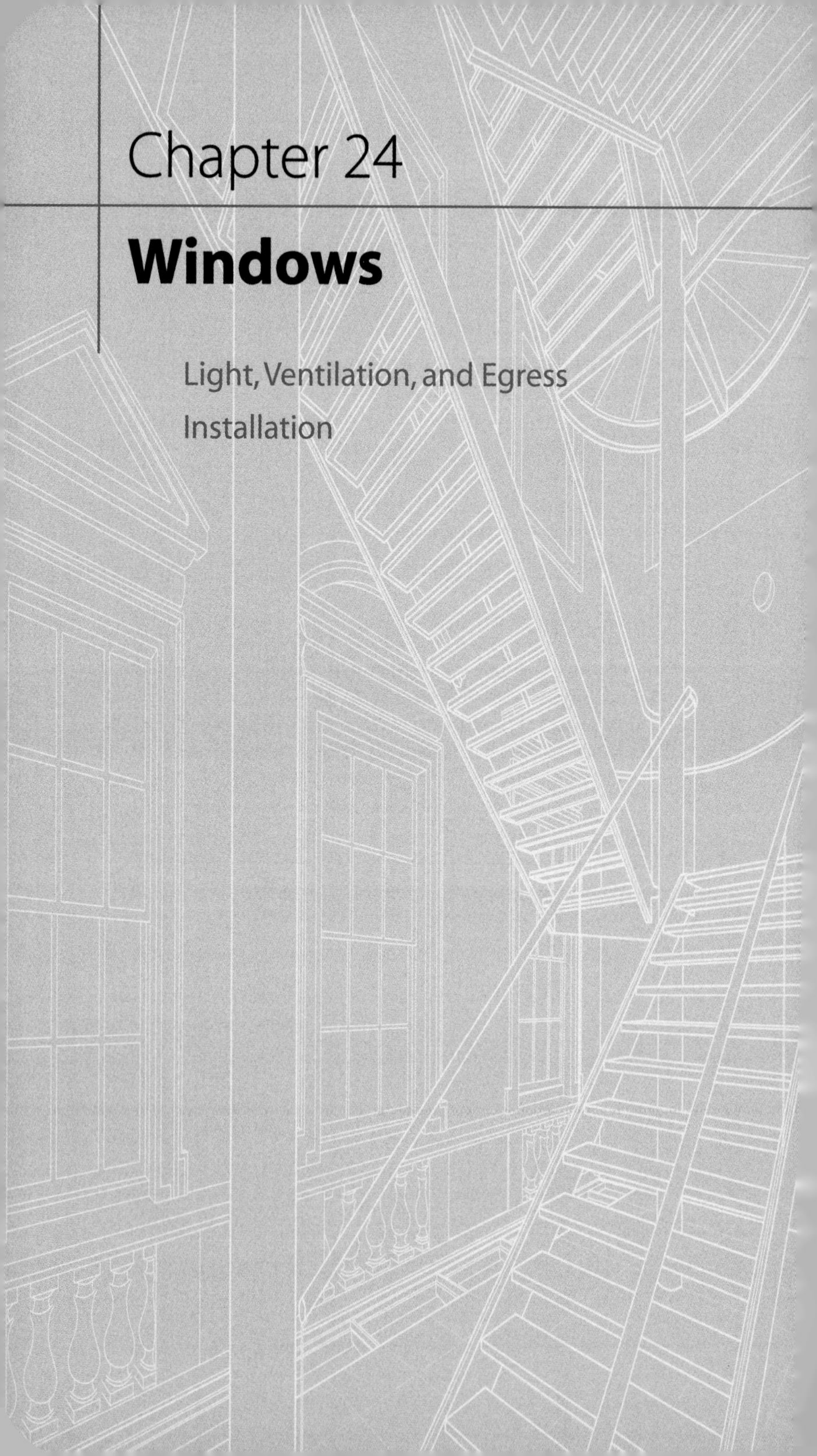

Chapter 24

Windows

Light, Ventilation, and Egress

Installation

Light, Ventilation, and Egress

Description

Window selection and location can make an important impact on building energy use and required emergency egress. An extensive variety of options—including shape, operation, materials, finishes, and hardware—make almost every window unique, and therefore may require closer attention when they are inspected in the field.

Careful selection of glazing type and arrangement, frame material, weather stripping, and hardware can reduce the need for heating or cooling and artificial lighting required by many state energy codes. Most residential projects use manufactured window units, composed of a self-contained frame and glazing assembly, which are fabricated in a variety of ways using different glazing, frame, and operating types. To reduce confusion when assessing window units, the National Fenestration Rating Council (NFRC) certifies and labels manufactured window units for basic thermal and optical properties based on whole window values. The NFRC standards for the basic thermal and optical properties of fenestration products are as follows: NFRC 100 for the U-factor, NFRC 200 for the solar heat gain coefficient (SHGC), NFRC 300 for visible light transmittance, and NFRC 400 for air leakage.

According to section R303.1 of the IRC, all habitable rooms must have an aggregate glazing area of not less than 8 percent of the given rooms floor area and, unless approved mechanical ventilation is provided, a minimum openable area of 4 percent for natural ventilation. The minimum net opening increases to 5.7 square feet in basements and sleeping rooms to meet emergency egress requirements of Section R310. Such openings shall be a minimum of 24 inches high and 20 inches wide. Unless artificial light and ventilation is provided, bathrooms require an aggregate glazing area of not less than 3 square feet, of which one-half must be operable. Screens, bars, and other coverings are allowable as long as they can be removed from the inside without special tools or excessive force.

Assessing Existing Conditions

In order to ensure windows will comply with light, ventilation, and egress requirements, verify the following conditions:

- Unit performance is verifiable through labels or certificate documentation.
- Windows that are installed to meet emergency egress requirements have a sill height not more than 44 inches above the floor.
- Required glazed openings open directly onto a public street or alley, or a yard located within the same property.
- Required glazed openings under a deck or cantilevered space have a minimum of 36 inches clear vertical height.

Acceptable Practices

Manufactured window units can be difficult to compare due to the variety of glass types, components, and construction methods available. Selections are often driven with performance, durability, and life-cycle costs in mind. Sealed, double-pane, insulating-glass units are considered to be standard. Other common options include single and triple panes, low-emissivity coatings, and argon-gas-filled inner spaces.

Common fabrication practices for manufactured window units include the following:

- Glazing unit structure: Multiple layers of glass improve thermal resistance and reduce heat loss attributed to convection between window layers. Additional layers provide more surfaces for low-E or solar-control coatings.
- Low-emittance coatings: Low-E coatings have a high rate of reflectance with long-wavelength infrared radiation, which reduces heat transfer. Low-E coatings may be applied directly to glass surfaces, which are then suspended in the air cavity between the interior and exterior glazing layers.
- Low-conductance gas fills: Although air is a relatively good insulator, other gases (such as argon, krypton, and carbon dioxide) have lower thermal conductivities. Using one of these nontoxic gases in an insulating glass unit can reduce heat transfer between glazing layers.
- Solar control glazings and coatings: Spectrally selective glazings and coatings absorb and reflect the infrared portion of sunlight, while transmitting visible daylight, thus reducing solar heat gain coefficients and resultant cooling loads.

- Warm edge spacers: Heat transfer through metal spacers used to separate glazing layers can increase heat loss and cause condensation to form at the edge of the window. "Warm edge" spacers use new materials and better design to reduce this effect.
- Weatherstripping designed for easy removal and replacement prolongs a window's performance level.
- Compression-sealed weatherstripping seals more tightly than sliding-sealed weatherstripping for less air and water infiltration and better thermal performance. Locking mechanisms, spaced at sufficient intervals, ensure tight sealing of compression-type weatherstripping.

Practices to Avoid

If window selection and placement is given careful consideration, many of the problems arising from lighting, ventilation, and egress needs can be met. Common construction practices to avoid include:

- Large expanses of windows in colder climates that will not receive any direct sun.
- Windows in warmer climates that receive direct sun.
- Windows placed near building exhaust or where fumes are present.
- Windows placed where intense glare of direct sunlight will fall in undesirable locations.

Installation

Description

Installation of manufactured window units varies as much as the fabrication methods among manufacturers. Regardless of the quality of the window unit, installation is critical to its performance and must follow manufacturer's instructions to avoid voiding warranties. General guidance when installing windows can be found in AAMA 2400, *Standard Practice for Installation of Windows with a Mounting Flange in Stud Frame Construction,* and ASTM E2112, *Standard Practice for Installation of Exterior Windows, Doors, and Skylights*; however, standard practices may be exceeded when more durable installation is desired.

Assessing Existing Conditions

In order to ensure the proper installation of manufactured window units, verify the following conditions:

- Proper sizing of the window and the rough opening. Allow for a 1/4-inch gap along all sides for adjusting.
- Rough openings are squared and level.
- Frames in rough openings are supported.

Acceptable Practices

In the installation of manufactured window units, weather-tight construction and consideration for the thermal movement of the frame material are of the upmost importance. Flashing, water/weather retarders, and joint sealants must be coordinated with window installation, and all components of an exterior wall must be compatible and installed undamaged, in the correct sequence and manner.

Conditions affecting the surface temperatures of the windows should also be addressed during installation to avoid condensation. Where warm inside air containing water vapor meets cold outdoor-air temperatures, the water vapor will turn to liquid, causing condensation. The moisture falls to the sill as it condenses, and therefore it is necessary to install a subsill of sheet metal, or other impervious material, with water-tight end dams and a slope to the exterior.

Common construction practices for installation include the following:

- Flashing should be installed around the outside of the window.
- Shims to level the window unit are nailed or glued in place.
- Insulation should be packed into gaps between the window and framing.

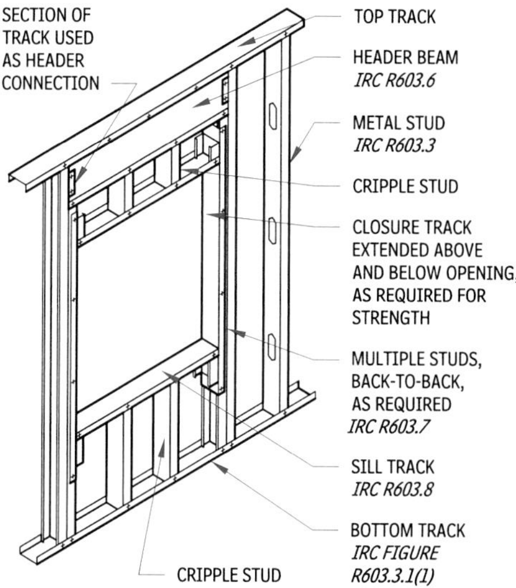

Figure 24.1 Framed openings for windows
AIA, *Architectural Graphic Standards for Residential Construction*, 2nd ed. Copyright 2010, John Wiley and Sons, Inc.

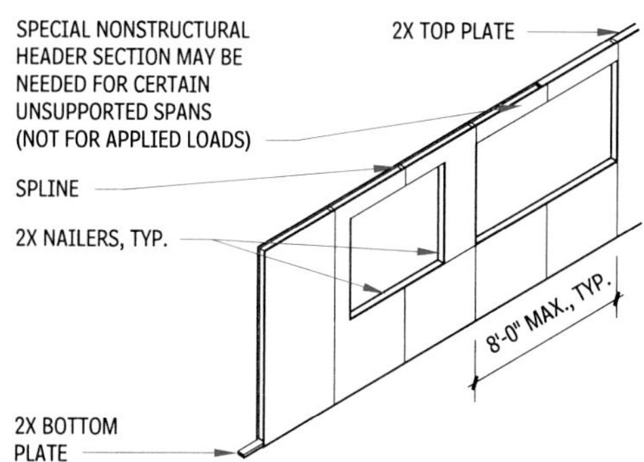

Figure 24.2 Window installation and flashing
AIA, *Architectural Graphic Standards for Residential Construction*, 2nd ed. Copyright 2010, John Wiley and Sons, Inc.

- Anchors should be the type, size, and compatible noncorrosive finish recommended by the manufacturer for the substrate.
- Anchors should be located and spaced according to the window manufacturer's recommendations.
- Single-point contact hardware provides uncomplicated operation; however, double-point contact hardware should be used where a more secure and weathertight window is required.

Practices to Avoid

Windows are an important part of every home in that they provide both a connection to and protection from the natural elements, while enhancing the visual beauty inside and outside of homes. Careful installation is necessary to ensure their lasting quality and comfort.

Common construction practices to avoid include the following:

- Do not pack insulation too tightly around the perimeter of window frames. This can cause distortion of the frame, failure of weather stripping and sealants, and glass breakage if they expand.
- Do not allow penetration in the horizontal portion of the sill. Penetration allows moisture to seep into the wall below.
- Frames in rough openings must be supported. Improperly supported frames can distort and sag, resulting in windows not operating smoothly, closing tightly, engaging hardware effectively, or being weathertight.

Resources

WITHIN THIS BOOK

- Chapter 2 Building Code Requirements
- Chapter 3 Accessibility Guidelines
- Chapter 12 Cold-Formed Metal Framing
- Chapter 15 Rough Carpentry
- Chapter 20 Exterior Wall Covering
- Chapter 27 Gypsum Board

REFERENCE STANDARDS

- AAMA 2400—Standard Practice for Installation of Windows with a Mounting Flange in Stud Frame Construction.
- ASTM E2112—Standard Practice for Installation of Exterior Windows, Doors, and Skylights

OTHER RESOURCES

- 2009 International Residential Code for One and Two-Family Dwellings. Washington, DC: International Code Council, Inc., 2009.
- American Institute of Architects, *Architectural Graphics Standards*, 11th ed. Hoboken, NJ: John Wiley and Sons, 2007.
- American Institute of Architects, *Architectural Graphic Standards for Residential Construction*, 2nd ed. Hoboken, NJ: John Wiley and Sons, 2010.
- National Fenestration Rating Council (NFRC), www.nfrc.org.
- American Architectural Manufacturer's Association (AAMA), www.Aamanet.org.

Chapter 25

Glazing

Safety Glazing

Mirrors

Safety Glazing

Description

Glazing, outside of manufactured window units, is often used for shower surrounds, railings, and mirrors, where according to Section R308.4 of the IRC it may be required to resist human impact loads and be labeled as safety glazing.

To qualify as safety glazing, glazing in doors or used as enclosures for tubs, showers or other wet areas must be tested in accordance with the Consumer Product Safety Commission (CPSC) 16 CFR 1201, *Safety Standard for Architectural Glazing Materials,* and comply with the test criteria for Category I or II. All other glazing may be tested in accordance with ANSI Z97.1, *Safety Glazing Materials Used in Buildings,* and comply with test criteria for Class A or B.

Table 25.1 Minimum Category Classification of Glazing Using CPSC 16 CFR 1201

Exposed Surface Area of One Side of One Lite	Glazing in Storm or Communicating Doors (Category Class)	Glazing in Doors (Category Class)	Glazed Panels Regulated by Item 7 of Section R308.4 (Category Class)	Glazed Panels Regulated by Item 6 of Section R308.4 (Category Class)	Glazed in Doors and Enclosures Regulated by Item 5 of Section R308.4 (Category Class)	Sliding Glass Doors Patio Type (Category Class)
9 square feet or less	I	I	NR[a]	I	II	II
More than 9 square feet	II	II	II	Ii	II	II

[a]NR means "No Requirement."

Table 25.2 Minimum Category Classification of Glazing Using ANSI Z97.1

Exposed Surface Area of One Side of One Lite	Glazed Panels Regulated by Item 7 of Section R308.4 (Category Class)	Glazed Panels Regulated by Item 6 of Section R308.4 (Category Class)	Glazed in Doors and Enclosures Regulated by Item 5 of Section R308.4[a] (Category Class)
9 square feet or less	NR[b]	B	A
More than 9 square feet	A	A	A

[a]Use is permitted only by the exception to Section R308.3.1.
[b]NR means "No Requirement."

Each pane of safety glazing must be identified, according to Section R308.1 of the IRC, with a manufacturer's designation or label specifying who applied the designation, the type of glass, and the safety standard to which it complies. Designation may be applied in a variety of ways, but must be permanent and not able to be destroyed. For safety glazing other than tempered glass, some local code officials will accept certificates or other evidence for confirming compliance with code.

Assessing Existing Conditions

In order for safety glazing to comply with code requirements, verify the following conditions:

- Glazing in hazardous locations is labeled, identified, or the building code official approves the use of a certificate to confirm compliance.
- Verify stability of mounting and seals.

Acceptable Practices

Many exceptions to required safety glazing locations exist. Common exceptions include decorative glazing, glazed openings through which a 3-inch sphere is unable to pass, glazing in doors that access a closet or storage area 3 feet or less in depth, mirrors mounted on a surface that provides continuous backing support, and glazing that has a horizontal railing installed in front of it. Verify all exceptions before accepting glazing.

Locations for safety glazing according to IRC Section R308.4 include:

- Glazing in fixed and operable panels of swinging, sliding, and bifold doors.
- Glazing within 24 inches of a door and with a bottom edge less than 60 inches above the floor.

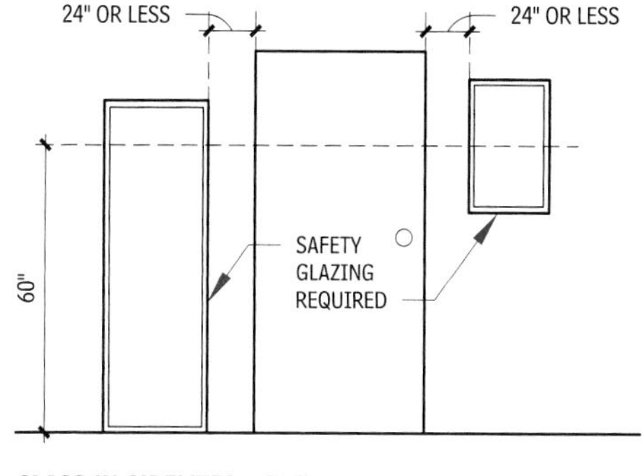

Figure 25.1 Glass requirements near doors
Source: AIA, *Architectural Graphic Standards for Residential Construction,* 2nd ed. Copyright 2010, John Wiley and Sons, Inc.

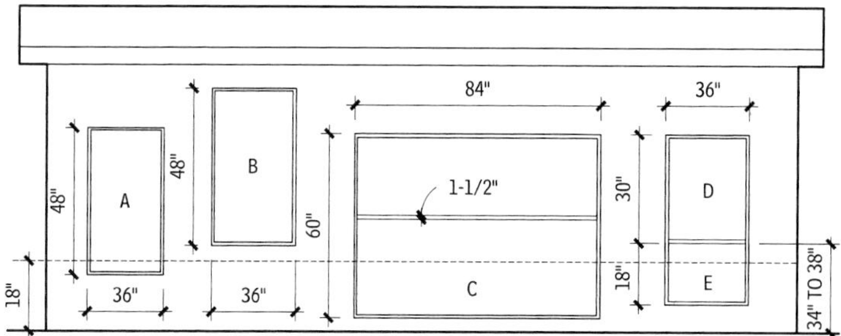

2010, John Wiley and Sons, Inc.

A—Safety glazing is required. Panel A is more than 9 sq. ft. in area, and its lowest edge extends to within 18" of the walking surface.

B & D—Safety glazing is not required. The lowest edge of the panel is more than 18" above the walking surface.

E—Safety glazing is not required. Panel E is less than 9 sq. ft. in area.

C—Safety glazing may be required. Panel C, being one piece of glass more than 9 sq. ft. in area and within 18" of the walking surface, is required to be of safety glazing materials, unless a horizontal member not less than 1-1/2" in width is located between 34" and 38" above the walking surface.

Figure 25.2 Glass requirements near walking surfaces
Source: AIA, *Architectural Graphic Standards for Residential Construction,* 2nd ed. Copyright 2010, John Wiley and Sons, Inc.

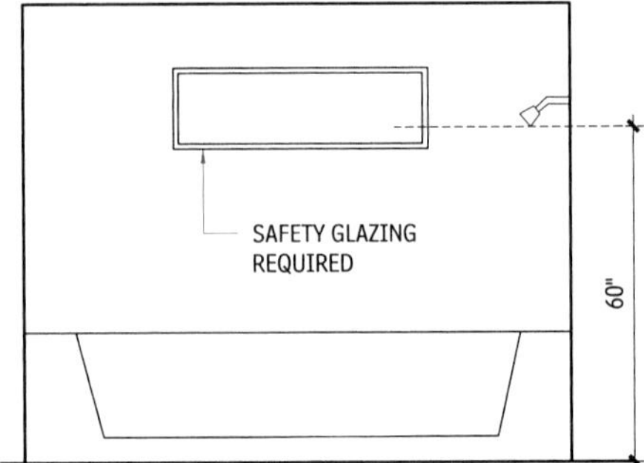

GLASS WITHIN SHOWER WALLS

Figure 25.3 Glass requirements in tub/shower enclosures
Source: AIA, *Architectural Graphic Standards for Residential Construction,* 2nd ed. Copyright 2010, John Wiley and Sons, Inc.

- Glazing panels that are larger than 9 square feet, with a bottom edge less than 18 inches and a top edge more than 36 inches above the floor, and within 36 inches of a walking surface.
- Glazing used in railings.
- Glazing enclosing or facing hot tubs, whirlpools, saunas, steam rooms, bathtubs, and showers where the bottom edge is less than 60 inches above any standing or walking surface.
- Glazing in walls or fences within 60 inches of the water's edge of any indoor or outdoor swimming pools, hot tubs or spas, with a bottom edge less than 60 inches above a walking surface.
- Glazing within 36 inches of stairways, landings or ramps, with a bottom edge less than 60 inches above adjacent walking surface.
- Glazing within 60 inches of the bottom tread of a stairway, with a bottom edge less than 60 inches above the nose of the tread.

Practices to Avoid

Common construction practices to avoid include:

- Clear glass where people are likely to walk into it

Mirrors

Description

Mirrors are created by coating clear or tinted glass with reflective silver, backed by copper, protected by epoxy paint. ASTM C 1503 offers recommendations for glass thicknesses for different applications and covers the requirements for silvered flat glass mirrors up to 1/4 inch thick, including minimum values for reflectance, silver coating appearance, coating resistance, blemishes, and dimensional and squareness tolerances. Safety glazing requirements for mirrors are addressed in the safety glazing topic. Where tempering is required, it must be performed before applying the silver coating but after cutting mirrors.

A high quality float-glass selected for lack of defects and dimensional tolerances is the most common glazing used for mirrors; however, ultraclear glass, which is ultra bright and reflects color more accurately than standard clear float glass, is another option. Most silver mirror coatings use a multilayered process. The third layer, which is offered by some manufacturers as a primer and top-coat process to improve corrosion resistance, is a protective paint coating, tough enough to resist damage from abrasion during cutting and edge fabrication. Since edge fabrication, which exposes edges of the metal coating to deterioration, is done after the final coat, it is important to seal edges after this operation.

Most unframed mirror applications are installed with mastic. Relying solely on mastic to support the weight of the mirror, however, is not recommended. Mechanical support is needed to support the weight of the mirror and to prevent the top edge of the mirror from pulling away from the substrates to which the mirror is attached.

Assessing Existing Conditions

In order to assess the proper installation of mirrors, verify the following conditions:

- Verify Section R308.4 in the IRC to determine if safety glazing is required.

- Verify an air space is located behind mirrors to allow air circulation.
- Third coat of silver coating is single or double coat process as specified.
- Verify warranty acceptance with mastic used.
- Mechanical supports are use at top and bottom of mirror.

Acceptable Practices

Common construction practices for mirrors include:

- 5- and 6-mm thicknesses are most common for applications where optical quality is a concern.
- Use of mirrors complying with safety glass requirements in areas not required by code for increased protection against breakage is desired.
- Mechanical bottom supports include angles, J-channels, clips, backsplashes, and baseboards.
- Top supports include J-channels and clips.

Practices to Avoid

Without its metal coating, a mirror is simply glass. Deterioration of the metal coating occurs when its edges are exposed to moisture or another substance that damages it. Common construction practices to avoid deterioration of mirrors include the following:

- Mirrors should not be installed in a manner that allows edges to be immersed in water for any length of time.
- Mirrors should not be installed over new plaster, new masonry, or freshly painted walls, which have high moisture content.
- Avoid cleaners that containing alkali, acid, or heavy ammonia bases.
- Do not apply cleaners directly to mirrors.

Resources

WITHIN THIS BOOK

- Chapter 23 Doors and Frames
- Chapter 24 Windows

REFERENCE STANDARDS

- 16 CFR 1201—Safety Standard for Architectural Glazing Materials
- ASTM C 1503—Standard Specification for Silvered Flat Glass Mirror
- ANSI Z 97.1—Safety Performance Specifications and Methods of Test for Safety Glazing Used in Buildings.

OTHER RESOURCES

- 2009 International Residential Code for One and Two-Family Dwellings. Washington DC: International Code Council, Inc., 2009.
- American Institute of Architects, *Architectural Graphics Standards*, 11th ed. Hoboken, NJ: John Wiley and Sons, 2007.
- American Institute of Architects, *Architectural Graphic Standards for Residential Construction*, 2nd ed. Hoboken, NJ: John Wiley and Sons, 2010.
- Glass Association of North America (GANA), www.glasswebsite.com.
- Insulated Glass Manufacturers Alliance (IGMA), www.igmaonline.org.

Part VIII

Finishes

Chapter 26

Plastering

Plastering (Walls and Ceilings)—Materials and Finishes

Plastering—Patches and Repairing

Plastering (Walls and Ceilings)—Materials and Finishing

Description

In days past, plaster walls were common in almost all homes and quality plastering for interior walls and ceilings was, and still is, an art. The development of gypsum board has made finishing walls a much simpler task, but some homeowners are still willing to pay the price in both time and money to have traditional plaster walls in their homes, since traditional three-coat plaster walls are stronger and more durable than gypsum board and provide increased fire and noise resistance as well. Plastering is a unique finish with a distinct look and can be applied as either a smooth or textured finish.

Conventional plaster types include gypsum and portland cement plasters. Both types of plaster have strict building code requirements that must be adhered to in both design and construction of interior and exterior plastering applications.

Table 26.1 Thickness of Plaster

Plaster Base	Finished Thickness of Plaster From Face of Lath, Masonry, Concrete	
	Gypsum Plaster	Cement Plaster
Expanded metal lath	⅝-in. minimum	⅝-in. minimum
Wire lath	⅝-in. minimum	¾-in. minimum
		⅞-in. minimum
Gypsum lath	½-in. minimum	¾-in. minimum
Masonry walls	½-in. minimum	½-in. minimum
Monolithic concrete walls	⅝-in. maximum	⅞-in. maximum
Gypsum veneer base	1/16″-in. minimum	¾-in. minimum
Gypsum sheathing	—	¾-in. minimum
Gypsum sheathing	—	⅞-in. minimum

Gypsum Plaster

Gypsum plaster can be applied over expanded-metal lath, masonry walls, monolithic concrete walls, gypsum lath, and wire-fabric lath. Some manufacturers state that gypsum plaster can be used in protected exterior areas; however, portland cement plaster is a better choice for any type of wet or exterior exposure. Gypsum plaster systems are more expensive than veneer plaster systems, but less expensive than portland cement plaster systems.

Gypsum plaster may be applied in two or three coats. Two-coat plaster is limited to vertical applications over gypsum lath and masonry substrates with enough texture to establish a strong bond with the base-coat plaster. Three-coat plaster is required over metal lath and other surfaces. Two-coat plaster saves time and, by omitting the metal lath, is less expensive than three-coat plaster. However, it has an increased risk of delamination or ghosting, which is telegraphing of the underlying mortar joints due to differences in suction.

Gypsum Veneer Plaster

Gypsum veneer plaster is a specially manufactured gypsum plaster that provides strength, hardness, and abrasion resistance. It consists of gypsum plaster applied in thin layers of one or two coats over unit masonry, monolithic concrete, cementitious backer units, and gypsum-based panels, specially manufactured for veneer plaster. Metal lath is not used with veneer plasters. Monolithic concrete and masonry substrates require more preparation work than gypsum base panels or cementitious backer units. Typically, gypsum veneer plaster has lower material costs, is installed more quickly, and dries faster than conventional plaster systems.

One-component systems are defined in ASTM C 843 as consisting of a single plaster material applied directly over an approved base in one coat. Such systems provide a hard monolithic surface finish at low cost and are suitable for use over gypsum-base panels or monolithic concrete substrates. A single layer is 1/16 inch to 3/32 inch total thickness for application to gypsum base panels. To help conceal surface imperfections in monolithic concrete substrates, veneer plaster manufacturers recommend a slight increase in material total thickness.

Two-component systems are defined in ASTM C 843 as consisting of two separate plaster materials mixed and applied as the base and finish coats. They provide a more durable and abrasion-resistant surface and can be finished to a truer plane than one-component systems.

They are suitable for use over gypsum or cementitious base panels, unit masonry, or monolithic concrete substrates. Two-component systems provide greater resistance to cracking, fastener pops, joint beading, and joint shadowing than one-component systems. In two-component systems, base and finish coats are 1/16- to 3/32-inch total thickness for each.

Veneer plaster compositions vary. Select plasters based on the requirements for surface hardness and smoothness. Standard veneer plasters are formulated with lime and alpha gypsum. High-strength veneer plasters, which do not contain lime, are more abrasion-resistant than standard veneer plasters. It is more difficult to produce a smooth surface with high-strength plasters; therefore, they cost more to apply. Conversely, more workable plasters are easier to apply, but their finish surface is not as hard. Lime increases plaster workability and coverage but reduces its strength and durability.

Portland Cement Plaster

Portland cement plaster can be applied over metal lath, unit masonry, and monolithic concrete, either by hand or by machine. It can be used on building exteriors and in wet areas of building interiors. However, portland cement plaster is not waterproof, and moisture can pass through it.

Traditional three-coat plastering involves two coarse or rough coats, covered by a smooth third finish coat.

First Coat—The Scratch Coat

- The first coat, called the *scratch coat,* is a mixture of lime or gypsum, aggregate (sand) and water. This mixture is applied in a thick layer about 3/8 inch thick to a wall covered with lath.
- After the first coat is applied, it is scratched or scored with a *scarifier* (comb) to create grooves for the second coat to help the second coat bond.

Second Coat—The Brown Coat

- After the first coat has dried sufficiently, the *brown* coat is applied. This is the same plaster mixture, and it again is applied in a layer about 3/8 inch thick. Once the wall has been plastered, a *browning rod* or straight edge is run across the surface to ensure that there are no holes in the plaster surface and the wall is smooth from top to bottom.

- Although the sand in the mixture theoretically provides enough texture for the third and final coat to bond with, a cement brush may be dragged across the surface to slightly roughen it and help hold the finish coat.

Third Coat—The Finish Coat

- After allowing the first two coats to dry thoroughly the final finish coat is applied. This coat is essentially a mixture of lime putty and water that is troweled on in smooth arcs with the trowel never leaving the wall to eliminate trowel marks.
- As the plaster begins to dry out, it is *water troweled* (sprayed with small amounts of water and troweled to a smooth finish).
- Once a plaster wall has dried thoroughly, it is ready to be primed and painted. There is no need to sand or smooth a properly finished plaster wall. In fact, sanding will only weaken the final finish.

Finishes

Plaster can be used as a finish for both interior and exterior applications. This chapter focuses on the interior applications. There are numerous methods and techniques for achieving the look that is desired.

Stucco

Stucco is a common term used to describe Portland cement plaster applied to exterior surfaces and is often used interchangeably with the term Portland cement plaster. Where used on exterior surfaces, it resists wind and rain penetration and deterioration from thermal changes, such as freeze-thaw cycles. Stucco is discussed separately in Chapter 20.

Plaster Bases

Plaster base is the industry's term for the lath or other backing to which the base plaster is applied. Metal bases include expanded-metal lath and wire-fabric lath; solid bases include concrete and masonry. Gypsum lath is a multilayered, laminated paper product.

Metal plaster bases reinforce base-coat plasters and is the most commonly used type of metal plaster base. During application, plaster is forced through lath meshes, creating a strong mechanical bond between the lath and plaster. Metal lath is mechanically fastened or wire tied to supports. Paper-backed, expanded-metal lath is available. Kraft-paper-backed lath is used to reduce plaster waste caused by "push through" (where hand applied) or "blow through" (where machine applied).

Gypsum base panels for veneer plaster is gypsum board surfaced with a specially treated, multilayer paper facing over a gypsum core designed for rapid veneer plaster application and finishing. The outer layers of the paper are highly absorptive and draw moisture rapidly and uniformly from the plaster mix so the mix bonds quickly to the panel and does not slide during application. The inner layers are chemically treated and form a barrier that prevents moisture from damaging the gypsum core and prevents it from softening or sagging.

Solid substrates for gypsum plaster include structurally sound unit masonry and monolithic concrete. Smooth concrete will not produce a good mechanical bond with gypsum plaster; sandblasting, bush hammering, or deep acid etching of the surface may be required. Masonry must be level and rough textured; the bond with plaster is improved by etching. If plaster will be applied directly to unit masonry or monolithic concrete, consider the application of bonding compound or the installation of self-furring, expanded-metal lath on these surfaces.

Plaster Finishes

Troweled finishes are hard, smooth finishes produced by using ready-mixed, gypsum finish-coat plaster or by mixing gypsum finish-coat plaster with lime putty. Troweled finish coats are not recommended for use over lightweight-aggregate base coats that are applied to expanded-metal lath; the combination of the flexible lath substrate and softer base coats may cause the harder finish coat to crack and spall.

Float finishes are sand-float finishes produced by mixing gypsum gaging plaster or gypsum Keene's cement with prepared lime and job-mixed aggregate.

Sprayed and textured finishes are most easily produced using ready-mixed plasters.

Artisan Plaster Finishes

A high level of skill and experience is required to realize the full potential of these historic plastering techniques. Several artisan finishes are produced in fresh plaster. Many decorative finishing products are marketed to imitate some of these historic finishing processes.

- Venetian plaster is a glossy plaster finish with remarkable depth and luster produced by applying thin layers of fine-grained plaster consisting of aged lime and marble powder and then burnishing the surface to a high polish.
- Marmorino is another finish using a plaster composed of lime and fine marble dust. The effect is a smooth finish with a matte sheen and cloudy variation of values resembling cut stone. It can be burnished to produce a glossy appearance.
- Lime paint applied as a wash or in thin layers and then wiped, sponged, or ragged creates a cloudlike mottling effect, producing the appearance of aged plaster.
- Sgraffito is a technique of applying layers of plaster tinted in contrasting colors and then scratching so as to produce an outline drawing. A combed wall surface is produced by dragging a comb-like tool over the prepared surface, producing stripes or waves.
- Fresco is a painting on damp, fresh, lime plaster with pigments having a glue or casein base. The lime of the plaster reacts with the binder of the pigments to form calcium carbonate, incorporating the pure pigments with the material of the wall as the plaster dries.

Assessing Existing Conditions

To ensure the proper installation of plastering materials and finishing, consider the following:

- Ensure proper plaster material storage and handling prior to installation.
- Plaster material manufacturers' written installation instructions and recommendations are followed for best application procedures.
- Substrate is structurally sound and support-spacing requirements for various configurations and weights of metal lath are supported per code requirements per Table 4.1 of ASTM 1063.
- Framing for walls and ceilings must meet minimum spacing requirements of local building codes to prevent problematic plaster installations.

Acceptable Practices

- Base- and finish-coat plaster mixes with high compressive strengths have improved resistance to damage from abrasion and impact, but require more time and effort.

- Lower-strength plaster mixes, which cost less than other mixes, can be used on surfaces not subject to normal contact, such as ceilings. They are easier to apply and work to achieve a smooth surface, resulting in increased production.
- Float or textured finishes may discourage hand and body contact because they have abrasive surfaces, but may take more effort to clean. Perlite aggregates can be used in mixes to reduce weight and improve fire resistance, but they produce softer plasters than sand aggregates.
- Fiber can be added to the plaster mixes at the jobsite to help reduce cracking and strengthen the plaster.
- Acrylic polymers may be added to improve flexural strength and workability of portland cement plaster.
- Air-entraining agents are often added to portland cement plaster where freeze-thaw cycling is anticipated.
- Rough-textured finishes used on exterior surfaces may accumulate dirt from the atmosphere. Consider smoother textures, like a sand-float finish, to reduce maintenance costs.
- Smooth-troweled finishes are seldom used because they show texture inconsistencies and cracks are more apparent.

Standard plaster accessories are attached to plaster bases. They are available in zinc, zinc-coated (galvanized) steel, and high-impact PVC. Zinc and PVC accessories are recommended by manufacturers for humid areas.

- An accessory made of expanded-metal diamond mesh that is available in 4- or 6-inch-wide strips is used to reinforce joints between sheets of gypsum lath. It can be used to reinforce joints between dissimilar plaster bases; however, consider requiring control joints at these locations.
- Control joints relieve expansion and contraction stresses in large plastered areas to prevent random plaster cracking. They should be installed where joints occur in the supporting construction. Control joints are available in metal and PVC.

Advantages and Disadvantages of Plaster Types

Gypsum plaster: Advantages of gypsum plaster include:

- Surfaces are abrasion resistant and appear more uniform than veneer plaster or gypsum board surfaces.
- Architectural features, such as vaulted ceilings and compound curves, can be installed with a smooth, monolithic appearance more easily than with veneer plaster or gypsum board.

Limitations of gypsum plaster include:

- Gypsum plaster is not recommended for use in areas subject to weather, moisture, or high humidity.
- Framing spacing and acceptable partition heights may be reduced from those used for veneer plaster or standard gypsum board assemblies because of lower deflection tolerances and greater weight.
- Drying must be strictly controlled as it may take as much as 30 to 60 days to fully dry before coatings or finishes can be applied.
- Primers containing polyvinyl acetate are unsuitable for use on finish-coat plasters that contain lime; the bond between the primers and plasters may fail and cause the prime coat and subsequent finish coats to delaminate from surfaces due to the alkalinity of the plaster.

Gypsum veneer plaster: Advantages of gypsum veneer plaster include:

- Installation is rapid and the plaster sets and dries quickly.
- Surfaces are abrasion resistant.
- Surfaces resist fastener pops and cracking.
- Smooth or textured finishes can be achieved.
- Finishes appear similar to conventional plaster finishes and are less expensive to install.
- Surfaces reduce gypsum panel joint shadowing under critical light conditions.

Limitations of gypsum veneer plaster include:

- It is not recommended for exterior use or use in areas subject to weather, moisture, or high humidity.
- Interior surface of exterior perimeter walls must be furred.
- Surfaces are less rigid than similar conventional plaster systems.
- Compound curves are more difficult to form than with conventional plaster systems.
- Veneer plaster is subject to joint beading and cracking under rapid drying conditions caused by low humidity, high temperatures, or drafts.
- Framing spacing and acceptable partition heights may be reduced from those used for standard gypsum board assemblies because of lower deflection tolerances.
- Ceramic tile cannot be directly applied to gypsum base panels; the surfaces must be plastered first.

Portland cement plaster: Advantages of portland cement plaster include:

- It resists weather, rot, fungus, and termites, and it does not deteriorate after repeated wetting and drying.
- Surfaces are abrasion-resistant.

Limitations of portland cement plaster include:

- Framing spacing and acceptable partition heights may be reduced from those used for gypsum plaster or standard gypsum-board assemblies because of lower deflection tolerances and greater weight.
- Control joints to limit plaster cracking must be closely spaced; spacing must be closer than in gypsum plaster.
- Greater thickness is required for portland cement plaster than for gypsum plaster to produce the same fire-resistance ratings. Fire-resistance-rated assemblies may require using lightweight aggregate (perlite) rather than sand.

Practices to Avoid

- Do not use gypsum plaster in wet areas of buildings, in exterior areas, or directly on the inside of exterior walls; portland cement plaster is recommended for these areas. Gypsum plaster will withstand occasional wetting and mild dampness and can be used in residential bathrooms (but not around shower stalls and bathtubs).
- Gypsum lath is not suitable for use with lime plasters or direct paint finishes, or for the direct application of tile.
- Gypsum lath should not be applied directly to exterior masonry or concrete surfaces. Interior surfaces of exterior walls should always be furred to provide an airspace between the lath and the exterior wall.

Plastering—Patching and Repairing

Description

Before beginning any plaster repair, be certain walls or ceilings are structurally sound and there are no concealed conditions. Existing plaster walls and ceilings found to be in need of repair can be successfully patched or repaired with the correct materials, methods, plastering tools, and some patience.

Plaster cracks are a normal occurrence and occur because plaster is fairly brittle and because of the movement of the house. Cracks at corners of doors and windows may run out at odd angles and are caused by the fact that houses settle over the years. Other wall and ceiling cracks may run in more or less straight lines and are generally caused by seasonal changes in humidity, which can cause a house to flex as the framing lumber behind the walls and ceilings expand and contract as it takes on (or gives up) moisture from the air. The only defense when dealing with such cracks is to maintain a constant level of humidity in the home. In light of these facts, plaster cracks seem to be inevitable over the lifespan of a house, and even repaired cracks may reappear over time.

Common Plastering Repairs

Cracks in Walls and Ceilings

Crack repairs can be made successfully by treating the cracks like new gypsum board seams. Begin by applying self-adhering fiberglass mesh tape over cracks. Apply successive layers of joint and topping compound to cover tape and disguise repair. After repair is dry, sand out any imperfections and uneven spots so that repair blends invisibly into the existing plaster. If desired, apply a final skim coat over the entire wall to fill dimples, hairline cracks, and other imperfections.

Cracked plaster ceilings may be easier and less expensively replaced rather than repaired, depending on the number of cracks and extent of damage. Installing a new gypsum board ceiling could be as simple as adding 1-inch by 4-inch strapping across the ceiling, hanging the gypsum board, then taping, and painting it.

Houses of historical significance registered with the National Register of Historical Places must be repaired within their specific guidelines.

Repairing Large Holes in Plaster Walls or Ceilings

Repairing large holes in plaster walls or ceilings must be done differently than smaller holes or cracks.

Mark a rectangle on the wall that includes the hole. With a knife or keyhole saw, cut out the rectangle, being careful not to break it. On a scrap piece of gypsum board, copy the section of the wall, then mark a frame about 2-inches wide around the section of wall. After cutting, remove the plaster from the paper backing for the entire 2-inch-wide frame. The 2-inch frame of paper will stick out like an ear all around, which will hold the patch in place. Spread patching plaster around the edge of the hole and around the edge of the patch. Put the patch in the hole and press the paper ears into the plaster and hold it while it sets. After patching is dry, sand lightly and paint.

Sagging Plaster Ceilings—When Plaster Is Disconnected from Lath

To learn if a sagging ceiling is a candidate for repair or must be replaced, start by checking to see how far the plaster layer has sagged. Push upward gently. If the plaster goes back into place with no more than 1/2 inch of play and without any crunching sounds, the ceiling can be repaired rather than having to replace it.

Start by drilling a series of injection holes into the ceiling with a 1/4-inch carbide-tipped drill bit. It is very important is to drill the holes into the lath and not the space between two laths; only drill through the plaster layer, not into the lath itself. Injection holes should be bored every three3 to 4 inches.

Squirt a little water into each hole with a spray bottle. This will dampen the old plaster and the old lath and help the glue dry more slowly, resulting in a better bond. Inject latex or acrylic glue into the hole until you can feel the plaster bulge very slightly. Wipe away the excess with a damp sponge.

Brace the ceiling and let the glue cure by pressing the ceiling upward until the plaster is back against the lath where it belongs. After 24 hours, remove the supports. Let the glue cure for another day, then scrape off the excess glue. Fill the holes with joint compound and repaint.

Removing Efflorescence from Plaster

Efflorescence is a condition where white salt deposits form on a plaster surface and appears as a fluffy powder substance. This is usually a sign of excessive amounts of moisture in the backup material, such as brick or concrete, or it may develop from soluble compounds within the adjacent masonry or in the soil. Efflorescence is generally not harmful to the plaster material, just unattractive. However, it should be removed from the surface as soon as possible.

Examine the plaster and substrate material for potential sources of moisture and make repairs as required before proceeding with the cleaning operation. Then, carefully remove any surface deposits with a clean, stiff fiber bristle brush and wipe the surface with a clean, damp cloth.

Plaster Loose Spots

Loose spots in plaster are fairly common in walls and ceilings of older houses. These bulging areas flex when pressed on and sound hollow when tapped. This indicates that the plaster has lost its bond with the lath. This condition can be repaired by installing gypsum board screws with plaster washers attached. Plaster washers are 1-1/4-inch steel disks made specifically for the purpose of keeping the screw from pulling through the plaster as it is placed into the soft plaster to help pull it back against the lath.

Assessing Existing Conditions

Assess existing condition of plaster walls and ceilings and consider the following procedures for patching and repairs:

- Before applying any product to the walls, walls must be clean and free of any peeling paint and flaking bits of old plaster, dirt, grime, or grease so the plaster can bond properly.
- After all loose plaster is removed, all cracks should be enlarged so that the top of the crack is at least 1/4 inch wide. Slightly dampen the areas to be patched with water just before applying any patching compound.
- Large holes in plaster may require repair to lath. This must be repaired before the plaster surface can be applied and repaired.

Acceptable Practices

- Most experts agree that it pays to practice repair techniques prior to beginning repairs on a wall surface that may be more inconspicuous or hidden by furniture after repairs are completed.
- Plaster patching should be done with patching plaster for best results. Powdered joint compounds that must be job-site mixed with water typically dry more quickly, form a harder finish, and bond better to old plaster than ready-mix compounds.

Practices to Avoid

- Do not repair a plaster wall or ceiling surface for cosmetic purposes without verifying its structural integrity first.
- Do not use common joint compound as a patching material. These products are only meant to be used with paper-faced gypsum board and will bond poorly to traditional plaster.

Resources

WITHIN THIS BOOK

- Chapter 20 Exterior Wall Covering
- Chapter 27 Gypsum Board

REFERENCE STANDARDS

- ASTM C 843—Standard Specification for Application of gypsum Veneer Plaster
- ASTM C 841—Standard Specification for Installation of Interior Lathing and Furring
- ASTM C1063—Standard Specification for Installation of Lathing and Furring to Receive Interior and Exterior Portland Cement-Based Plaster

OTHER RESOURCES

- 2009 International Residential Code for One and Two-Family Dwellings. Washington, DC: International Code Council, Inc., 2009.
- American Institute of Architects, *Architectural Graphics Standards*, 11th ed. Hoboken, NJ: John Wiley and Sons, 2007.
- American Institute of Architects, *Architectural Graphic Standards for Residential Construction*, 2nd ed. Hoboken, NJ: John Wiley and Sons, 2010.

Chapter 27

Gypsum Board

Gypsum Board Materials

Gypsum Assemblies

Gypsum Finishing

Gypsum Board Materials

Description

Proper selection and installation of gypsum board panels are necessary to construct partition assemblies. Common residential gypsum board panel types include the following:

- *Regular:* Most vertical interior partitions are constructed with 1/2-inch regular core gypsum board panels. 1/4-inch and 3/8-inch thickness are also available but should only be used in double-layer applications.
- *Type X gypsum board:* Stronger than regular gypsum board, Type X provides greater fire resistance. It is generally 5/8-inch thick and most commonly used in fire-resistance-rated wall and ceiling assemblies. High-strength 1/2-inch thick ceiling board is also acceptable.
- *Acoustical gypsum board panels:* These sandwich a sound-absorbing viscoelastic polymer-based laminate layer between two thin layers of gypsum board, offer enhanced acoustical properties, and can be used where sound is a concern.
- *Mold and moisture resistant gypsum board panels:* Commonly referred to as green board, these panels have silicone-modified cores with a reduced capacity to absorb water and surface papers treated with antimicrobial chemicals to resist the growth of mold. Mold and moisture resistant gypsum panels should be used in intermittently wet areas such as bathroom walls that are not part of the bathtub or shower areas. Partitions at wet areas should be constructed of cementitious backer units.

Assessing Existing Conditions

In order to ensure the proper installation of gypsum board panels, verify the following conditions:

- Wood framing members are not less than 1½ inches thick.
- Wood framing members are not spaced more than 24-inches on center.
- Metal framing members are not less than 1¼ inches wide.

- Metal framing flanges face one direction.
- Framing member attachment surfaces do not vary more than 1/8 inch from the plane of adjacent framing members.

Acceptable Practices

In the installation of gypsum board panels, consideration must be given to the structural and thermal movement to avoid cracking. Panels should be isolated where structural movement may impose a direct load and expansion joints should be used in large areas of gypsum board, including:

- Ceilings that exceed 2500 square feet in area
- Walls that are over 30 feet in length
- Change in direction of ceiling framing

Common construction practices for installation of gypsum board panels include the following:

- Apply gypsum board panels to ceiling before wall surfaces.
- Locate joints in panels so that no joint will align with the edge of an opening, unless control joints are required.
- Install gypsum board panels a minimum of 1/4 inch above the floor.
- Full-height nonrated partitions may have gypsum board extending above the ceiling or fully enclosing studs.
- Apply panels at right angles or parallel to framing.
- Locate all edges and ends (except perpendicular edges) on framing members. Bearing surface at corners or angles shall be 3/4 inch minimum. End joints shall be staggered.
- Set fasteners with the head slightly below the surface of the board.
- Locate fasteners at gypsum board edges or ends a maximum of 3/8 inches from the edge or end.
- Maximum on center fastener spacing:
    - Nails: Ceiling, 7 inches. Walls, 8 inches.
    - Screws for 16-inches on center framing: Ceiling, 12 inches. Walls, 16 inches.
    - Screws for 24-inches on center framing: Ceiling, 12 inches. Walls, 12 inches.

Edge configurations include square or tapered with square, beveled, or rounded returns, and should be selected with the final appearance in mind. Treated joints at squared edges are more noticeable than others. *Prefilled edges increase labor and material costs but increase joint strength and minimize joint imperfections.*

Wood or metal support framing for gypsum board panels is most common in residential construction. Gypsum board panel thickness, number of layers, and orientation affect the spacing and other requirements of framing members, as tabulated in ASTM C754. Closer spacing than required of studs is common since it improves visual flatness and the strength of the partition.

International Residential Code Table R702.3.5 indicates mechanical attachment requirements for gypsum board panels; Table 27.1 shows some of the common applications. Screw attachment methods are more common, but single or double nailing, and adhesive and nailing methods can also be used for wood framing.

Practices to Avoid

Since gypsum board panels will either be exposed to view or the substrate for another material, it is important to protect them and install them appropriately. Common construction practices to avoid include the following:

- Interior gypsum board panels shall not be installed where they are directly exposed to the weather or to water.
- Board edges should not be forced together.
- End joints on opposite sides of a partition shall not occur on the same stud.
- Insulation blankets, or the flanges of the facing of insulation blankets, should not be attached to the face of the framing members to which gypsum board panels are to be attached.

Table 27.1 Minimum Thickness and Application of Gypsum Board

Thickness of Gypsum Board (inches)	Application	Orientation of Gypsum Board to Framing	Maximum Spacing of Framing Members (inches)	Maximum Spacing of Fasteners (inches)		Size of Nails for Application to Wood Framing
				Nails	Screws	
Application without Adhesive						
$\frac{1}{2}$ in.	Ceiling	Either direction	16 in. oc	7 in. oc	12 in. oc	13 gage, $1\frac{3}{8}$-in. long, $\frac{19}{64}$-in. head; 0.098-in. diameter, $1\frac{1}{4}$-in. long, annular-ringed; 5d cooler nail, 0.086-in. diameter, $1\frac{5}{8}$-in. long, $\frac{15}{64}$-in. head; or gypsum board nail, 0.086″-in. diameter, $1\frac{5}{8}$-in. long, $\frac{9}{32}$-in. head
$\frac{1}{2}$ in.	Ceiling	Perpendicular	24 in. oc	7 in. oc	12 in. oc	
$\frac{1}{2}$ in.	Wall	Either direction	24 in. oc	8 in. oc	12 in. oc	
$\frac{1}{2}$ in.	Wall	Either direction	16 in. oc	8 in. oc	16 in. oc	
$\frac{5}{8}$ in.	Ceiling	Either direction	16 in. oc	7 in. oc	12 in. oc	13 gage, $1\frac{5}{8}$-in. long, $\frac{19}{64}$-in. head; 0.098-in. diameter, $1\frac{3}{8}$-in. long, annular-ringed; 6d cooler nail, 0.0092-in. diameter, $1\frac{7}{8}$-in. long, $\frac{1}{4}$-in. head; or gypsum board nail, 0.0915-in. diameter, $1\frac{7}{8}$-in. long, $\frac{19}{64}$-in. head
$\frac{5}{8}$ in.	Ceiling	Perpendicular	24 in. oc	7 in. oc	12 in. oc	
$\frac{5}{8}$ in.	Wall	Either direction	24 in. oc	8 in. oc	12 in. oc	
$\frac{5}{8}$ in.	Wall	Either direction	16 in. oc	8 in. oc	16 in. oc	
Application with Adhesive						
$\frac{1}{2}$ in. or $\frac{5}{8}$ in.	Ceiling	Either direction	16 in. oc	16 in. oc	16 in. oc	Same as above for $\frac{1}{2}$-in. and $\frac{5}{8}$-in. gypsum board, respectively.
$\frac{1}{2}$ in. or $\frac{5}{8}$ in.	Ceiling	Perpendicular	24 in. oc	12 in. oc	16 in. oc	
$\frac{1}{2}$ in. or $\frac{5}{8}$ in.	Wall	Either direction	24 in. oc	16 in. oc	24 in. oc	

Gypsum Assemblies

Description

Gypsum board assemblies composed of gypsum board panels, support framing and accessories, are wall and ceiling systems that have been proven to meet strength, sound, or other characteristics. The most common gypsum board assemblies used in residential construction include the following:

- *Fire-resistance-rated:* Using fire-rated sealant at all joints, penetrations and openings, multiple layers or fire-rated gypsum board panels, and surface-to-surface construction; fire-resistance assemblies are given an hour rating indicating the period of time they will withstand and confine the spread of fire. Ratings range from one to four hours and are chosen by code-defined separations between adjacent occupancies and spaces.
- *Acoustical:* Acoustical assemblies have a sound transmission class (STC) rating that defines its performance under controlled laboratory conditions. Each assembly dictates the support framing methods and materials, as well as sealants and insulation at voids to control the mass, resiliency, and absorption of the wall.
- *Mold- and moisture-resistant:* Under the right conditions, mold can grow on almost any surface. Provide building materials that cannot properly dry out or vent, supplying the moisture and organic food source for mold spores, and mold will grow on every surface. Mold- and moisture-resistant assemblies use water-resistant products, air spaces, and proper placement of vapor retarders to address moisture vapor migration and avoid mold growth.

Field installation of assemblies must be identical or within allowable tolerances of proven assemblies to produce desired performance or acceptance.

Assessing Existing Conditions

Allowable tolerances are important to note when assessing gypsum board assemblies. Framing tolerances for partitions address the plumbness and level of the studs to ensure a strong, solid wall. In most cases, tolerances of the final finish surface will be of most concern. Trim pieces when installed poorly can extend an edge out by 1/8 inch or more.

In order to ensure the proper installation of gypsum board assemblies, verify the following conditions:

- Acoustical sealant is applied at perimeter edges of panel surfaces at both sides of assembly.
- Acoustical sealant is applied at all gaps, openings, and penetrations.

Acceptable Practices

Common construction practices for gypsum board panel assemblies include the following:

- Use multilayer partitions at acoustical and fire-resistance-rated partitions.
- Use steel studs rather than wood at acoustical partitions.
- Stagger wood stud placement or use resilient channels at acoustical partitions.
- Use sound attenuation insulation at acoustical partitions.
- Seal perimeter edges and all openings or penetrations at acoustical and fire-resistance-rated partitions.
- Use mold- and moisture-resistant gypsum board panels at bathroom, kitchen, and other intermittently wet walls.

Recommended allowable tolerances for gypsum board panel light-gauge framed assemblies include the following:

- Plumbness and level of studs shall be within 1/8 inch in 10 feet.
- Attachment surface of framing members shall not vary more than 1/8 inch from plane of the face of adjacent framing members.
- Stud spacing shall not vary by more than 1/8 inch from required.

Recommended allowable tolerances for gypsum board panel wood-framed assemblies include the following:

- 3/8 inch in any 32-inch vertical measurement
- 1/4-inch in 10 feet across ceilings

Practices to Avoid

To ensure the safety or intended function of a residential project, it is important to verify that gypsum board assemblies are constructed identically to tested systems to qualify for stated ratings:

- Installation of full-height acoustical or fire-resistance-rated partitions after ceiling installation.
- Installation of back to back devices in 3¾-inch fire-resistance-rated partitions.
- Use of mold- and moisture-resistant panels at wet areas such as shower or bathtub surrounds. Use a cementitious backer board instead.
- Use of mold- and moisture-resistant panels over vapor retarder. This may cause moisture to be trapped.
- Use of mold- and moisture-resistant panels at ceilings. The spacing of the joists may need to be closer or a thicker panel may be required.

Gypsum Finishing

Description

Gypsum board can be used as the substrate for a variety of materials creating the need for several levels of finishing. The type and application method of tape and joint compounds define minimum requirements for each level.

Setting-type and drying-type joint compounds should be used appropriately based on the project conditions. Setting-types, which are available as job-mixed powders, harden to produce a high-strength joint by chemical action and are not susceptible to shrinking. Since they are not affected by humidity, they are commonly used on exterior surfaces. Their high strength makes them difficult to finish. Drying-type compounds are available as ready mixed or job-mixed powders. They shrink as they dry, and thus require a minimum of 24 hours drying time between coats. Setting-type taping compounds used with all-purpose drying-type compounds often produce a strong joint that resists cracking.

Textured finishes can be applied to gypsum board panels for both visual effect and as a finish to mask imperfections. Sand, orange peel, and knock down are common textured finishes that can be applied as paint, a special coating, or as the same topping compound used for joint treatment. Mold- and moisture-resistant gypsum board panels should be used where a textured finish is used to avoid sag from excessive moisture in the finish. Since many variables affect the texture finish appearance, a mockup is also recommended.

Assessing Existing Conditions

In order to ensure the proper finishing of gypsum board panels, verify the following conditions:

- Gypsum board panels are free of nail pops, high shoulders, ridging and beading, pealing, and paper blistering that will affect final decoration.
- Gaps are a maximum of 1/4 inch wide.
- Proper edge treatment and joint compound are used.
- Review mockup.

Acceptable Practices

Guidelines from GA-214, *Recommended Levels of Gypsum Board Finishing*, are summarized as follows:

LEVEL 0:

- *Requirements*: No taping, finishing, or accessories required.
- *Uses*: Temporary construction or where final decoration has been determined.

LEVEL 1:

- *Requirements*: All joints and interior angles shall have tape set in joint compound. Surface shall be free of excess joint compound. Tool marks and ridges are acceptable.
- *Uses*: Above ceilings, in attics, and in areas where the wall would generally be concealed. Accessories are optional.

LEVEL 2:

- *Requirements*: All joints and interior angles shall have tape embedded in joint compound and wiped with a joint knife, leaving a thin coating of joint compound over all joints and interior angles. Fastener heads and accessories shall be covered with a coat of joint compound. Surface shall be free of excess joint compound. Tool marks and ridges are acceptable. Joint compound applied over the body of the tape at the time of tape embedment shall be considered a separate coat of joint compound and shall satisfy the conditions of this level.
- *Uses*: Water-resistant gypsum backing board (ASTM C 630) is used as a substrate for tile; may be used in garages, storage, or other, similar areas where surface appearance is not of primary concern.

LEVEL 3:

- *Requirements*: All joints and interior angles shall have tape embedded in joint compound and one additional coat of joint compound applied over all joints and interior angles. Fastener heads and accessories shall be covered with two separate coats of joint compound. Joint compound shall be smooth and free of tool marks and ridges.
- *Uses*: Areas that are to receive heavy- or medium-texture (spray or hand-applied) finishes before final painting, or where heavy-grade wall coverings are to be applied as the final decoration. This level of finish is not recommended where smooth, painted surfaces or light to medium wall coverings will be used.

LEVEL 4:

- *Requirements*: All joints and interior angles shall have tape embedded in joint compound, two separate coats of joint compound applied over all flat joints, and one separate coat of joint compound applied over interior angles. Fastener heads and accessories shall be covered with three separate coats of joint compound. All joint compounds shall be smooth and free of tool marks and ridges.
- *Uses*: This level should be used where flat paints, light textures, or wall coverings are to be applied. In critical lighting areas, flat paints applied over light textures tend to reduce joint photographing. Gloss, semigloss, and enamel paints are not recommended over this level of finish.
    - The weight, texture, and sheen level of wall coverings applied over this level of finish should be carefully evaluated. Joints and fasteners must be adequately concealed if the wall covering material is lightweight, contains limited pattern, has a gloss finish, or any combination of these finishes is present. Unbacked vinyl wall coverings are not recommended over this level of finish.

LEVEL 5:

- *Recommendations*: All joints and interior angles shall have tape embedded in joint compound, two separate coats of joint compound applied over all flat joints, and one separate coat of joint compound applied over interior angles. Fastener heads and accessories shall be covered with three separate coats of joint compound. A thin skim coat of joint compound, or a material manufactured especially for this purpose, shall be applied to the entire surface. The surface shall be smooth and free of tool marks and ridges.
- *Uses*: This level of finish is highly recommended where gloss, semigloss, enamel, or nontextured flat paints are specified or where severe lighting conditions occur.

Practices to Avoid

Since the finishing of gypsum board panels can often affect a material being applied over it, it is important ensure the quality of the finish. Common construction practices to avoid include:

- Use of topping compounds as a first coat or tape compound.
- Improper joint compound or sealant application, which may cause compound shrinkage and cracking.

Resources

WITHIN THIS BOOK

- Chapter 22 Expansion Control
- Chapter 26 Plastering
- Chapter 28 Tiling
- Chapter 30 Painting, Staining, and Wall Covering

REFERENCE STANDARDS

- ASTM C475/C475—Standard Specification for Joint Compound and Joint tape for Finishing Gypsum Board
- ASTM C754—Standard Specification for Installation of Steel Framing Members to received Screw-Attached Gypsum Panel Products
- ASTM C840—Standard Specification for Application and Finishing of Gypsum Board
- ASTM C1396—Standard Specification for Gypsum Board
- ASTM E119—Standard Fire Tests of building Construction Materials
- Gypsum Association GA-214—Recommended Levels of Gypsum Board Finishing, Washington, DC, 2007
- Gypsum Association GA-216—Application and Finishing of Gypsum Board, Washington, DC, 2010

OTHER RESOURCES

- 2009 International Residential Code for One and Two-Family Dwellings. Washington, DC: International Code Council, Inc., 2009.
- American Institute of Architects, *Architectural Graphics Standards*, 11th ed. Hoboken, NJ: John Wiley and Sons, 2007.
- American Institute of Architects, *Architectural Graphic Standards for Residential Construction*, 2nd ed. Hoboken, NJ: John Wiley and Sons, 2010.
- National Gypsum Company, *Gypsum Construction Guide*. 12th ed. Charlotte, NC 2006, www.nationalgypsum.com.
- USG Corporation, *The Gypsum Construction Handbook*, 6th ed. Kingston, MA: R. S. Means Company, Inc., 2009, www.usg.com.
- Gypsum Association, www.gypsum.org.

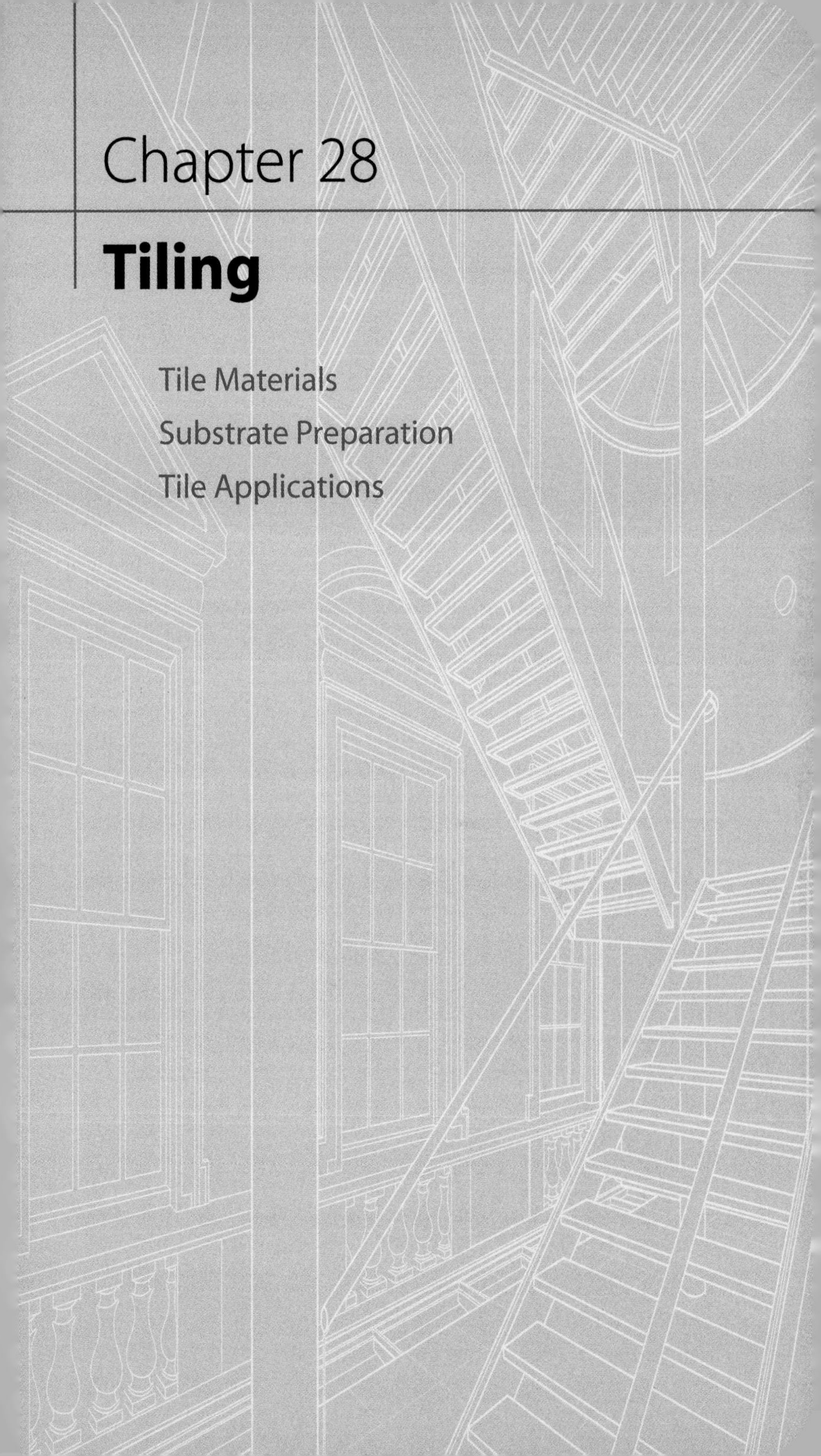

Chapter 28

Tiling

Tile Materials

Substrate Preparation

Tile Applications

Tile Materials

Description

There are many different methods that can be used to install tile, the materials that are used is generally based on where the tile is to be placed and how much use or abuse the tile will receive. The *Handbook for Ceramic Tile Installation* by the Tile Council of North America, Inc. (TCNA) is the leading reference book used when choosing how tile should be installed.

The basic components of any tile installation are the tile, grout, mortar, adhesives, mortar beds, and underlayment or tile backing units. Tiles come in many forms and sizes, common tile used in residential construction include ceramic, porcelain, glass, and clay tiles. In addition to standard sizes most tiles also come in a large format size. Large format in all tiles, except glass tile, is considered to be tiles 8 by 8 inches in size or larger and can come in square or rectangular shapes. A large format glass tile is considered to be 3 by 3 inches or larger.

Grout for tile comes in sanded or unsanded portland cement grout, and epoxy grout.

Mortars are a paste consisting of sand, cement, and water and are used to attach tile to an uncured mortar bed or are also used to install tile in a thin-set application. Mortars come in three types, dry-set mortar, polymer-modified portland cement mortar and exterior glue plywood (EGP) latex portland cement mortar. Polymer-modified portland cement mortar is similar to dry-set mortar but has a latex additive added that provides better adhesion, reduces water absorption, and has a greater bond strength and resistance to shock and impact. EGP latex portland cement mortar has a polymer additive that improves bonding between tile and plywood in thin-set applications. Organic adhesive is a premixed organic compound that is only used for interior applications and generally only in residential or light commercial construction.

Mortar beds include both thick- and thin-bed methods. Thick-bed methods use a setting bed, usually of portland cement mortar and are either bonded or unbonded to the substrate. Advantages of the thick-bed method include allowing some minor leveling to be accomplished in placing the setting bed and allowing the setting bed to be independent of the substrate.

Cementitious backer units and fiber-cement underlayment are suitable substrate materials for walls over bathtubs, shower receptors, and similar areas where optimum water resistance is required. The cut edges of these two products do not require treatment with a water-resistant adhesive or sealant to prevent deterioration of the backing.

A cleavage membrane is a thin layer of material within a tile assembly that is loose laid (floating) or mechanically attached but not bonded. Cleavage membranes are incorporated below the mortar setting bed in thick-bed installations when the substrate can be damaged by water. In addition, the cleavage membrane separates the backing surface from the mortar setting bed and tile, allowing the setting bed to be unbounded and free floating, thus preventing reflective cracking. Cleavage membranes are moisture resistant but do not necessarily form an impermeable membrane that will hold water, they are intended to provide other materials some protection from moisture and vapor.

Waterproof membranes, like cleavage membranes, can be loose laid or bonded to substrate with manufacturer's recommended adhesive. In some installations they can also be bonded to the top of the mortar bed with the tile installed in a thin-bed method. Prior to placement of tile or mortar bed, these membranes should be tested for leaks. This is accomplished by plugging the drain and filling the area with water.

Assessing Existing Conditions

Prior to installation of tile materials substrate tolerances should be verified when installing tile in thin-bed applications.

- Substrate tolerances for flatness of substrate in thin-bed applications shall be not greater than 1/4 inch in 10 feet or 1/16 inch in 1 foot.
- For plywood subfloors thickness variation between plywood sheets shall not exceed 1/32 inch.

Acceptable Practices

Tile Council of North America, Inc., *Handbook for Ceramic Tile Installation* is the most widely used guideline for the installation of ceramic tile and includes design and construction guidelines.

- Choosing the correct tile for a floor finish: Porcelain tile is the harder than ceramic tile and it has a lower rate of water absorption; therefore, it will stain less. Porcelain tile is generally more expensive than ceramic tile.
- If wood base is used in locations subject to wetting due to mopping or splashing of water, the joint between floor tile and wood base should be sealed with a silicone sealant to prevent wicking of water into wood base.

Practices to Avoid

- Glazed tile with a slip coefficient of less than 0.60 (wet) should not be used in areas subject to wetting, like foyers, mud rooms or outside showers.
- Do not use high-gloss ceramic tile on countertops, it will show scratches.

Tiling Substrate Preparation

Description

Surface preparation for tile, because of its hardness, is critical for a long-lasting floor or wall finish. Substrate movement is one of the leading causes of tile failure. It is important to have a sound, clean, and dimensionally stable surface to place tile on using either a thin-bed method or thick-bed method. Substrates that will be subjected to frequent wetting should have a backing material that is not affected by water such as cast-in-place concrete, concrete slab on grade, suspended concrete slabs, cementitious backer units or masonry. If a substrate is used that can be affected by water, is not continuous, is cracked or dimensionally unstable then a membrane should be placed over the substrate. The membrane is used to separate the backing surface from the setting bed and tile.

Plywood is the only wood product that is recommended as a substrate for tile and is used for interior floors, counter and vanity top applications. Plywood, in order to be used as a substrate for a horizontal surface, must be fabricated using fully waterproof adhesive and have an exposure durability rating of Exposure 1 or Exterior Grade. The plywood must be installed in accordance with ANSI A108.01. The minimum thickness required for plywood as a subfloor for setting tile shall be 19/32 inch.

Assessing Existing Conditions

In order to ensure the proper installation of ceramic tile, verify the following conditions:

- Concrete surfaces must be fully cured, free of form release compounds, curing compounds, paint, and dusting of concrete.
- Masonry surfaces have fully cured mortar joints, no efflorescence, loose mortar or surface material.
- Wall construction guidelines:
  - Wood studs: Minimum 3-1/2-inch depth
  - Metal studs: 20 gage (0.039 inches or heavier)
  - Stud spacing: 16 inches on center

- Floor construction guidelines:
  - Recommended joist spacing 16 inches on center maximum, except in certain tile installations, where joist spacing can be a maximum 24 inches on center.
  - Minimum 19/32-inch-thick plywood subfloor. Building movement joints are in place and, if sealant is used, the sealant is fully cured.
  - The flange of floor drains are attached to substrate and penetrations through substrates are properly set and secure.
- Substrates for ceramic tile countertops shall have cabinetry or supports for countertops solidly set.

Acceptable Practices

- Movement joint guidelines for substrates: Building expansion joints should continue through tile surface should match joint.
- Floor underlayment requires 1/8-inch gap between sheets with 1/4-inch gap between underlayment and vertical wall surfaces. This allows for plywood movement.

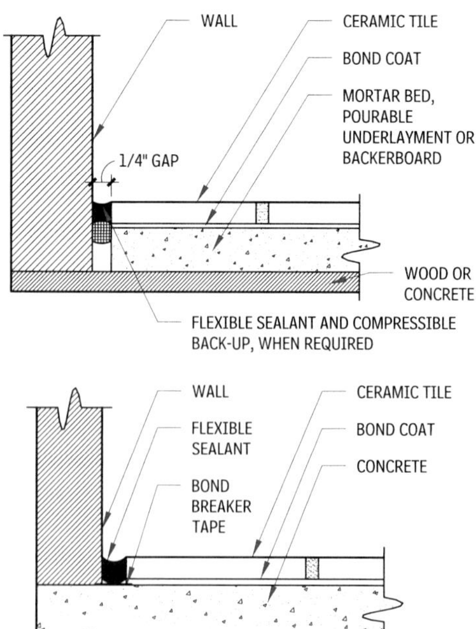

Figure 28.1 Perimeter joints
Source: TCNA Handbook, 2009

- Substrates for walls:
  - Appropriate substrate includes gypsum board, cementitious backer units, or gypsum plaster.
  - Gypsum board shall be attached with screws or nails spaced not more than 8 inches on center. Gypsum board shall not be adhesive applied.
  - Nail/screw heads and alkali-resistant joint tape shall receive one coat of joint compound and shall cure completely before beginning tile installation.
- Substrates for bathtub and shower walls:
  - Cementitious backer unit
  - Coated glass-mat water-resistant gypsum backer board.
  - Embed 2-inch-wide alkali-resistant glass fiber mesh tape in skim coat of mortar over joints, corners, and fasteners. Allow to fully cure.
  - Penetrations in at wet locations: Where substrate has been cut, openings shall be sealed with flexible water-repellant sealant such as an elastomeric sealant, Type S, Grade NS, Class 25.
- Substrates for shower floors:
  - If subfloor is not sloped to drain, either a cement mortar fill can be used to slope to drain or a preformed sloped insert can be provided that is approved for use in shower applications and is a suitable substrate for mortar bed.
  - Blocking between studs shall be provided at base of wall to support shower pan.
- Substrates for counters:
  - Two layers of plywood.
  - One layer of plywood and one layer cementitious backer unit.
  - 1 × 6 inch solid wood substrate.

Practices to Avoid

- Wood-based panel products will expand and contract and should not be used as a substrate, including particleboard, composite panels, oriented strand board, lauan plywood, and softwood plywood.
- Gypsum board or gypsum plaster should not be used as a substrate in wet areas.
- If a mortar setting bed is used, the setting bed is not intended to slope; it should be a consistent thickness.
- Avoid butting underlayment sheets together, to allow for movement without buckling.

Tile Applications

Description

There are two setting methods for tile installations *thin-bed method* and the *thick-bed method.*

The thin-bed method uses a cement mortar to attach tile to the substrate. The thick-bed method places a reinforced or nonreinforced mortar bed on the substrate between 1 inch and 1-3/4 inches thick, then uses a cement mortar to attach the tile to the mortar bed. The decision on which installation method to use is based on the type of use the surface will get.

Grouting of ceramic tile is the final step in the installation of tile. Portland cement is the base for most grouts and is modified to provide specific qualities such as whiteness, mildew resistance, uniformity, hardness, flexibility, and water resistance. There are also non–cement-based grouts such as epoxies that offer properties that are not possible with cement based grouts.

In residential construction, common types of grout are portland cement grout, polymer-modified grout, and epoxy grout. There are two types of portland cement grout: sand-portland cement grout, which is job-site mixed, and standard cement grout, which is factory-mixed. Polymer-modified grout is also a cement-based grout, but has a latex admixture that is added in place of mixing water. Epoxy grout is a non-cement-based grout that employs epoxy resin and coarse silica fillers in the grout mixture.

Grout used in installations with heavy use, including floors and countertops, may benefit from being sealed for protection; however, sealers must be reapplied periodically to remain effective. Grout sealers come in penetrating sealers or a membrane-forming sealers. Penetrating sealers are used to seal grout joints, while membrane-forming sealers are used to seal the surfaces of unglazed floor tile as well as grout joints. In most cases, for horizontal grout joints, whether for countertops or walking surfaces, it is a good idea to apply a grout sealer to all grout joints. Sealer does not need to be applied to epoxy grout joints.

Acceptable Practices

Some of the common TCNA methods for various applications are indicated below.

FLOOR INSTALLATIONS IN PLACES SUCH AS A FOYER OR MUD ROOM:

- Wood substrate : TCNA Method F150
- Concrete Substrate: TCNA Method F116

WALL INSTALLATIONS IN DRY AREAS SUCH AS KITCHEN BACKSPLASHES:

- Gypsum board substrate: TCNA Method W243

WALL INSTALLATIONS IN WET AREAS SUCH AS SHOWERS AND BATHTUB SURROUNDS:

- Cementitious backer unit—bathtub: TCNA Method B412
- Cementitious backer unit—shower: TCNA Method B415

Countertop Installations

- Wood substrate: TCNA Method C511

Movement Joints in and Between Surfaces

- TCNA EJ171F: Interior movement joints should be placed in each direction between 20 foot and 25 foot centers.
- TCNA EJ171G or EJ171I: Where tile work abuts vertical wall surfaces.
- TCNA EJ171B: Joints in building structure should continue through tile surface, and tile joint should match joint width in building structure.
- Countertops: If countertop has a tile backsplash, provide movement joint at base of backsplash at joint with countertop.

Practices to Avoid

- Do not run tile or substrate over building joints in concrete.
- In wet locations, use waterproof membrane to protect substrate from moisture and buckling of substrate.
- Do not use gypsum board or gypsum plaster as tile backing in wet areas.
- In shower installations, mortar bed should not be allowed to plug weepholes in drain assembly; crushed stone or broke tile should be placed directly around drain assembly.
- Use of light-color grout is not recommended in high use areas.

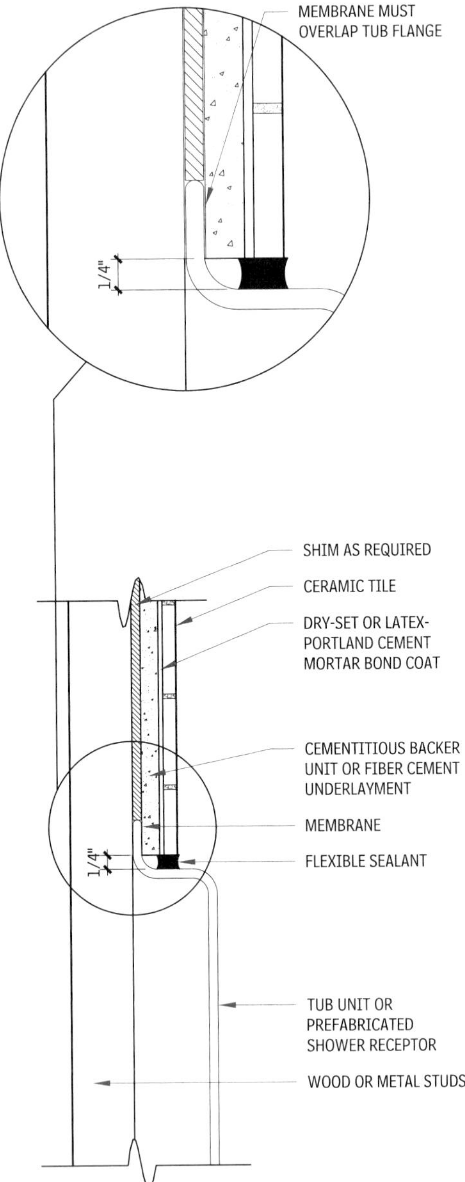

Figure 28.2 Bathtub/shower walls, cementitious backer
Source: TCNA Handbook, 2009

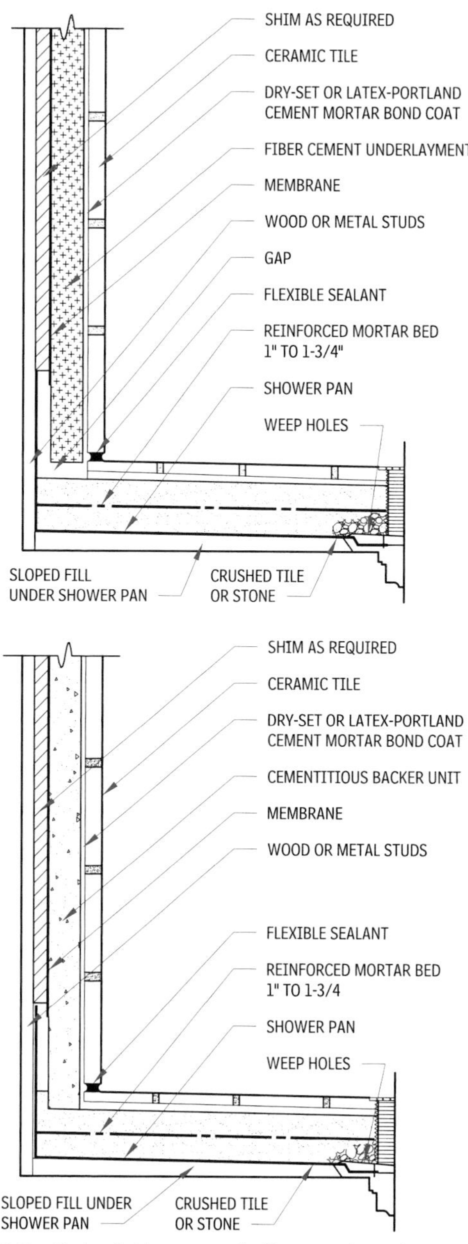

Figure 28.3 Bathtub/shower walls, fiber-reinforced water-resistant cementitious backer board
Source: *TCNA Handbook*, 2009

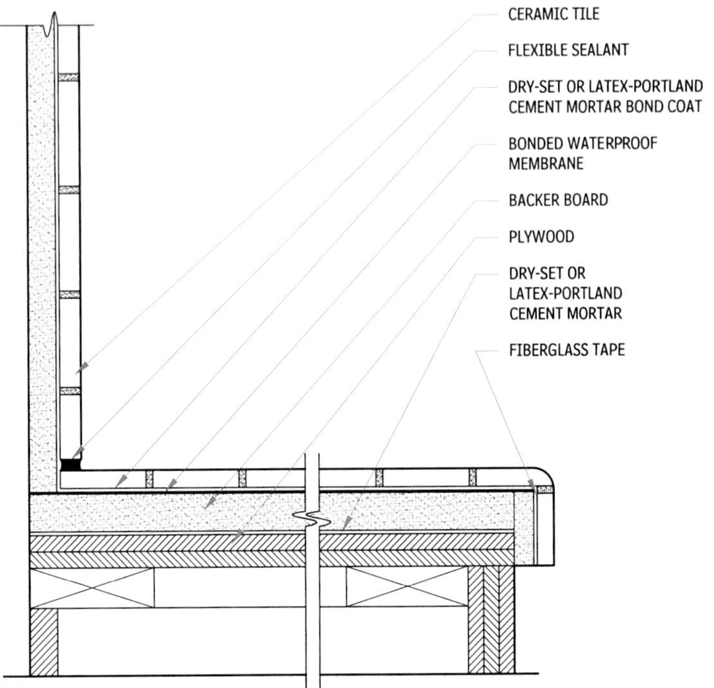

Figure 28.4 Countertops, wood base for installation of countertops
Source: TCNA Handbook, 2009

Resources

WITHIN THIS BOOK

- Chapter 14 Common Work Results for Wood, Plastics, and Composites
- Chapter 27 Gypsum Board

OTHER RESOURCES

- 2009 International Residential Code for One and Two-Family Dwellings. Washington, DC: International Code Council, Inc., 2009.
- American Institute of Architects, *Architectural Graphics Standards*, 11th ed. Hoboken, NJ: John Wiley and Sons, 2007.
- American Institute of Architects, *Architectural Graphic Standards for Residential Construction*, 2nd ed. Hoboken, NJ: John Wiley and Sons, 2010.
- *Handbook for Ceramic Tile Installation.* Anderson, SC: Tile Council of North America, 2009.

Chapter 29

Flooring

- Wood
- Resilient
- Carpet

Wood

Description

Solid wood flooring, regardless of width or length, is one piece of wood from top to bottom. Engineered wood consists of either three or five layers or plies of plywood placed under a top layer of finish wood, mechanically pressed and adhered together with wood grains running in different directions, which makes it more dimensionally stable than solid wood. Engineered flooring is preferred for areas prone to attracting moisture and subjected to elevated levels of humidity, where solid wood may not be suitable (e.g., basements). Acrylic impregnated floors are made by a process of acrylics being injected into the wood itself, which creates a very hard and durable floor. This type of wood flooring is most commonly used in commercial applications, but can be used in residential construction if required.

Both solid and engineered wood flooring are available in strips, planks, or parquet styles. Strip flooring is linear flooring. Plank flooring is also linear; however, it is wider than strip. Parquet is a geometric design made up of a series of wood pieces.

Acceptable Practices

Common construction practices for wood flooring include the following:

- Before installing wood flooring, stack it indoors for a few days to allow the wood time to adjust to the home's humidity level.
- Plan to install the flooring perpendicular to the flooring joists.
- After marking the positions of floor joists along a wall for reference, cover subfloor with a layer of 15-pound asphalt felt to provide some moisture protection and minimize squeaks.
- Gaps between strip hardwood floorboards should not exceed 1/8-inch in width at the time of installation.
- If flooring creates a change of level to a hallway or adjoining room, install a reducer strip for a smooth transition.
- Lippage in wood strips greater than 1/16-inch is considered excessive.

- Voids in floor finish that are readily visible from a distance of 6 feet under normal lighting conditions are considered excessive.
- Protection from sunlight/UV rays is recommended to avoid wood color fading.
- Verify that hardwood floor is not loose from its substrate.
- If excessive knots and color variations are observed in strip hardwood flooring, verify that grade intended has been installed.

Practices to Avoid

When installing wood flooring, common construction practices to avoid include the following:

- Avoid installing solid wood flooring in below-grade areas or near wet areas due to possible moisture damage.
- There should be no slivers or splinters observed in wood strip flooring.
- Do not allow liquid to remain on the surface of any wood flooring product for extended periods of time, as this may cause permanent damage.
- Do not use cleaning products on wood flooring unless it is a product recommended by the flooring manufacturer.
- Cupping is caused by gaining or losing moisture on one side faster than on the other. Cups in strip hardwood floorboards should not exceed 1/16 inch in height to a 3-inch maximum span measured perpendicular to the long axis of the board.
- Crowned flooring is actually convex cupping, and occurs when flooring loses some excess moisture, shrinks on the underside and flattens, leaving the edges of strips lower than the centers. If the flooring is sanded with boards cupped and edges high, the high edges of boards are cut flat by the sanding machine, if done correctly. In profile, after sanding, the boards will then have abnormally thin edges—flat on top, with edges of the reverse side of boards still curved upward, or cupped. If these boards later dry and flatten to their original position, the thin edges recede, leaving the top of boards convex (edges lower than the centers) and the back again flat against the subfloor.

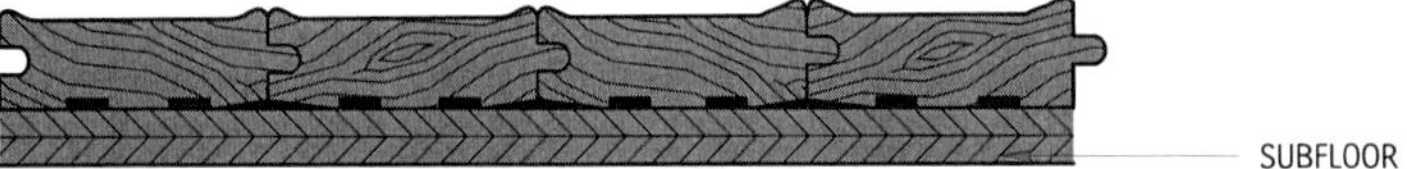

Figure 29.1 Cupped flooring

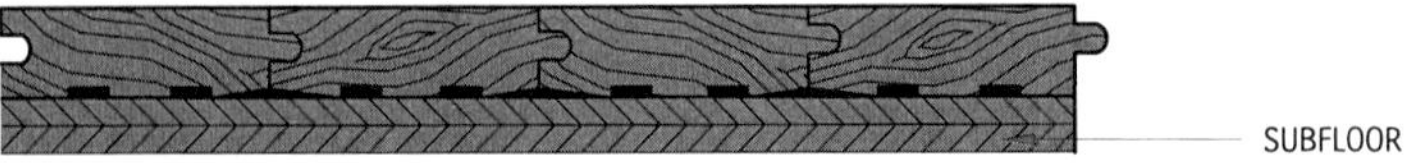

Figure 29.2 Flooring sanded flat

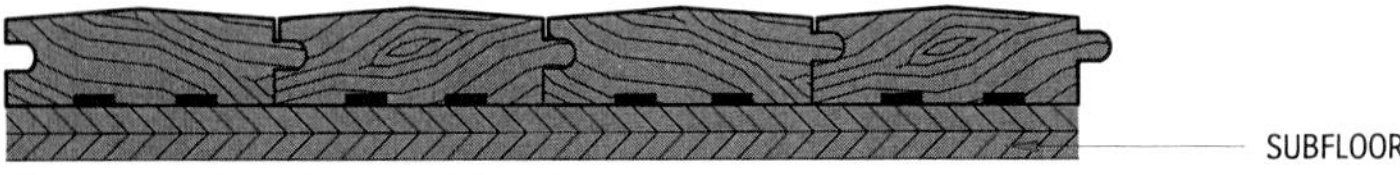

Figure 29.3 Crowned flooring

Resilient

Description

Resilient flooring includes vinyl, linoleum, rubber, cork, and laminate materials. Most of these materials are available in roll/ sheet goods, tiles, and planks, and are typically adhered to a clean, dry floor substrate.

Sheet vinyl flooring is the most commonly used resilient flooring type in residential construction. Vinyl is a product that, once cut, is extremely difficult to patch or repair. Therefore, the initial installation is vital to the life of the vinyl and its performance. Proper floor preparation is an absolute must when working with sheet vinyl. Installing underlayment, when needed, is just as important as installing the vinyl.

Two types of backing are available for sheet vinyl, with felt being the most common. Fiberglass is a newer construction format; it is a structural layer and makes the product more dimensionally stable. It will not curl, allows the vinyl to lie flat, and has a cushioned vinyl backing that provides added underfoot comfort.

Vinyl composition tile (VCT) is a more dense and durable product than sheet vinyl. VCT is popular primarily because of its durability and cost efficiency; however, since it requires a polished wax finish, high maintenance may discourage its use for residential applications.

Linoleum flooring is a sheet or tile product and has regained popularity in recent years. Made of linseed oil, natural resin, powdered cork, limestone, wood flour, and pigments, it is naturally bacteria resistant, antimicrobial, antistatic, and is considered an environmentally friendly product. Sheet products are bonded to a fiber backing (typically burlap); tile is bonded to a polyester backing.

Rubber floors, though more commonly used in commercial applications, are becoming popular for residential use. Durability, slip resistance, shock absorbency, and ease of installation and maintenance make them an attractive flooring option. Rubber flooring is available in either rolls or tiles, but tile is generally better suited to use on a residential scale. While other materials crack, gap, and loosen when installed on subflooring that is anything but perfectly even and level, rubber, with its flexibility, is much more forgiving.

Cork flooring is probably the most environmentally friendly wood flooring product available and is made from the bark of the cork tree. Cork has natural sound deadening characteristics and buoyancy for underfoot comfort. Cork is available in tiles, planks, as well as cork planks that have wood veneers applied to them. Cork flooring can be purchased finished in either wax or urethane, or can be field finished if desired. Some manufacturers offer tiles with a clear PVC vinyl wear layer for more endurance.

Laminate flooring is composed of wood-chip composite on the back and a thin surface layer made of resin-infused paper that displays a photograph of the material intended to depict (i.e., wood, stone, ceramic tile, etc). This makes it nearly indistinguishable from the actual material photographed. Available in planks and tiles, laminate flooring is renowned for its ability to resist scratches and scrapes, holds up well to moisture, and is easy to maintain. It comes with a tongue and groove edge and is available in a variety of different install formats, such as glue down, click-lock, and floating floor methods.

Assessing Existing Conditions

In order to ensure the proper installation of resilient flooring, verify the following conditions:

- Good lighting is necessary for proper observation of substrate conditions and material issues.
- Seams or shrinkage gaps at joints/seams in vinyl flooring should not exceed 1/32 inch in width. Where dissimilar materials abut, gaps should not exceed 1/16 inch.
- Resilient flooring should not lift, bubble, or detach.
- Bubbles resulting from trapped air and that protrude higher than 1/16 inch from the floor are considered excessive.
- Readily visible nail pops on resilient flooring are considered excessive.
- Depressions or ridges observed in resilient flooring are because of subfloor irregularities.
- Flooring patterns at seams shall be aligned to within 1/8 inch.
- Resilient floor tiles should be securely attached to the floor.
- Corners of adjoining resilient floor tiles should be aligned to within 1/8 inch.

Acceptable Practices

For a quality installation of resilient flooring, considerations must include the following:

- Concrete slab is tested for moisture content and is in compliance with that listed in resilient flooring manufacturer's written installation instructions, and either ASTM F1869 or ASTM F2170.
- Each room should be carefully measured prior to installation to ensure adequate flooring materials are on hand.
- Subfloor preparation in accordance with building codes requirements, ASTM Standards, and resilient flooring manufacturer's recommendations must be done properly and is critical to a successful resilient flooring installation.
- Resilient flooring can be installed over concrete, hardwood, plywood, or an existing resilient floor as long as the subfloor is smooth, flat, and dry and properly prepared. A floor leveler to smooth textured surfaces, fill in grooves, or patch irregularities may be used, in accordance with both manufacturer's instructions.
- Adhesives used for application must be as recommended by resilient flooring manufacturer, with their installation instructions followed correctly. Remember that the type of backing determines how resilient flooring can be installed.
- A permanent HVAC system must be operational before installing the resilient flooring, and it should be installed only after other trades have finished.
- Resilient flooring and accessories at the job site should be kept at room temperature (min. 65°F/18.3°C and max. 100°F) for at least 48 hours before, during, and after installation. When using reactive adhesives, such as epoxies, the room temperature should not exceed 85°F during installation. Thereafter, temperature should be maintained above a minimum of 55°F.
- Resilient, homogeneous sheet flooring products are intended for interior locations only.
- Use appropriate underlayment as recommended by the flooring manufacturer, and install and prepare it according to the specific underlayment manufacturer's written instructions.
- Seam visibility should be kept to a minimum, with seams positioned so that, as often as feasible, main traffic runs parallel to, rather than across, the seam.
- Heat-welded seams are formed by melting a vinyl rod between edges of vinyl sheets and must be done by trained installers using special equipment.

- Protect any welded seam from dust and traffic with seam covers as recommended by flooring manufacturer.
- Use the resilient floor as little as possible for at least 24 hours after installation is complete to minimize indentation while adhesive sets.
- Check appearance of entire installation and use proper cleaner (in accordance with flooring manufacturer's recommendations) to remove any adhesive on the surface of flooring, walls, or adjacent surfaces.
- Linoleum will grow slightly in the width and shrink slightly in the length of the material when placed into wet adhesive. Linoleum flooring has specific installation requirements and instructions that differ from other resilient flooring types. Particular attention must be paid to linoleum manufacturer's written instructions to ensure a quality installation.
- When installing several rolls of linoleum in one area, read manufacture's sequence numbers on back of flooring and only install rolls that are within 20 numbers of each other; install rolls in sequential order.
- Linoleum Color Change: "Drying room yellowing," sometimes referred to as "seasoning bloom," is a natural phenomenon that occurs during the manufacturing process of all linoleum. As linoleum cures in the drying room, a yellowish cast may develop on the surface due to the oxidation of the linseed oil. This is not a product defect. Any change in the product's appearance because of this yellow cast is temporary and disappears after exposure to either natural or artificial light. The time required for the yellow cast to disappear ranges from a few hours to several weeks, depending on the type and intensity of the light source. Typically, the yellow cast disappears more quickly with exposure to natural light. The application of floor finishes will not interfere with the dissipation of the yellow cast. Disappearance of the yellow cast will not occur on areas not exposed to light.
- Linoleum flooring will not retain a shiny finish without either a protective top coat or regular cleaning and waxing maintenance.
- Cork flooring has specific installation requirements and instructions that differ from other wood flooring types. Particular attention must be paid to cork manufacturer's written instructions to ensure a quality installation.

Practices to Avoid

Construction practices to avoid include the following:

- Marking pens, felt-tipped markers, or waxed crayons must not be used to write on the vinyl backing, nor used to mark layout on the under floor, as they could bleed through and stain the material.

- If material is flattened or distorted during storage or transporting prior to installation, do not attempt to install it.
- Excessively high or low interior air relative humidity and temperatures will influence curing times of flooring adhesive materials. Those conditions during installation should be avoided.
- Avoid moving heavy furniture or allowing rolling load traffic on the resilient floor for at least 72 hours after installation.
- Linoleum flooring is not recommended for full bathroom installations.
- Cork flooring can be damaged by excessive use of water or pooling of water on the floor surface.
- Cork flooring is not recommended for below-grade applications (basements), as excessive moisture can cause the cork to swell.
- Because some materials used during the installation of resilient flooring may be flammable, be certain no sources of ignition or open flame exist near those materials.

Carpet

Description

Carpet adds warmth and comfort, and is quieter than hard surface flooring in one's home. To make an informed choice about carpet, consider your budget, how much traffic the carpets will receive and how much maintenance is required. Wool carpet is expensive, has an excellent crush resistance, and moderately resists stains. Nylon, polyester, and olefin carpets may have built-in static control, have excellent abrasion and crush resistance, and clean easily. Tufted carpet accounts for the bulk of carpet on today's residential market and is made in cut pile, loop pile, and cup and loop pile styles. All carpet types are available in many styles, patterns, fibers, textures, and performance characteristics.

Padding is also an important consideration in the investment and life of your carpet. It is worth spending money on good padding to prolong the life of carpet, increase its comfort, and provide sound insulation. Pads are constructed from flat rubber, foam, felt, or rubberized felt.

Assessing Existing Conditions

In order to ensure the proper installation of carpeting, you need to verify the following conditions:

- Of vital importance prior to ordering or installing carpet is confirmation that room measurements are correct and seam placement is reviewed.
- Prior to installation, inspect carpet for correct style, color, texture, and visible defects. Report concerns to retailer immediately.
- Use low-emitting adhesives when adhesives are required; contact carpet retailer if objectionable odors persist.
- Install carpet in accordance with carpet industry installation standards found in CRI *Carpet Installation Standard*.
- All newly installed carpet should be vacuumed thoroughly.

Acceptable Practices

Acceptable practices for a quality carpeting installation includes the following:

- Be certain the ventilation system is in proper working order before carpet installation begins, and operate the system with maximum outdoor air during and after installation for 48 to 72 hours.
- It is not unusual for carpet seams to show, but a visible gap in carpet seams is not acceptable.
- When stretched, a secured properly, wall-to-wall carpeting should not be loose or separate from the points of attachment.
- Ensure seams run the length of the area.
- Consider carpet pads with antimicrobial treatments that combat odors and mold, a solid moisture barrier that keeps spills from penetrating, and hypoallergenic attributes.
- Carpet padding must provide full coverage of flooring surface to avoid "dead spots" in finished carpet surface.
- Use walk-off mats at all entrances to absorb soil and moisture. Clean mats regularly so they don't become sources of soil themselves.
- Use a quality pad under carpet, particularly on stairs. A good pad gives better resilience underfoot and extends the life of your carpet.
- Move heavy furniture occasionally to avoid excessive pile crushing.
- Protect your carpet from prolonged periods of direct sunlight with blinds, shades, or awnings.
- Vacuum thoroughly and frequently, particularly in high-traffic areas, to remove the dry soil. As particles of dry soil work down into the pile, they are more difficult to remove and can scratch the fibers, leading to premature wear of the carpet.
- Remove spills and stains promptly.
- Clean your carpet every 12 to 18 months according to the manufacturer's recommendation.
- Carpet padding thickness should not exceed 7/16-inch.
- Carpet is attached to tackles strip along wall and NOT stapled to the floor.
- Carpet padding seams should be installed at right angles to carpet seams.
- Carpet padding seams should be taped and stapled to the floor.
- Carpet has been power stretched 1.5 percent.

Practices to Avoid

For a quality carpeting installation avoid the following conditions:

- Indoor temperature is less than 65 degrees
- Seams located in pivot areas
- Seams located perpendicular to doorways
- Primary light source is perpendicular to seam
- Carpet pile does not run in the same direction
- Exposed carpet edges are not protected with metal strip or molding

Resources

WITHIN THIS BOOK

- Chapter 7 Cast-in-Place Concrete
- Chapter 14 Common Work Results for Wood, Plastics, and Composites
- Chapter 15 Rough Carpentry
- Chapter 16 Finish Carpentry

REFERENCE STANDARDS

- ASTM F1869—Standard Test Method for Measuring Moisture Vapor Emission Rate of Concrete Subfloor Using Anhydrous Calcium Chloride
- ASTM F2170—Standard Test Method for Determining Relative Humidity in Concrete Floors Using in situ Probes
- CRI, *Carpet Installation Standard*, 1st ed. Dalton, GA: The Carpet and Rug Institute, 2009

OTHER RESOURCES

- 2009 International Residential Code for One and Two-Family Dwellings. Washington, DC: International Code Council, Inc., 2009.
- American Institute of Architects, *Architectural Graphics Standards*, 11th ed. Hoboken, NJ: John Wiley and Sons, 2007.
- American Institute of Architects, *Architectural Graphic Standards for Residential Construction*, 2nd ed. Hoboken, NJ: John Wiley and Sons, 2010.
- *The Carpet Primer*. Dalton, GA: Carpet and Rug Institute, 2009.
- Carpet and Rug Institute, www.carpet-rug.org.

Chapter 30

Painting, Staining, and Wall Covering

Painting

Description

There are two categories of paints: water-based latex paints and oil-based paints. Oil-based paints are commonly called *alkyd* paint. Water-based latex paint, as the name implies, has as its main component water. Oil-based paint has as its main component solvent.

Characteristics of latex paints, in comparison to solvent-based paints, include greater durability because it is flexible and porous. Latex paint also has better color retention, chalk resistance, and dries quicker than oil-based paints. Latex paints are very versatile and can be applied to many different surfaces with appropriate preparation and primer, have very little odor, and are not combustible. One of the biggest advantages of latex paint is the ability to clean up with soap and warm water.

Oil-based paints are best known for their excellent adhesion to the substrate and hard surfaces, but over time, the hard surface oxidizes and can get brittle and chip if hit. Some drawbacks of using oil-based paints are the strong odor, solvent cleanup of equipment, and the flammability potential of materials used for cleanup. Drying and recoating times can also be an issue—oil-based products can take anywhere from 8 to 24 hours to dry.

Properly prepared surfaces are critical to the performance of paint. Moisture, dirt, grease, mill scale, rust, concrete dust, or other materials on surfaces create barriers between substrates and coatings. Surfaces must be dry, clean, and in sound condition before paints are applied. A minimum 28-day curing period for concrete, mortars, and grouts before paint application is recommended. Curing is not the same as drying; therefore, additional time might be required for substrates to dry thoroughly.

Surfaces should be primed, either factory primed or field primed. Factory priming provides a more uniform and controlled prime coat and provides a better surface to apply field finish coats. If surfaces are to be field primed, the appropriate primer should be used.

Assessing Existing Conditions

Prior to priming surfaces, verify that surfaces are ready for the primer:

- All new surfaces should be primed—either factory primed or field primed.
- All loose, blistered, or chipped paint should be removed. If paint is removed to bare wood, gypsum board, or plaster, the surface should be primed.
- Verify that surfaces to be painted are properly prepared and ready to receive paint. Preparation can include the following:
  - Gypsum board surfaces are taped and sanded, and surfaces are fully cured.
  - Gypsum board textures are complete and fully cured.
  - Wood trim is securely attached to wall surface.
  - Fasteners are set and filled.
  - Sealant joints are fully cured.
  - Paintable latex sealant has been used on joints that will be painted.
- Sand all glossy surfaces prior to application of paint.

Acceptable Practices

The basis of a good paint system is the primer. Care should be taken to prep the surface for the primer. All surfaces should be clean and dry prior to application of the primer. The following are primers for different substrates.

- Interior primers:

  Gypsum board or plaster surfaces should be primed with a 100 percent acrylic latex primer.
  Wood surfaces—open grain woods or woods containing sapwood use a high-hiding solvent thinned primer. This type of primer will block stains from "bleed-through" of the wood grain.
  Wood surfaces—closed grain woods use a 100 percent acrylic primer or a high-hiding solvent thinned primer.
  Fiberglass surfaces, if not factory primed, use a 100 percent acrylic primer.

- Exterior primers:

  Wood surfaces—open grained woods use either a 100 percent acrylic primer or an oil-based (alkyd) primer.

  Fiberglass surfaces, if not factory primed, use a 100 percent acrylic primer.

Aluminum surfaces use a quick drying metal primer.
Concrete surfaces use a 100 percent acrylic prime.

- For top coats and intermediate coats, it is recommended to use a 100 percent acrylic resin paint. Acrylic latex is breathable, flexible, and dries quickly for recoating. Acrylic latex is mildew resistant and cleans up with soap and water. Appropriate for use on interior or exterior surfaces.
- For interior trim, an oil-based enamel is recommended. Oil-based enamel provides a hard finish that adheres well to substrates. Oil-based enamels take longer to dry for recoating; can take up to 12 hours.
- Minimum 50°F /maximum 90°F for application of paints.

Paints come in different gloss levels. Traditional gloss levels are flat, eggshell, or satin, semigloss, and gloss. The more gloss a paint finish has, the better the surface is for serviceability or cleanablilty.

In bathrooms and kitchens, an eggshell, satin, or semigloss would be recommended. The semigloss would give you the best cleanability, and would have the highest gloss level.

Generally, if ceilings are painted a different color than the walls, ceilings are painted with a flat paint. Walls can be either a flat, eggshell, or satin gloss, depending on how much cleanability is desired on the wall surfaces.

Wood trim, when painted, is generally painted with a satin or semigloss finish.

Practices to Avoid

- Oil-based paints should not be applied to concrete or masonry surfaces subject to constant dampness or intermittent saturation with water. These conditions can cause the coating to blister due to the coating's nonporous nature.
- Oil-based paints should not be applied directly to galvanized surfaces.
- Avoid using paints within a single paint system from different manufacturers. If this is unavoidable, obtain written verification from paint manufacturers that paints are compatible.
- Acrylic latex paints cannot be applied over chalky or powdery surfaces. If existing substrate shows signs of chalking, surface must be properly cleaned, primed, then painted with an acrylic latex.

Staining/Transparent Finishes

Description

The *Architectural Woodwork Standards* (first edition) classifies staining and transparent finishes into three general categories: economy grade, custom grade, and premium grade. These different grades establish finish quality.

The purpose of finishing products with stain and/or a transparent finish is to provide a protective surface. The protective surface protects the end product from damage due to moisture, contaminants, and handling. It also is a means to enhance or alter the natural beauty of the wood.

Wood trim and paneling require that all exposed surfaces be finished. Exposed surfaces for wood trim and paneling are defined as any surface exposed to view after installation. With wood paneling, however, it is required that the backside of the paneling be finished to act as a balancing finish for the panel so that the panel does not warp or bow.

Exterior stains are oil-based, to help with penetration into wood surfaces. Exterior staining of wood surfaces helps protect those surfaces from UV degradation by the use of semitransparent color in the stain. In addition most stains include a water-repellant additive that keeps water from penetrating the wood and destroying the wood fiber and a mildewcide to prevent the growth of mildew.

Transparent finishes are not recommended for exterior surfaces due to the effect of UV rays on the transparent coatings. In addition, many transparent coatings are not breathable, which does not allow the escape of moisture from the wood surface and can cause transparent coatings to fail.

Assessing Existing Conditions

For interior woodwork and cabinetry:

- Verify that all wood trim is installed and fasteners are set and filled with matching wood filler.
- In custom and premium installations, end joints of scribing shall be beveled and corners of scribing to be mitered.

- In custom and premium installations, color-compatible caulking is permitted, but shall not exceed 1/8 inch in width.
- In economy-grade installation, scribing is not required.

For exterior woodwork:

- Verify that wood is firmly attached and fasteners are set.
- If wood to be stained is pressure treated, it needs to weather for 6 months before application of stain.

Acceptable Practices

Visual inspection of exposed surfaces for interior woodwork and cabinetry for finish quality can be done according to Table 30.1.

Exterior woodwork preparation:

- Air temperature should be between 50°F and 85°F for stain.
- Clean surfaces with a mixture of tri sodium phosphate (TSP), household bleach, and water using a low-pressure garden sprayer. Agitate with brush or broom.
- Power wash surfaces with minimum 500 psi power washer.
- Allow surfaces to dry.
- Sand surfaces in direction of grain with 50 to 80 grit sandpaper, if surfaces are rough from cleaning.

Practices to Avoid

- Interior finish systems are usually not compatible with each other. Do not intermix systems. This could cause quality and performance problems.
- Finish systems often fail because too much top-coat material is applied. Application rates should be as recommended by manufacturer.

Table 30.1 Visual Tests Applicable to Exposed Surfaces

Surface Condition	Premium	Custom	Economy
Finish sanding scratches	Not permitted	Inconspicuous beyond 3 feet	Inconspicuous beyond 6 feet
Orange peel (slight depression in surface, similar to the skin of an orange)	Not permitted	Inconspicuous beyond 3 feet	Inconspicuous beyond 6 feet
Runs (running of wet finish film in rivulets)	Not permitted	Not permitted	Inconspicuous beyond 3 feet
Sags (partial slipping of finish film creating a curtain effect)	Not permitted	Inconspicuous beyond 3 feet	Inconspicuous beyond 6 feet
Blistering (small, swelled areas like water blisters on human skin)	Not permitted	Not permitted	Inconspicuous beyond 3 feet
Blushing (whitish haze, cloudy)	Not permitted	Not permitted	Inconspicuous beyond 3 feet
Checking, crazing (crowfeet separation or irregular line separation)	Not permitted	Not permitted	Inconspicuous beyond 3 feet
Cracking (formation like dried mud)	Not permitted	Not permitted	Inconspicuous beyond 3 feet
Glue spots	Not permitted	Not permitted	Inconspicuous beyond 3 feet
Filled nail holes	Inconspicuous beyond 3 feet	Inconspicuous beyond 6 feet	Inconspicuous beyond 9 feet
Field repairs and touch-ups	Inconspicuous beyond 3 feet	Inconspicuous beyond 6 feet	Inconspicuous beyond 9 feet

Wall Covering

Description

Wall coverings are often selected as an alternative to paint in applications where increased durability is required or the appearance of a texture or pattern is desired. Types of wall coverings include vinyl, woven glass-fiber, textile, wood veneer, and wallpaper. Though any wall covering can be used, wallpaper is the most common type used in residential construction.

Most wall coverings, except some textures and murals, have a pattern repeat. The repeat is the vertical distance between one point on the pattern to the identical point vertically. This pattern repeat is an integral part of the design, and can range from an inch or less, up to as much as the width of the wall covering or more.

A pattern number and dye-lot or "run number" is printed on each roll of wall covering. A pattern number identifies a particular design and color way of a pattern. The dye-lot number represents a particular group of rolls that are printed on the same print run. Different dye-lot numbers could signal variables such as a possible change of color tone, a change in the vinyl coating, or a change in the embossing process.

Before deciding which wall covering to use, consider your local climate and the design features of the home. Any wall covering can be installed in a dry or properly ventilated building. However, in hot humid climates, condensation inside the exterior wall might cause unusual moisture accumulation, that might, in turn, increase the possibility of mold growth. The key is to either eliminate the source of moisture and air infiltration or to ensure that water vapor in the wall cavity can escape to the building's interior or through the wall surface to the exterior environment. Proper wall construction, insulation, use of air barriers, and moisture vapor barriers can keep condensation from forming inside the wall system.

Common characteristics and definitions for wall coverings:

- *Scrubbable* means that the wall covering can withstand scrubbing with a brush and a prescribed detergent solution. Washable means that the wall covering can withstand occasional sponging with a prescribed detergent solution.

- *Stain resistance* is the ability to show no appreciable change after the removal of different types of stains such as grease, butter or coffee.
- *Abrasion resistance* is the ability to withstand rubbing, scraping, or scrubbing.
- *Colorfastness* is the ability to resist change or loss of color caused by exposure to light.
- *Peelable* means that the decorative surface and ground may be drypeeled from the wall, leaving a continuous layer of the substrate on the wall. This remaining substrate can be used as a liner for hanging new wall covering. Peelable paper is recommended for ease of wall covering replacement.
- *Strippable* means that the wall covering can be drystripped from the wall, leaving a minimum of paste or adhesive residue and without damage to the wall's surface.
- *Prepasted* means that the substrate of the wall covering has already been treated with an adhesive that is activated by water.

Whether a particular wall covering is strippable, peelable, washable, and so on is shown on the label of the wall-covering bolt. Figure 30.1 shows symbols used internationally to indicate wall-covering characteristics.

Assessing Existing Conditions

- Before installing wall coverings, check each roll to ensure uniformity in color and pattern.
- Remove all switch plates, outlet plates and wall fixtures that are not permanent prior to installing wall coverings; if removing any type of electrical obstacle, remember to disconnect the source of electricity.
- Verify that wall surfaces are clean, dry, sound, and properly prepared to receive wall covering, in accordance with wall covering manufacturer's installation instructions.

	NO DESIGN PATTERN MATCH		SPONGEABLE		SINOPABLE
	STRAIGHT ACROSS DESIGN PATTERN MATCH		WASHABLE		PEELABLE
	DROP MATCH		SUPER-WASHABLE		PRE-PASTED
50/25	DROP PATTERN REPEAT DISTANCE OFFSET		SCRUBBABLE		PASTE-THE-WALL
	DIRECTION OF HANGING		SUFFICIENT LIGHT FASTNESS		DUPLEX
	REVERSE ALTERNATE LENGTHS (STRIPS)		GOOD LIGHT FASTNESS		CO-ORDINATED FABRIC AVAILABLE

INTERNATIONAL WALLCOVERING SYMBOLS

Figure 30.1 International wall covering symbols

- Any wall irregularities should be corrected with appropriate wall repair materials.
- Any loose paint must be removed from the wall. Glossy and semigloss paint should be sanded to dull the surface and a coat of adhesion primer should be applied before the installation of wall covering.

What to do if there is mold:

- Visible stains (red, pink, yellow, and black) on the wall coverings can indicate mold growth behind the wall covering.
  Find and eliminate the source of moisture. If the source is not eliminated, the mold will return.
- Any mildew stains should be sealed with a good-quality stain primer.
- If mold growth is not extensive (affecting less than 10 square feet of the wall surface) and the mold has not degraded the surface, vacuum the mold away with a HEPA-filtered unit. Any mold or mildew should be cleaned from the wall surface with a solution of two cups of household bleach per gallon of water. Rinse and allow to dry.
- If the mold growth is more extensive than 10 square feet of the wall surface, consult local Department of Health for cleanup experts.

Acceptable Practices

- Ensure that the wall is free of contaminants such as dust, dirt, and mildew. Joints and spackled areas should be thoroughly cured and sanded smooth.
- If wall coverings are thin enough to be semitransparent and thus allow dark images caused by wall patching to show through, prime the wall with a pigmented wall covering primer/sealer, or use a lining paper.
- Remove old wall coverings and residual adhesive, since it can be a food source for mold and make bonding to the wall surface uneven and difficult. Prime wall with a good-quality wall covering primer that contains a biocide; follow manufacturer's instructions for application. Keep tools and supplies clean; cleanliness reduces the mold-growth risk by minimizing food and spores.
- Use the minimum quantity of adhesive that is required; less adhesive and water on the wall covering encourages faster drying. Be certain to keep air circulating after installation to allow the adhesive to dry quickly.

If wall covering to be hung has a pattern, determine what type of pattern match it has. The three major types of pattern matches are:

- *Random match:* In this type of pattern, the pattern matches no matter how adjoining strips are positioned. Stripes are the best examples of this type match. It is generally recommended to reverse every other strip to minimize visual effects such as shading or color variations from edge-to-edge. Note that any random match will produce less waste since there is no repeat distance to take into account.
- *Straight across match:* This match has design elements that match on adjoining strips. Every strip will be the same at the ceiling line.
- *Drop match:*
    - *Half-drop match*: Every other strip is the same at the ceiling line and the design elements run diagonally. It takes three strips to repeat the vertical design.
    - *Multiple-drop match*: A match that takes four or more strips before the vertical design is repeated. Similar to drop match except that it takes more strips to repeat the first strip.

Practices to Avoid

- Before hanging new wall coverings, make sure the wall is structurally sound and completely dry, with no excessive moisture or condensation, free of grease, staining markers, and mold. Never install wall coverings on a wet wall.
- Avoid installing vinyl wall coverings on the inside of an ouside wall bcause it acts as a vapor barrier and can trap moisture, creating possibilities for mold growth.
- Avoid using a dull blade when cutting wall coverings as it can result in ragged edges
- Avoid allowing adhesives and dirt to contact wall covering pattern surface.
- Avoid installing wall coverings in temperatures below 50°F. Doing so may encourage smoothing out a strip smoothly and bubbles and blisters to occur.

Resources

WITHIN THIS BOOK

- Chapter 16 Finish Carpentry
- Chapter 23 Doors and Frames
- Chapter 24 Windows
- Chapter 27 Gypsum Board

OTHER RESOURCES

- 2009 International Residential Code for One and Two-Family Dwellings. Washington, DC: International Code Council, Inc., 2009.
- American Institute of Architects, *Architectural Graphics Standards*, 11th ed. Hoboken, NJ: John Wiley and Sons, 2007.
- American Institute of Architects, *Architectural Graphic Standards for Residential Construction*, 2nd ed. Hoboken, NJ: John Wiley and Sons, 2010.
- Corky Binggeli, *Field Guide to Commercial Interiors*. Hoboken, NJ: John Wiley and Sons, 2009.
- Wallcovering Association, www.wallcoverings.org.

Part IX

Utility Services

Chapter 31

Plumbing

Piping

Water Heaters

Water Closets and Bidets

Lavatories, Sinks, and Faucets

Bathtubs and Showers

Piping

Description

Piping is used to carry liquid, most commonly drainage, waste and vent and supply and distribution. The International Residential Code and the International Plumbing Code provide detailed requirements necessary for appropriate design.

Assessing Existing Conditions

Low water pressure can be due to:

- Undersized piping
- Mineral deposits that have collected over time and narrowed the diameter of the pipe

Acceptable Practices

Pipe Material

Cast-Iron Pipe

Cast-iron pipe is used for nonpressure, sanitary, and stormwater gravity drainage service, above and below grade. The most commonly used pipe above grade is hubless, service-weight cast iron; below grade it is service-weight, hub-and-spigot pipe, with compression gaskets.

Steel Pipe

Steel pipe is manufactured either seamless (extruded) or welded. Wall thickness, known as *schedule,* ranges from schedule 5 (thinnest) to schedule 160 (thickest). Steel pipes can be joined by welding, or with flanges or threaded joints.

Copper Tube

Available as either hard (annealed) or drawn (soft) temper, seamless copper tubes can be joined by soldering, brazing, flared joints, and flanges.

- Types K, L, and M (thickest to thinnest walls) are used primarily for potable water service. Type L hard temper is often used aboveground, and type K soft temper is used underground.

- Type ACR is available only in small diameters and soft temper and is generally used for air conditioning and refrigeration service. It can be joined with flared fittings or by soldering.
- Type DWV for drainage, waste, and vent, this tubing is used for drainage service and is joined by soldering. It has the thinnest wall of any copper product.
- Type G is primarily used for fuel gas service. It is joined by using soldering and flange fittings.

Brass Pipe

Brass pipes (BR) are made of an alloy of copper and zinc, the proportion of copper varies from 85 percent (in red brass) to 67 percent (in yellow brass). Brass pipe is joined by threading, soldering, brazing, or using flanged fittings.

Larger brass pipes are used for potable water and sometimes for branch drainage lines. Fittings and castings made from an alloy different than the pipe may not be suitable for potable water service.

Plastic Pipe

Plastic has become the material of choice for piping systems used to convey a variety of liquids, including sewage, water, liquid fuel, and fuel gases. To convey potable water, plastic pipe must be listed by NSF International.

Thermoplastics, the most commonly used pipe materials, soften when heat is applied and reharden when cool, so the pipe can be extruded or molded into shapes. Thermosetting plastics must be cured by heating or with a curing chemical to achieve permanent shapes; once shaped, they cannot be reformed. Plastic pipe can be joined with heat fusion, flanged joints, solvent cement, or threaded pipe of schedule 80 wall thickness or greater.

Subclassifications of plastic pipe are based on the pipe material; the two most common are polyolefins and fluoroplastics.

- *SDR* means standard dimensional ratio. The SDR is found by dividing the average outside diameter of a pipe by the wall thickness.
- *DR* means dimensional ratio and is often incorrectly used interchangeably with SDR. The DR is found in the same way as the SDR and means the same thing, but is used when a product does not have the preferred SDR number established by prevailing standards.
- *OD* is the designation used when the outside diameter of a pipe is the controlling factor in its selection.

- *ID* is the designation used when the inside diameter of a pipe is the controlling factor in its selection.
- *PR* is a designation used when the pressure rating is the controlling factor in the selection of a pipe.
- *Schedule* is a designation used to match the standard dimensions for metallic pipe sizes. The pressure rating of the pipe varies with pipe size.

Pipe Joints

A joint is required to connect pipe to other pipe, a fitting, or a piece of equipment. The joint type selected for a particular application depends on the pipe material and wall thickness, pipe contents, system pressure, system temperature, disassembly requirements, and the applicable plumbing code.

Common pipe joints are as follows:

- Caulked joints
- Compression gasket joints
- Compression coupling joints
- Threaded joints
- Solvent cement joints
- Soldered and brazed joints
- Flared joints
- Welded joints
- Flanged joints
- Heat-fused joints

Pipe Insulation

The primary purpose of insulation is to retard the flow of heat and water vapor from pipes, ducts, and equipment. An insulation system consists of the insulation itself, a jacket to cover it, and, if needed, an additional jacket to provide specific characteristics, such as weather protection or the ability to be repeatedly cleaned.

Code limitations for flame spread and the amount of smoke developed, established for components in fireproof and noncombustible buildings, apply to these insulation system elements.

Water Heaters

Description

There are three type of water heaters: instantaneous-type, semi-instantaneous type, and storage-type water heaters. In residential construction, the storage-type water heaters are the most common. For storage-type water heaters, the size of the water heater, in gallon capacity, will be determined by the number people in the house, the types and quantities of plumbing fixtures, and how often they will be used in one hour. Table 31.1 provides an example of how to determine how large a water heater is required for a house with four occupants.

Water heaters should have a "first hour rating" (FHR) within 1 or 2 gallons of the peak hour demand. Each water heater, based on the fuel source, has the FHR listed somewhere on the unit. In the previous example, a 57- to 61-gallon water heater should be selected.

Instantaneous-type water heaters are generally located close to the plumbing fixture to be served. Water is heated by passing water through coils, which are surrounding an electric or gas heat source.

Table 31.1 Calculating Water Heater Size Requirements

Use	Hot Water Demand	Times Used during 1 hour	Gallons Used in 1 hour
	(per usage)		
Shower	12	× 3	= 36
Bathtub	9	× 1	= 9
Shaving	2	× 1	= 2
Hands and face washing	4	×	=
Hair shampoo	4	× 3	= 12
Hand washing	4	×	=
Dishwasher	14	×	=
Food preparation	26	×	=
Clothes washer	32	×	=
Total first hour rating			59 gallons

Temperature control of water is very poor, due to the speed at which the water is being heated.

Semiinstantaneous-type water heaters are similar to instantaneous-type water heaters except that they have a small storage tank (2 to 6 gallons).

Assessing Existing Conditions

Verify the following in the field:

- In seismic zones, the water heater should have a seismic strap around the tank that is securely fastened to the wall. The seismic strap should be located within the upper third of the water heater height.
- If the water heater is located in the garage, the ignition source shall be a minimum of 18 inches above adjacent grade.
- If the water heater is not protected from motor vehicle impact, it shall be a minimum height of 6 feet above the garage floor.
- If water heater is located in an unconditioned space, it shall be insulated to a minimum of R-2.
- Water heaters shall be located and connected to provide access for observation, maintenance, servicing, and replacement.

Acceptable Practices

- If a water heater is installed in a bedroom or a bathroom, it shall be in a sealed enclosure so that combustion air is not taken from the living space.
- Fuel-fired water heaters located in a separate room shall be provided with combustion air, either from other interior spaces or from outside air. Combustion air from inside the building can be provided by two openings, one at the top and one at the bottom of wall into another room in the building. Obtaining combustion air from outside the building can be accomplished by placing a single vent directly to the outside, either through an outside wall or through an outside ventilated attic space. Combustion air can be provided through mechanical ventilation, provided ignition of the water heater burner is interconnected with the mechanical air supply so that the air supply is on whenever the burner is on.
- Where water heaters are located in areas where leaking water will cause damage, the water heater shall be provided with a galvanized steel drain pan a minimum of 1-1/2 inches deep. Drain pan shall be

drained by a minimum 3/4-inch indirect waste pipe. The drain pipe shall terminate at a floor drain or shall terminate at the exterior of the building a minimum 6 inches and maximum of 24 inches above adjacent grade.

- Water heaters shall be equipped with a pressure and temperature relief valve.

Practices to Avoid

- Fuel-fired water heaters shall not be installed in storage closets.
- Water heater relief valve discharge pipes shall not be directly connected to a drainage system but should discharge to drain pan, floor drain or outdoors, so that it is visible to the occupants, as discharge from the relief valve signals a problem.

Water Closets and Bidets

Description

Water closets (toilets) and bidets generally have two parts—a receptor for waste, which includes the drain trap, and a flushing or water supply mechanism. Most are made of vitreous china. These plumbing fixtures are generally grouped according to their flushing action, which affects the bowl type, flushing mechanism, and mounting method.

Two common types of residential type toilets are gravity flush tank, which is the most common, and the pressure-assisted flush tank:

- *Gravity flush tank:* Water enters the tank through a ball cock and is stopped when the float valve reaches a predetermined level. The handle raises the flapper to release the water in the tank into the fixture and stops when the flapper closes. Gravity flush tanks require 10 psi water pressure.
- *Pressure-assisted flush tank:* Water enters a pressure tank installed inside an outer tank, partially filling the tank and compressing the air inside. When flushing is started, the air pressure causes the quick release of water into the fixture. Pressure-assisted flush tanks require 30 psi water pressure.

Bidets are similar to a sink or lavatory; they have hot- and cold-water valves, a bowl similar to a toilet, a spray mechanism in the center of the bowl, and a drain.

Assessing Existing Conditions

Common leaks in toilets:

- Verify that wax gasket ring where base of toilet and sewer line connect is well seated. A leak in this joint can destroy flooring and substrate.
- If a toilet continues to run after flushing, there are two potential problems. First, check the drain hole in the bottom of the tank, as there could be an obstruction or the perimeter of the hole could be dirty, allowing water to pass. The other problem could be that the tank float could be not properly adjusted, which would not allow the ball cock valve to completely close.

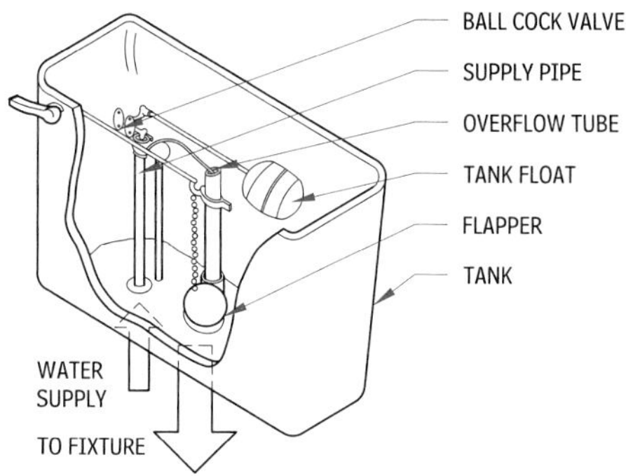

GRAVITY FLUSH TANK

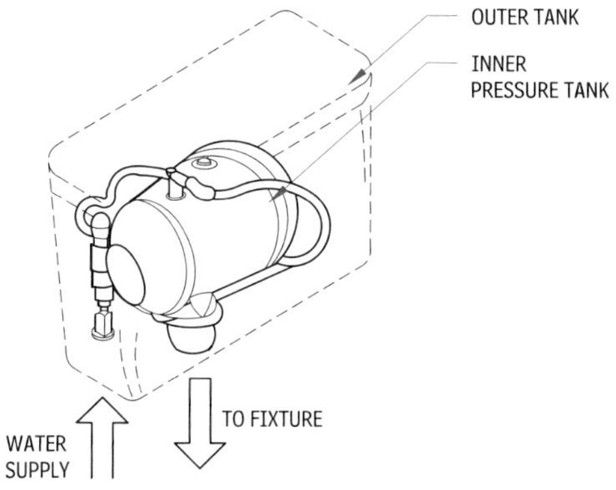

PRESSURE-ASSISTED FLUSH TANK

Figure 31.1 Gravity flush task and pressure assisted flush tank
Source: AIA, *Architectural Graphic Standards for Residential Construction,* 2nd ed. Copyright 2010, John Wiley & Sons, Inc.

Acceptable Practices

Accessible toilets:

- Toilets should be located minimum of 16 to 18 inches away from any wall on the side next to the toilet.
- Clear space in front of the toilet should be a minimum of 2 feet, 6 inches wide by 4 feet long.

Lavatories, Sinks, and Faucets

Description

Built-in lavatories come in a variety of sizes and shapes, typically oval, rectangular, or circular. Built-in sinks may include single-, double-, and triple-bowl sinks. More specialized fixtures include corner-bowl sinks, units with integral drainboards, and pedestal sinks, which can be free-standing or the sink can be wall hung with a pedestal placed under the sink to hide the trap. Both lavatories and sinks may be self-rimming, where the rim is integral to the unit. Rimless units are available for undercounter installations. Lavatory bowls may also be mounted on top of a countertop.

Faucets come in many shapes and sizes. The difference is in how water is delivered from the spigot. There are two basic types. Hot and cold water can be operated from individual valves (two-handle faucet), which are then mixed together as they exit the spigot. Hot and cold water can also be mixed within the same valve, which requires operation of only one valve (single lever), then exits the spigot. Faucets can be manually operated or they can be electronically operated by sensor.

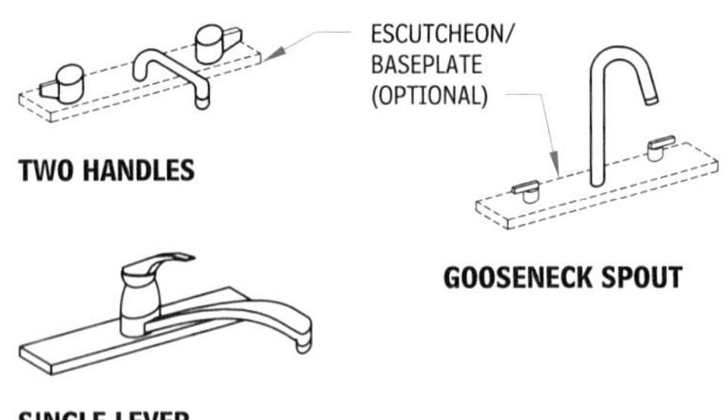

Figure 31.2 Two-handle and single-lever faucets
Source: AIA, *Architectural Graphic Standards for Residential Construction,* 2nd ed. Copyright 2010, John Wiley & Sons, Inc.

Assessing Existing Conditions

Following are some common causes of leaks.

Faucet:

- Fittings on water supply lines are not tight. Check hot and cold fittings for tightness on shut-off valves at wall. Check tightness of fittings on faucet supply lines. If fittings on faucet still leak, verify that Teflon tape or plumbers putty was used on the threads of the supply lines. If fittings on shut-off valves are leaking, verify that the proper seals were installed on the connections to the valves.
- Leaking water under the faucet body can be caused by loose fittings or loose body connection. A new faucet is generally provided either with a black rubber factory seal that is to be placed under the faucet body, or if stated in the installation instructions, plumber's putty should be placed under the faucet body prior to installation on sink.

Lavatory/sink:

- If there is a leak under the lavatory or sink, it may be caused by forgetting to place plumbers putty under the flange of the drain assembly.

Acceptable Practices

Accessible lavatories:

- Faucets should not require more than 5 pounds of force to operate and should not require any pinching, grasping, or twisting of the wrist to operate the mechanism.
- Lavatories are required to have a clear space of 30 by 48 inches and should have knee space under the lavatory to allow a wheelchair-bound individual to roll up under the lavatory.
- Wall-hung lavatories should not have any sharp or abrasive surfaces underneath the lavatory.
- Drain and water pipes should be insulated or protected from contacting wheelchair-bound users.

Standard heights:

- Bathroom lavatory height: 30 to 31 inches
- Kitchen sink heights: 36 inches

Bathtubs and Showers

Description

Bathtubs are available in many shapes, sizes, and styles, including rectangular, corner, and oval. Three types of installation are common, including recessed, drop-in, and freestanding. Cast iron and enameled steel bathtubs are available but fiberglass and acrylic units are currently the most common material for these fixtures.

Whirlpool bathtubs are usually made of fiberglass-reinforced acrylic, which can be fabricated in a variety of shapes. Air mixed with water streams through jets in the side of the tub, giving the whirlpool its soothing, therapeutic character. Pumps range from 1/2 to 3 horsepower, and the intensity of the flow varies accordingly. Inline heaters are recommended to keep the water warm without refilling the tub.

Built-in bathtubs have an integral apron and tiling flange, for installation in a three-wall alcove. Drop-in designs are intended for deck-mounted installations and typically have integral feet that support the weight of the unit. Many whirlpool bathtubs are drop-in units, though manufacturers may offer built-in units with a removable apron for access to the pump.

Showers may be integrated with bathtubs or be separate elements within the bathroom. If the shower is a part of the bathtub, then the surround and tub are generally fabricated from fiberglass or acrylic material.

Shower enclosures are generally three-sided, with an impervious finish. A shower door or curtain completes the enclosure. These enclosures, also known as *shower stalls,* consist of a shower pan with water-resistant walls which can be site built or can be a one-piece fiberglass or acrylic enclosure. Shower pans are designed to slope to the drain.

Assessing Existing Conditions

Verify the following in the field:

- Plumbing piping should be complete before installation of tub or shower units.

- Generally, tub and shower units have flanges at the edges of the unit that can be let into the stud framing so that the gypsum board can lay flat against the studs in the wall. An option is to attach the tub or shower flange directly to the stud, then fur out the stud to the ceiling to allow the gypsum board to lay flat on the stud wall.

Acceptable Practices

- Protect fiberglass or acrylic materials from grit, which could scratch the finish surface of the tub or shower unit.
- Verify that the tub is level.
- Any seams or joints between different materials should be sealed with a silicone, mildew-resistant bathtub sealant.

Resources

WITHIN THIS BOOK

- Chapter 3 Accessibility Guidelines

REFERENCE STANDARDS

- ASTM B43—Standard Specifications for Seamless Red Brass Pipe, Standard Sizes
- ASTM B88—Standard Specification for Seamless Copper Water Tube
- ASTM B306—Standard Specification for Copper Drainage Tube

OTHER RESOURCES

- 2009 International Plumbing Code. Washington, DC: International Code Council, Inc., 2009.
- 2009 International Residential Code for One and Two-Family Dwellings. Washington, DC: International Code Council, Inc., 2009.
- American Institute of Architects, *Architectural Graphics Standards*, 11th ed. Hoboken, NJ: John Wiley & Sons, 2007.
- American Institute of Architects, *Architectural Graphic Standards for Residential Construction*, 2nd ed. Hoboken, NJ: John Wiley & Sons, 2010.

Chapter 32

Heating, Ventilating, and Air Conditioning

Ducts, Registers and Diffusers

Description

Ducts, registers, and diffusers are the basic components that make up an air distribution system for residences. Typically, they include a system for both supply of conditioned air and return of room air. A properly designed system should meet all of the following requirements:

- Provide conditioned air to satisfy all room heating and cooling requirements
- Provide a pressure drop across the air handler that is within specifications
- Prevent polluted air from entering the residence
- Provide balanced air flows between the supply and return systems
- Minimize temperature fluctuations between the air handler and supply register

Assessing Existing Conditions

Assessing the installation of the air distribution system (ducts, registers, and diffusers) falls into these categories:

- Mechanical integrity
- Air movement
- Insulation

Mechanical Integrity

- All joints in air distribution system are mechanically fastened and sealed.
- No components are crushed, torn or otherwise damaged.

Air Movement

- System is balanced between supply and return.
- There are no leaks in the system.

Insulation

- Exterior ducts are required to be insulated.
- Best practice is to provide insulation on distribution ductwork.

Duct Materials

Rigid ductwork, whether it is round or rectangular, is typically constructed from G-60 coated galvanized steel. The advantages of using rigid sheet metal ductwork include the fact that it is lightweight and durable, can be easily fabricated in both rectangular and round shapes, and can be used with most HVAC systems.

Flexible ductwork has gained popularity in the residential market because it is easy to use and is very cost effective. It is constructed from blanket insulation covered with a flexible vapor-barrier jacket. Flexible ductwork can be connected to rigid ductwork through a series of clamps. The biggest disadvantage of flexible ductwork is that during installation, it can easily be crimped so that airflow is restricted and the proper volume of air is not reaching its destination.

Registers, Diffusers, and Grilles

- A register is a grille with an operable damper or a control the air pattern. Opposed blade dampers provide a more uniform air flow.
- A diffuser directs the airflow perpendicular to adjacent surfaces.
- Grilles are fixed louvers that have not operable damper. In residential construction, the most common grille is for return air.

Table 32.1 Guidelines for Ductwork Sizing

Air Volume	Rectangular Duct					Round Duct
50 CFM	6 × 4 in.					5 in.
100 CFM	8 × 4 in.	6 × 6 in.				6 in.
200 CFM	14 × 4 in.	8 × 6 in.				8 in.
300 CFM		12 × 6 in.	8 × 8 in.			9 in.
500 CFM		18 × 6 in.	12 × 8 in.	10 × 10 in.		11 in.
700 CFM		24 × 6 in.	16 × 8 in.	12 × 10 in.		12 in.
1000 CFM			22 × 8 in.	16 × 10 in.	14 × 12 in.	14 in.

Acceptable Practices

- Place diffusers so that air will move over the face of windows and outside walls. This will minimize the formation of condensation.
- Locate return air grilles on inside walls.
- Stretch flexible duct so that is tight and not allowed to drape. This will assist in maximum air flow.
- Reduce duct size away from unit to maintain velocity.
- Return airflow cubic feet per minute (CFM) needs to be equal to or great than the supply air CFM.
- Seal seams of ductwork and insulate when in unconditioned environments such as crawl spaces or attics.

Practices to Avoid

- Placing return air grille near high humidity spaces such as bathrooms

Ventilation and Exhaust Systems

Description

Ventilation and exhaust for a dwelling can be provided through natural ventilation or mechanical exhaust systems. Natural ventilation occurs through the use of windows, openings, and vents. Mechanical ventilation requires the use of a fan to pull air out of a space.

Whole-house ventilation and local exhaust are the primary methods of ventilating a residence. Whole-house ventilation removes air from the entire space; this helps to remove contaminants in the air that are caused by the people, the materials, and the activities in the space. Local exhaust removes contaminants within a contained space such as a bathroom or kitchen. Source control addresses exhausting contaminants that can be anticipated, such as a garage.

Assessing Existing Conditions

Attics and crawlspaces can be designed to be either ventilated or nonventilated (sealed) spaces. When designed as a ventilated space, the code assumes the space is naturally ventilated and vents are required to allow natural air flow to ensure that moisture is removed from the space.

Toilet rooms and bathrooms are required to be ventilated, and similar to attic and crawlspaces, this may be accomplished either naturally with a window or, if it is an interior space, through ventilation equipment, which is required to exhaust the air directly to the outdoors.

Acceptable Practices

Whole-House Ventilation

15 to 20 air changes per hour is typical.

Exhaust Ventilation Systems

- Reduces the inside air pressure to below the outdoor air pressure.
- Makeup air infiltrates through building envelope and vents.
- Works best in cold climates.
- May introduce undesirable humidity in warm/humid climates.
- Typically, a single fan is connected to a centrally located single exhaust point.

Supply Ventilation Systems

- Increases the inside air pressure to above the outdoor air pressure.
- Air escapes through building envelope and local exhaust.
- Works best in hot or mixed climates.
- May cause condensation in cold climates when interior space is humid.
- If outside air is not mixed prior to introduction into the space, cold spots and drafts may occur.
- Typically, a single fan is connected to a centrally located single exhaust point—reverse system of exhaust ventilation systems.

Balanced Ventilation Systems

- Introduces and exhausts an equal amount of air.
- Air escapes through building envelope and local exhaust.
- Appropriate in all climates; more expensive to install and operate than either exhaust or supply ventilation systems.
- No method for controlling the transfer of humidity.
- Typically, there are two separated sets of fans and ductwork.

Energy Recovery Ventilation Systems

- Controlled method of ventilating a home while minimizing energy loss.
- Heat is transferred from the warm inside air that is being exhausted to the fresh air that is being introduced.
- This is the most expensive system to install, but costs are recovered by reduced heating and cooling costs.
- Works best in extreme winter or summer conditions.

Local Exhaust

Local exhaust systems may improve the effectiveness of the whole-house ventilation. *The International Residential Code* requires a minimum air flow rate for exhausting bathrooms and toilet rooms when natural ventilation is not used:

- Kitchens
  - 100 cfm intermittent
  - 25 cfm continuous

- Bathrooms/toilet rooms
  - 50 cfm intermittent
  - 20 cfm continuous

Source Control

Source control is the most cost-effective approach to protecting indoor air quality. Products that contain hazardous materials can be encased or sealed to minimize their off-gassing capabilities. In some cases, standard equipment maintenance or adjustment can greatly reduce the level of the contaminants in the space. This, along with increased natural ventilation, will help.

Heating and Cooling Systems

Description

Climate-control systems may be classified as either active or passive in nature. Passive systems use no purchased energy resources. Normally, they are assembled of "architectural" building elements doing double duty, such as glazings, walls, floors, and finishes, and require design coordination.

Active climate-control systems use purchased energy resources and employ task-specific, single-purpose elements, such as pumps, fans, ducts, and diffusers. In the broadest sense, the term *air conditioning* means that a quantity of air is:

- Mixed with the required amount of outside (fresh) air
- Filtered to remove specified amounts of particulate and/or gaseous elements
- Heated and/or cooled by an appropriate temperature control system
- Humidified or dehumidified
- Ionized, ozonated, or otherwise treated
- Delivered to the conditioned spaces and distributed in a quiet, draft-free manner

Assessing Existing Conditions

The size of the air conditioning unit is measured in tons. The capacity of the air conditioning unit is measured in British thermal units (Btu). It takes 12,000 Btu per hour to melt one ton of ice in a 24-hour period; thus, a 3-ton unit would have a capacity of 36,000 Btu per hour.

For heating systems, the efficiency of the unit comes into play. A heating unit that has a capacity of 80,000 Btu per hour and is 90 percent efficient will have an actual heat output of 72,000 Btu per hour.

HVAC Equipment Types

Condensing Furnaces

Condensing furnaces are high-efficiency units that extract heat from exhaust gasses, to the point at which water and combustion byproducts are condensed out of the gasses.

Condensing furnace is highly recommended for colder climate areas, where heating costs are a major portion of the annual utility bill.

When units are oversized for the space, the unit will short cycle. This may cause condensation and thus corrosion in the unit.

Direct-Expansion Systems

The term *direct expansion* means that a chemical refrigerant is used in the refrigeration circuit to remove heat. Direct-expansion systems come in "cooling only" mode, or in specially designed heat pumps that can furnish either heating or cooling.

The most common direct-expansion system is the packaged unit installed through the wall or in a window. These can also be floor-mounted in or out of the air-conditioned space, or located on the roof.

Direct-expansion system can also be known as a "split" system, in which the heat rejection components of the condenser and compressor are packaged separately and can be located remotely from the evaporator and fan, which must be in the air-conditioned space. The two subassemblies, which are attached to the system with refrigerant piping, may be as close as on opposite sides of a wall or up to 100 feet away from each other.

Furnaces

Warm air furnace units are designed primarily for residential heating. Cooling can be added to these units by installing a cooling coil downstream from the furnace, with a refrigerant compressor and condenser located remotely outside the building.

Since all variations of warm air heating systems recirculate their air within the building envelope, it is a crucial design requirement to leave adequate return air passage from each space supplied with air to the furnace room. The efficiency of a furnace is measured by annual fuel utilization efficiency (AFUE).

Radiant Heating Systems

Radiant heating systems transfer heat from hot water tubing (or electric cables) embedded in the floor or ceiling to a medium that will distribute heat to the specified space. The choice of hot water or electric cable heat is made based on installation, energy, and total life-cycle costs.

Properly designed and operated radiant heating systems will provide greater comfort, at lower operating costs, than other heating systems because of the inherent nature of the human body's thermal functions. About 70 percent of the body's heat is transferred by radiation (via electromagnetic waves, like light), 25 percent by convection (via air or water), and 5 percent by conduction (via physical contact).

In terms of overall system configuration, a radiant floor, wall, or ceiling is equivalent to a radiator, convector, or any other terminal heating element. The primary caveat is that a suitable control system must be provided, to ensure that floor surface temperatures do not rise above 75°F or, if ceiling systems are used, above 120°F. Thermostats for radiant systems can generally be set several degrees lower for heating than thermostats for other types of systems. Finished floors should not be of a thermal insulating material; ceramic tile or wood flooring would be suitable.

Humidity Control

In a humid environment, during the summer, properly sized air conditioning equipment will operate almost continuously to maintain humidity and temperature control.

By controlling humidity in a room, the room temperature can typically be warmer than if the humidity is not controlled.

Acceptable Practices

- Pitch exhaust piping a minimum of 1/4 inch per foot so condensate can drain.
- AFUE for a noncondensing fossil-fueled, warm-air furnace is 78 percent.
- AFUE for a condensing fossil-fueled boiler is 80 percent.

Practices to Avoid

- Using indoor air for combustion; it may contain traces of household chemicals that can cause corrosion.
- Oversizing equipment; bigger is not better in this case, and may actually shorten the life of the equipment.
- Sizing HVAC equipment based solely on square footage, or on the original equipment.

Resources

WITHIN THIS BOOK

- Chapter 31 Plumbing
- Chapter 33 Electrical

OTHER RESOURCES

- 2009 International Residential Code for One and Two-Family Dwellings. Washington, DC: International Code Council, Inc., 2009.
- American Institute of Architects, *Architectural Graphics Standards*, 11th ed. Hoboken, NJ: John Wiley & Sons, 2007.
- American Institute of Architects, *Architectural Graphic Standards for Residential Construction*, 2nd ed. Hoboken, NJ: John Wiley & Sons, 2010.
- Air Conditioning Contractors of America (ACCA), Arlington, Virginia:
  - *Manual D: Residential Duct Systems*
  - *Manual G: Selection of Distribution Systems*
  - *Manual J—HVAC Residential Load Calculation*
  - *Manual T: Air Distribution Basics for Residential and Small Commercial Buildings*
- Air Diffusion Council (ADC), Schaumburg, Illinois:
  - *Flexible Duct Performance & Installation Standards*
- North American Insulation Manufacturers Association (NAIMA), Alexandria, Virginia:
  - *Residential Fibrous Glass Duct Construction Standards*
  - *A Guide to Insulated Air Duct Systems*
- Sheet Metal and Air Conditioning Contractors' National Association, Inc. (SMACNA), Chantilly, Virginia:
  - *Residential Comfort System Installation Standards Manual*
  - *Fibrous Glass Duct Construction Standards*
  - *HVAC Duct Construction Standards—Metal and Flexible*

Chapter 33

Electrical

Panelboards

Description

The panelboard, also called a service panel or *load center*, is the distribution point for all the cables and wires in a residence. The panel houses the fuses and circuit breakers, which provide overcurrent protection.

The main service panel (the first panel downstream from the meter base), will always need a main breaker to protect all down-stream wiring. Panels without a main breaker are called "lugs only" panels, and are used for subpanels—(panels that feed off a breaker within the main service panel).

Assessing Existing Conditions

Installation of the panelboard should be reviewed during rough-in construction and after finishes are installed. Verify the following:

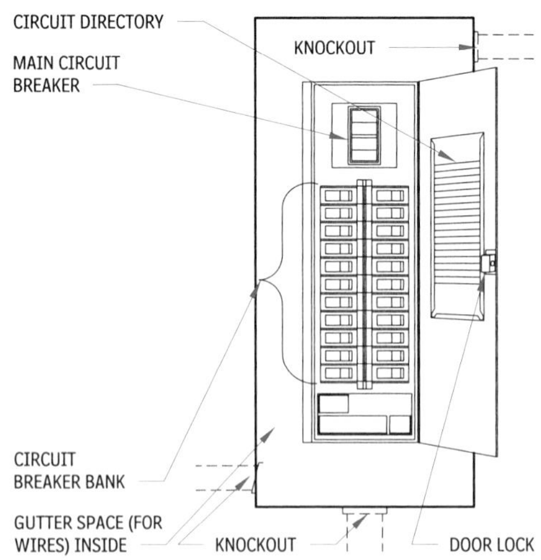

Figure 33.1 Panelboard
Source: AIA, *Architectural Graphic Standards for Residential Construction,* 2nd ed. Copyright 2010, John Wiley and Sons, Inc.

Rough-in

- Panelboard is located to allow minimum working space and clearances
- Location and rating of panelboard overcurrent device
- Protection for cables entering and around the panelboard
- Panelboard zone is free of nonelectrical utilities or equipment

Finish

- Gaps between panelboard and finishes are within required maximum range
- Face of panelboard relative to wall complies with code
- Cables and conductors entering cabinet protected from abrasion
- Panelboard circuits and switches clearly marked with specific purpose or use, including spares

Acceptable Practices

Workspace and Clearances

- Service panels should be installed vertically, not horizontally, unless the manufacturer has listed the panel for horizontal installation. Panels should not be installed in bathrooms, where water and drain lines are overhead, in any unprotected locations, or where panel doors cannot be opened at least 90°.

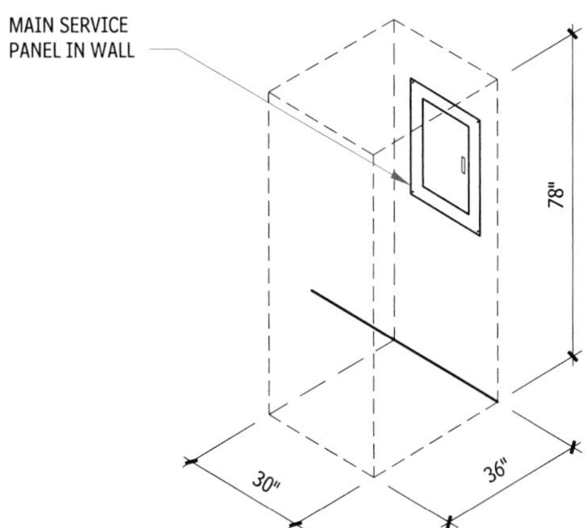

Figure 33.2 Main service panel clearances
Source: AIA, *Architectural Graphic Standards for Residential Construction,* 2nd ed. Copyright 2010, John Wiley and Sons, Inc.

- Clearance distances are measured from the energized parts of panelboards without covers; and from the panelboard face for enclosed models. *IRC E3405.2*
- For panelboards wider than 30 inches, the clear workspace width must be increased to match the width of the panelboard. *IRC E3405.2*
- The space equal to the width and depth of the panelboard and extending from the floor to 6 feet above the panelboard, or to the structural ceiling is to be dedicated electrical space. With a few minor exceptions, equipment, piping, etc. of other utilities and systems is not allowed in that zone. *IRC E3405.3*
- Provide artificial lighting for panelboards located indoors. *IRC E3405.6*

Panelboards and Connections

- Joining conductors of dissimilar materials, such as copper and aluminum, copper and copper-clad aluminum, or aluminum and copper-clad aluminum, can only be done using devices listed for the purpose and condition of the application. Inhibitors and compounds may be suitable for the application. *IRC E3406.8*
- Panelboard circuits are required to be marked to clearly identify their specific purpose or use. Spare positions must also be marked. *IRC E3706.2*
- When mounted in wood-stud wall or other combustible wall types, the front edge of the panelboard cabinet must be flush with or project forward from the wall finish. Panelboards mounted in noncombustible walls can have the front edge recessed 1/4 inch maximum from the wall finish. *IRC E3907.3*
- Insulated conductors 4 American Wire Gauge (AWG) or larger entering a panelboard cabinets must be protected by a substantial fitting that is smoothly rounded and insulated, or substantial insulating material secured in place. *IRC E3906.1.1*

Table 33.1 Panelboard Dimensions

Maximum Number of Circuits	Box Dimensions		
	Width	Height	Depth
12	9–15 in.	13–20 in.	3¾–4⅝ in.
20	9–15 in.	20¼–24 in.	3¾–4⅝ in.
30	12–15 in.	30–33½ in.	34–39 in.
40	14–15 in.	34–39 in.	4–4⅝ in.

Most residential panels are designed to fit between studs nailed on 16–inch centers, making them about 14-1/2 in. wide. The only difference between higher and lower amperage panels is the height of the panel. Slots in the upper and lower plates are open, to allow the cables to exit the stud cavity.

Overcurrent Protection (Breakers)

- The panelboard must be protected by an overcurrent protection device located inside the panelboard or remotely on the supply side of the panelboard. The device cannot have a rating greater than the panelboard. *IRC E3706.3*
- Panels come with solid or slotted tabs. Solid tabs fit full-size breakers only, while slotted tabs fit two-in-one breakers. Panels with full-size tabs are preferred over panels with slotted tabs. Although slotted tab panels make it possible to have a large number of breakers in a small panel, this arrangement should be avoided whenever possible because it crowds many wires into a small space in the panel.

Practices to Avoid

- In marking panelboards, do not use designations that may be temporary, such as "Tom's room" or "spare room."
- Keep water pipes and other utilities clear of electrical panels.
- Do not use panelboard workspace for storage. *IRC E3405.4*
- Do not locate panelboards or overcurrent protection devices in clothes closets, bathrooms, or over the steps of a stairway. *IRC E3405.4*

Wiring, Cabling, and Devices

Description

Wiring, cabling, and devices include components that receive power from the source, typically a local utility company, and distribute it throughout the residence to devices, outlets, switches, etc. This section should be reviewed with the previous section on panelboards; and the following sections on lightning and surge protection, and lighting, for a better understanding of the electrical power distribution system for a home.

In addition to power distribution, communication systems also form part of the network of electrical wiring and devices common in residential construction. For more information on those systems, turn to Chapter 34, "Electronic Safety and Security."

Assessing Existing Conditions

Wiring, cabling, and device installation can be broken down into two basic categories: rough-in and finish. In order to ensure proper installation of wiring, cabling, and devices, verify the following:

Rough-in

- Electrical wiring is installed to supply all device locations.
- Electrical device boxes for outlets are located at a minimum as required by code.
- Electrical device boxes are installed at the proper height.
- All cable is supported and protected as required by code.
- Metallic electrical device boxes are grounded.
- Cable bends meet required minimum radius.

Finish

- All service equipment and disconnects are permanently marked.
- Overhead service entrance meets clearance requirements.

- Gaps between electrical device boxes and plaster or gypsum board are in accordance with code.
- Receptacle faceplates do not extend past the outlet device.

Acceptable Practices

Electrical Service Entrance

- Overhead service-entrance lines should be installed above National Electrical Code (NEC) minimum requirements to allow for some sag due to ice and heat.
- Service-entrance conductors without jackets are required to have a minimum clearance of 10 feet at the lowest point above sidewalks and finished grade. The minimum clearance is increased to 12 feet over residential property and driveway. *IRC E3604.1*
- Service-entrance conductors without jackets are required to have a minimum clearance of 3 feet from windows, doors, porches, balconies, ladders, stairs, etc. *IRC E3604.1*
- Overhead service-entrance conductors are required to have a vertical clearance of at least 8 feet from a roof that has a slope of less than 4 in 12, unless the roof surface has pedestrian traffic. *IRC E3604.2.1*
- Overhead service-entrance conductors are required to have a vertical clearance of at least 3 feet from a roof that has a slope of at least 4 in 12. *IRC E3604.2.1*
- The minimum clearance over the roof for overhead service-entrance conductors may be reduced to 18 inches when it passes over an outside overhang only. Not more than 6 feet of conductor length can pass over not more than a 4-foot roof overhang measured horizontally. *IRC E3604.2.1*
- When minimum clearances above grade cannot be maintained across a span, a lift pole must be added.
- A service-entrance disconnect that disconnects all conductors in a building from the service-entrance conductor is required either outside the residence or inside, nearest the point of the service-entrance. It needs to be permanently marked as a service disconnect. This disconnect is cannot be installed in a bathroom. *IRC E3601.6.1*
- A service-entrance disconnect can have a maximum of six switches or circuit breakers either installed in a group or in a single enclosure. *IRC E3601.7*

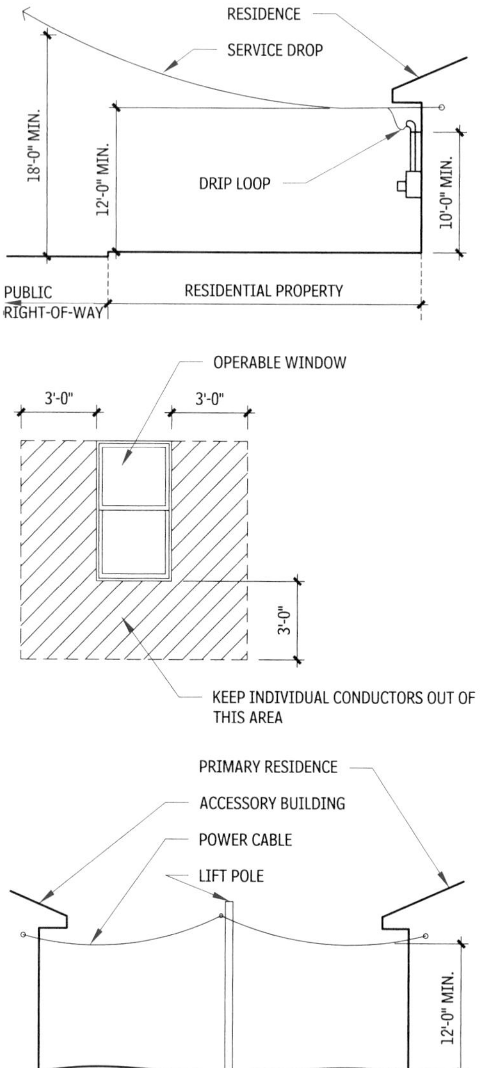

Figure 33.3 Clearances for overhead service entrance

Source: AIA, *Architectural Graphic Standards for Residential Construction,* 2nd ed. Copyright 2010, John Wiley and Sons, Inc.

Branch Circuits

- A minimum of two 20-amp branch circuits are required to serve wall and floor outlets in the kitchen, pantry, breakfast area, dining area, or similar area. A minimum of two 20-amp branch circuits are required to serve the kitchen countertop outlets. Either or both of these

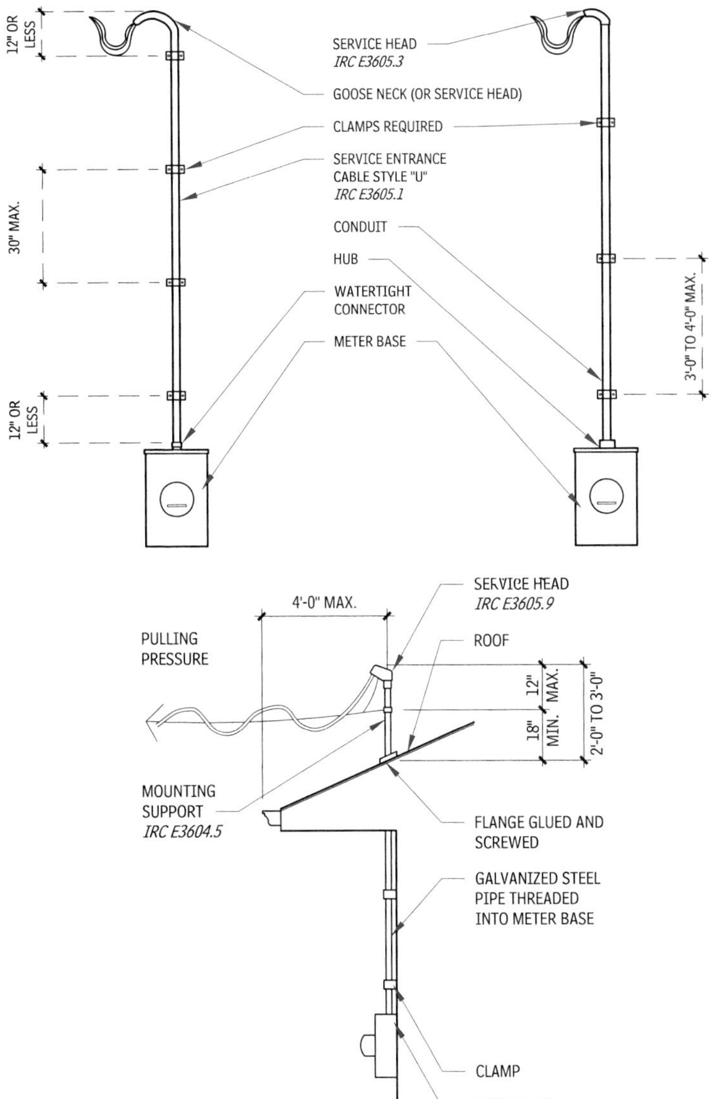

Figure 33.4 Attachment details
Source: AIA, *Architectural Graphic Standards for Residential Construction,* 2nd ed. Copyright 2010, John Wiley and Sons, Inc.

branch circuits may be used to supply other outlets in the same kitchen, pantry, breakfast, and dining area. *IRC E3703.2*

- Kitchen ranges with a rating of 8.75 kVA or more shall be supplied by a branch circuit with a minimum rating of 40 amps. *E3702.9*

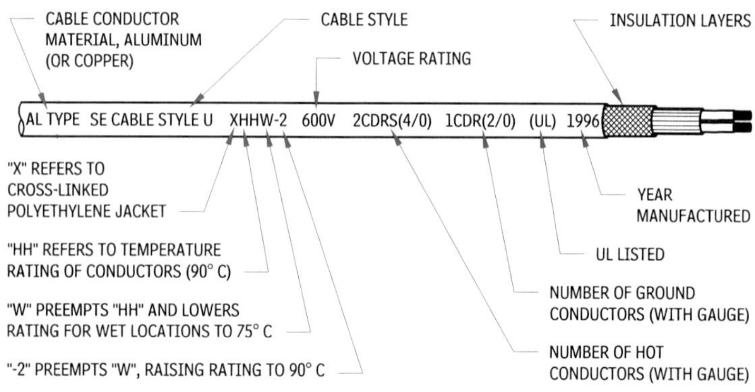

Figure 33.5 Service entrance (SE) cable
Source: AIA, *Architectural Graphic Standards for Residential Construction,* 2nd ed. Copyright 2010, John Wiley and Sons, Inc.

- A minimum of one 20-amp branch circuit is required for outlets in the laundry area. This circuit shall serve only outlets in the laundry area. *IRC E3703.3*
- A minimum of one 20-amp branch circuit is required to supply bathroom receptacles.

Required Outlet Locations

- In every kitchen, family room, dining room, den, breakfast room, living room, parlor, sunroom, bedroom, recreation room, and similar rooms, receptacle outlets must be installed so that no point measured horizontally along the floor line in the wall is more than 6 feet from a receptacle outlet. *IRC E3901.2*
- Countertops along the walls in kitchens, pantries, breakfast rooms, dining rooms, and similar areas shall have outlets installed so that no point along the wall line is more than 24 feet, measured horizontally, from an outlet. *IRC E3901.4*
- Countertops along the walls in kitchens, pantries, breakfast rooms, dining rooms and similar areas that are 12 feet or wider shall have an outlet. *IRC E3901.4.1*
- Countertops along the walls in kitchens, pantries, breakfast rooms, dining rooms, and similar areas that are separated by range tops, refrigerators, or sinks shall be considered separate countertops for the purpose of calculating outlets. *IRC E3901.4.4*
- Island countertops in kitchens, pantries, breakfast rooms, dining rooms, and similar areas shall have at least one outlet when the island is at least 24 inches long and 12 inches wide. *IRC E3901.4.2*

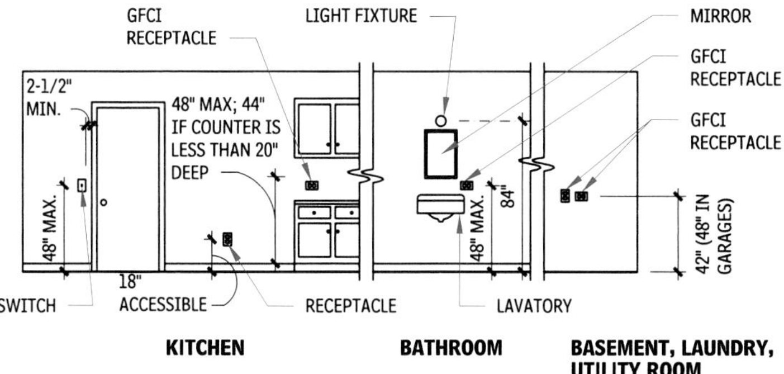

Figure 33.6 Switch and outlet locations
Source: AIA, *Architectural Graphic Standards for Residential Construction,* 2nd ed. Copyright 2010, John Wiley and Sons, Inc.

- Countertop outlets are required to be located not more than 20 inches above the countertop. Outlets are not allowed to be installed face up in a countertop. *IRC E3901.4.5*
- Outlets intended to serve specific appliances, such as laundry equipment, must be installed within 6 feet of the appliance. *IRC E3901.5*
- Bathrooms need at least one wall outlet to be installed within 36 inches of the outside edge of the lavatory basin. The outlet is required to be installed in a wall adjacent to the lavatory, or on the side or face of the lavatory cabinet. If installed in the cabinet, the outlet cannot be more than 12 inches below the countertop. *IRC E3901.6*
- One exterior outlet is required at the front and back of each dwelling that opens onto grade. The outlet must be located 6 feet, 6 inches maximum above grade. *IRC E3901.7*
- Balconies, porches, or decks that open off the dwelling and are 20 square feet or larger need an outlet located not more than 6 feet, 6 inches above the floor. *IRC E3901.7*
- Hallways measuring 10 feet or longer need at least one outlet. *IRC E3901.10*
- At least one communication outlet is required to be provided in a residence by the 2008 National Electrical Code (NEC).

Cable and Wire

Typically, *wire* refers to a single strand of copper or aluminum used to route electricity. Wires are spun together and put in a single jacket to form a conductor. A *cable* is typically several wires or conductors in a single jacket. The diameter of a wire is called its *gauge,* and measured

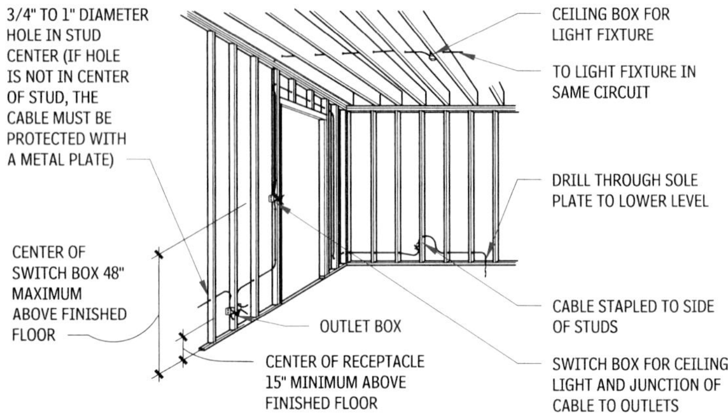

Figure 33.7 Typical wiring in wood construction
Source: AIA, *Architectural Graphic Standards for Residential Construction,* 2nd ed. Copyright 2010, John Wiley and Sons, Inc.

(in the United States) in accordance with American Wire Gauge (AWG) standards: the smaller the number, the larger diameter of the wire.

- When aluminum cable is used, coat conductors with an antioxide.
- In residential construction 14, 12, and 10 gauge are most common.
- The most common cable/wire used in residences is nonmetallic sheath (NM) cable for dry locations.
- For outdoor direct burial, underground feeder (UF) cable is common if allowed by local code.

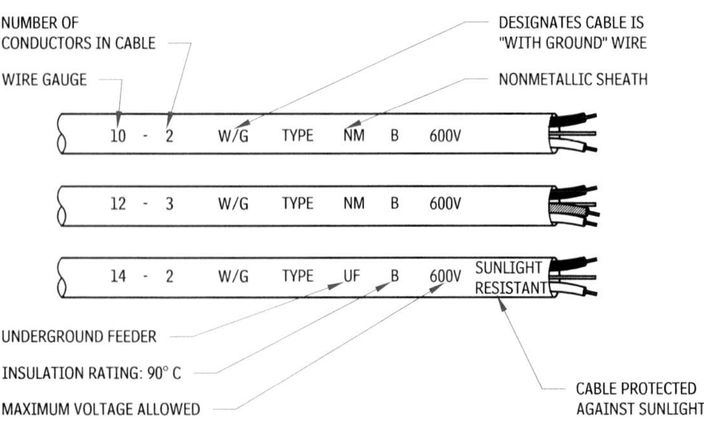

Figure 33.8 NM and UF wire markings
Source: AIA, *Architectural Graphic Standards for Residential Construction,* 2nd ed. Copyright 2010, John Wiley and Sons, Inc.

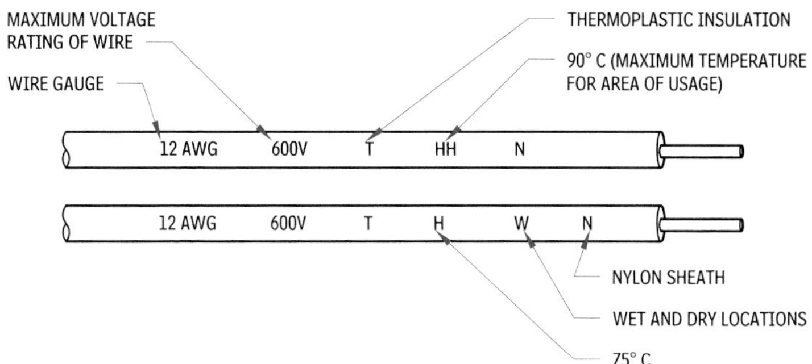

Figure 33.9 THHN and THWN wires.
Source: AIA, *Architectural Graphic Standards for Residential Construction,* 2nd ed. Copyright 2010, John Wiley and Sons, Inc.

- THHN cable is commonly used in dry conditions in residences when conduit is required. THWN is similar to THNN except that it has a temperature rating of 75°C in both wet and dry locations.
- For information on restrictions on cutting and notching wood framing members see Chapter 15, Rough Carpentry
- Bored holes in framing members for wiring must be at least 1-1/4 inches from the edge of the framing member, or it must be protected with a steel plate. *IRC Table E3802.1*
- Provide bushings or grommets to protect wiring run through openings in metal framing. *IRC Table E3802.1*
- For wiring in rigid or flexible conduit, a maximum of four 90-degree bends are allowed between junction boxes. *IRC Table E3802.1*
- For wiring in rigid or flexible conduit, a maximum of four 90-degree bends are allowed between junction boxes. *IRC Table E3802.1*
- NM and UF cable must be supported at 4 feet, 6 inch intervals maximum. Flat cable cannot be stapled on edge. *IRC Table E3802.1*
- NM and UF cable typically must be supported, at most, 12 inches from every electrical device box or other termination. *IRC Table E3802.1*
- In attics with permanent stair or ladder access, wiring and cable run across the top of floor joists, or within 7 feet of floor joists across the face of rafters or studding, guard strips are required. The guard strips must be at least as high as the cable. *IRC E3802.2*
- In attics with permanent stair or ladder access, wiring and cable run across the top of floor joists, or within 7 feet of floor joists across the face of rafters or studding, guard strips are required within 6 feet of the nearest edge of the attic entrance. The guard strips must be at least as high as the cable. *IRC E3802.2*
- For bends in NM and SE cable, the radius of the inner edge must be at least five times the diameter of the cable. *IRC E3802.5*

Electrical Device Boxes

- All metal electrical device boxes are grounded. *IRC E3905.2*
- Wiring entering electrical device boxes must be secured to the box; except that in some instances nonmetallic-sheathed cable is not required to be secured to a box not larger than 2-1/4 inches by 4 inches (wall or ceiling) and where the cable is fastened within 8 inches of the box. *IRC E3905.3.2*
- Nonmetallic electrical device boxes can only be used with nonmetallic-sheathed cables. *IRC E3905.3*
- When nonmetallic-sheathed cable and nonmetallic electrical device boxes are used, the cable, including the sheath, must extend at least 1/4 inch into the electrical device box. *IRC E3905.3.1*
- All electrical device boxes for floor outlets must be listed specifically for that use. *IRC E3905.8*
- Electrical device boxes and junction boxes must be installed so that the wiring inside can be accessed without removing parts of the building, of excavating paving or earth. *IRC E3905.11*
- Electrical device boxes installed in wet locations must be listed for that use. *IRC E3905.12*
- For electrical device boxes mounted flush in plaster or gypsum board, the gap between the edge of the box and the finish cannot be more than 1/8 inch. *IRC E3906.6*
- Metal cover plates for electrical device boxes shall be grounded. *IRC E3906.10*

Electrical Devices

- All receptacle faces must either be flush with or protrude from a nonmetallic cover plate.
- In residences 15-amp and 20-amp, 125-volt receptacles are required to be tamper-resistant.

Practices to Avoid

Cable/Wire

- Do not use cable to support other cable, raceways, etc. *IRC E3904.3.1*
- Do not bundle cables together for more than 2 feet, or the current carrying capability of the conductors must be reduced. *IRC E3705.3*
- Cable gauges larger than 4/0 aluminum and 2/0 copper are stiff and heavy, making them difficult to install. This size restriction limits panel

size to 200 amps; therefore, a 400-amp service would have two 200-amp panels.

Required Outlet Locations

- Do not install outlets face up in a countertop. *IRC E3901.4.5*
- Switched outlets do not count in meeting the code-required minimum for outlet number or location.

Lightning and Surge Protection

Description

The National Electrical Code (NEC) provides basic grounding and protective measures against lightning. These measures guard people against shock or electrocution when they are inside—as well as guard against the risk of lightning-sparked fires.

Beyond these basic safeguards, other measures can be taken to protect structures and equipment. This section primarily deals with these protection systems.

Assessing Existing Conditions

In order to evaluate the effectiveness of your lightning protection for structures and equipment you should determine the following:

- The threat of damage due to a lightning strike
- The type of lightning protection system you are using
- The systems or equipment you are protecting

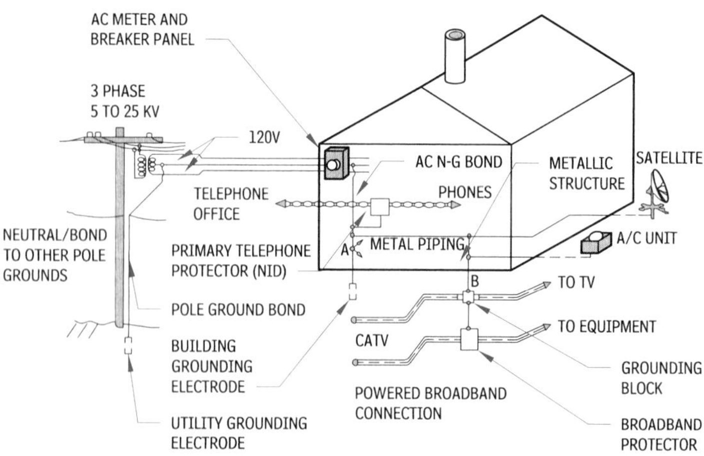

Figure 33.10 Basic grounding and protection

Source: AIA, *Architectural Graphic Standards for Residential Construction,* 2nd ed. Copyright 2010, John Wiley and Sons, Inc.

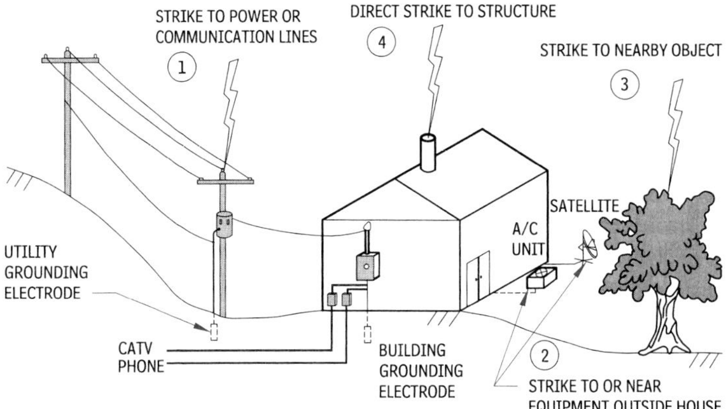

Figure 33.11 Potential lightning strikes
Source: AIA, *Architectural Graphic Standards for Residential Construction,* 2nd ed. Copyright 2010, John Wiley and Sons, Inc.

Figure 33.11 shows how lightning strikes can damage property and equipment. The types of strikes are numbered in order of decreasing frequency (with "1" being the most frequent).

Acceptable Practices

There are four basic types of lightning protection for structures and equipment:

1. Lightning protection system (LPS)
2. Building service-entrance surge protection
3. Signal-service surge protection
4. Point-of-use surge protection

Lightning Protection System (LPS)

An LPS is useful in the rare event of a direct lightning strike to the structure. LPS systems can be quite expensive.

Building Service Entrance Surge Protection

There are two types of surge protection devices that can be used at the building service entry:

- *Surge arrestor*—installed upstream or downstream of the building main disconnect. If installed upstream, must carry a UL Surge Arrestor listing.
- *Transient voltage surge suppressor (TVSS)*—installed downstream of the building main disconnect.

Signal Service-Entrance Surge Protection

If the signal service entrance is located with the building's AC power service entrance, surge protection for all utilities should be brought together and bonded to a common ground point.

Point-of-Use Surge Protection

Equipment located outside a building, such as compressors, well pumps, and pool heaters may suffer damage from a surge induced by a lightning strike. Installation of a surge protector (SP), can prevent such damage.

Practices to Avoid

- The National Electrical Code (NEC) specifically forbids the use of a separate ground rod for individual lines, equipment, and protectors, unless the separate ground rod is connected (bonded) to the building ground.
- For electronic equipment connected to both AC power and signal service, surge protection must be provided for both.

Lighting

Description

Lighting is critical to a space and is dependent on use of the space and the user. There are many things that need to be considered with lighting: the type of fixture and the type of lamp (bulb), the location of the fixture, and how the fixture is operated. The code provides minimum standards for lighting and their installation. It is best to also follow the recommendations of the manufacturer for a light fixture so as to not provide the potential for a fire.

Assessing Existing Conditions

Lighting installation can be broken down into two basic categories: rough-in and finish. In order to ensure proper installation of lighting, verify the following:

ROUGH-IN

- Electrical device boxes for lighting are installed in proper locations.
- Electrical device boxes for light switches are installed in proper locations.
- Electrical device boxes are installed for connection of any remote transformers or ballasts.
- Electrical device box types are correct for each application.
- Electrical device boxes are mounted to be flush with finishes.
- Electrical device boxes are adequately supported.

FINISH

- Installed fixtures are appropriate for boxes.
- Installed fixtures maintain code-required clearances.
- Fixtures are adequately supported.
- Switching devices are correct for locations, fixtures, and lamping.
- Lamping is correct for fixture.
- Track fixture voltage and total wattage are within track limitations.
- Total wattage of low-voltage fixtures is less than maximum wattage for transformers.

Acceptable Practices

Required Light Locations

- All habitable rooms and bathrooms must have one wall-switch-controlled light fixture. In other than kitchens and bathrooms, switched receptacles are acceptable. *IRC E3903.2*
- All interior stairs must be illuminated. Interior stairs shall have lighting in the immediate vicinity of each landing, or directly over each stairway section. *IRC R303.6.1*
- Exterior stairs shall be illuminated in the vicinity of the top landing, or in the vicinity of the bottom landing for stairs leading from grade to a basement. *IRC R303.6.1*
- Wall-switch-controlled light fixtures must be provided in hallways. (Wall switch not required if remote, central, or automatic switching is installed.) *IRC E3903.3*
- Wall-switch-controlled light fixtures must be provided at all egress doors. (Wall switch not required if remote, central or automatic switching is installed.) *IRC E3903.3*
- Wall-switch-controlled light fixtures must be provided in attached garages and detached garages with electrical power. *IRC E3903.3*
- Provide lighting in attics, under-floor spaces, utility rooms, and basements when they are used for storage or contain equipment that requires servicing. Lighting should be located near the equipment that requires servicing. *IRC E3903.4*

Clothes Closets

- Surface-mounted incandescent of LED light fixtures with enclosed light source can be installed on the wall above the door or on the ceiling, provided that there is a 12-inch minimum clearance between the fixture and the nearest storage. *IRC E4003.12*
- Surface-mounted and recessed fluorescent light fixtures can be installed on the wall above the door or on the ceiling, provided that there is a 6-inch minimum clearance between the fixture and the nearest storage. *IRC E4003.12*
- Recessed incandescent of LED light fixtures with enclosed light source can be installed on the wall above the door or on the ceiling, provided that there is a 6–inch minimum clearance between the fixture and the nearest storage. *IRC E4003.12*

Required Switch Locations

- Provide wall switches at each landing for interior stairways that have six or more risers (not required for lights that are always on or automatically controlled). *IRC R303.6.1*
- Exterior lighting shall be switched from inside the dwelling (not required for lights that are always on or automatically controlled). *IRC R303.6.1*
- In lieu of wall switches, remote, central, or automatic switching is permitted for lighting in hallways, stairways, and at exterior egress doors. *IRC E3903.3*
- Switches for lighting in attics, under-floor spaces, utility rooms, and basements can be either wall-mounted or integral to the light fixture; but should be located at the typical entry to the space.

Light Levels

Light level typically refers to the amount of light on a surface. Commonly known as *illuminance*, light levels are measured in candela per square foot, or footcandles (fc). Multiplying fc by 10.76 will give the equivalent metric unit: *lux*.

Table 33.2 Illuminance Target Values for Various Indoor Activities

Group	Category	Visual Task	FC
Task only occasionally involves reading or close visual scrutiny	A	Public spaces	3
	B	Simple orientation	5
	C	Simple tasks	10
Normal visual tasks	D	Tasks of high contrast and large size	30
	E	Either low contrast or small size	50
	F	Low contrast and small size	100
Critical visual tasks	G	Task lighting for difficult or critical visual demands	300

Note: Illuminance categories and general footcandle recommendations for different visual demands. Multiply fc by 10.76 to obtain lux.

- All habitable rooms are required to have a certain amount of glazing. However, the glazing is not required if certain conditions are met. One of the conditions is for artificial light that produces an average illumination of 6 fc over the area of the room, measured at 30 inches above the floor. *IRC R303.1*
- Lighting for interior stairs must provide at least 1 fc, measured at the center of each tread and at the center of all landings. *IRC R303.6*

Consider several factors when determining light levels:

- Age of users
- Contrast level of the task
- Duration of the task
- Critical importance of visual error

Electrical Device Box Types

For the most part, the different types of electrical device boxes are discussed in the previous chapter; however, here are a few issues that relate directly to electrical device boxes for lighting:

- Electrical device boxes for light fixtures that mount flush to the finished surface must be completely enclosed when the light fixture is mounted, and must be capable of supporting the weight of the light fixture. *IRC 3905.5*
- Electrical device boxes for ceiling lights must support a light fixture weighing up to 50 pounds. *IRC E3905.6*
- Electrical device boxes for supporting ceiling fans must be marked as suitable for that purpose. They are not allowed to support ceiling fans weighing more than 70 pounds. *IRC E3905.9*
- Electrical device boxes for supporting ceiling fans weighing more than 35 pounds must be marked as suitable for that purpose, and also indicate the maximum weight they are capable of supporting. They are not allowed to support ceiling fans weighing more than 70 pounds. *IRC E3905.9*

Light Fixture Types

- Ceiling-mounted light fixtures that weigh more than 50 pounds shall be supported independently of the electrical device box they are connected to unless the electrical device box is listed and marked for the maximum weight to be supported. *IRC 3905.7*
- Recessed light fixtures shall be either marked as "Type IC" or shall have at least 1/2-inch clearance from combustible materials. *IRC E4004.8*

- Recessed light fixtures shall be either marked as "Type IC" or have at least 3-inch clearance from insulation. *IRC E4004.9*
- Lighting track 4 feet or shorter shall have two supports. Longer track sections shall be supported at every 4 feet minimum (unless track is rated for longer spans). *IRC E4005.5*
- Surface-mounted fluorescent or LED light fixtures installed in clothes closets shall be identified for this use. *IRC E4003.12*

Damp and Wet Locations

- Light fixtures installed in wet locations must be marked "SUITABLE FOR WET LOCATIONS." *IRC E4003.9*
- Light fixtures installed in damp locations must be marked "SUITABLE FOR DAMP LOCATIONS." *IRC E4003.9*
- Light fixtures located within 8 feet, measured vertically, above the bathtub rim or shower threshold, and within 3 feet, measured horizontally, of the bathtub rim or shower threshold, must be approved for use in damp locations. *IRC E4003.11*
- Light fixtures that are subject to shower spray shall be approved for use in wet locations. *IRC E4003.11*

Energy Efficiency

The 2009 version of the *International Residential Code for One and Two Family Dwellings* (IRC) includes energy-efficiency requirements for lighting systems. Section N1104 states that a minimum of 50 percent of the lamps in permanently installed lights must be high-efficiency lamps. The IRC defines high-efficiency lamps as compact fluorescent or linear fluorescent size T-8 or smaller with a minimum efficacy of:

- 60 lumens per watt for lamps over 40 watts
- 50 lumens per watt for lamps over 15 watts to 40 watts
- 40 lumens per watt for lamps 15 watts or less

It is also important to check state and local codes. Not all states have adopted the IRC energy-efficiency requirements. California, for instance, has developed its own residential energy-efficiency standards.

The ENERGY STAR program, developed by the U.S. Environmental Protection Agency Department of Energy, lists guidelines, as well as certifies products, to help in compliance with energy-efficiency code mandates.

Lamping

Incandescent Lamps

Incandescent lamps come in several sizes and shapes. Their generic label takes the form WWSDDBB. Other terms may be used for colored lamps, lamp base, or manufacturer-specific features.

- W: Watts of power
- S: Shape, including general-service A-lamps, reflector lamps, elliptical reflectors, PAR (pressed aluminized reflector), candle, globe, and decorative shapes
- D: Diameter of the lamp bulb, in eighths of an inch
- B: Beam spread characteristic, if applicable: spot or flood

Halogen Incandescent Lamps

Halogen incandescent lamps are available in both line-voltage and low-voltage, low voltage is currently most common. Some low-voltage fixtures require locating a transformer remotely.

Fluorescent Lamps

Fluorescent lamps are identified by designations such as F40T12CW. The labeling format is generically FSWWTDD-CCC, and is coded as follows:

- F: Fluorescent lamp. Germicidal shortwave UV lamps are designated G.
- S: Shape or style of lamp. No letter indicates the typical straight tube; circline lamps are designated C.
- WW: Power in watts.
- CCC: CW = cool white (about 4,100°K), color. W = white (about 3,500 °K), and WW = warm white (about 3,000°K). Manufacturers may use special designations for specific products, such as SPX.
- T: Tubular bulb.
- DD: Diameter of tube, in eighths of an inch.

Light-Emitting Diode (LED) Lamps

LED lamps operate on direct-current voltage, and are polarity-sensitive; improper connection can destroy them. Otherwise, they have an extremely long life, typically about 10 years. LEDs usually fail by gradual dimming, rather than sudden burnout. They are also insensitive to vibration and temperature.

Practices to Avoid

Bathrooms

- Pendant, cord-connected and chain-, cable-, or cord-suspended light fixtures are not allowed to be within 3 feet horizontally and 8 feet vertically of a bathtub rim or shower threshold. *IRC E4003.11*
- Ceiling fans are not allowed to be within 3 feet horizontally and 8 feet vertically of a bathtub rim or shower threshold. *IRC E4003.11*
- Track lighting is not allowed to be within 3 feet horizontally and 8 feet vertically of a bathtub rim or shower threshold. *IRC E4003.11*

Clothes Closets

- Pendant light fixtures shall not be used. *IRC E4003.12*
- Incandescent light fixtures with exposed or partially exposed bulbs shall not be used. *IRC E4003.12*

Track Lighting

Do not use track lighting in the following locations: *IRC E4005.4*

- Where it is likely to be damaged
- In wet or damp locations
- Where subject to corrosive vapors
- In hazardous locations
- Where concealed
- Where it will extend through walls or partitions
- Less than 5 feet above the finished floor (unless protected from damage or low voltage)

Resources

WITHIN THIS BOOK

- Chapter 34 Electronic Safety and Security

REFERENCE STANDARDS

- NFPA 70—National Electrical Code, National Fire Protection Association (NFPA)

OTHER RESOURCES

- 2009 International Residential Code for One and Two-Family Dwellings. Washington, DC: International Code Council, Inc., 2009.
- American Institute of Architects, *Architectural Graphics Standards*, 11th ed. Hoboken, NJ: John Wiley and Sons, 2007.
- American Institute of Architects, *Architectural Graphic Standards for Residential Construction*, 2nd ed. Hoboken, NJ: John Wiley and Sons, 2010.
- Institute of Electrical and Electronics Engineers (IEEE), *How to Protect Your House and Its Contents from Lightning: The IEEE Guide for Surge Protection of Equipment Connected to AC Power and Communications Circuits*. New York: IEEE Press, 2005.
- Illuminating Engineering Society of North America (IESNA), www.iesna.org.
- International Commission on Illumination (CIE), www.cie.co.at.
- National Electrical Manufacturer Association (NEMA), www.nema.org.

Chapter 34

Electronic Safety and Security

Electronic Safety and Security

Description

Electronic safety and security equipment includes systems and components designed to sense the presence of danger in the home and alert the residents in a timely manner.

Types of devices:

- Smoke alarms
- Heat detectors/alarms
- Carbon monoxide alarms
- Home intrusion alarms

It is increasingly common for detection and alarm systems to be brought together under one central control panel. This "home automation" system (also known as "smart homes") can also control lighting, appliances, entertainment systems, thermostats, irrigation, data systems, and others. The various systems can be connected by several means:

- AC power wiring
- Telephone lines
- Wireless (radio signal)
- Structured wiring (coaxial cable, CAT 5 wire, fiber optics)

A potential risk of using a home automation system is that the failure of a key component can interrupt the entire system.

Assessing Existing Conditions

Planning system types and device and controller locations early in the design/construction process allows for the installation of power and connectivity wiring at the same time the AC power wiring is installed. Waiting until later in the process is much more labor intensive and disruptive, as finishes may be damaged. In order to ensure that the electronic safety and security equipment is installed properly, you should verify the following conditions:

- Electrical boxes for devices are installed in proper locations.
- Power wiring and boxes are installed for devices needing AC power.
- Connection wiring and boxes are installed for devices needing connectivity.
- Electrical device box locations for mounting detection devices are clear of all potential obstructions/interference.
- Ground-fault protection is included for connectivity wiring.

Acceptable Practices

The *IRC* requires installation of smoke detectors and carbon monoxide detectors/alarms in new construction and during renovation of existing structures.

Smoke Alarms

IRC Section R314 Smoke Alarms—requirements:

- Install in each sleeping room.
- Install outside each separate sleeping area.
- Install on all levels of a residence, including basements and finished attics.

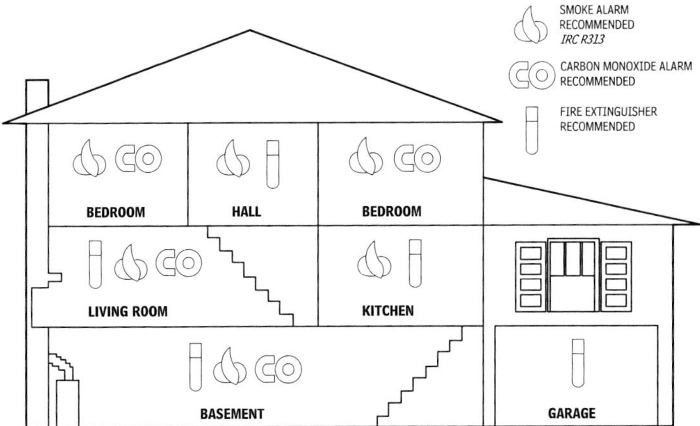

Figure 34.1 Recommended locations for alarm system and safety devices
Source: AIA, *Architectural Graphic Standards for Residential Construction*, 2nd ed. Copyright 2010, John Wiley and Sons, Inc.

- Multiple smoke alarms must be interconnected.
- Alterations to existing structures requiring a permit trigger requirements for smoke alarms to be installed in accordance with new construction.
- Devices shall be hardwired into the residence's AC power (unless not on commercial power system).
- Devices shall have battery backup.

Types:

- *Ionization chamber:* This is the best detector for fires that start with flame but put out little smoke.
- *Photoelectric:* This is best for detecting smoldering-type fire start.

Installation:

- See "IRC Section R314 Smoke Alarms—requirements" above.
- Mounted on wall or ceiling.
- If mounted on the ceiling, the alarm cannot be less than 4 inches from a wall.
- If mounted on wall, the alarm can be no lower than 12 inches and no higher than 4 inches from ceiling.
- In kitchens, the alarm must be photoelectric type or equipped with alarm-silencing feature.

Refer to NFPA 72 for more complete requirements regarding smoke alarms.

Heat Detectors/Alarms

Reference Standards:

- National Fire Protection Association: NFPA 72

Types:

- *Fixed temperature detector/alarm:* An alarm sounds when temperature exceeds a fixed mark—typically 135°F for habitable spaces and 200°F to 225°F for attics.
- *Rate-of-rise detector/alarm:* An alarm sounds when the ambient temperature rises a fixed amount over a certain period of time—typically 15°F per minute.
- *Combination detector/alarm:* This includes both fixed-temperature and rate-of-rise detection methods.

Installation:

- Use in combination with smoke alarms.
- Use where smoke alarms are problematic—for example, cooking spaces and close to fuel-fired appliances.

Carbon Monoxide Alarms

IRC Section R315 Carbon Monoxide Alarms—requirements:

- Install outside each sleeping area.
- These are required for residences with fuel-fired appliances.
- These are required for residences with attached garages.

Types:

- *Biomimetic detector/alarm:* Typically battery operated, they are sensitive to temperature and humidity.
- *Oxide semi-conductor detector/alarm:* These are the most common type, typically plugs into wall, sensitive to moisture.
- *Electrochemical detector/alarm:* These are the least common but most accurate. The alarm typically plugs into wall, has a short sensor life, and is expensive.

Installation:

- Recommended one alarm installed on each level of a residence, including basement.

Home Intrusion Alarms

Home intrusion alarms fall into three basic categories:

- *Hard-wired: connected to AC power supply:* Low-voltage wiring is used to connect other system devices; recommend battery backup.
- *Wireless:* Many system components are battery powered and use radio frequencies to connect to the control panel.
- *Stand-alone:* This combines arming, detection and alarm in a single unit either battery power or plugged into an outlet. It has a limited area of coverage.

There are five types of components used in the assembly of a home intrusion alarm system:

- *Control panel:* Generally runs off AC house current with a battery backup. The control panel coordinates all of the other components.

- *Arming station:* Most use touch pad or key fob to activate system; also available with high security key activation.
- *Sensors:* These could include panic buttons; perimeter protection such as magnetic contacts and glass-break sensors; interior protection such as infrared, photoelectric, ultrasonic and microwave sensors.
- *Alarms:* Siren, bell, annunciator and/or strobes are options.
- *Monitoring system:* 24-hour professional monitoring is available; system connects to monitoring station over telephone lines.

Practices to Avoid

Smoke Alarms

The *IRC* only allows smoke detectors power solely by battery to be installed in very limited and specific applications and only when renovating existing structures. If battery-powered smoke detectors are used, they should be equipped with a low-battery warning light. Limitations to smoke alarm installation are as follows:

- Shall not be installed within 36 inches (measured horizontally) of a door to a kitchen or bathroom containing a shower or tub.
- Shall not be installed within 36 inches (measured horizontally) of an HVAC supply register.
- Shall not be installed within 36 inches (measured horizontally) of the tip of a ceiling fan.
- Should not be installed less than 12 inches from fluorescent light fixtures.
- Should not be installed where temperatures are regularly below 40°F.
- Should not be installed in insect-infested areas.

Refer to NFPA 72 for more complete requirements regarding smoke alarms.

Heat Detectors/Alarms

- Heat detectors should be used only in combination with smoke alarms, not as a sole means of fire detection.

Resources

WITHIN THIS BOOK

- Chapter 33 Electrical

REFERENCE STANDARDS

- Underwriters Laboratories, Inc., UL 2034—Standard for Safety Single and Multiple Station Carbon Monoxide Alarms, 3rd ed., 2008
- Underwriters Laboratories, Inc., UL 217—Single and Multiple Station Smoke Dectectors, 6th ed. with 2 addenda
- National Fire Protection Association, NFPA 72—National Fire Alarm and Signaling Code, 2010

OTHER RESOURCES

- 2009 International Residential Code for One and Two-Family Dwellings. Washington, DC: International Code Council, Inc., 2009.
- American Institute of Architects, *Architectural Graphics Standards*, 11th ed. Hoboken, NJ: John Wiley and Sons, 2007.
- American Institute of Architects, *Architectural Graphic Standards for Residential Construction*, 2nd ed. Hoboken, NJ: John Wiley and Sons, 2010.

Index

D

Z